THE FALSE CHRIST
—*The 8th King*

THE FALSE CHRIST
—The 8th King

The Abomination That Makes Desolate and the Time of the End

Last-day Events As Foretold
in Daniel and Revelation

MONTY L. GOHL, M.D.

Prism House Media
Port Charlotte, Florida

The False Christ—The 8th King
The Abomination That Makes Desolate and the Time of the End
Last-day Events as Foretold in Daniel and Revelation

Cover design by Bill Kirstein
Electronic Makeup by Toy Shop Productions

Additional copies of this book are available at: http://www.TheFalseChrist.org

Library of Congress Control Number: 2004117473

Gohl, Monty
    The False Christ—The 8th King The Abomination That Makes Desolate and the Time of the End Last-day Events as Foretold in Daniel and Revelation / Monty L. Gohl, M.D.

1. The False Christ   2. The 8th King   3. The Abomination That Makes Desolate
4. Time of the End   5. Last-day events   6. Daniel and Revelation   7. Bible–Prophecies

Includes bibliographical references.

ISBN 0-9748-088-1-4

Published by Prism House Media, Port Charlotte, Florida

Printed by Review and Herald Publishing Association

First Edition

DEDICATION

This book is dedicated to the "wise" who, at the time of the end,
"shall make many understand" (Daniel 11:33).

Table of Contents

Section IV—The Time of the End

Section V—Summary—The False Christ and the Eighth King

INTRODUCTION/BACKGROUND

Several years ago I became interested in the books of Daniel and Revelation and how they relate to last-day events. I began to wonder if there wasn't more to the story than had already been revealed. Ellen G. White suggests that more truth will be revealed in the last days but how and when that would occur is unclear.[1]

At about that time I ran across a book by Robert Smith, M.D., titled *The Sixth King*, which posed a fascinating question: are we now living in the last days? His book forced me to reassess long held assumptions about certain prophetic interpretations such as the 1260-day prophecy of Daniel 12. Although, I do not completely agree with Dr. Smith's interpretation of last-day events, I will always be in debt to him for prompting me to re-evaluate biblical prophecy in general and last-day events in particular.

In studying the book of Daniel, it is apparent that Daniel's prophecies cover world history from Daniel's time to Christ's Second Coming in both symbols and real events. In Daniel 11 and 12, we see a shift away from predominantly symbols to a combination of symbols and actual events. It appears that Daniel 12 is focused on time of the end events beginning with the time of trouble in verse one. Where are the events described that precede this time of trouble? The answer is hidden in the last portion of Daniel 11. In studying the book of Revelation, it became apparent that the emphasis of the first 14 chapters is primarily on what happens to God's people and then the emphasis switches to what happens to the wicked from chapters 15-20. This does not mean that God's people are not included in these later chapters, but the emphasis is more on the wicked, especially in chapters 15-18 and 20. My main focus of study became the first 14 chapters of the book of Revelation, because this is where I expected to find details of last-day events affecting God's people. However, as will be seen later, Revelation 17 became equally important.

One question that concerned me was why we do not seem to have more guidance in scriptures about the most critical time period in earth's history. It is estimated that more than six billion people are living on earth today.[2] Why isn't there more information in the scriptures to help guide all of those living at the end of time? Daniel gives an excellent outline of world history in prophecy but appears to shortchange last-day events. John, in the book of Revelation, appears to give a historical overview of the church but again seems to give limited time to last-day events. Why did Daniel overlook the time of the end? Why did John not give more guidance on last-day events? These are questions, which this book will attempt to answer. It is the author's conviction that God has revealed far more than we have previously understood.

PROPHECY: SOURCE OF HOPE
HISTORICAL OR REPETITIVE?

Prophecy is often viewed as all or none. In other words, prophecy is often seen as having only one real interpretation. This concept is reinforced by the presence of multiple ideas and interpretations, which make a single interpretation much more appealing. Unfortunately, the concept that only one true application of a given Bible prophecy exists is incorrect and unsubstantiated in the Bible. God's mind and His abilities should not be limited by our small intellects. Just because we can't understand something doesn't take away its existence. God's mind is far greater than our mind and He is able to give many meanings to the same verse. Indeed, many scholars and Christians through the years have found many applications to the same verse. Similarly, in prophecy, God did not limit prophecy to one application. There are multiple examples in both the Old and New Testaments of prophecies with more than one application.

As we study a prophecy we often see several applications, all of which may apply. A given prophecy may have a literal local application, a spiritual application now or later, a symbolic future application, or more than one future application.

For example, the seven churches of Revelation 1, 2, and 3 had a literal local application, because these were real churches that existed in John's day. They also had a future application representing seven consecutive time periods of history. In addition, they also have had spiritual applications to many churches throughout the years with the same spiritual characteristics as each of these seven churches. Some prophecies have more than one future application. For example, Matthew 24 is a prophecy about the destruction of Jerusalem that was fulfilled in A.D. 70 but it is also a prophecy about last-day events for God's people.

Since prophecy can have more than one application, it is important to understand the purpose of prophecy. If we understand that prophecy is one of God's methods to save souls for eternity, then we can understand why God would want prophecy to apply to all ages. This explains why God uses prophecy in vague terms, so that it can be interpreted differently throughout the ages. God does not and will not destroy hope. Just because a prophecy worked to save souls 200 years ago does not mean that it cannot have another application later in time that will further instill hope and save additional souls. "For now we see in a mirror dimly, but then face to face. Now I know in part; then I shall understand fully" (1 Corinthians 13:12). Our understanding now is still incomplete but it will continue to grow until the end of time and beyond.

To view all prophecy as having only a historical application is to limit God's ability to communicate with us. It assumes only one possible interpretation when clearly there are other applications that may apply. Many Old Testament prophecies, which applied to literal Israel, also apply to spiritual Israel and therefore have dual applications. These same prophecies often had individual spiritual applications as well. Since Revelation is a book of multiple prophecies, it is important to approach it with an open mind recognizing that God can and does have more than one possible application in mind for many of these prophecies.

God does not reveal everything at once. God actually hides the truth from us at times, because we are not ready for it to be revealed. This is shown in Luke 9:45, where God hid the truth about Jesus upcoming death from the disciples. "But they did not understand this saying, ***and it was concealed from them, that they should not perceive it;*** and they were afraid to ask him about this saying" (Luke 9: 45) (emphasis supplied).

Prophecy is written to establish and maintain hope. This is why God does not give all of the details at once. He wrote prophecy in such a way as to maintain hope. This means that He will not tell you when He is coming, since that would harm all those living much earlier. For example, if the Bible said Jesus was coming in the year 2010, imagine how those living in the year A.D. 100 would have felt. They would have had difficulty getting motivated to prepare for His soon coming. Hope in a soon coming is a powerful motivator and God will not destroy that hope.

Because God is God, He is not limited to one or two possible correct interpretations. He can write a prophecy, which can give hope to those living in the year A.D. 70 and yet apply also to those living in the last days. This book will not suggest that prior applications of prophecies were incorrect or not God ordained. God has intended all along to use prophecy as a means to instill hope and to save souls and He will continue to do so until He returns. Ellen G. White suggests that further light will be given in the last days and yet many of us are unwilling to even consider any new light.[3]

There are several approaches used to explain prophecy. Two approaches that are acceptable in interpreting prophecy are the historical approach and the repetitive approach. The historical approach treats prophecy as historical. Using this approach some believe that the majority of the prophecies in the book of Revelation were fulfilled prior to the 1840s.

Another approach to interpreting prophecy is called the repetitive approach. This concept suggests that when God gives a prophetic message it can have more than one application down through history. Matthew 24 and many Old Testament prophecies are consistent with this repetitive approach. This repetitive approach often leads to either a dual or sometimes a triple application of a given prophecy.

The question arises as to why some will not accept a repetitive view of prophecy. The following are some reasons why a dual application or repetitive approach is often rejected. First, a new interpretation can be seen as destabilizing the individual's faith foundation. They see any new idea as false because they already have the truth. Any new idea therefore threatens or weakens the truth. Second, the repetitive approach puts the individual at risk. If all prophecy is historical then most of the bad events described in Revelation have already happened and there is less to fear for the future. This concept gives the believer false security. They do not need to concern themselves with the rest of Revelation because it is past history and does not apply to them. Third, some believers will reject a repetitive approach because the interpretation is new and was not specifically taught by the church in the past. This concept assumes that the church has already been given all prophetic interpretation to the end of time. This approach suggests that further Bible study is of no value.

There are also some dangers that are implicit in relying totally on a historical approach. First, if one relies on the historical approach for interpreting prophecy then there is no need to search the scripture, since the events have already occurred.

Second, there is no sense of urgency to understand these prophecies, since they are all in the past and therefore do not affect the current situation. Third, God's Word is no longer applicable to the current temporal environment, since the events are all in the past. Fourth, the historical approach leads to a lack of preparation for coming events, since it is assumed that the events have already occurred.

The repetitive approach to prophecy is consistent with what God has revealed in the past regarding prophetic interpretation. Many prophecies have had dual or triple applications, which make them repetitive by definition. This book will endeavor to give the historical viewpoint and then where appropriate endeavor to give an alternative or dual application. This book will not dismiss, belittle, or replace any previous historical interpretations. These interpretations were God inspired for previous generations and provided hope and salvation for many souls. Any new interpretations must also lead to the salvation of others. These dual applications are not meant to replace the historical applications and in many situations both applications apply simultaneously.

God reveals only what is needed for a given generation to be ready for His coming. This concept has been proven throughout the ages. The reformers who began the Reformation, which ended the Dark Ages, were only given the truths they needed for their time. Luther was given light on salvation by faith but not on the 2300-day prophecy. God does keep some things hidden until the time is right. In Luke 9:44 Jesus told His disciples that "the Son of man is to be delivered into the hands of men." This was critical information that the disciples needed, however, the next verse states, "But they did not understand this saying, *and it was concealed from them, that they should not perceive it*" (Luke 9:45) (emphasis supplied). God concealed this message of Jesus' death from Jesus' disciples because they were not ready for it. God reveals prophecy only when the time is right.

We are now living in the last days. It is time for us to wake up and open our eyes. God is about to begin the final chapter of earth's history. He has given us ample warning and has revealed these last-day events in Daniel and Revelation.

[1] White, Ellen G., *Counsels to Writers and Editors*, (Pacific Press Publishing Association, Nampa, Idaho) 1946, p. 35.

[2] United Nations, *World Population Prospects: The 1994 Revision*, U.S. Census Bureau, International Programs Center, International Data Base and unpublished tables, 1994.

[3] White, Ellen G., *Counsels to Writers and Editors*, (Pacific Press Publishing Association, Nampa, Idaho) 1946, p. 35.

Section I

The Abomination
That Makes Desolate

Matthew 24
The Sign of the End

When Jesus was asked "what will be the sign of your coming and the close of the age?" (Matthew 24:3), His disciples were asking the question which every Christian wants answered. What will be the sign that tells us Jesus' coming "is near, at the very gates" (Matthew 24:33). Jesus' initial answer is the same in all three gospel accounts: Matthew 24:4, 5; Mark 13:5, 6; and Luke 21:8. He said "take heed that no one leads you astray" (Matthew 24:4). At first glance, this seems like a strange answer and yet, it is His answer. Jesus is warning that a great deception will occur. Jesus is warning that false Christs will appear. He then goes on to expand this idea warning not to believe these false Christs or believe their signs and wonders. He continues to add other events that will occur prior to His Second Coming such as wars, famines, earthquakes, and persecution. However, His initial answer is consistent in each of the three gospels. It appears that Jesus is warning us of a special delusion that will deceive "if possible even the elect" (Matthew 24:24).

> Matthew 24:3: *"As he sat on the Mount of Olives, the disciples came to him privately, saying, 'Tell us, when will this be, and what will be the sign of your coming and of the close of the age?'"*

Jesus' disciples are asking, "when will this be"? This question refers to Jesus' statement in Matthew 24:2: "there will not be left here one stone upon another, that will not be thrown down." Jesus was referring to the temple in Jerusalem. This temple was the main source of pride to the nation of Israel but Jesus was foretelling its destruction. Historically, this occurred in A.D. 70 when Jerusalem was overrun by the Roman army. However, there will be another application of these events in the last days. In the last days, this rebuilt temple will be destroyed again at the resurrection of the two witnesses (discussed in Revelation 11 (first part)—The Two Witnesses). The disciples then ask another question "What will be the sign of your coming and the close of the age?" This question is what all Christians down through the ages have asked. What is "the sign" of Jesus coming? What is "the sign" that the time of the end is near? Jesus gives His answer in Matthew 24:4.

> Matthew 24:4: *"And Jesus answered them, 'Take heed that no one leads you astray.'"*

This is Jesus' answer! Jesus is warning them of a deception. Jesus is warning that people will be led astray. Jesus is telling His disciples that "the sign" will be deception. He is suggesting that someone will try to deceive and mislead God's people in the last days. Jesus will expand on this answer several times in the next few verses. He will also give other signs, but His emphasis in Matthew 24 is clearly deception. This deception will be by false Christs and false prophets (Matthew 24:5,

9

11, 15, 23, 24, 26). Jesus' answer continues in Matthew 24:5.

> Matthew 24:5: *"For many will come in my name, saying,*
> *'I am the Christ,' and they will lead many astray."*

Jesus is predicting "many will come" who will claim to be Christ returned. These false Christs will "lead many astray." This prophecy has been fulfilled many times through the ages and continues to be fulfilled today. However, there will be a special fulfillment in the last days. This special fulfillment in the last days will be discussed under Matthew 24:14.

> Matthew 24:6: *"And you will hear of wars and rumors*
> *of wars; see that you are not alarmed; for this must take*
> *place, but the end is not yet."*

Jesus warns that wars will be common in the last days but not to be alarmed. These wars must occur but they are not the sign. He says "this must take place, but the end is not yet." In other words, the wars are not the sign the disciples are looking for. The disciples wanted "the sign" of the close of the age (Matthew 24:3).

> Matthew 24:7, 8: *"For nation will rise against nation, and*
> *kingdom against kingdom, and there will be famines and*
> *earthquakes in various places; all this is but the beginning*
> *of the sufferings."*

Jesus is predicting international warfare, which will lead to famine. He is also predicting earthquakes, which will lead to famine and starvation. All these events have occurred many times in earth's history. However, these events will be increased in the last days. These events are also foretold in Revelation under the seven seals, seven trumpets, and seven last plagues (discussed in Revelation 6—The Seven Seals; Revelation 8 and 9—The Seven Trumpets; and in Revelation 16—The Seven Last Plagues). The world is currently experiencing a significant increase in the number of earthquakes. However, Jesus says "all this is but the beginning of the sufferings." Jesus is saying this is not the sign but only the beginning. The "end is not yet" (Matthew 24:6). This verse suggests that natural disasters such as earthquakes will precede this final sign but are not the sign.

> Matthew 24:9: *"Then they will deliver you up to*
> *tribulation, and put you to death; and you will be*
> *hated by all nations for my name's sake."*

Historically, this verse has been fulfilled many times through the ages. However, it will have a special application in the last days. In the last days, there will be a "great tribulation" which Jesus describes in Matthew 24:21. This great tribulation is similar to Daniel's "time of trouble" in Daniel 12:1. However, another tribulation is also described by Daniel, just prior to the time of trouble. In this tribulation some "shall fall by sword and flame, by captivity and plunder, for some days" (Daniel 11:33). Clearly, some of God's people will die during this earlier tribulation. This earlier tribulation has been called the preliminary time of trouble.

Jesus states that His people will be "hated by all nations." This prophecy will be fulfilled in the last days by Babylon when "all nations drink the wine of her impure passion" (Revelation 14:8). When all the nations accept Babylon's false teachings, they will be rejecting God's truth. They will then attempt to force their falsehoods upon God's people, which will lead to the persecution of God's true followers. This persecution begins with the second angel's message (Revelation 14:8) and is described as war on the saints (Revelation 13:7). This prophecy has a special application at the time of the third angel's message (Revelation 14:9-11) when the nations will attempt to enforce the mark of the beast (discussed in Revelation 13 (last part)— The Mark of the Beast).

Jesus then gives the reason why God's people will be hated. They will be hated "for my name's sake." This prophecy has also been fulfilled through the ages but will have special meaning in the last days. Millions have died through the ages for Jesus' name. They refused to worship any other god. In the last days there will be a special application of this verse. As will be shown later in this discussion, there will be a false Christ in the last days. Jesus is warning His disciples about this false Christ in Matthew 24. Those who reject the false Christ and claim Jesus as the only true Christ in the last days will be hated by all nations. One of the identifying characteristics of God's people in the last days is that they will "have the faith of Jesus" (Revelation 14:12). It is this belief in Jesus' name and in His salvation, as opposed to accepting the false Christ, which will cause persecution to fall on God's people during the last days.

> Matthew 24:10: *"And then many will fall away,*
> *and betray one another, and hate one another."*

This prophecy has also been fulfilled many times through the years since Christ's first advent. It was especially fulfilled during the persecution seen in the Dark Ages. This prophecy however, will be fulfilled again during the last days. This prophecy suggests that families will be divided over their relationship with Christ. It also suggests that "many will fall away and betray one another." This prophecy will be fulfilled again when the false Christ convinces many that he has returned to save them. Those who accept this false Christ will betray those who reject him.

> Matthew 24:11: *"And many false prophets will arise*
> *and lead many astray."*

Historically, this prophecy has also been fulfilled many times through the ages since Christ predicted it. This prophecy will again be fulfilled during the last days and has seen many recent examples. The emphasis is on deception. This is the sign that Jesus is warning about. Do not be deceived.

> Matthew 24:12: *"And because wickedness is multiplied,*
> *most men's love will grow cold."*

This text has also been fulfilled many times throughout the ages; however, it will have a special application in the last days. Once the false Christ has begun to reign, he will be able to change God's Law. Once God's Law is changed, wickedness will multiply. This wickedness will lead to love growing "cold." This will especially be seen in the false Christ's capital city, which will be called "Sodom and Egypt"

(Revelation 11:8). It will be called Sodom because of its immorality and Egypt because of its rejection of the true God.

> Matthew 24:13: *"But he who endures to the end will be saved."*

This verse connects these prophecies to "the end." Jesus is describing last-day events. Jesus is describing the salvation of God's people after this tribulation is over. He will describe this salvation again in Matthew 24:30, 31 where He is seen "coming on the clouds of heaven" to rescue His people. Those who endure are also described in Revelation 14:12 as those who have the "endurance of the saints." They are those who keep God's Commandments and keep faith in the true Jesus (Revelation 14:12). In other words, they reject the false Christ.

> Matthew 24:14: *"And this gospel of the kingdom will be preached throughout the whole world, as a testimony to all nations; and then the end will come."*

This verse tells us that the good news or gospel will be preached throughout the whole world prior to "the end." The "end" refers to Jesus' Second Coming. This preaching will go to all the nations. All the nations at the end will reject the truth. All the nations will hate God's people because of Jesus' name (Matthew 24:9). These nations are those who have accepted the false Christ and Babylon's wine (Revelation 14:8 and Revelation 17:2). God's people will give these same nations the truth about Babylon's falsehoods and Satan as the false Christ. This is described in Daniel 11:32-33 where God's people are called "wise" and the wise will "make many understand." The nations will be warned before the end comes. The good news about the true Christ will be shared by the "wise" with those who have accepted the false Christ (Daniel 11:31-33).

> Matthew 24:15: *"So when you see the desolating sacrilege spoken of by the prophet Daniel, standing in the holy place (let the reader understand)."*

Historically, this verse has been applied to the overthrow of Jerusalem in A.D. 70.[1] The "desolating sacrilege" has been applied to the Roman armies which overran Jerusalem and destroyed the temple not leaving one stone upon another.

However, this verse also has a last-day application. The context of Matthew 24 suggests this verse should be applied to last-day events because the preceding and following verses all refer to last-day events. Jesus now states "So." This word indicates a declaratory statement. Jesus is now going to answer the disciples question again. Jesus is now going to describe the deception He warned of in Matthew 24:4. Jesus is now predicting the signal event, which is "the sign" His disciples asked for in Matthew 24:3. This is the answer to His disciples' question. This "desolating sacrilege" is the sign which signals the "close of the age" (Matthew 24:3). This "desolating sacrilege" is the signal to flee for their lives. This "desolating sacrilege spoken of by the prophet Daniel" is the "abomination that makes desolate" (Daniel 11:31 and Daniel 12:11), it is "the transgression that makes desolate" (Daniel 8:13) and it is the "one who makes desolate" (Daniel 9:27). Jesus' initial answer to His disciples was to "take heed that no one leads you astray" (Matthew 24:4). Now He says that when you see this "desolating sacrilege" it is time to flee (Matthew 24:16). What is the connection between the two statements? Who is this "desolating sacrilege"? Why is he "standing in the holy place"? Why is it important for the reader to "understand"? These questions will be answered in the chapters discussing Daniel 8, 9, 11, and 12—The Abomination That Makes Desolate.

In Matthew 24, Jesus explains that the sign in the last days will focus on false Christs and the false prophets which point to the false Christs. The issue is deception. Then He describes His Second Coming twice (Matthew 24:27, 30, 31) to compare it to the false Christ's coming. In Matthew 24:30, He describes His Second Coming as "the sign of the Son of man." He is describing His sign, as the manner of His coming, as opposed to the sign of the false Christ. Jesus is comparing His coming in the clouds to the fake return of the false Christ. The false Christ will be seen "in the wilderness" and "in the inner rooms" (Matthew 24:26). Jesus coming will be "on the clouds" and that is His "sign" (Matthew 24:30). Jesus will not walk on this earth at His Second Coming. The sign of "the close of the age" that the disciples asked for (Matthew 24:3) will be the false Christ coming to stand "in the holy place." This "desolating sacrilege" is the final false Christ. This "desolating sacrilege" is the "abomination that makes desolate" which was "spoken of by the prophet Daniel" (Daniel 11:31).

"As the crowning act in the great drama of deception Satan himself will personate Christ. The church has long professed to look to the Savior's advent as the consummation of her hopes. Now the great deceiver will make it appear that Christ has come. In different parts of the earth, Satan will manifest himself among men as a majestic being of dazzling brightness, resembling the description of the Son of God given by John in the Revelation. Revelation 1:13-15. The glory that surrounds him is unsurpassed by anything that mortal eyes have yet beheld . . . He heals the diseases of the people . . . This is the strong, almost overmastering delusion" (*The Great Controversy*, page 624).[2] This almost overpowering delusion is Satan as the false Christ. He is the "desolating sacrilege" who will stand "in the holy place."

Jesus refers us to Daniel in order for us to recognize this final sign of the end. The scriptural cross-references refer you to three texts in Daniel: Daniel 9:27; Daniel 11:31; and Daniel 12:11. Jesus is referring to these prophecies and connecting them to last-day events. Each of these texts will be discussed in detail in the following chapters: Daniel 8, 9, 11, and 12—The Abomination That Makes Desolate. It is important to note that Jesus Himself applied Daniel 9:27 to the false Christ in the last days and not to Himself! Daniel 9:27 speaks of one week of prophetic time or seven years. This same seven years will appear again in Revelation 11:3, 9. Jesus applies the seven years spoken of by Daniel to Satan and not to Himself! Satan, as the "one who makes desolate," will cause the sacrifice and offerings to cease (Daniel 9:27). The "desolating sacrilege" is the "desolater" (Daniel 9:27).

This "desolating sacrilege" or the "abomination that makes desolate" (Daniel 11:31) is the final false Christ. This will be Satan impersonating Jesus Christ. This "sacrilege" is what upset Daniel so much and which he could not understand (Daniel 12:8). Only the "wise" in the last days will understand (Daniel 12:10). All of the prophecies in Daniel, which relate to this abomination, have a last day's application, which is why Jesus said "let the reader understand." These dual applications will be discussed further in the remaining chapters in Section I: The Abomination that Makes Desolate.

The phrase "standing in the holy place" is important. When the abomination is finally seen "in the holy place" that is the time to flee (Matthew 24:16). Thus, "the sign" of the "close of the age" (Matthew 24:3) is when Satan occupies the holy place. The holy place is the front compartment of the sanctuary or temple of God. God's temple was in Jerusalem.

Today, many in the world are focused on Jerusalem as shown by the following facts:

- *Millions of dollars have been raised to fund the rebuilding of the temple in Jerusalem.[3]*

- *The descendants of the tribe of Levi (the priesthood) have been identified genetically through DNA studies in preparation for their service in the temple.[4]*

- *The furnishings of the temple are being rebuilt and prepared for the restoration of the temple services.[5]*

- *The pure red heifer needed for the temple dedication has been identified.[6]*

Daniel foresaw this abomination "set up" in Daniel 11:31. This abomination would "profane the temple" (Daniel 11:31). Satan will set up his kingdom in Jerusalem and claim to be Christ returned. This is confirmed in Revelation 11:7, 8 where Satan is described as the "beast that ascends" who is in the city "where their Lord was crucified."

- *Jesus foretold the sign of the end and the sign He foretold is the false Christ ministering in the temple in Jerusalem.*

The "sign" the disciples were asking for in Matthew 24:3 will occur when Satan assumes his throne as the false Christ in Jerusalem and begins to minister in the rebuilt temple.

> Matthew 24:16: *"then let those who are in Judea flee to the mountains."*

Historically, this verse was fulfilled in A.D. 70 when Rome overran Jerusalem. This warning, however, will apply again. During the last days when the abomination is set up in the holy place, God's people are told to flee to the mountains. When God's people see the abomination or false Christ set up in Jerusalem and ministering in the temple then it is time to flee to the mountains. The phrase "those who are in Judea" applies to all of God's people at that time, not just to those in the Middle East. The time of the great tribulation and the mark of the beast are soon to follow.

> Matthew 24:17: *"let him who is on the housetop not go down to take what is in his house."*

This verse stresses the importance of fleeing immediately. Once the false Christ takes over as king of Israel and begins his ministry in the temple, persecution of God's people will increase rapidly. This is the time to flee to the mountains. It should be noted that the deserts are not the place to hide. There are several important reasons why this is true, which will become apparent in discussions later on in this book. The reader is referred to the chapters on Revelation 8, 9 and 13. The issue is not just fleeing to a remote place. The deserts can be very remote and unpopulated. However, the global temperature will be rising and the deserts will become intolerable. Also the water supply will become an issue in the last days. Both of these facts suggest that the mountains are the place to flee to.

> Matthew 24:18: *"and let him who is in the field not turn back to take his mantle."*

This verse repeats the concept of the prior verse. Make haste and do not delay. There will be no time for packing. God's people should have been prepared prior to this because if they are not many will suffer unnecessarily. It is critical that God's people recognize this sign and flee before it is too late.

> Matthew 24:19: *"and alas for those who are with child and for those who give suck in those days!"*

This verse again repeats the warning. When the abomination is set up (Daniel 11:31) it is to time flee. Those with small children and those who are pregnant will have an especially difficult time. However, they still must flee. Each of these verses reiterates the same concept. The only safety will be found in fleeing to remote and isolated areas in the mountains. Once the abomination that makes desolate is set up, his power will be far reaching.

> Matthew 24:20: *"Pray that your flight may not be in winter or on a sabbath."*

This verse again repeats the importance of flight to safety. Jesus is emphasizing how critical it will be to flee from this abomination before it is too late. Regardless of the weather, it will be imperative to flee to isolated areas in the mountains. Jesus repeats His warning four times (Matthew 24:17, 18, 19, 20). Jesus is strongly emphasizing the importance of this deception.

> Matthew 24:21: *"For then there will be great tribulation, such as has not been from the beginning of the world until now, no, and never will be."*

Jesus is now describing a unique event, which will only occur once in the history of the world. This "great tribulation" will occur after the "abomination that makes desolate" is "set up" (Daniel 11:31). This "great tribulation" occurs after the desolating sacrilege is seen standing in the holy place. This is clear because he says, "*then* there will be great tribulation*" (emphasis supplied). This "great tribulation":

1) Occurs after the desolating sacrilege is seen standing in the holy place.
2) Will never be equaled in the history of the world, past, present, or future.
3) Is the same as the time of trouble that Daniel is describing in Daniel 12:1 "such as never has been since there was a nation till that time."

Daniel is describing the exact same events as Jesus is describing! Daniel's time of trouble (Daniel 12:1) also occurs after the abomination is "set up," which occurs in Daniel 11:31 prior to the events of Daniel 12:1. Daniel is describing time of the end events just prior to Jesus' Second Coming. This "great tribulation" will occur after the ascension of the false Christ or Satan to the throne in Jerusalem where he will minister in the temple of God in "the holy place" (Matthew 24:15).

> Matthew 24:22: *"And if those days had not been shortened, no human being would be saved; but for the sake of the elect those days will be shortened."*

This verse again only applies to the last-day events. It is referring to the time of great tribulation, which will only occur at the time of the end. Jesus says that things will be so severe that no one will survive unless God cuts this time period short. God will do this by bringing His wrath on the wicked in the form of the seven last plagues (Revelation 15:1). This verse suggests that God can shorten the length of Satan's reign and will do so in order to protect His people. This verse will have its fulfillment during the Battle of Armageddon (discussed in Revelation 16—The Seven Last Plagues).

> Matthew 24:23: *"Then if any one says to you, 'Lo, here is the Christ!' or 'There he is!' do not believe it."*

This verse returns to Jesus' initial answer to the disciple's question "what will be the sign" (Matthew 24:3). Jesus is again emphasizing that deception is the issue and the false Christ will be the method. The abomination is the false Christ. The false Christ will first appear working miracles in many places and many people will accept him because of those miracles. This will eventually lead to the false Christ being "set up" (Daniel 11:31) as "the abomination" in Jerusalem. Jesus is warning not to believe anyone who claims to know where Christ is physically located. He continues by explaining why not to believe them when they say He is here. He then describes His true coming in the clouds and compares it to the coming of the false Christ.

> Matthew 24:24: *"For false Christs and false prophets will arise and show great signs and wonders, so as to lead astray, if possible, even the elect."*

Again, Jesus reiterates the key to His answer to what the sign is. The answer is: do not be deceived. The method is the false Christ. In the last days Satan will pose as the final false Christ. Satan, as the false Christ or antichrist will employ false prophets to support his claim. These false prophets will work wonders and miracles in his name and point people to Satan as the returned Christ. Satan will work even greater miracles and convince the Christian world that he has returned to establish peace on earth. Satan's miracles will be powerful enough "to lead astray, if possible, even the elect." In Ellen G. White's book, *The Great Controversy,* page 624, we read, "As the crowning act in the great drama of deception, Satan himself will personate Christ... In gentle, compassionate tones he presents some of the same gracious, heavenly truths, which the Savior uttered; he heals the diseases of the people... This is the strong, almost overmastering delusion."[6]

Matthew 24:25: *"Lo, I have told you beforehand."*

Jesus again is trying to warn His disciples that this deception is extremely powerful. He is telling them that He has warned them beforehand so they can withstand this almost overwhelming delusion.

> Matthew 24:26: *"So, if they say to you, 'Lo, he is in the wilderness,' do not go out; if they say, 'Lo, he is in the inner rooms,' do not believe it."*

Jesus repeats once more His warning. If someone says that Christ is in the wilderness or in the city or in this church or at this synagogue, do not believe it. Jesus has now repeated His warnings and His answer to what is the sign multiple times in this chapter. The warning is not to be deceived and the sign is the deceiver being "set up" (Daniel 11:31) or "standing in the holy place" (Matthew 24:15). The following verses in Matthew 24 relate to "the sign": Matthew 24:3, 4, 5, 11, 15, 23, 24, and 26. *Jesus' answer to His disciples' question is: the sign of My coming will be a false Christ who will come in the last days and stand in God's holy temple and deceive, if possible, the very elect.*

> Matthew 24:27: *"For as the lightning comes from the east and shines as far as the west, so will be the coming of the Son of man."*

Jesus now gives the sign of His coming. Jesus gives this description of His coming in order for the elect to know the difference between His coming and the appearance of the false Christ. Satan will not be allowed to counterfeit Jesus Christ's Second Coming in the clouds. Satan will be allowed to walk the earth as the false Christ and reign as the false Christ but he cannot counterfeit Jesus' coming in the clouds. Jesus gives this description to show the difference between His coming and the coming of the false or anti-Christ. Jesus Christ coming will be worldwide and visible to all men. His coming will be seen "as the lightning comes from the east and shines as far as the west." Jesus' coming will not be secret or invisible. His coming will not be in the desert or at a local church or in one of the inner rooms. He will not rapture His people secretly!

> Matthew 24:28: *"Wherever the body is, there the eagles (vultures) will be gathered together."*

The context of this verse is in connection with end-time events and particularly with Jesus' Second Coming, since He has just described His coming in the clouds.

This suggests a connection to Revelation 19:17, 18, and 21. In Revelation 19:17, the destruction of the wicked is pictured as "the great supper of God" where the birds will eat the flesh of the wicked. This verse is describing the end result of the wicked at the Second Coming, when they will be destroyed and eaten by the vultures.

> Matthew 24:29: *"Immediately after the tribulation of those days the sun will be darkened, and the moon will not give its light, and the stars will fall from heaven, and the powers of the heavens will be shaken."*

This event clearly occurs at the end of time, since it follows the tribulation and precedes Jesus' Second Coming. This same event is described in Joel 2:31: "The sun shall be turned to darkness, and the moon to blood, before the great and terrible day of the Lord comes." Also, this event is described as part of the sixth seal in Revelation 6:12,13: "the sun became black as sackcloth, the full moon became like blood, and the stars of the sky fell to the earth as the fig tree sheds its winter fruit when shaken by a gale." These events occur immediately after the tribulation and have not yet occurred as some have suggested in the past. Some have applied the events of the sixth seal to the time period of 1750 to 1840.[7] However, this is inconsistent with the rest of the sixth seal, which describes events at the time of the Second Coming (discussed in Revelation 9— The Seven Trumpets: The First and Second Woes).

At the end of time, nature will reflect God's wrath as God demonstrates His power over nature. This is power Satan has claimed as his own because he claims to be Christ. The sun will refuse to shine and the moon will be darkened and the stars will fall just prior to Jesus appearing in the clouds of heaven. This is shown in the next text which begins with "then."

> Matthew 24:30: *"then will appear the sign of the Son of man in heaven, and then all the tribes of the earth will mourn, and they will see the Son of man coming on the clouds of heaven with power and great glory."*

This is the second time Jesus describes His coming in His answer to His disciples' question about what will be the sign. He does this to specifically compare His coming to that of the false Christ or the abomination that makes desolate. He wants it to be crystal clear that His coming is worldwide and in the clouds as opposed to the false Christ who will appear on earth "in the wilderness" or "in the inner rooms" (Matthew 24:26).

Jesus also calls His appearance in the clouds His "sign." He does this to show what His "sign" is compared to "the sign" of the "close of the age" (Matthew 24:3). Jesus' "sign" is His coming on the clouds. Jesus "sign" is how He comes: He will come in the clouds of heaven. The sign that the disciples asked about: "the sign" of the "close of the age" (Matthew 24:3) is the false Christ when he becomes "the abomination that makes desolate" (Daniel 11:31). Jesus calls this the "desolating sacrilege" (Matthew 24:14). Jesus is calling attention to the difference between His real coming and the false coming of the anti-Christ.

Jesus describes His coming as "on the clouds of heaven with power and great glory." Jesus' description is paralleled by Paul's description in 1 Thessalonians 4:17 where Paul describes the saved being "caught up together with them in the clouds to meet the Lord in the air." This is the seventh plague, which is poured "into the air" (Revelation 16:17). Jesus will not touch the earth at His Second Coming. Jesus will bring His people up to Him in the clouds. Satan will not be allowed to counterfeit this.

> Matthew 24:31: *"and he will send out his angels with a loud trumpet call, and they will gather his elect from the four winds, from one end of heaven to the other."*

Jesus will not touch the earth but will send His angels to gather His elect. His "elect" are the righteous saved, both those resurrected and those living at His Second Coming. Jesus' angels will gather the saved from all four corners of the earth represented by the "four winds." They will then be caught up "in the clouds to meet the Lord in the air" (1 Thessalonians 4:17). Jesus will not walk the earth working miracles nor will He be found in the inner rooms.

> Matthew 24:32: *"From the fig tree learn its lesson; as soon as its branch becomes tender and puts forth its leaves, you know that summer is near."*

Jesus now introduces an object lesson. This object lesson relates to the last-day events He has been describing as the answer to His disciples' question about the sign. This object lesson involves the fig tree. Jesus is saying that you can tell by the fig tree's branches and leaves that summer is near. He is going to apply this object lesson to the last-day events. Jesus is saying that we should be able to recognize when the time is near by the events He has described in the previous verses.

> Matthew 24:33: *"So also, when you see all these things, you know that he is near, at the very gates."*

Jesus is telling us that when we see the "desolating sacrilege" of Matthew 24:15 or the "abomination that makes desolate" of Daniel 11:31 set up in the holy place that we can know that His coming is near "at the very gates." Many Christians feel that any information that suggests that Jesus' coming is near or that outlines last-day events cannot be correct because it might give us an idea relating to when Jesus' return would occur. Jesus clearly disagrees with this concept. Even though no one can know "that day and hour" (Matthew 24:36) **we can know that it is near "at the very gates"** (emphasis supplied).

> Matthew 24:34, 35: *"Truly, I say to you, this generation will not pass away till all these things take place. Heaven and earth will pass away, but my words will not pass away."*

Jesus' statement in this verse has often been misunderstood. Some have thought He was referring to His current generation. However, in the context of these verses it appears that He is actually referring to the generation that exists when the abomination appears. This generation will not pass away before Christ returns. The generation that exists when the abomination is set up will exist when Jesus returns. *This generation will not pass away before Jesus returns but will be destroyed when Jesus returns, except for those who are part of the elect.* This living elect is described in Revelation 7:3, 4 as the 144,000 who are sealed (discussed under Revelation 6:17 and Revelation 9:4 in the chapters on the Seven Seals and the Seven Trumpets). Jesus' statement "heaven and earth will pass away, but my words will not pass away" is reiterating the significance of His prophecy. Jesus is saying that even though the world "will pass away" His prophecy is accurate and will not fail. Jesus is implying that heaven and earth will come to an end with this generation but His words will never pass away.

SUMMARY

Matthew 24 gives Jesus' answer to His disciples' question "What will be the sign of your coming and of the close of the age?" (Matthew 24:3). Jesus answer involves a false Christ. Jesus' initial answer was "take heed that no one leads you astray" (Matthew 24:4). Jesus continues to give His answer in the next several verses by describing false Christs more than any other sign. He then links "the desolating sacrilege" described in Daniel 9:27, Daniel 11:31, and Daniel 12:11 to the sign of the close of the age. Jesus refers the reader to Daniel. Jesus applies Daniel 9:27 to the last days. He does not apply Daniel 9:27 to Himself. He states that the "desolating sacrilege" will be followed by the great tribulation and then followed by His Second Coming. Jesus then again warns against being misled by false Christs. He finally describes His Second Coming on the clouds as His "sign" (Matthew 24:30) in order to compare His sign to "the sign" of the false Christ, who will come walking on the earth to mislead mankind. Jesus also points to those living at the time of the abomination as the last generation prior to His coming. Jesus' answer to what is the sign of the close of the age is that the "desolating sacrilege" or the abomination that makes desolate is the sign. This abomination is the final false Christ, who is Satan, who will deceive the world in the last days. This abomination is referred to in Daniel 8, 9, 11, and 12. In Daniel 8:13, this "desolating sacrilege" is called "the transgression that makes desolate." In Daniel 9:27, this "desolating sacrilege" is called "the one who makes desolate." In Daniel 11:31 and in Daniel 12:11, this "desolating sacrilege" is called "the abomination that makes desolate." In order to understand the events which surround the establishment of this "desolating sacrilege," we must study each of these prophecies. These prophecies are all related to this abomination and therefore to the last-day events. It is important that the "reader understand" that Jesus made this connection and that Jesus himself applies Daniel 9:27 as well as Daniel 11:31 and Daniel 12:11 to last-day events. The following graph outlines the events described in Matthew 24.

Matthew 24

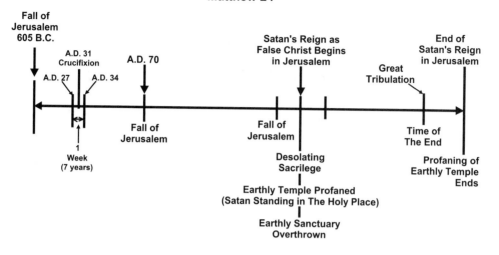

1 Nichol, Francis D. (Ed.). *The Seventh-day Adventist Bible Commentary,* (Review and Herald Publishing Association, Washington, D.C.) 1957, Vol. 5, p. 499.
2 White, Ellen G., *The Great Controversy* (Pacific Press Publishing Association, Nampa, Idaho) 1950, p. 624.
3 Price, J. Randall.(2004), *The Jewish Voice Today* (electronic version). Copyright 2004. Retrieved November 3. 2004, from http://dunamai.com/articles/Israel/third_temple_built.htm
4 Ibid.
5 Hubbard, R. Dean, (1998). *U. S. Ministers and Israeli Rabbis are Joining Hands in a Restoration Ministry* (electronic version). Retrieved November 3, 2004, from http://www.templemount.org/heifer.html
6 White, Ellen G., *The Great Controversy* (Pacific Press Publishing Association, Nampa, Idaho) 1950, p. 624.
7 Nichol, Francis D. (Ed.). *The Seventh-day Adventist Bible Commentary,* (Review and Herald Publishing Association, Washington, D.C.) 1957, Vol. 7, p. 779.

Daniel 8
The Abomination and the Sanctuary

Daniel 8 introduces Daniel's third vision, which covers the world's history from Babylon's reign down to the end of time. Daniel has previously been shown an "image" and a "stone" in Daniel 2:35, which represented world history extending from Babylon through Media-Persia, Greece, Rome, and finally to the Second Coming. The image is destroyed by the stone "cut out by no human hand" (Daniel 2:32). Daniel's second vision of world history involved four beasts: a lion, a bear, a leopard, and a "terrible and dreadful" beast with a little horn (Daniel 7:7). It also included a court scene with the judgment of the world portrayed (Daniel 7:9, 10).

The third vision of Daniel covers the same historical time frame as the previous visions. The ram represented Media-Persia (Daniel 8:21) and the he-goat represented Greece (Daniel 8:22). The little horn represented pagan Rome and Papal Rome. Pagan Rome followed Greece as the next world power and then was followed by the Papacy, which took over from pagan Rome as the world's leader. There appears to be a dual application in Daniel 8:9-14 since both pagan Rome and Papal Rome can be understood to fulfill this prophecy. It depends on whether this prophecy is applied to the heavenly or earthly sanctuary. This prophecy can represent the literal earthly sanctuary in Israel, which pagan Rome overran, or it can represent the heavenly sanctuary in which case the Papacy fulfills this prophecy. Papal Rome took away the "continual burnt offering" and "cast down" truth (Daniel 8:11-12).[1]

> Daniel 8:11: *"It magnified itself even up to the Prince of the host; and the continual burnt offering was taken away from him, and the place of his sanctuary was overthrown."*

Historically, this text has been applied to either pagan Rome or to the Papacy. However, another application of this prophecy is possible. These verses are describing a power, which will magnify itself even up "to the Prince of the host." The "Prince of the host" is Christ referred to in Daniel 8:25 as the "Prince of princes." This same power will take away the continual burnt offering from the Prince of Hosts and overthrow His sanctuary.

The continual burnt offering mentioned in this verse refers to the sacrifice of animals in the Hebrew sanctuary, which pointed forward to Jesus as the Lamb Slain (Revelation 5:6). This power pictured as a horn will replace Jesus as the Lamb Slain and also overthrow His sanctuary. In the last days, Satan will impersonate Christ on earth and he will cause the real daily sacrifice or continual burnt offering to lose its effect for all those who accept Satan as Christ. This will take the "continual burnt offering" away "from him." This will make Jesus "offering" of no value to those who believe Satan's lies. This will overthrow Jesus' sanctuary on earth. The earthly sanctuary or temple will become Satan's. This will effectively destroy the sanctuary that Daniel was hoping to see re-established. In the last days, Satan as the false Christ will fulfill this prophecy again by rebuilding and occupying the temple in Jerusalem. This would explain Daniel's sudden illness at the end of this prophecy.

> Daniel 8:12: *"And the host was given over to it together with the continual burnt offering through transgression; and truth was cast down to the ground, and the horn acted and prospered."*

The "host" here refers to God's people since in the previous verse Jesus is described as the Prince of the host. This suggests that God's people will be ruled or controlled by this power. This will occur when Satan gains control as Christianity's leader in the last days. Satan and his kingdom are represented by the horn. The continual burnt offering will be taken over by Satan when he claims to be Christ returned to earth. When Satan takes over the temple services in Jerusalem he will act as God and forgive sins. When this occurs, transgression or sin will have replaced the continual burnt offering. Satan will replace Jesus' true sacrifice or burnt offering with Satan's false religion. Once this has occurred, truth will be "cast down to the ground" and Satan as the false Christ will prosper as the world's spiritual leader.

> Daniel 8:13: *"Then I heard a holy one speaking; and another holy one said to the one that spoke, 'For how long is the vision concerning the continual burnt offering, the transgression that makes desolate, and the giving over of the sanctuary and host to be trampled under foot?'"*

The holy ones talking are angels or God's spokesmen who are introduced here in order to ask an extremely important question. This question is asked in order for Daniel and future generations to understand how long this horrible situation would last. The answer is critical and relates to all the events described in the previous three verses. There are four separate but related symbols:

1) the continual burnt offering,
2) the transgression that makes desolate,
3) the giving over of the sanctuary,
4) and the trampling underfoot of God's people.

How you define these four symbols will determine how you interpret the answer found in Daniel 8:14. If you define the sanctuary as the heavenly sanctuary then the taking away of the burnt offering would represent pagan and Papal Rome's attempt to replace Jesus as Priest and Savior with salvation by works and a false priesthood.[2] The host being "trampled underfoot" would represent the persecution of God's people during the reign of the Papacy (A.D. 538 to 1798). The "transgression that makes desolate" would refer to pagan and Papal Rome's false religions, which dominated God's people before and during the Dark Ages.[3] This interpretation of Daniel 8:13, 14 is critical to an understanding of the investigative judgment process, which began in 1844 (discussed in Appendix (1)—The Investigative Judgment). This judgment process is also described in Daniel 7:9-14, Revelation 4:2-8, and Revelation 5:1-10 (discussed in Revelation 4 and 5—The Judgment Scene). This interpretation was God ordained and led to many converts to Christianity in the 1800s and 1900s and up to the present time.

However, since God is a God of hope, He has given us a second application to this prophecy, which will apply in the last days. This second application does not negate or replace the previous application any more than applying Matthew 24 to events in A.D. 70 negates its application to last-day events. Matthew 24 clearly has a dual application to last-day events since Jesus refers to Daniel 9:27 and the "desolating sacrilege" (Matthew 24:15) as the sign "of the close of the age" (Matthew 24:3). In Matthew 24:15, Jesus connects Daniel 9:27 to last-day events. These last-day events are described in 2 Thessalonians 2:4 where the man of sin "takes his seat in the temple of God, proclaiming himself to be God." This lawless one will come "with all power and with pretended signs and wonders" (2 Thessalonians 2:9).

Applying Daniel 8:13 to last-day events it becomes clear that the "transgression that makes desolate" represents Satan as the false Christ. The "giving over of the sanctuary" will occur when Satan establishes his false kingdom in Jerusalem and sets up his false religion in the sanctuary (rebuilt temple). This will destroy the "continual burnt offering," which represents Jesus' death for sin. The real "burnt offering" will be replaced with Satan's false religion claiming that he is Christ. If this is not an abomination, what is? From Satan's throne in Jerusalem, he will attempt to destroy God's true worshipers and "make war on the rest" of God's people (Revelation 12:17). This trampling of God's people will continue until Christ's Second Coming.

> Daniel 8:14: *"And he said to him, 'For two thousand*
> *three hundred evenings and mornings; then the*
> *sanctuary shall be restored to its rightful state.'"*

This time prophecy has been viewed in two different ways. Historically, "two thousand three hundred evenings and mornings" has been thought of as 2300 days if you consider an evening and morning as equal to one day (Genesis 1:5, 18, 13, 19, 23, and 31). Using this approach, 2300 prophetic days would equal 2300 literal years. This is based on one prophetic day equals one literal year (Ezekiel 4:6 and Numbers 14:34). In Daniel 9:24, "seventy weeks of years" is cut off or decreed for God's people. This 70 weeks or 490 days (70 times 7) is prophetic of 490 years, which began "at the going forth of the word to restore and build Jerusalem" (Daniel 9:25). This 70 week period was cut off from the original 2300-year prophecy of Daniel 8:14. Daniel 9:24-27 is the angel Gabriel's answer to Daniel's lack of understanding of his vision in Daniel 8. This lack of understanding is evidenced in Daniel 8:27: "I was appalled by the vision and did not understand it."

Daniel was appalled by the fact that time would go for so long and that Satan would ultimately occupy God's sanctuary and seat of authority in His temple. This 2300-day prophecy began in 457 B.C. when Artaxerxes's decree went forth to restore and rebuild Jerusalem. This 2300-year prophecy ended in 1844 when the heavenly sanctuary was to be cleansed.

This cleansing or restoration of the sanctuary is represented by the Day of Atonement services in the Old Testament. This was the yearly cleansing of sin from the most holy place of the sanctuary. This process involved removing the sins of God's people from the sanctuary's most holy place. These sins were removed or cleansed on the Day of Atonement by the slaying of a lamb and the ministering of the lamb's blood in the most holy place. This cleansed or restored the sanctuary. These sins were then symbolically transferred to a living scapegoat, which was then sent into the wilderness to die.

This cleansing of the sanctuary typifies the investigative judgment in heaven, which began in 1844 and is still ongoing. The investigative judgment is the process whereby the heavenly sanctuary is cleansed of the sins of God's people. The investigative judgment involves cleansing only those sins, which have been placed in God's temple or sanctuary. This judgment involves only those who claim to be God's people, just as the earthly cleansing process only involved God's people. The unrepentant have never brought their sins to the sanctuary to be forgiven and, therefore, their sins have not accumulated in the sanctuary.

Those who have transferred their sins into the heavenly sanctuary by accepting God's plan of salvation will have their records reviewed. Their records are contained in a book in heaven. This book or scroll is described in Revelation 5:1 as "written within and on the back, sealed with seven seals." Only Christ the Lamb "slain" and the "Lion of the tribe of Judah" (Revelation 5:5-6) can open this book. Only Jesus Christ has earned the right to open this book through His death. His death is what allowed His saint's names to be written in the book in the first place. For a further discussion of the investigative judgment the reader is referred to Appendix (1)—The Investigative Judgment.

The investigative judgment began in 1844 as prophesied in Daniel 8:14. However, there is also a dual application that applies to the last days. Other scholars have interpreted "two thousand three hundred evenings and mornings" as a total figure. In other words, this would represent 1150 evenings plus 1150 mornings, which would total 2300. This would equal 1150 total days (if an evening plus a morning equal one day). In the last-day application, this could represent either 2300 literal days or 1150 literal days at the time of the end. It should be noted that if this text had said 2300 "days" then there would be only one possible interpretation. However, it describes "evenings and mornings," which allows an alternative interpretation. God wrote this text in such a way as to allow both interpretations. This was not accidental. As will be discussed later, 1150 literal days is the more likely interpretation for the last-days application, since this is consistent with the time prophecies of both Daniel 12 and Revelation 11.

A time of the end application is apparent in Gabriel's explanation to Daniel, since he specifically refers to the time of the end. It will become apparent later in the discussion on Daniel 11 that in the book of Daniel "the time of the end" is a very specific time period (Daniel 11:35,40).

> Daniel 8:17, 19: *"So he came near where I stood; and when he came, I was frightened and fell upon my face. But he said to me 'Understand, O son of man, that the vision is for the time of the end'. . . He said, 'Behold, I will make known to you what shall be at the latter end of the indignation; for it pertains to the appointed time of the end.'"*

In both of these verses Gabriel tells Daniel that the 2300-day prophecy applies to the "time of the end." The "vision is for the time of the end" and it "pertains to the appointed time of the end." Later in Daniel 11 and 12 "the time of the end" is linked to the time of trouble and also to the abomination that makes desolate. The book of Daniel has a specific "time of the end." It is associated with the very last-day events of earth's history. This "time of the end" involves events that have not yet occurred. Daniel's "time of the end" did not occur in 1844. Gabriel also states he is going to tell Daniel what occurs at the "latter end of the indignation." This latter end is mentioned again in Daniel 8:23, which refers to Satan. The "indignation" refers to the abomination that makes desolate. The "indignation" will involve "the time of the end." The "indignation" represents the antichrist pretending to be the true Christ.

> Daniel 8:23: *"And at the latter end of their rule, when the transgressors have reached their full measure, a king of bold countenance, one who understands riddles, shall arise."*

Gabriel is explaining the prophecy of Daniel 8 because Daniel did not understand it. Historically, this text has been applied to the development of pagan Rome, which followed the breakdown of ancient Greece.[4] It was thought that the four divisions of Greece were described in Daniel 8:22. Papal Rome then followed pagan Rome and Daniel 8:24, 25 was interpreted as describing both pagan and Papal Rome's attacks on God's people and on His Son the "Prince of princes."

However, there is another interpretation that is consistent with the previous dual application of Daniel 8:8-14. This application would apply Daniel 8:23 to the time of the end events, which is consistent with Daniel 8:17, 19 where Gabriel connects this vision to the time of the end. In this context, "when the transgressors have reached their full measure" refers to last-day events when Satan has control over the world, which will cause transgression to reach its full potential.

The "king of bold countenance" who "understands riddles" refers to Satan as he pretends to be Christ and works miracles which "lead astray if possible, even the elect" (Matthew 24:24). His "bold countenance" refers to his appearance as a mighty angel pretending to be Christ returned. This countenance will mimic the description of Jesus in Revelation 1:13-15. Satan's ability to interpret the scriptures and his claims to be their author, which will effectively destroy the scriptures as an effective witness of the true Christ, can be seen as a fulfillment of this phrase describing his mental ability.

> Daniel 8:24: *"His power shall be great, and he shall cause fearful destruction, and shall succeed in what he does, and destroy mighty men and the people of the saints."*

Historically, this text has been applied to the Papacy as it grew in power and persecuted God's people. However, it also describes Satan as he gains control of Christianity and the so-called Christian nations. Satan's power as the false Christ will include control of Rome as the eighth king (Revelation 17:11). Satan will "cause fearful destruction, and shall succeed in what he does." Satan's primary focus beyond gaining world control will be to destroy "the people of the saints." In order for Satan to gain control of the world, he will have to destroy many "mighty men."

Daniel 8:25: *"By his cunning, he shall make deceit prosper under his hand, and in his own mind, he shall magnify himself. Without warning he shall destroy many; and he shall even rise up against the Prince of princes; but, by no human hand, he shall be broken."*

Historically, the first part of this verse has been applied to the Papacy.[5] Papal Rome did magnify itself and "make deceit prosper." Papal Rome destroyed millions of people during the Dark Ages who refused to accept her doctrines. The Papacy did rise up against the Prince of princes, Jesus, by taking away His authority to forgive sin and placing it in the priest's hands.

However, in the dual application involving last-day events, Satan also fulfills each of these prophecies. Clearly, when Satan attempts to impersonate Christ, he is rising up against the Prince of princes and he is also magnifying himself as is predicted in this verse. This is a fulfillment of Isaiah 14:12 where Satan is called the "Day Star." In Isaiah 14:14 Satan declares "I will make myself like the Most High."

Satan as the false Christ will reinterpret scriptures and claim to be the author of God's Word. This reinterpretation will "make deceit prosper." This is when God's two witnesses will be dead but not buried (Revelation 11:9). The two witnesses are the Old and New Testaments. Once Satan has control of Christianity as the false Christ he will be able to "destroy many" without warning. Clearly, Satan's cunning does fulfill this verse.

The fact that he will not be broken by "human hand" again connects this verse to Satan. In Daniel 2:44, we see that God sets up His own eternal kingdom and destroys the world's last kingdom. This is portrayed by using the image of a stone "cut out by no human hand" (Daniel 2:34, 45). This represents Satan's last kingdom being destroyed not by man but by God Himself. This phrase "by no human hand" confirms that Daniel 8:25 is referring to the same event. Daniel 8:25 is referring to Satan's kingdom, which is set up in the last days, being destroyed not by man but by God. This connects this prophecy to the time of the end and to Satan as the false Christ. The phrase "rise up against the Prince of princes" refers to the final battle between Satan and Christ (Revelation 17:13, 14 and Revelation 19:19).

Daniel 8:26: *"The vision of the evenings and the mornings which has been told is true; but seal up the vision for it pertains to many days hence."*

This verse ends the explanation given at that time to Daniel regarding the 2300 evenings and mornings. In Daniel 9:22-27, Daniel is given a further explanation regarding this vision. This explanation comes in answer to Daniel's prayer for his people, and for wisdom and understanding (Daniel 9:22).

This vision was to be sealed up, but not the entire book. This vision pertained to "many days hence" and related to time of the end events. This sealing suggests a connection to Daniel 12:9 where that vision was sealed "until the time of the end." Indeed, the vision in Daniel 12 also concerns the "abomination that makes desolate" (Daniel 12:11), which is described in Daniel 8:13 as the "transgression that makes desolate."

> Daniel 8:27: *"And I, Daniel, was overcome and lay sick for some days; then I rose and went about the king's business; but I was appalled by the vision and did not understand it."*

Daniel was greatly upset by this vision to the point of physical illness because he did not understand its meaning. In addition, he "was appalled" or astonished by the vision. Daniel was looking forward to the reestablishment of Israel as a kingdom and also the reestablishment of the temple services in Jerusalem. This vision showed that God's sanctuary would be overrun by evil and destroyed and that a "transgression that makes desolate" would be set up (Daniel 8:13). That alone would be enough to make Daniel physically ill, however, the time prophecies would also have upset him because of the long delay before Christ's return. Regardless of whether you view this vision as a prophecy of a future investigative judgment to begin in 1844 and/or as a prophecy of Satan's attempt to impersonate Christ's return at the end of time, the message is still appalling. Daniel's lack of understanding is clear in his final statement "I was appalled by the vision and did not understand it." Daniel 9 continues God's explanation of this prophecy.

SUMMARY

There is a dual application for Daniel 8:11-14. It can and does apply to Papal Rome through history as it opposed God's true believers. It correctly predicts an investigative judgment that began in 1844. However, it also applies to Satan as the abomination that makes desolate when he becomes the world's spiritual leader in the last days. Satan will truly cast truth "down to the ground" and trample God's people under foot. The 2300-day prophecy also has a dual application in the last days.

The question asked in Daniel 8:13 is "how long is the vision concerning the continual burnt offering, the transgression that makes desolate, and the giving over of the sanctuary" and the "host to be trampled under." The answer in Daniel 8:14 is "For two thousand and three hundred evenings and mornings; then the sanctuary shall be restored to its rightful state." This would mean that the time from the trampling of the "host" to the restoration of the sanctuary would be 2300 evenings and mornings, which can be interpreted as 1150 days. In this application, 2300 can be considered as a total number of evenings and mornings, in other words 1150 evenings and 1150 mornings. This time period would then represent 1150 days (discussed in Revelation 13 (last part)—The Mark of the Beast).

The loss of the "continual burnt offering" represents Satan replacing Jesus who is the Lamb Slain. The "giving over of the sanctuary" represents Satan taking over the rebuilt earthly temple in Jerusalem. The establishment of the "transgression that makes desolate" represents Satan as the false Christ, which will occur at the inauguration of the eighth king (discussed in Revelation 17 (second part)—The Eighth King). The eighth king is the abomination that makes desolate. The trampling of the host will be the result of Satan's actions as the eighth king. These actions will lead to the enactment of the buy-sell law described in Revelation 13. This trampling of the host occurs during Satan's reign. Satan's reign in Jerusalem ends with the destruction of Jerusalem (Revelation 11:13), which will cleanse the earthly sanctuary of Satan. These two applications of Daniel 8:13, 14 are shown on the following chart, which is followed by Appendix (1)—The Investigative Judgment.

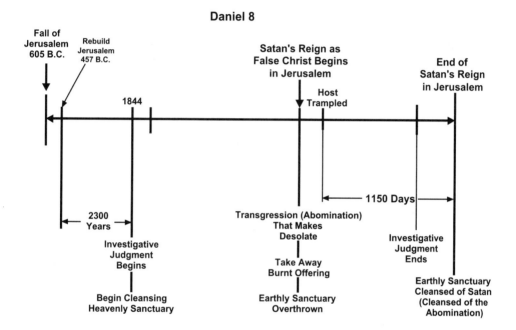

Daniel 8

Appendix (1)
The Investigative Judgment

The cleansing or restoring of the sanctuary described in Daniel 8:14 marks the end of the 2300-year prophecy. This time period began in 457 B.C. with the order to restore and rebuild Jerusalem (Daniel 9:25) and ended in 1844. The restoration of the heavenly temple began in 1844. This restoration will restore the temple to its original state prior to the fall of man. This restoration or cleansing of the heavenly temple has been called the investigative judgment. The reason for this terminology is based upon the scenes described in both Daniel 7:9, 10 and Revelation 4:2-4 both of which describe a court room scene. God the Father, the Ancient of Days, is seated on His throne with 24 thrones placed around His throne. The books are opened and the "court sat in judgment" (Daniel 7:10). This courtroom scene involves "the Lamb" who was slain (Revelation 5:12). He is the only One who can open the book because He is the One who died to place the names in this book (Revelation 5:8, 9). This judgment process involves 24 elders who are seated on 24 thrones (Revelation 4:4). This judgment process also involves an accuser (Revelation 12:10) which is Satan.

The purpose of this judgment process in heaven is shown in the Day of Atonement service in the earthly sanctuary service. This Day of Atonement service occurred only once a year and was done to cleanse the sanctuary of the sins of Israel, which had accumulated in the sanctuary during the previous year. The yearly ministry or Day of Atonement was designed to cleanse the sanctuary of sin (discussed on the following page). The daily ministry of the sanctuary was designed to cleanse the individual of his sins. When an Israelite sinned, he was required to bring an offering in order to remove the sin from himself. He would bring a lamb to the sanctuary, the lamb would be slain, and its blood would be ministered in the sanctuary. The sacrifice of the lamb symbolized Jesus' death for our sins and our cleansing from those sins. This cleansing of sin and transferring of the sin into the sanctuary only occurred for those who brought their offering and placed their sins on the offering. This represents God's people who claim Him as their God and Jesus as their Savior. This transfer of sins into the sanctuary did not involve the wicked who never asked for forgiveness or brought their sins to the sanctuary. Their sins are not transferred to the sanctuary and therefore, their sins are not involved in the cleansing of the sanctuary either on earth or in heaven. *The cleansing of the heavenly sanctuary only involves the sins of God's people or those who have claimed Him as their God.* It is important to note that the sinner was cleansed once he brought his lamb and sacrificed it. Similarly God's people are cleansed once they accept Jesus' sacrifice for them as their Lamb Slain. What then is the purpose of cleansing or restoring the heavenly sanctuary? What is being restored? What is being cleansed? Who is being judged and by whom and for what purpose?

In order to understand this process, we must understand the Day of Atonement service. Once a year on the Day of Atonement a special unblemished lamb was sacrificed by the high priest and its blood was ministered in the most holy place where

God's Ark of the Covenant was located. The most holy place could only be entered by the high priest. If he entered the most holy place with unforgiven sins he would die, because sin cannot exist in God's presence. The ark symbolized God's presence and His throne. Once the high priest ministered the blood in the most holy place, he then symbolically took those sins upon himself and carried them out of the sanctuary and placed them on a scapegoat. This goat was then led into the wilderness and released to die alone in the wilderness.

This process symbolized God's plan of salvation. The sins transferred represent only the sins of God's redeemed, since the wicked will die for their own sins (Revelation 20:12-14). The Lamb Slain is Jesus whose death forgives our sins for eternity. The most holy place represents God's throne room in heaven and the ark represents God's presence on His throne. The High Priest also represents Christ as He ministered His blood for our sins. He is our Advocate or defense lawyer in the court-room scene, who claims His blood as the reason we can be saved. The accuser is Satan (Revelation 12:10-12) and he is also represented by the scapegoat, who will be sent to the wilderness at the Second Coming. This wilderness is described as a "bot-tomless pit" (Revelation 20:1-3). If our sins are forgiven by Christ's death as our Lamb Slain, then why does God need an investigative judgment? What is the purpose of this judgment? Who is being judged?

In order to answer these questions, it is necessary to understand what the great controversy involves. The great controversy is between God and Satan. Satan claims that God is not fair. Satan claims that God's rules or Commandments are unjust. Satan claims that God cannot be trusted. Satan claims that God is not all-loving but selfish. These claims allowed Satan to mislead one-third of the angels in heaven (Revelation 12:4, 9). Jesus' death on the cross answered each of these questions. Jesus' death proved God is love. Jesus' life proved God's Law was just and fair. Jesus' life and death proved that God is more than fair and can be trusted. Jesus' death allowed sinners to be saved if they would accept His free gift (Ephesians 2:8, 9). If God has proven His love for mankind and has shown He is trustworthy, then why have an investigative judgment? The answer is inherent in God Himself. God does not want sin to ever occur again and God knows that doubt is the beginning of sin. If God's creatures were to ever doubt His fairness in allowing sinners to be saved then sin could arise again. *The purpose of the investigative judgment is to assure that sin will never arise again.* This judgment is not to convince God whom to save. God already knows who is safe to save. God does not make mistakes, only we do! The investigative judgment is not like our courts where the jury decides the verdict and the judge determines the punishment. God has already decided our case based on our response to His gift of His Son. The investigative judgment does not determine our salvation based on the 24 elders' decisions. God is the only One capable of making the right decision and only He will decide our case. God's decision is made based on our response to His love and our actions, which reflect that response. Satan claims we are unworthy to be saved but the Lamb Slain offers His blood to cover our sins.

What then does the investigative judgment determine? The investigative judg-ment allows Satan the opportunity to question God's fairness regarding each person saved and allows Christ the opportunity to defend His people. The investigative judg-ment allows God to blot out the sins of the saved for eternity. This blotting "out" of our sins (Acts 3:19) cleanses the heavenly sanctuary. Thus, the heavenly sanctuary is cleansed of sin and restored to its prior sin free state. These sins will be placed symbolically on the scapegoat (Satan) who was responsible for sin. This does not mean that Satan pays the penalty for these sins because Jesus has already died to remove these sins from God's people. During the investigative judgment, everyone who has claimed God as their Savior or King will have their records reviewed. The wicked, who never accepted God, will not be involved in this judgment process. Their review process will occur after the Second Coming when their cases are reviewed by the saved saints (1 Corinthians 6:2, 3). The investigative judgment also allows the universe, as represented by the 24 elders, to review each case and agree or disagree with God's decisions. However, ultimately, there will be no disagreement because God is never wrong! *This judgment process allows the universe to question God's decisions in order for the universe to never again raise the issue of God's trustworthiness.* In this sense the investigative judgment parallels our appeals court process. In the appeals court, the issue is the process of the trial and not so much the outcome. In the appeals court process, the judge's actions and lawyer's actions and proper use of evidence are at issue. This is similar to the process with the investigative judgment. God is allowing His decisions to be examined before He goes to claim back His redeemed. This process will assure that no doubt will ever arise again regarding God's trustworthiness throughout eternity. This process will reinforce trust in God and will eliminate the possibility of sin ever arising again. *This process will restore heaven and God's throne to a state of perfect trust, which existed before Satan allowed doubt to lead to sin. This process will also cleanse sin from heaven once and for all and blot it out. This will restore the heavenly sanctuary "to its rightful state"* (Daniel 8:14).

[1]   Nichol, Francis D. (Ed.). *The Seventh-day Adventist Bible Commentary,* (Review and Herald Publishing Association, Washington, D.C.) 1957, Vol. 4, p. 843.
[2]   Ibid.
[3]   Ibid.
[4]   Ibid., p. 845.
[5]   Ibid., p. 846.

Daniel 9
The Abomination and the Final Week

Daniel's plea to God for understanding of the vision in Daniel 8 was answered in Daniel 9. Daniel 9:23 states "At the beginning of your supplications a word went forth, and I have come to tell it to you, for you are greatly beloved; therefore consider the word and understand the vision." This verse is referring to the prior vision of the "two thousand and three hundred evenings and mornings" of Daniel 8:14, which Daniel did not understand. The angel, Gabriel, goes on to explain the 70 week prophecy which relates to Daniel's people and his holy city (Daniel 9:24). This prophetic time period was to begin at the "going forth of the word to restore and build Jerusalem" and end at the "coming of an anointed one" (Daniel 9:25). This Anointed One was Jesus and He was "to finish the transgression, to put an end to sin, and to atone for iniquity, to bring in everlasting righteousness" (Daniel 9:24).

> Daniel 9:26: *"And after the sixty-two weeks, an anointed one shall be cut off, and shall have nothing; and the people of the prince who is to come shall destroy the city and the sanctuary. Its end shall come with a flood, and to the end there shall be war; desolations are decreed."*

This text states "after the sixty-two weeks," however, the first seven weeks are described in Daniel 9:25. The total is 69 weeks or 483 years (seven times 69) (one prophetic day equals one literal year: Numbers 14:34). This text prophesied that Jesus, the Anointed One, would come 69 weeks after the decree to restore and rebuild Jerusalem. This decree would also signal the beginning of the 2300-year prophecy of Daniel 8:14. This "Seventy weeks of years" was "decreed" (Daniel 9:24) or cut off from the rest of the vision and set aside for Israel. The decree to rebuild Jerusalem occurred in 457 B.C. when the Media-Persian king Artaxerxes allowed the Israelites to return to Jerusalem. Jesus came right on schedule and began His ministry in A.D. 27 and fulfilled this prophecy. Jesus was "cut off" with "nothing" in the midst of the last prophetic week when He died on the cross for our sins. Therefore, Jesus fulfilled the prophecy of the 70 weeks or 490 years.

There is, however, another portion of this prophecy which applies after Christ's first advent. The phrase "and the people of the prince who is to come shall destroy the city and the sanctuary" introduces another time period. Historically, this "prince" has been interpreted by some as pagan Rome and "the people" as the Romans, who destroyed Jerusalem and it's temple in A.D. 70.

However, there appears to be a dual application to last-day events since this verse also states "to the end there shall be war." This suggests that this new time period extends to the time of the end. Also, the next verse refers to the time of the end when it refers to the "one who makes desolate" (Daniel 9:27). This "one who makes desolate" is seen having "the decreed end" poured out on him (Daniel 9:27). This decreed end suggests the final judgment of Satan. As has been shown earlier, the "transgression that makes desolate" (Daniel 8:13) is a description of Satan in the last days. In the context of the last days, the "prince who is to come" is Satan who will come in the place of the "anointed one." Satan, impersonating Christ, will establish his rule in the city "where their Lord was crucified" (Revelation 11:8). He will truly destroy Jerusalem and the temple service in terms of its ability to save mankind. With Satan on the throne in Jerusalem and ministering in the temple, Jerusalem will become "Sodom and Egypt" (Revelation 11:8).

This is further described in 2 Thessalonians 2:1-8. Second Thessalonians 2:1 begins "Now concerning the coming of our Lord Jesus Christ and our assembling to meet him." Paul then goes on to explain that Jesus has not yet come as some have reported, but that certain events must occur prior to His coming. Second Thessalonians 2:3, 4 states "Let no one deceive you in any way; for that day will not come, unless the rebellion comes first, and the man of lawlessness is revealed, the son of perdition, who opposes and exalts himself against every so-called god or object of worship, so that he takes his seat in the temple of God, proclaiming himself to be God." In 2 Thessalonians 2:9, 10 Paul further states "The coming of the lawless one by the activity of Satan will be with all power and with pretended signs and wonders, and with all wicked deception for those who are to perish, because they refused to love the truth and so be saved." The "man of lawlessness" or "man of sin" (2 Thessalonians 2:3) is Satan who will take over God's temple and work miracles to deceive the world into believing that Satan is Christ returned. This same event is being described in Daniel 9:26. Satan is "the prince who is to come" and his people will destroy the city and the sanctuary. The word "its" in Daniel 9:26 can be translated "his." "His" would then refer to the "prince who is to come." This prince is Satan.

"Its end shall come with a flood" can also refer to Jerusalem's end in A.D. 70 or to Jerusalem's end at the time of the end when Satan is reigning in Jerusalem and the world converges on Satan's capital city in the final battle. Truly "to the end there shall be war" and "desolations are decreed."

> Daniel 9:27: *"And he shall make a strong covenant with many for one week; and for half of the week he shall cause sacrifice and offering to cease; and upon the wing of abominations shall come one who makes desolate, until the decreed end is poured out on the desolator."*

Historically, many have applied the pronoun "he" to Christ and then applied the "half of the week" to the middle of the seven years of the last prophetic week of the "Seventy weeks of years" (Daniel 9:24). Christ began His public ministry in A.D. 27. He was crucified in A.D. 30 in the middle of this seven-year period and in A.D. 34 the gospel went to the Gentiles. When the gospel went to the Gentiles, this ended the "Seventy weeks of years" of Daniel 9:24, which were set aside for the Jewish nation. Christ's death is interpreted as the cause of the ceremonial sacrifices and offerings to cease. This interpretation is certainly correct. However, it requires a change of subject matter in the middle of the verse to interpret the last half of the verse, since the "desolator" is clearly not referring to Christ.

In Matthew 24:15, Jesus applies this text to the last days. Jesus does not apply this text to Himself! Jesus is answering the disciples question "what will be the sign of your coming" (Matthew 24:3). Jesus' answer is that a false Christ will appear who will deceive "if possible, even the elect" (Matthew 24:24). This false Christ is the "desolating sacrilege spoken of by the prophet Daniel, standing in the holy place" (Matthew 24:15). If Jesus applies this text to Satan in the last days then we also should apply it to Satan in the last days (discussed in Matthew 24—The Sign of the End).

The application of this verse to Satan, which is consistent with the prior verse, does not require changing subject matter in the middle of the verse in order to interpret it. This verse is a continuation of the prior verse regarding end-time events. Other scholars have suggested that in this verse the "he" applies to the prince who comes to destroy the city referred to in Daniel 9:26. This interpretation is consistent with the prior verse and suggests that Satan is the prince who "shall destroy the city" (Daniel 9:26). Also as noted previously the word "its" in Daniel 9:25 can be interpreted "his." His end "shall come with a flood" (Daniel 9:25) would then refer to the prince "who is to come" which is Satan. If the word "his" applies in Daniel 9:25, then this further connects the "he" in Daniel 9:27 to Satan and not to Christ.

When this verse is applied to Satan and last-day events, then the "week" referred to in this verse is not a part of the 70 weeks, but stands alone as an end-time prophecy. Each one of Daniel's prior prophecies has always extended to the end of time and this would be consistent with Daniel's prior prophecies. Applying this "week" to last-day events does not negate applying it to the 70 weeks and to Christ but rather gives a dual application to last-day events. The phrase "he shall make a strong covenant with many for one week," when applied to last-day events, suggests a final prophetic week or seven years during which Satan will finally become the world's spiritual and temporal leader. This has a certain appeal in regards to symmetry. God created this world in seven days or one week. The gospel to literal Israel involved one week. In the midst of that week, Jesus was "cut off" (Daniel 9:26). God also gives Satan seven years to complete his work and allows Satan to reign for one-half of that week. During this seven year period Satan will become the spiritual leader of Protestant Christianity as the false Christ returned and the leader of Catholicism as the eighth king (discussed in Revelation 17 (second part)—The Eighth King). From this platform of leadership he will eventually set up his kingdom in Jerusalem and will "trample over the holy city" (Revelation 11:2). He will successfully kill God's two witnesses (the Old Testament and the New Testament) by becoming the sole authority and interpreter of the Bible (Revelation 11:8).

And "for half of the week he shall cause sacrifice and offering to cease." This sentence suggests that Satan will effectively destroy the sanctuary service for one-half of the week. This time period is three and one-half years and is the same time period described in Revelation 11:9 as three and one-half days (one prophetic day equals one literal year). This is the time period when Satan will rule as the spiritual leader of the world in his new capital city, Jerusalem. This is predicted in Revelation 11:8, where the city is described as the city "where their Lord was crucified." This is also the same time period, which is referred to in Revelation 11:2 as the "forty-two months" when the "holy city" will be trampled over.

This is also the same time period that Daniel describes in Daniel 12 (discussed in Daniel 12—The Abomination and the Time of Trouble). In answer to Daniel's question "How long shall it be till the end of these wonders" (Daniel 12:6) came the response "a time, two times, and half a time." Since "a time" equals one year this is equivalent to three and one-half years. This 1260 days or three and one-half years of Daniel 12:6 is the same time period as described in Revelation 11:9 and Daniel 9:27. Satan causes "sacrifice and offering to cease" because he replaces worship of the true God and Christ with worship of him as the false Christ. Truly, Jerusalem will be "Sodom and Egypt" (Revelation 11:8). Sodom represents uncontrolled immorality and Egypt represents the worship of false gods. When Satan reigns as the "desolating sacrilege" (Matthew 24:15) in Jerusalem, Jerusalem will become the center of immorality and false worship.

And "upon the wing of abominations shall come one who makes desolate." This clearly suggests that abominations will characterize the "one who makes desolate." When Satan impersonates Jesus Christ this will be the ultimate abomination. Satan, the Devil, the consummate liar, replacing Jesus, the Son of God, the Word of Truth. This abomination will be the greatest abomination ever to occur on this earth, with Satan, the source of death, masquerading as Jesus, the source of life. This abomination will truly desolate those who are true believers and who recognize Satan as the false Christ. This abomination will also "desolate" all those who believe his lies. Those who accept him as Christ will be led to perdition with him.

The phrase "until the decreed end is poured out on the desolator" clearly refers to the end of time. The "decreed end" will come initially at the Second Coming of the true Christ in the clouds of heaven with His angels. At that time Satan will be seized: "he seized the dragon, that ancient serpent, who is the Devil and Satan, and bound him for a thousand years" (Revelation 20:2). The "desolator" in this text is Satan and the "decreed end" will be imprisonment in "the pit" (Revelation 20:3) for 1000 years followed by total destruction, which is described in Revelation 20:10.

SUMMARY

In summary, we can see that the prophecy of Daniel 9:26, 27 has a dual application. It can be applied to Christ being "cut off" in the midst of His last prophetic week or seven years. It can also be applied to Satan being "set up" (Daniel 11:31) in the midst of his last prophetic week or seven years. Satan is the abomination that makes desolate, and when he pretends to be Christ returned, he will cause "sacrifice and offering to cease." Satan will trample over the holy city and then the "decreed end" will come.

The following facts support this dual application. First, Jesus himself applies Daniel 9:27 to the last days and refers to it as His answer to what the sign of His Coming would be (Matthew 24:15). Jesus does not use this text to refer to His First Advent but applies it to His Second Advent. The "desolating sacrilege" (Matthew 24:15) about whom Jesus warns is the "one who makes desolate" and "the prince who is to come." Second, the subject matter of Daniel 9:27 relates to "the prince who is to come" who will destroy the city rather than to the Anointed One. This prince, who will destroy the city in the last days, is Satan. Third, the last half of Daniel 9:26 and Daniel 9:27 are describing "desolations" that will occur in the last days when Satan reigns as the false Christ. Fourth, Satan is given half a week or three and one-half years during which the sacrifice and offering will cease. This is consistent with the prophecy of the two witnesses in Revelation 11:8 (discussed in Revelation 11 (first part)—The Two Witnesses). It is also consistent with Daniel 12:7 when God's peoples' power is "shattered" for three and one-half years (discussed in Daniel 12—The Abomination and the Time of Trouble). Finally, the "desolater" of Daniel 9:27 is Satan who is described as "Abaddon" in Revelation 9:11 which means the Destroyer. The following graph outlines Daniel 9:24-27 along with Daniel 8:9-14 and Daniel 8:23-26.

Daniel 8 and 9

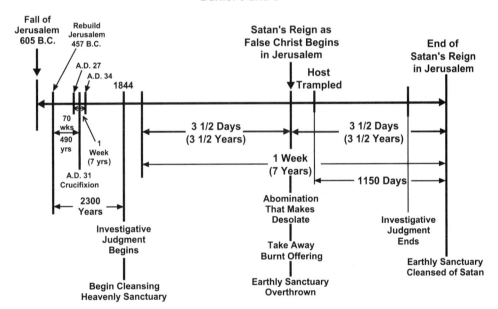

Daniel 11
The Abomination
and the Time of the End

In order to understand the abomination that makes desolate, we must also examine Daniel 11. In Daniel 11, Daniel begins another world history prophecy. He has covered these events at least three different ways in prior chapters. In Daniel 2, world history was explained by the symbols of the golden image and the stone that destroyed it. In Daniel 7, world history was explained by the symbols of the four beasts and the little horn. In Daniel 8, world history was explained by the symbols of the ram, the he-goat, and the little horn. Each of the prior prophecies covered the time period from Daniel's day to the end of time. However, very little information was given describing actual last-day events.

In the prophecy about the golden image, the rock is shown destroying the other kingdoms and "it shall stand for ever" (Daniel 2:44). In the prophecy about the four beasts in Daniel 7, last-day events are described in verses 13 and 14, which describe Christ receiving His kingdom from the "Ancient of Days." They are also described in verses 26 and 27, which describe a judgment scene and Christ receiving His kingdom.

The prophecies of Daniel 8:10-14 and 23-26 have a dual application and apply historically as well as to the last days (discussed in Daniel 8—The Abomination and the Sanctuary). However, even though Daniel 8 gives us more information about last-day events than Daniel 2 or Daniel 7, it mainly emphasizes what happens to God's holy city and His sanctuary. These prophecies do not explain about events in the rest of the world. These prophecies do not explain about God's people in the last days. These prophecies do not explain how last-day events relate to each other.

In Daniel 11 and 12, Daniel attempts to explain these events. Daniel 11 and 12 must be taken as a continuous whole. Daniel begins the story again at his time and takes us to the end of this world's history or the "end of the days" (Daniel 12:13).

The critical transition to last-day events occurs in Daniel 11:29. This verse has historically been applied to pagan Rome.[1] However, in Daniel 11:31, we see that "the abomination that makes desolate" is set up. Historically, Daniel 11:31 has been applied to pagan Rome and also to Papal Rome.[2] However, as will be shown later this text also applies to Satan as the false Christ. Daniel 12 covers events related to the time of trouble (Daniel 12:1), which are clearly time of the end events. However, we must also include Daniel 11:40-45, since these verses begin with the phrase "at the time of the end" (Daniel 11:40). It appears Daniel 12:1 connects to Daniel 11:40 since Daniel 12:1 begins "at that time." The phrase "at that time" appears to refer back to the "time" mentioned in Daniel 11:40. Therefore, at least a portion of Daniel 11 is a time-of-the-end prophecy connected to Daniel 12.

We already know that Satan's last great deception will be to pretend to be Christ returned and that this will occur shortly prior to the end of time.[3] This deception is the "abomination that makes desolate" and this event is described in Daniel 11:31. This means that last-day events apply from Daniel 11:29 onward, since Daniel 11:29, 30 are related to Daniel 11:31 in the time sequence.

> Daniel 11:29: *"At the time appointed he shall return and come into the south; but it shall not be this time as it was before."*

The phrase "at the time appointed" must be taken as a signal of an important event. Daniel 11:27 states that "the end is yet to be at the time appointed," which suggests that there is a connection between the end time and "the time appointed." The subject matter "he" of Daniel 11:29 is the same as the subject matter "him" described in Daniel 11:31, who sets up the abomination that makes desolate. The "abomination that makes desolate" (Daniel 11:31) is a last-day event, which occurs just prior to the "time of the end" events of Daniel 11:40 through Daniel 12:1.

Daniel 11 can only be understood using Israel as the reference point for all the compass directions. This means that the king of the north represents countries north of Israel, for example, Turkey. The king of the south represents countries south of Israel, for example, Egypt. The king of the west would represent countries west of Israel, such as Greece. The king of the east would represent countries east of Israel, such as Syria. Depending on the historical time period, these kingdoms would change names but not locations. For example, Babylon was east of Israel and is now occupied by Iraq. Understanding that the compass location is centered on Israel allows us to determine what countries are involved in each description.

Another important aspect, related to interpreting Daniel 11, is to understand that a king may represent a nation or a spiritual entity or a single person. Historically, Daniel 11:31 has been applied to the Papacy, which is a spiritual entity, which is similarly described in Daniel 7:24, 25.[4] However, a dual application applies here. These verses can also describe Satan who seeks "to magnify himself" when he pretends to be Christ returned. Daniel 11:29 suggests that he will attack the south (Egypt) and will initially fail.

> Daniel 11:30: *"For ships of kittim shall come against him, and he shall be afraid and withdraw, and shall turn back and be enraged and take action against the holy covenant. He shall turn back and give heed to those who forsake the holy covenant."*

This suggests that Satan's initial attempt to overthrow Egypt will fail. Historically, some have thought that the "holy covenant" represents Jerusalem being overthrown in A.D. 70.[5] However in the context of this verse, it appears to represent a belief or relationship. This covenant can be forsaken or broken suggesting a belief or relationship rather than a city.

In Exodus 31:16, God describes His Sabbath as a "perpetual covenant" with His people. Prior to Satan's final overpowering delusion, when he attempts to impersonate Christ returned, there will be an effort to make the world accept a false Sabbath. This change in God's Law, to require Sunday keeping in place of the true seventh-day Sabbath, will represent the seal or mark of the beast foretold in Revelation 14:9 and Revelation 13:16, 17 (discussed in Revelation 13 (last part)— The Mark of the Beast). This Sunday law will be a clear attack on God's "perpetual covenant" of Exodus 31:16. This attack on Egypt appears to occur after the passage of the universal Sunday law. This is suggested in Daniel 11:26, since the holy covenant is attacked prior to this invasion. Those who forsake or reject the holy covenant will support this law. In the context of these verses, the holy covenant represents God's Law or His Ten Commandments and more specifically the fourth commandment relating to His Sabbath.

In Genesis 2:3 we read "So God blessed the seventh day and hallowed it, because on it God rested from all his work which he had done in creation." The seventh day is a memorial to the true Creator of the universe. In the last days Satan will pretend to be the Creator and will attempt to change God's Law to prove he has that power as well as to lead men astray.

Exodus 20:8 states "Remember the sabbath day to keep it holy . . . for in six days the Lord made heaven and earth, the sea, and all that is in them, and rested the seventh day; therefore the Lord blessed the sabbath day and hallowed it." This is the fourth commandment of God's Ten Commandments. This commandment was established to honor the Creator of the universe. Satan will attempt to change God's Law by creating a false Sabbath and will demand worship of himself as the creator.

The seventh-day Sabbath is not only a "perpetual covenant" (Exodus 31:16) to remind us that God is our Creator but also to remind us "that you may know that I, the Lord, sanctify you" (Exodus 31:12). The Sabbath is a reminder of our salvation through Jesus' death for us. Satan will also attack this aspect of God's covenant because he will claim to be Christ returned and will demand worship of himself as the false Christ.

Following the institution of this Sunday law, Satan will consolidate the world behind him as he impersonates Christ returned. Once he has taken over as the world's leader of both Protestantism and Catholicism he will attempt to occupy Christianity's birthplace. That birthplace is Israel. Satan will argue that the Jews rejected him and killed him and now the world needs to help him take his rightful place in Jerusalem as leader of the world. This will lead to an overthrow of Israel so that Satan can occupy Jerusalem as Christ returned.

> Daniel 11:31: *"Forces from him shall appear and profane the temple and fortress, and shall take away the continual burnt offering. And they shall set up the abomination that makes desolate."*

This verse suggests that Israel will be overrun in order for the "abomination" to be set up. This is confirmed in Luke 21:20 which describes "Jerusalem surrounded by armies" when the abomination or "desolation" is set up. Once Satan has occupied Jerusalem, he will be able to influence the world spiritually, claiming to be Christ returned. The continual burnt offering represents Christ's true sacrifice for mankind. Satan will effectively replace this and will "take away the continual burnt offering." Clearly, God's temple will be profaned by Satan's presence as the false Christ, which is "the abomination that makes desolate." In Malachi 2:11, Judah's abominations are linked to profaning "the sanctuary of the Lord." This same event was described by Paul in 2 Thessalonians 2:3, 4: "the man of lawlessness" or "son of perdition" is seen exalting himself and taking "his seat in the temple of God, proclaiming himself to be God." Both Daniel 11:31 and 2 Thessalonians 2:3, 4 suggest that the temple in Jerusalem will be rebuilt.

> Daniel 11:32: *"He shall seduce with flattery those who*
> *violate the covenant, but the people who know their God*
> *shall stand firm and take action."*

The "covenant" described here is the "holy covenant" of Daniel 11:28, 30 which Satan had attacked prior to being "set up" as the abomination that makes desolate (Daniel 11:31). This holy covenant is God's Law and specifically His fourth commandment regarding the Sabbath. Satan will "seduce" with praise those who reject God's Law and accept his false Sabbath. Satan as the false Christ will now claim that God's Law, which he (Satan) wrote, has been misunderstood and only he can explain what it really means. Those who choose to believe Satan, as the false Christ, will think they are serving God but they will actually be rejecting God's covenant (the Sabbath) and accepting Satan's mark in their "forehead" or "hand" (Revelation 14:9). The people who "know their God" will not be misled by this false god claiming to be Christ returned. Because they "know their God" they will "stand firm and take action." To "know" God in this sense means having a close personal relationship with Him. These people are described in Revelation 12:17 as those "who keep the commandments of God and bear testimony to Jesus." These people will recognize Satan as the false Christ and will "take action" to warn others of their danger and of the soon coming of the real Jesus Christ, their Savior and Lord.

> Daniel 11:33: *"And those among the people who are wise*
> *shall make many understand, though they shall fall by*
> *sword and flame, by captivity and plunder, for some days."*

Those described here as "wise" are God's people who do not accept Satan as Christ. These "wise" people are the same people Daniel describes in Daniel 12:3 as those "who are wise shall shine like the brightness of the firmament; and those who turn many to righteousness, like the stars for ever and ever." These people are "wise" because they do not get misled by Satan's overpowering delusion. They do not accept Satan as the returned Christ and they warn others of his lies. These people will turn many away from Satan and sin and turn them to righteousness. These same people are also mentioned in Daniel 12:10 as those "who are wise *shall understand*" (emphasis supplied). These people shall "purify themselves, and make themselves white, and be refined" (Daniel 12:10). They will understand the prophecies of Daniel 12, which Daniel did not understand. They will be made white through Jesus' robe of righteousness (Revelation 3:5). These "wise" people of God will have studied the scriptures, especially Daniel and Revelation, and will be able to explain to others why Satan is an impostor and how he fulfills these prophecies. It is important to understand that the "wise" of Daniel 11:33, who appear after Satan's abomination is set up, are the same "wise" as described in Daniel 12:3, 10. This further connects Daniel 11:29-39 with the last days and the time of trouble (Daniel 12:1).

However, there is a price that will be paid. Many of these "wise" followers of the true God will suffer and fall to "sword and flame" and many will be imprisoned. Some of those who die during this period are depicted under the fifth seal in Revelation 6:9-11 as crying out to God "how long before thou wilt judge and avenge our blood?" Many of these "wise" followers will live through the "time of trouble" of Daniel 12:1 and will make up the "hundred and forty-four thousand sealed" of Revelation 7:4. These will be sealed "upon their foreheads" (Revelation 7:3). They are protected by God during the fifth trumpet because they have God's seal "upon their foreheads" (Revelation 9:4). God's last day seal or mark is His seventh-day Sabbath. Satan's mark or seal is his false Sabbath or Sunday law. All mankind will be sealed prior to the Second Coming, either with God's seal or Satan's seal (discussed in Revelation 13 (last part)—The Mark of the Beast).

> Daniel 11:34: *"When they fall, they shall receive a little help. And many shall join themselves to them with flattery."*

The phrase "When they fall, they shall receive a little help" has been interpreted by some authors to suggest that the deaths of some of God's people led to the creation of leaders who brought others to the truth.[6] This text also suggests that some people will join the true believers but will not be truly converted. This will appear to be a help to God's people but actually it will work against them. Many of God's people will be captured and imprisoned because of these insincere conversions.

> Daniel 11:35: *"and some of those who are wise shall fall, to refine and to cleanse them and to make them white, until the time of the end, for it is yet for the time appointed."*

This text clearly connects to Daniel 12:10, which describes the "wise" as those who "understand" and as those who are "refined" and "make themselves white." This text again shows that the "wise," about whom Daniel is talking, are the same group of people in both Daniel 11 and in Daniel 12. These are the people who live during the time of the "abomination that makes desolate" and some of them will also live to the "time of the end." These are God's people, who understand the last day prophecies of Daniel 12, and many of them will live to see Jesus' Second Coming.

The phrase "until the time of the end" connects this group to the "time of the end" which is described in Daniel 11:40-45. This verse also shows that God's people will die "until the time of the end." This is seen in the phrase some "shall fall." In this context to fall means to die. This verse also suggests that at "the time of the end" God's people will no longer die. This is consistent with the concept of the close of probation when God's righteous people will "still do right, and the holy still be holy" and the evildoers will "still do evil" (Revelation 22:11). The close of probation coincides with Daniel's "time of the end" and will overlap with the "time of trouble" of Daniel 12:1. It will simultaneously coincide with the events of Daniel 11:40-45, which occur at "the time of the end." The close of probation represents the time in the world's history after which no one else will change their mind and accept Jesus as their Savior.

Daniel 11:40-45 describes several battles, which occur over a period of time prior to the final battle on earth. These battles occur during "the time of the end" (Daniel 11:40). Therefore, "the time of the end" in the book of Daniel is the time period just prior to Christ's return and not just the time of His return. During this time period the "wise" will no longer "fall" (die). This time period is called the close of probation time period. At the close of probation God's people will no longer "fall" (die). God's people and the world are sealed forever at this time. This is "the time of the end" but not the end of time.

At the "time of the end" the sealing of God's people has been completed. All of God's people will be sealed or marked prior to the close of probation. All of the 144,000 of Revelation 7:3, 4 have been accounted for and are sealed. The entire wicked are also sealed at this time. This sealing occurs prior to the fifth trumpet because during the fifth trumpet Satan cannot harm those who have God's seal "upon their foreheads" (Revelation 9:4). Daniel's "time of the end" marks the close of probation and the sealing of God's people.

> Daniel 11:36: *"And the king shall do according to his will;*
> *he shall exalt himself and magnify himself above every god,*
> *and shall speak astonishing things against the God of gods.*
> *He shall prosper till the indignation is accomplished; for*
> *what is determined shall be done."*

Historically, this text has been applied by some to the Papacy and others have applied this text to France.[7] However, in the context of the time of the end, this "king" is Satan who will attempt to "magnify himself" and exalt himself above all gods, including the one true God. This has always been Satan's goal, to become God (Isaiah 14:14). Satan will try to accomplish this by impersonating Christ on earth.

The phrase "and the king shall do according to his will" relates to time of the end events because Satan has never been able to do according to his will in regard to humanity. Satan has been controlled by God's rules of engagement. If God had not controlled Satan or limited Satan's powers, Satan would have already destroyed the world and all of God's people. This control is demonstrated in Revelation 7:1 where God's four angels are holding back the four winds of strife. Daniel 11:36 suggests God is now allowing Satan to "do according to his will."

This release of God's control over Satan is described in Revelation 9:1. The star fallen from heaven to earth is Lucifer and he is given the key to open "the shaft of the bottomless pit" (Revelation 9:2). Satan is bound by circumstances represented by "the bottomless pit." These circumstances are God's rules of engagement, which God enforces in order to protect all of mankind. In the fifth trumpet (Revelation 9:1), God now allows Satan partial freedom to "do according to his will." It should be noted that Satan is referred to as king during the fifth trumpet (Revelation 9:11). In the sixth trumpet, God further releases Satan when He withdraws His four angels who are bound at the Euphrates (Revelation 9:15). These events occur just prior to Jesus' Second Coming, which is the seventh trumpet (discussed in Revelation 11 (last part)—The Seventh Trumpet).

The only time when Satan will be able "to do according to his will" occurs just prior to the Second Coming and during "the time of the end." The context of this text suggests the time of the end, since this ongoing description of Satan is followed by Daniel 11:40, which clearly relates to the "time of the end." Also, Daniel 12:1 states "at that time" which connects "the time of trouble" to the "time of the end" in Daniel

11:40. Satan will be involved in the time of trouble as well as the time of the end. Both of these texts are connected in time to the actions of Satan described in Daniel 11:36-39. The actions of Satan described in Daniel 11:36-39 immediately precede "the time of the end" (Daniel 11:40) during which the "indignation is accomplished" or completed and Jesus will return.

Satan will "speak astonishing things against the God of gods." Satan will claim to be God on earth, as Christ, and will claim the power to interpret God's Word. Satan will attempt to nullify God's Word and will effectively kill it as prophesied in Revelation 11:7-8. Satan will not be satisfied with anything short of the total destruction of God's true followers. Satan will "prosper till the indignation is accomplished." The "indignation" refers to Satan as the false Christ ruling the world in Jerusalem. This will occur because God is going to allow Satan to demonstrate what happens to a world run by sin. What "is determined shall be done" means that God's plan will be completed.

> Daniel 11:37: *"He shall give no heed to the gods of his fathers, or to the one beloved by women; he shall not give heed to any other god, for he shall magnify himself above all."*

Historically, this verse has been applied to the Papacy, which magnified itself above all other religions, even taking the place of God on earth.[8] Some have applied this verse to France, when it replaced all gods with atheism.[9] However, in the context of the last days and the context of the "abomination that makes desolate" (Daniel 11:31), this verse has much greater meaning. When Satan takes over as the world's spiritual leader and then later as the world's king, he is not going to allow any other gods to replace him. The false gods he had men worship in the past will certainly not be worshiped by him. Satan is capable of worshiping only one god, himself. Satan will claim to be God, who has returned as Christ to save mankind from all of the problems that Satan has created. He certainly will not worship the true Christ, "the one beloved by women," because he will claim to be Christ returned. Satan will "magnify himself above all," first as the Christ returned and then later as the world's king.

> Daniel 11:38: *"He shall honor the god of fortresses instead of these; a god whom his fathers did not know he shall honor with gold and silver, with precious stones and costly gifts."*

Historically, this verse has been applied to the worship of Mary the mother of Jesus, who was thought to represent "the god of fortresses."[10] Worship of Mary did replace many pagan gods that were worshiped previously. Mary was offered many gifts and precious stones and still is today! Others have applied this text to the worship of reason in France.[11] However, in the context of the last-day events, this verse suggests that Satan will honor the god of fortresses, instead of the prior false gods of his predecessors.

It appears Satan will honor this "god" with riches including silver, gold, and precious stones. This "god of fortresses" represents the leading world power at the time of the end. This "god of fortresses" is called this because of its political and economic power. This "god" is the same power that John described in Revelation 13:11: "Then I saw another beast, which rose out of the earth; it had two horns like a lamb and it spoke like a dragon." This lamb-like beast coexists with "the first beast, whose mortal wound was healed" because it exercises its authority "in its presence" (Revelation 13:12). The first beast is the Papacy whose "mortal wound" was healed in 1929 when its right to exist as a nation was restored by Italy. The lamb-like beast is the United States of America. At the time of the end, the United States of America will support both Protestantism and Catholicism and will support Satan as the world's leader of all Christianity (discussed in Revelation 13 (last part)—The Mark of the Beast).

This "god of fortresses" represents Satan's relationship with the United States as it supports and helps establish Satan's kingdom. Satan's kingdom will require military support in order to carry out his plans. The United States will provide that support.

> Daniel 11:39: *"He shall deal with the strongest fortresses*
> *by the help of a foreign god; those who acknowledge him he*
> *shall magnify with honor. He shall make them rulers over*
> *many and shall divide the land for a price."*

Historically, this verse has been applied by some to France when it divided its land taken from the royalty and gave it to the common man.[12] Others have applied this verse to the Papacy suggesting that the Papacy divided up the world in the past.[13] However, this verse appears to be connected to the prior verse and the "foreign god" refers to the previous "god of fortresses." This "foreign god" is actually the strongest country in the world, the one country who could "deal with the strongest fortresses." The only country that could fulfill this prediction in the last days is the United States of America. "Those who acknowledge him he shall magnify with honor." This statement suggests that those world leaders who do not resist Satan as the world's leader will be honored by Satan and allowed to continue as rulers under Satan. Those who refuse to "acknowledge him" will cause Satan to "deal with" them with the help of the "foreign god."

The last phrase in Daniel 11:39, "and shall divide the land for a price," suggests how Satan will finance his kingdom. Satan will sell off conquered lands as part of his plan to control the world and keep its leaders under his control. This verse also may point forward to Revelation 17:12 when the beast or eighth king gives authority to ten kings for "one hour," which occurs just prior to the Second Coming of Jesus Christ.

> Daniel 11:40: *"At the time of the end the king of the south*
> *shall attack him; but the king of the north shall rush upon*
> *him like a whirlwind, with chariots and horsemen, and*
> *with many ships; and he shall come into countries and*
> *shall overflow and pass through."*

Historically, this verse has been applied by some to Egypt (the king of the south) who was overrun by Turkey (the king of the north).[14] Turkey then overran Israel (the "glorious land" of Daniel 11:41). In the context of this verse, however, applying this verse to Egypt and Turkey in the late 1700s and early 1800s does not fit the beginning statement of the verse, which says "at the time of the end." If we apply this to the real "time of the end" then it is referring to the time after Satan becomes the "abomination that makes desolate" Daniel 11:31, which precedes this verse.

This "time of the end" is the same "time of the end" mentioned in Daniel 11:35. This is the time when the wise will no longer fall. This is the close of probation. This overlaps "the time of trouble" of Daniel 12:1. This is the time when God's people are sealed. This is the time when the investigative judgment ends. This is the time when the seven last plagues begin to fall (discussed in Revelation 16—The Seven Last Plagues).

We must be consistent when reading these verses. Daniel 11:29-45 are chronological and indeed introduce Daniel 12:1. Daniel 12:1, in terms of timeframe, parallels Daniel 11:40-45. Daniel 11:31-45 describes events, which occur in Israel, while Daniel 12:1-13 describes what happens to God's people during the same time period. Satan has already established his kingdom in Jerusalem prior to Daniel 11:40, which is describing an attack upon Satan from the south.

This suggests an attack by Egypt and those countries aligned with Egypt "at the time of the end." It is probable that some of Islam will reject Satan's rule as the world's situation deteriorates. It appears Satan will receive help from the north. This could represent Europe but the actual countries cannot be determined at this time. This invasion force will march through the countries north of Israel in order to protect Satan's throne.

> Daniel 11:41: *"He shall come into the glorious land. And tens of thousands shall fall, but these shall be delivered out of his hand; Edom and Moab and the main part of the Ammonites."*

Historically, this verse has been thought by some authors to represent the Turks who overran Palestine, "the glorious land," in the early 1800s.[15] The same Turks were unsuccessful in overrunning the Arabian tribes, which were descendants of Edom, Moab and the Ammonites. However, to apply this verse to the 1800s is to ignore its context, which suggests this is a "time of the end" event (Daniel 11:40). This verse suggests that the army of the north that appears to come to Satan's rescue will "come into the glorious land" (Palestine) and will kill tens of thousands in the process. This verse also suggests that certain Arabian neighbors will be spared from this carnage. The Arabian countries surrounding Israel are economically important to the world because of their oil supply. This may be why they are protected in this situation.

> Daniel 11:42: *"He shall stretch out his hand against the countries, and the land of Egypt shall not escape."*

Historically, Egypt was overrun by the Turks in 1805. However, since this is a time of the end event, this verse is describing the army of the north, along with Satan, attacking Egypt and overthrowing Egypt at the time of the end. This would be in response to Egypt's initial attack against Palestine in Daniel 11:40.

> Daniel 11:43: *"He shall become ruler of the treasures of gold and of silver, and all the precious things of Egypt; and the Libyans and the Ethiopians shall follow in his train."*

Historically, this verse has been interpreted by some as having been fulfilled when the Turks overran Egypt in 1805 and subsequently made Egypt pay them huge amounts of gold and silver.[16] However, since this is a time of the end event, which occurs after the abomination is set up (Daniel 11:31), this has not yet been fulfilled. This verse suggests Egypt, Libya, and Ethiopia, after they are overrun, will pay tribute in silver and gold to Satan and his supporters from the north.

> Daniel 11:44: *"But tidings from the east and the north*
> *shall alarm him, and he shall go forth with great fury to*
> *exterminate and utterly destroy many."*

Historically, this text has been applied by some to the attack of the Arabian countries (east) and Russia (north) on the Turkish Empire during World War I.[17] During this time period, the Turks killed many Armenian Christians. However, since this verse describes time of the end events after the abomination is set up, this has not yet occurred. This verse suggests that Satan becomes alarmed when he hears news of an impending attack. This attack appears to originate in the north and east. In Revelation 9:14, the final event prior to Jesus' Second Coming is related to the great river Euphrates. The four angels which "are bound at the great river Euphrates" are released (Revelation 9:14). After these angels are released, a massive battle occurs described in Revelation 9:16-19.

Daniel 11:44 also parallels Revelation 16:12 where the sixth angel pours out his bowl "on the great river Euphrates" and its water is "dried up" which prepares "the way for the kings from the east." Both the sixth trumpet (Revelation 9:13-21) and the sixth plague (Revelation 16:12-16) involve the Euphrates river and warfare. Both of these events occur at the end of time just prior to Jesus' Second Coming, which is the seventh plague (Revelation 16:17-21) (discussed in Revelation 16—The Seven Last Plagues) and the seventh trumpet (Revelation 11:15-19). Both of these events are universal in scope involving the whole world and involving Satan who claims to be the world's king.

It appears that a colossal battle will occur in the Middle East involving Satan's kingdom. This attack will involve those countries which border the Euphrates (kings of the east) as well as countries from the north. Daniel is describing the same events at the end of time that John described. This appears to represent the world's last battle which is Armageddon (Revelation 16:16).

> Daniel 11:45: *"And he shall pitch his palatial tents*
> *between the sea and the glorious holy mountain; yet he*
> *shall come to his end, with none to help him."*

Historically, this verse was thought by some to describe the Turks during World War I when they moved their headquarters onto Mount Scopas, one of Jerusalem's holy mountains.[18] The Turks were then abandoned by Germany and subsequently overrun by the Allies. However, this verse is actually describing the end of the story of this world's history. That story is really about Satan and his rebellion against God. The context of Daniel 11:40-45 involves the "time of the end." This verse is describing Satan's "palatial tents," which are overrun at the end of time with no one "to help him." This refers to the Second Coming of Christ and

His final battle with Satan when Satan is finally overcome. This battle is described in Revelation 19:11-21 and also in Revelation 17:14.

SUMMARY

It can be seen that Daniel 11 has a dual application, beginning with Daniel 11:29. This dual application is describing last-day events. These events include the attack on the "holy covenant" (Daniel 11:30), which is God's Sabbath, and the setting up of the "abomination that makes desolate" (Daniel 11:31), which is Satan as the eighth king. This prophecy also describes God's people who are pictured as "wise" (Daniel 11:33) because they understand the last-day events. They are "wise" because they refuse to accept Satan as the false Christ and refuse to accept Satan's mark which is his false Sabbath. Satan's attack on the "holy covenant" is accomplished with the passage of a universal Sunday law. In the book of Revelation these "wise" are described as saints or "those who keep the commandments of God and the faith of Jesus" (Revelation 12:14). This definition of saints matches the description of the "wise" found in Daniel 11. They keep God's Commandments by not accepting the false Sabbath and violating the holy covenant. They keep faith in the true Jesus by not accepting the false Christ who is the "abomination that makes desolate."

Daniel 11 continues by describing Satan and his activities during the last days. Satan will kill many of God's people until the "time of the end" when the close of probation occurs. This "time of the end" in Daniel overlaps the time of trouble (Daniel 12:1). Satan as the abomination that makes desolate, will impersonate Christ returned. He will magnify himself above God. He will profane God's temple. He will rule the world from Jerusalem. Daniel closes this chapter with a description of Satan's occupation of Israel and his ultimate overthrow. Daniel 11 then leads into Daniel 12, which continues to describe what happens to God's people during the same time period as described in Daniel 11:31-45. Daniel 12 will be discussed in the chapter "The Abomination and the Time of Trouble." The following graph illustrates the events discussed in Daniel 11.

Daniel 11

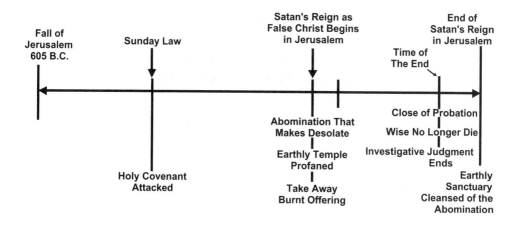

---

[1] Nichol, Francis D. (Ed.). *The Seventh-day Adventist Bible Commentary,* (Review and Herald Publishing Association, Washington, D.C.) 1957, Vol. 4, p. 872.

[2] Ibid., p. 874.

[3] White, Ellen G., *The Great Controversy* (Pacific Press Publishing Association, Nampa, Idaho) 1950, p. 624.

[4] Nichol, Francis D. (Ed.). *The Seventh-day Adventist Bible Commentary,* (Review and Herald Publishing Association, Washington, D.C.) 1957, Vol. 4, p. 872.

[5] Ibid.

[6] Ibid., p. 874.

[7] Ibid., p. 875.

[8] Ibid., p. 876.

[9] Ibid.

[10] Ibid.

[11] Ibid.

[12] Ibid.

[13] Ibid, p. 877.

[14] Gresham, Joe W., *The Wise Shall Understand*, Copyright 1996, J. W. Gresham, Fort Worth Texas, p. 72.

[15] Ibid.

[16] Ibid.

[17] Ibid, p. 731.

[18] Ibid.

Daniel 12
The Abomination
and the Time of Trouble

Daniel 12 continues Daniel's description of last-day events. This chapter is an explanation of events that parallel the events of Daniel 11:31-45. Daniel 11 introduces last-day events in Daniel 11:29 and then introduces the abomination that makes desolate in Daniel 11:31. This abomination is reigning at the time of the end when Daniel 12 begins.

> Daniel 12:1: *"At that time shall arise Michael, the great prince who has charge of your people. And there shall be a time of trouble, such as never has been since there was a nation till that time; but at that time your people shall be delivered, every one whose name shall be found written in the book."*

This verse begins by connecting Daniel 12 to Daniel 11. This verse connects Daniel 12:1 to Daniel 11:40, which is the last verse which mentions time. In Daniel 11:40, the time period is "the time of the end." The time of trouble described in Daniel 12:1 will occur "at that time." At that time refers back to the "time of the end" (Daniel 11:40). Therefore, it appears that the events of Daniel 11:40-45 must parallel some of the events of Daniel 12 since both occur during the time of the end and both reach to the end of time. This is reinforced in Daniel 12:9 where Daniel is told that these "words" are to be "shut up and sealed until the time of the end." The "words" referred to in Daniel 12:9 relate particularly to the message of Daniel 12. The phrase "at that time" in Daniel 12:1 suggests that the "time of trouble" occurs "at the time of the end" (Daniel 11:40).

Historically, some have suggested that Michael is one of the covering cherubs which stand in God's presence. This concept suggests that Michael and Gabriel are similar and that both are angels. However, Michael is called "the great prince" and there is only one "great prince." Michael "the great prince" refers to Jesus Christ.

In Jude 9, Michael is called the Archangel. In 1 Thessalonians 4:16, the voice of the Archangel raises the dead. In John 5:28, it is Jesus' voice that will raise the dead. Jesus is the Archangel. Jesus is "the great prince." He is the Prince of princes. In Revelation 12:7, Michael (Jesus) is shown fighting against Satan and overcoming him. Michael, who "has charge of your people," is the Son of God and He will return for His people at the Second Coming.

The "time of trouble" is described as "such as never has been since there was a nation till that time." This time of trouble specifically relates to God's people even though the entire world will be in trouble. This is shown by the phrase "at that time your people shall be delivered." It is Daniel's people or God's people who will be delivered at that time. The phrase "at that time" is repeated twice in this verse. The time referred to is "the time of the end" described in Daniel 11:35 and Daniel 11:40. This time of the end is when God's people, who are called the "wise," shall no longer "fall" (Daniel 11:35). The only time in history before the Second Coming when God's people will no longer die is at the close of probation. This close of probation is described in Revelation 22:11 as the time when the filthy will "still be filthy" and the holy will "still be holy." This close of probation occurs at the end of the investigative judgment, which is currently ongoing in heaven. This investigative judgment is reviewing the records of those who will be saved. This investigative judgment involves "the book" which contains the names of God's people.

The "book" referred to in Daniel 12:1 is described in the New Testament as the "book of life" (Revelation 3:5, Revelation 13:8, Revelation 20:12, and Philippians 4:3). This "book" is involved in the judgment (Daniel 7:10, Revelation 20:12-15). Those who are delivered safely through the time of trouble will be God's people whose names are "written in the book" (discussed in Revelation 4 and 5—The Judgment Scene). The reference to "the book" in this text further connects the "time" of this verse to the close of the investigative judgment when this book is being reviewed.

The phrase "at that time your people shall be delivered" can be applied to "the time of the end" (Daniel 11:35) or to the end of time. The end-of-time application means Jesus will save His people at the Second Coming. The time-of-the-end application means that God's people are now sealed with God's seal in their foreheads. The 144,000 of Revelation 7:3, 4 will be sealed with God's seal "upon their foreheads" at the close of probation and the end of the investigative judgment. This is when Jesus or Michael "shall arise" or stand up. Michael "shall arise" is describing the end of Jesus ministry in the heavenly court as our "Lamb standing, as though it had been slain" (Revelation 5:6). This is the end of the investigative judgment. This is when the temple is filled with smoke "and no one could enter the temple" (Revelation 15:8). Michael "shall arise" means that God will now begin to pour out His wrath on this earth (Revelation 16:1). Michael "shall arise" means that God will now avenge His faithful slain (Revelation 5:10).

> Daniel 12:2: *"And many of those who sleep in the dust of the earth shall awake, some to everlasting life, and some to shame and everlasting contempt."*

At first glance this verse seems not to be connected to the prior verse. In the prior verse Daniel described the worst time of trouble the world would ever see and he also described those who were delivered by God. Those who are delivered by God are those saved at the Second Coming because they remained faithful to Him. This next verse now describes those who were faithful and also some who were not faithful but all of whom died. This verse emphasizes that God will be faithful to His people even if they die. God will raise some just prior to the Second Coming. These people are described in Daniel 12:3 as "wise." They are also described in Daniel 11:33, 35 and Daniel 12:10 as "wise." All of these verses are referring to the same group who will witness for God prior to the "time of the end" (Daniel 11:35) and during the "time of trouble" (Daniel 12:1). Some of these wise "shall fall, to refine and cleanse them and to make them white, until the time of the end, for it is yet for the time appointed" (Daniel 11:35). The time of the end in Daniel 11 is not the end of time. This is shown in Daniel 11:40-45 where multiple battles occur after "the time of the end." Probation closes at "the time of the end" and after that the wise will no longer die. In other words, the wise will no longer die once the time of trouble begins. The time of trouble begins with the close of probation.

This resurrection of the dead who are raised to everlasting life is a special resurrection just prior to the Second Coming of Christ. This special resurrection involves "all who have died in the faith of the third angel's message" (*The Great Controversy*, page 637).[1] This will allow God's people who suffered and died during the time after the mark of the beast to see the final events and participate in the Second Coming. This is not the resurrection described at the Second Coming when "the Lord himself will descend from heaven with a cry of command, with the archangel's call, and with the sound of the trumpet of God. And the dead in Christ will rise first; then we who are alive, *who are left,* shall be caught up together with them in the clouds to meet the Lord in the air; and so we shall always be with the Lord" (I Thessalonians 4:16, 17) (emphasis supplied). The phrase who are left (alive) suggests that many will die prior to His Second Coming.

There is another group resurrected who will rise not to "everlasting life" but to "everlasting contempt" and shame. This group is unique. This special resurrection occurs just prior to the Second Coming in order for this group to see the event they scoffed. This is not the resurrection of the wicked described in Revelation 20:13, 14. The wicked, which are raised in this special resurrection, include those "who pierced him" (Revelation 1:7) as well as "the most violent opposers of His truth and His people" (*The Great Controversy*, page 637).[2] This special resurrection will occur shortly before Christ's Second Coming.

> Daniel 12:3: *"And those who are wise shall shine like the brightness of the firmament; and those who turn many to righteousness, like the stars for ever and ever."*

This verse is a promise to those who are "wise" that they shall shine forever. This is a promise that they shall live forever in glory. The "wise" in this text are those who witness to others and "turn many to righteousness" during the last days. They will be purified and made white and refined (Daniel 11:35 and Daniel 12:10). Some of them will fall by the "sword and flame" but they "shall make many understand" (Daniel 11:33). They are "wise" because they "shall understand" the last-day events, which Daniel did not understand (Daniel 12:10).

It is clear that the "wise" of Daniel 12:3 are the same as the "wise" of Daniel 11:33, 35 and Daniel 12:10. Both groups understand, both groups will be refined and made white, both groups will witness to others, and both groups exist at the time of the end. It is also apparent that Daniel 12:1 connects to Daniel 11:40 regarding the timing of these events. These connections place these events in direct association with the "abomination that makes desolate" (Daniel 11:31). This association will be made even stronger when Daniel receives his answer to "what shall be the issue of these things?" in Daniel 12:11. We find in Daniel 12:11 that the answer involves the "abomination that makes desolate."

Daniel 12:4: *"But you, Daniel, shut up the words, and seal the book, until the time of the end. Many shall run to and fro, and knowledge shall increase."*

This verse tells us that the time of trouble is linked to the "time of the end." This time of trouble is clearly a last-day event and because it is not related to Daniel's time he is told to "seal the book." This message regarding the time of trouble would be unsealed or opened up at the "time of the end." This same phrase is used to introduce certain events of history relating to Israel's last days in Daniel 11:40. This suggests that these events in Daniel 11:40-45 will occur simultaneously with the time of trouble.

It is significant that the "abomination that makes desolate" is "set up" prior to the "time of the end" (Daniel 11:31 compared to Daniel 11:40). This is also shown in Daniel 11:31-35 where the abomination is set up but the "wise" refuse to accept this abomination and some of the wise "fall" or die until "the time of the end" (Daniel 11:35). This same "transgression that makes desolate" described in Daniel 8:13, 14 is also linked to the "time of the end" in Daniel 8:17, 19.

In other words, the abomination is set up prior to the wise witnessing against it. They are wise because they recognize him as a liar and the "father of lies" (John 8:44). They are wise because they recognize him as the false Christ. They are wise because they refuse to accept his false Sabbath. They are wise because they "keep the commandments of God and bear testimony to Jesus" (Revelation 12:17). They are wise because they refuse to accept Satan as the true Christ.

In Revelation 12:17, "the dragon was angry with the woman, and went off to make war on the rest of her offspring." The dragon is Satan (Revelation 12:9). The woman represents God's people or church and the "rest of her offspring" represents God's remnant church or people at the time of the end. The reason the dragon or Satan is angry is easily understood in the light of the circumstances in the last days. Satan has set himself up as the Messiah, Christ returned. He has declared Sunday as his Sabbath and changed God's Law but a small group of people refuse to accept this change of the Law. This refusal to accept his seal or mark will result in their inability to buy or sell (Revelation 13:17) (discussed in Revelation 13 (last part)—The Mark of the Beast). However, this inability to buy or sell will not cause them to renounce God's Law. Satan is also angry because they refuse to accept him as Christ. Satan will be king of the world but this remnant will not accept him and will continue to "bear testimony to Jesus" (Revelation 12:17). They will completely reject his claim to be Christ. His claim to be Christ and his enthronement as Christ in Jerusalem is "the abomination that makes desolate" (Daniel 11:31).

The truly "wise" referred to in Daniel 11:33, 35, Daniel 12:3 and Daniel 12:10 are those who reject Satan as Christ and reject his authority over them. Daniel 11:35 tell us that "some of those that are wise shall fall . . . until the time of the end." Historically, this has been applied to those who died during the Dark Ages.[3] However, another application clearly fits this verse. The time of trouble is linked to the "time of the end." The "time of the end" follows "the abomination that makes desolate" being set up in Daniel 11:31. "The abomination that makes desolate" is Satan as the false Christ who persecutes God's people, the remnant. The remnant are those who reject the false Christ, they are the "wise" who "shall make many understand" (Daniel 12:10 and Daniel 11:33).

Some of this remnant will die prior to the "time of the end" (Daniel 11:35). However, Daniel 11:35 suggests that they will stop dying at "the time of the end." Daniel 11:35 states "and some of those who are wise shall fall . . . *until the time of the end*" (emphasis supplied). "Shall fall" until, suggests that at the time of the end the falling will cease. This is consistent with the close of probation when no further death of God's righteous followers will occur. Thus, Daniel's time of the end is the close of probation.

John in Revelation 22:11 describes a time when "the righteous still do right" and "the evildoer still do evil." At the close of probation everyone will have chosen either to accept Satan's lies or to accept Jesus' truths. All decisions for or against God will have been completed as they relate to salvation. Once this time of probation has closed no one else will be converted and once this occurs no more righteous will die because there is no one who will be influenced by their deaths and no point in their dying. This cessation of the righteous dying is described in Daniel 11:35 when it refers to "the wise" dying until "the time of the end." This further connects the wise to the very last remnant of God's church. *It is important to note that the time of the end in Daniel 11 is not the end of time.* This is shown in Daniel 11:40-45 because all of the events described in these verses occur during "the time of the end" (Daniel 11:40) prior to Jesus Second Coming, which occurs at the end of time.

"Many shall run to and fro, and knowledge shall increase." One interpretation of this phrase is that scientific knowledge will be greatly expanded in the last days and that travel will be increased.[4] However, the biblical context suggests that the "knowledge" referred to in this phrase refers to biblical knowledge expanding and that running "to and fro" refers to running through the Bible increasing knowledge.[5] Certainly, Bible knowledge has increased, especially as it relates to the books of Daniel and Revelation. This increase in understanding led to worldwide reformations in the nineteenth and twentieth centuries. However, it appears that at the "time of the end" a special understanding of Daniel will occur. This "understanding" is linked to the "wise" (Daniel 11:33 and Daniel 12:10) and these "wise" are linked to the abomination that makes desolate (Daniel 11:31-33) who persecutes them. The abomination is linked to the time of the end. *The special understanding that occurs at the time of the end will be the understanding of who the abomination that makes desolate is and the need to warn others.* The wise will "stand firm and take action" (Daniel 11:32).

> Daniel 12:5: *"Then I Daniel looked, and behold two others stood, one on this bank of the stream and one on that bank of the stream."*

Daniel is standing by the Tigris River discussed in Daniel 10:4. He suddenly sees two more angels, one on each side of the river. Daniel had been listening to Gabriel (Daniel 9:21) explain the world's last-day events (Daniel 11:2). Now, two more angels appear with "a man clothed in linen" (Daniel 12:6). The presence of these two angels is not explained. However, they can be considered witnesses to the oath that will be taken in Daniel 12:7. In Old Testament times two witnesses were considered an adequate proof of truth. There could also be some symbolism here related to the two witnesses of Revelation 11 who will be involved in the last-day events.

> Daniel 12:6: *"And I said to the man clothed in linen, who was above the waters of the stream, 'How long shall it be till the end of these wonders?'"*

The man clothed in linen was previously described in Daniel 10:5, 6 as having His loins "girded with gold of Uphaz. His body was like beryl, his face like the appearance of lightning, his eyes like flaming torches, his arms and legs like the gleam of burnished bronze, and the sound of his words like the noise of a multitude." This man is also described in Revelation 1:13-15: "one like a son of man, clothed with a long robe and with a golden girdle round his breast; his head and his hair were white as white wool, white as snow; his eyes were like a flame of fire, his feet were like burnished bronze, refined as in a furnace, and his voice was like the sound of many waters." This Son of Man is Jesus Christ. This Man "clothed in linen" is Jesus Christ.

This Man clothed in linen was standing "above the waters of the stream." This Man was not limited to standing on the ground. This Man appears to be in charge because Daniel now asks Him "How long shall it be till the end of these wonders?" This man is Michael who will arise "at that time" (Daniel 12:1). He is the One who "has charge of" God's people and he is the "great prince" (Daniel 12:1).

Daniel asks "How long shall it be till the end of these wonders?" Daniel wants to know how long this abomination will last (Daniel 11:31). How long will the wise (God's people) continue to be persecuted? When will God's people "be delivered" (Daniel 12:1)? Daniel is clearly concerned about these "time of the end" events (Daniel 11:40), which include the time of trouble.

> Daniel 12:7: *"The man clothed in linen, who was above the waters of the stream, raised his right hand and his left hand toward heaven; and I heard him swear by him who lives for ever that it would be for a time, two times, and half a time;* **and that when the shattering of the power of the holy people comes to an end all these things would be accomplished"** *(emphasis supplied).*

The Man "clothed in linen" is Jesus Christ who is answering Daniel's question. Jesus begins by raising both hands and swearing by "him who lives forever." Jesus is swearing by God the Father and by the Holy Spirit and by Himself! Raising one hand is usually accepted as a pledge that your testimony is true. However, Jesus raises both hands suggesting a solemn oath taken before His two witnesses, standing one on each side of the river. Clearly, the answer is important if Jesus has to take an oath before giving it. Jesus' answer includes a time prophecy: "that it would be for a time, two times and half a time." A "time" in biblical prophecy is equal to one year. One year on the Jewish calendar is 360 days. Two "times" or two years is 720 days and a "half a time" or half a year is 180 days. Therefore, three and one-half times equals 360 days plus 720 days plus 180 days or 1260 days.

Historically, since this time span is identical to Daniel 7:25, which also introduced a 1260-day prophecy, it was assumed that this prophecy covered the same time period as Daniel 7:25. The 1260 days of Daniel 7:25 represent 1260 years (one prophetic day equals one literal year). Daniel 7:25 applies to the time from A.D. 538 to 1798 when Papal Rome ruled the world and persecuted God's true believers. Daniel 7:25 describes a power, which speaks "words against the Most High" and persecutes God's people. However, this kingdom loses its power when its head is mortally wounded (Revelation 13:3, 12). This mortal wound occurred in 1798 long before the events that Daniel is describing in chapter 12 which involve the time of the end (compare Daniel 11:35, 40 with Daniel 12:1). A time of the end application of this verse is not consistent with a Dark Ages application to the years A.D. 538 to 1798.

There are several reasons why the time period described in this verse should be applied to last-day events.

> **First,** Daniel did not understand Jesus' answer. Daniel had previously been shown the world's history in Daniel 7 as well as in Daniel 9. Daniel understood the 1260-year prophecy of Daniel 7, but he did not understand the 1260-day prophecy of Daniel 12.

> **Second,** Ellen G. White connects this prophecy to the time of the end. She states "let us read and study the twelfth chapter of Daniel. It is a warning that *we shall all need to understand before the time of the end"* (emphasis supplied) (*Last-day Events*, page 15).[6]

> **Third,** the context of Daniel 12 is clearly about last-day events. Daniel 12 is a continuation of Daniel 11. Daniel 11 introduces last-day events in Daniel 11:29, 31, and 40.

> **Fourth,** Daniel 12 begins with the time of trouble, which is clearly a time-of-the-end event.

Where then does this 1260-day prophecy fit in the last-day events? The key to understanding this prophecy is found in Revelation 11: the story of the two witnesses, the Old Testament and the New Testament (discussed in Revelation 11 (first part)— The Two Witnesses). The two witnesses are "in sackcloth" for 1260 days (Revelation 11:3), then they are dead for 1260 days (Revelation 11:9). The beast "that ascends" will kill them (Revelation 11:7). This beast is Satan who ascends his throne as the eighth king and is the abomination that makes desolate (previously discussed under Daniel 8, 9, and 11). This abomination is Satan as the false Christ. This abomination is described in Daniel 11:31 and is set up in Jerusalem (Revelation 11:8, Daniel 11:31, and Matthew 24:15). When Satan as the false Christ becomes the world's spiritual leader or eighth king (Revelation 17:11), he will now be able to shatter "the power of the holy people." When Satan becomes the spiritual leader of the world as the false Christ returned, he will claim to have the right to interpret his Bible. He will claim that he wrote God's Holy Word and mankind has misunderstood it. Satan will deceive the world into believing his lies and destroy God's Word as an effective witness. God's Word will then be dead but "not buried" (Revelation 11:8, 9) because the world will think they now understand the scriptures better than before!

God's peoples' "power" will be shattered because their strongest witnessing tool will be dead for the non-believers. Imagine trying to witness to a non-believer who thinks you do not understand God's Word as well as he does! Imagine witnessing about God's truth when God's truth has been turned into lies. God's peoples' power to help save others will be shattered when the world will no longer listen to their interpretation of God's Word because they believe the false Christ's interpretation. God's peoples' power will also be shattered because the world will think Christ has returned and they no longer need to prepare for His Second Coming. When God's people try to convince the world they need the true Christ in their lives, the world will ridicule them pointing to the false Christ and his signs and wonders. Satan's miracles as the false Christ will make it almost impossible for nonbelievers to accept the true Christ. Finally, God's peoples' power will be shattered because Satan, the dragon of Revelation 12 will "make war on the rest of her offspring" (Revelation 12:17). Her offspring represent God's people who will be hunted down by Satan and his followers because they "keep the commandments of God and bear testimony to Jesus" (Revelation 12:17). God's true believers will not accept Satan's mark, which would require them to break God's Law (discussed in Revelation 13 (last part)—The Mark of the Beast). God's true believers will refuse to accept Satan as Christ, but will "bear testimony to Jesus."

The 1260 days of Daniel 12:7 represents a last day's prophecy. This time period begins after Satan becomes the eighth king and the spiritual leader of the world. This will occur when the world accepts him as the false Christ, which is the "abomination that makes desolate" (Daniel 11:31). This occurs in the midst of the week (Daniel 9:27): the last prophetic week of earth's history. This 1260 days is the same time period as the three and one-half years during which God's two witnesses are dead (Revelation 11:9,11). This 1260 days is the same 1260 days prophesied in Revelation 12:14 described as a "time, and times, and half a time" when the dragon (Satan) rules the world and seeks to destroy God's remnant. This is the same "half of the week" described in Daniel 9:27 when Satan shall cause "sacrifice and offering to cease." This is the same time period as the 42 months in Revelation 11:2 during which Satan and "the nations" will trample over the holy city. This occurs when Satan as the "beast that ascends" occupies the city "where their lord was crucified" (Revelation 11:7, 8). This 1260-day period represents the last three and one-half years of Jerusalem's history, during which Satan will finally be allowed to rule this world, first as spiritual king (the eighth king) and finally as world king (Revelation 9:11).

> Daniel 12:8: *"I heard, but I did not understand. Then I said,*
> *'O my Lord, what shall be the issue of these things?'"*

Daniel did not understand this prophecy. Daniel particularly did not seem to understand the time element.[7] Daniel had understood the prior 1260-year prophecy of Daniel 7:25 and the 2300-year prophecy of Daniel 8:14, after they were explained, but he did not understand this prophecy. This suggests that this prophecy was different from the prior 1260-year prophecy, which he understood. Daniel asks again "what shall be the issue of these things?" Daniel is referring to the abomination that makes desolate and to the time of trouble and asking what will be the outcome. Daniel knows that Jesus overcomes at the end but he is concerned about God's people during these last-day events. How will they survive the time of the end?

> Daniel 12:9: *"He said, 'Go your way, Daniel, for the words are shut up and sealed until the time of the end.'"*

Daniel is persistent. He asks Jesus twice what will happen. Jesus responds by telling Daniel to "go your way." This phrase means stop asking since it does not affect you now. The answer is not critical for Daniel to know. The answer is important only for those who live at the "time of the end." Jesus tells Daniel "the words are shut up and sealed ***until the time of the end"*** (emphasis supplied). The time of the end occurs after the abomination that makes desolate appears, which is described in Daniel 11:31, 35. The time of the end correlates with Daniel 11:40-45, which is introduced by the phrase at "the time of the end." The time of the end involves the time of trouble since Daniel 12:1 refers back to Daniel 11:40. The time of trouble will be preceded by a preliminary time of trouble, which will begin shortly after Satan begins his reign as the abomination that makes desolate (the world's false Christ) (discussed in Revelation 17 (third part)—The Eighth King). This preliminary time of trouble occurs when the buy-sell law is enacted (discussed in Revelation 13 (last part)—The Mark of the Beast). This preliminary time of trouble will occur during the reign of the abomination that makes desolate. It will be followed by the actual time of trouble. The actual time of trouble of Daniel 12:1 will occur after Satan begins his reign as world king and the sealing of God's people has occurred (Revelation 9:4, 11). This occurs at Daniel's time of the end (Daniel 11:35, 40) when the investigative judgment ends and probation closes. The time of trouble for God's people "such as never has been since there was a nation" (Daniel 12:1) corresponds with the reign of Satan as world king.

Ellen White suggests that the book of Daniel is unsealed in the book of Revelation.[8] The key to understanding Daniel 12 is contained in Revelation 11, 13, and 17. The book of Daniel is now about to be completely unsealed, because we are rapidly approaching the time of the end.

> Daniel 12:10: *"Many shall purify themselves, and make themselves white, and be refined; but the wicked shall do wickedly; and none of the wicked shall understand; but those who are wise shall understand."*

The "wise" of this end-time period were mentioned initially in Daniel 11:33. They are "wise" because they do not accept the abomination that makes desolate (Daniel 11:31). This abomination is Satan pretending to be Christ returned to earth. They are "wise" because they do not violate God's holy covenant, which is His Sabbath. Satan will attack God's holy covenant (Daniel 11:28, 30, 32). Satan attacks God's covenant by replacing it with his own day of worship. Daniel 11:28, 30 show that this attack will occur prior to the abomination that makes desolate being "set up" (Daniel 11:31). These verses show that the enactment of the Sunday law will precede the setting up of the abomination that makes desolate.

The "wise" will not accept this false Sabbath or change in God's Law. They are "wise" because they refuse to go along with the world, which will claim that Jesus has returned as the eighth king (discussed in Revelation (second part)—The Eighth King). They are "wise" because they "know their God" (Daniel 11:32). They are "wise" because they "stand firm and take action" (Daniel 11:32). They are "wise" because they "shall make many understand" (Daniel 11:33). Some of these wise "shall fall" or die "until the time of the end" (Daniel 11:35), which is the close of probation. They "shall purify themselves, and make themselves white, and be refined." This refers to the persecution they will experience as the "wise" in the last days. These wise shall "shine like the brightness of the firmament" (Daniel 12:3).

They are "wise" because they understand the last-day events and recognize Satan as the abomination that he is instead of the Christ he claims to be. These "wise" of Daniel 11 and 12 are called "saints" in Revelation 14:12. They are saints because "they keep the commandments of God and the faith of Jesus" (Revelation 14:12). These saints reject the false Sabbath thereby keeping God's Commandments and reject the false Christ, thereby keeping the faith of Jesus. This is exactly what the "wise" will do.

"But the wicked shall do wickedly; and none of the wicked shall understand." Once Satan is established as the abomination that makes desolate or the false Christ, he will encourage the wicked to "do wickedly." Jerusalem will become "Sodom and Egypt" (Revelation 11:8) because Satan will eliminate God's Law by killing it (discussed in Revelation 11 (first part)—The Two Witnesses). Once the world believes Satan is Christ returned and God's Word has been reinterpreted by Satan, the wicked will become even more evil.

The most critical issue that determines wisdom during the last days is recognizing Satan as the false Christ. The wise will know who he is and "understand" but "none of the wicked shall understand." The wicked have accepted Satan as the false Christ and therefore none of them shall "understand" that he is the abomination that makes desolate. But "those who are wise shall understand." They are wise because they understand who the abomination that makes desolate is and they help others understand (Daniel 11:32, 33). They are wise because they understand the prophecies of Daniel 11 and 12.

> Daniel 12:11: *"And from the time that the continual burnt offering is taken away, and the abomination that makes desolate is set up, there shall be a thousand two hundred and ninety days."*

This verse mentions two events which also occur together in Daniel 11:31 and in Daniel 8:14. Also, they are both alluded to in Daniel 9:27 where it states "he shall cause sacrifice and offering to cease; and upon the wing of abominations shall come one who makes desolate." Daniel 12:11 combines these two events and associates a time period of 1290 days. This 1290 prophetic day time period could equal 1290 literal years, with one prophetic day equaling one literal year.

Historically, this time period was thought to have begun in A.D. 508 when Clovis, King of the Francs, was converted and the Visigoths were overrun. Historicists (those who accept the historical approach to prophetic interpretation) suggest that the taking away of the "burnt offering" started the 1290-year prophecy and link this to the conversion of King Clovis.

Historicists then add 1290 years to A.D. 508 which gives 1798, which was the end of Papal supremacy. Using this approach, the Papacy is the abomination, which ended in 1798. They also suggest that the setting up of "the abomination" is the beginning of the Papacy and that this started the 1260-year prophecy of Daniel 12:7. They suggest that both prophecies end in 1798.[9]

However, we have seen that in the last days the abomination that makes desolate is clearly Satan as the false Christ. This has been shown in Daniel 8:11-14, in Daniel 9:27 and in Daniel 11:31 (discussed in Daniel 8, 9, and 11—The Abomination That Makes Desolate). When Satan sets up his kingdom as the false Christ, he will also take away the burnt offering. The burnt offering represents Jesus sacrifice for our sins. When Satan is set up as the false Christ, he will interpret God's Word, since he will claim to be the author. God's Word is what reveals the true Jesus to us. This will no longer be available to the world if they believe Satan's lies. Once Satan ascends the throne as the eighth king, he will eliminate the world's need for a Lamb Slain. The burnt offering represents Jesus as our Lamb Slain. The world will see no need for the real Jesus because they already have a false Christ as their king.

Some have assumed that the "continual burnt offering" begins this time period and the "abomination that makes desolate" ends this time period. However, both of these events occur together in Daniel 8:14, Daniel 9:27, Daniel 11:31, and in Daniel 12:11 and are not separate but simultaneous events. The assumption that these two events mark either end of this time period is inconsistent with all the other texts, which discuss these same events and always place them together. In none of the prior references to both of these events (Daniel 8:14, 9:27, and 11:31) are they considered separate events in time but are always linked together in time as simultaneous events. Both of these events occur together at the beginning of this time period. The end of this time period is simply not given in Daniel 12. The next verse actually implies an ending, which occurs after this time period of 1290 days.

In Revelation 11:11, 12, the two witnesses are raised at the end of the 1260 days and ascend to heaven. This is followed by an earthquake in Jerusalem, Satan's capital city (Revelation 11:13). Satan's followers are terrified and they "gave glory to the God of heaven" (Revelation 11:13). The world has not yet come to an end, but the third woe is soon to come (Revelation 11:14). It appears that Satan's followers will finally lose faith in him because he is not able to prevent an earthquake in his own city! Their faith in Satan has already been eroded by the plagues, which God has been pouring out. This loss of confidence in Satan will then spread to the world and cause Satan ultimately to divide up his kingdom into ten kingdoms (Revelation 17:12). Satan would never voluntarily yield any of his power to others! This text states "there shall be a thousand two hundred and ninety days." Because this is a last days prophecy it should be considered a literal 1290 days that begins with Satan being "set up" as the abomination (Daniel 11:31). This abomination is the false Christ and the eighth king of Revelation 17:11. Satan's control of the world and his rule as the world's king will end 1290 days after he ascends his throne. This will be followed by the short reigns of the last ten kings and then Jesus will return.

Daniel 12:12: *"Blessed is he who waits and comes to the thousand three hundred and thirty-five days."*

Historically, this time prophecy has been applied to A.D. 508 through 1844.[10] This application suggests that God's people were blessed in 1844 when Daniel's prophecy of 2300 years was understood. Those who accept this interpretation start the 1260-year time period at A.D. 538 but start the 1290 year and the 1335 year time periods at A.D. 508. However, the context of Daniel 12 suggests that this time period belongs to the "time of the end." Since no new starting point is given and this text suggests waiting through the prior events, it is reasonable to assume that this time period begins at the same time as the 1290-day time period of the prior verse and the 1260-day time period of Daniel 12:7. This verse states "blessed is he who waits." This waiting refers to enduring Satan's attacks until the end of time. This waiting refers to waiting for the Lord's return. In Dr. Robert Smith's book, *The Sixth King*, he applies this verse to God's people just prior to the Second Coming. He suggests that God's people who wait will be blessed when they hear God's voice announcing His soon return.[13] However, this could also represent the time when God's saints are raised in the special resurrection described in Daniel 12:2 just prior to the Second Coming. Another possibility is that this verse is referring to the onset of the seventh trumpet. It is unknown how long a time it will take to complete the seventh trumpet and the seventh plague but certainly all of God's people who "wait" for this event will be blessed. Jesus said we would know when the time of His coming was near. "So also, when you see all these things, you know that he is near, at the very gates" (Matthew 24:33). In Matthew 24, Jesus was referring to the same events that Daniel is describing. Jesus says that when we see these things we can know that His coming is imminent. Jesus says that we can know that He is "at the very gates" (Matthew 24:33). Once the ten kings reign Jesus Second Coming is truly "at the very gates" (Matthew 24:33).

Daniel 12:13: *"But go your way till the end; and you shall rest, and shall stand in your allotted place at the end of the days."*

Jesus is telling Daniel for the second time to "go your way." In other words, Daniel is not to worry but to do his job until the end. Daniel would die and "rest" in his grave until "the end of the days." Daniel is promised that he will be raised prior to the end of the world. Daniel was going to be able to see these last-day events which he did not understand.[12]

SUMMARY

Daniel 12 describes the world's last-day events. It begins with the time of trouble and then describes a special resurrection at the end of time. Daniel's answer to "how long" is answered with three time prophecies all of which relate to the "abomination that makes desolate." This abomination or false-Christ will shatter God's people's power for 1260 days. This correlates with the three and one-half years of Revelation 11, which ends when God's two witnesses are raised. The shattering of God's people's power occurs when Satan becomes the official interpreter of God's Word. This will occur when Satan takes his throne as the abomination that makes desolate or the false Christ. This abomination will rule for 1290 days and then will be forced to divide up his kingdom. God's people will be blessed if they wait for 1335 days because at that point they will know their Lord is coming for them soon. The following graph outlines the events of Daniel 12.

Daniel 12

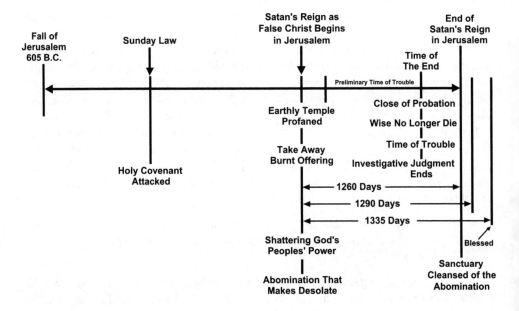

1   White, Ellen G., *The Great Controversy* (Pacific Press Publishing Association, Nampa, Idaho) 1950, p. 637.
2   Ibid.
3   Nichol, Francis D. (Ed.). *The Seventh-day Adventist Bible Commentary,* (Review and Herald Publishing Association, Washington, D.C.) 1957, Vol. 4, p. 874.
4   Ibid. p. 879.
5   Ibid.
6   *White, Ellen G., Manuscript Release 228 (1903),* Quoted in *Last-day events* (Pacific Press Publishing Association, Nampa, Idaho) 1992, p. 15.
7   Nichol, Francis D. (Ed.). *The Seventh-day Adventist Bible Commentary,* (Review and Herald Publishing Association, Washington, D.C.) 1957, Vol. 4, p. 880.
8   White, Ellen G., *Testimonies to Ministers and Gospel Workers*, (Pacific Press Publishing Association, Nampa, Idaho) 1923, p. 115.
9   Nichol, Francis D. (Ed.). *The Seventh-day Adventist Bible Commentary,* (Review and Herald Publishing Association, Washington, D.C.) 1957, Vol. 4, p. 881.
10 Ibid.
11 Smith, Robert N. Jr., *The Sixth King,* Copyright 1993, Robert N. Smith, Jr., M.D., Fort Worth, Texas, p. 51.
12 White, Ellen G., *Prophets and Kings*, (Pacific Press Publishing Association, Nampa, Idaho) 1917, p. 537.

SUMMARY
Section I—The Abomination
That Makes Desolate

In Matthew 24, Jesus answers the most important question for our time: "what will be the sign of your coming and of the close of the age?" (Matthew 24:3). Jesus' answer was "Take heed that no one leads you astray" (Matthew 24:4). Jesus then explains His answer by describing the false Christs and false prophets who will appear (Matthew 24:5, 11, 23, 24, and 26). However, "the sign" of Jesus' soon coming (Matthew 24:3) is found in Matthew 24:15. "So when you see the desolating sacrilege spoken of by the prophet Daniel, standing in the holy place (let the reader understand)" (Matthew 24:15). Jesus is telling His disciples that the last great deception will be a false Christ standing in the holy place and this is the sign of His soon coming and the close of the age. Jesus emphasizes the importance of this event to God's people by warning them to flee immediately (Matthew 24:16-20). He tells them not to "take what is in his house" or to "turn back to take his mantle" (Matthew 24:17, 18). When God's people see this false Christ "standing in the holy place" (Matthew 24:15), they are to "flee to the mountains" (Matthew 24:16). The very urgency of the instructions to flee confirms the importance of this event. Jesus continues His explanation by describing a "great tribulation" which follows the reign of this false Christ (Matthew 24:21). This "great tribulation" is the same event as Daniel's "time of trouble" and both are described as the worst trouble this world has ever seen (Daniel 12:1, Matthew 24:21). The association of this tribulation with the desolating sacrilege further connects the desolating sacrilege to the last-day events.

Jesus then compares His "sign" with the sign of "the close of the age" (Matthew 24:30, Matthew 24:3). Jesus' sign is His "coming on the clouds" as compared to the coming of the false Christ "in the wilderness" or "in the inner rooms" (Matthew 24:26). Jesus also describes His Second Coming as "the lightning comes from the east and shines as far as the west" (Matthew 24:27) to further emphasize the difference between the false Christ's coming and His Second Coming. The "sign of your coming and of the close of the age" (Matthew 24:3) is the false Christ "standing in the holy place" (Matthew 24:15).

Jesus refers us to Daniel to understand these events. Jesus refers us to those verses in Daniel, which relate to the desolating sacrilege. It is important to recognize that Jesus applies Daniel 9:27 to last-day events. He also applies Daniel 11:31 and Daniel 12:11 to last-day events, since all three of these verses refer to the same desolating sacrilege or the abomination that makes desolate. Jesus applies Daniel 9:27 to Satan as the false Christ who will "cause sacrifice and offerings to cease" for one "half of the week." Satan will "make a strong covenant with many for one week" (Daniel 9:27) and in the middle of that week he will begin his reign as the false Christ. These events are outlined in the graph at the end of this summary.

Daniel 8 discusses a little horn, which magnifies itself (Daniel 8:11). Historically, this little horn has been applied to the Papacy. However, there is a dual application, which will apply in the last days. In the last days, this horn represents Satan as the false Christ who will magnify himself "even up to the Prince of the host" (Daniel 8:11). Satan will take away "the continual burnt offering" (Daniel 8:11), which represents Jesus' true sacrifice for mankind, and replace it with himself as the false Christ. Satan will overthrow "the place of his sanctuary" (Daniel 8:11). This refers to the temple in Jerusalem which will be rebuilt, when Satan reigns as the false Christ. God's people are "the host" who are given over to Satan (Daniel 8:12) and "trampled under foot" (Daniel 8:13). Satan will "cast down" truth (Daniel 8:12) since he is "the father of lies" (John 8:44).

Daniel 8:13 asks the question "For how long is the vision" which concerns the transgression that makes desolate, the continual burnt offering, and "the giving over of the sanctuary and host to be trampled under foot." The answer is that the sanctuary will be restored to its rightful state after "two thousand and three hundred evenings and mornings." This verse has a dual application. Historically, the investigative judgment in heaven began at the end of this 2300-year prophecy in 1844 and is ongoing. However, this abomination will occur again in the last days and the host and the sanctuary will again be trampled under foot. This abomination will occur again when Satan reigns as the false Christ in Jerusalem. The trampling of God's host will begin with the passage of the economic penalties to enforce the Sunday law. This will occur after Satan's reign in Jerusalem has begun. This trampling of the host and the sanctuary will continue for 2300 evenings and mornings or 1150 days and will end when Satan loses his power. Both of these applications of Daniel 8:14 are shown on the graph at the end of this summary.

Daniel 9 completes the vision of Daniel 8. Daniel 9:24-27 describes 70 weeks or 490 years, which correctly predicted Jesus' ministry. However, a dual application exists for Daniel 9:26, 27, which applies to the last days. This dual application is confirmed by Christ's own use of Daniel 9:27 to apply to the last-day events. The "desolating sacrilege" (Matthew 24:15) is the sign of the close of the age (Matthew 24:3). This desolating sacrilege is Satan as the false Christ. Satan is going to "make a strong covenant with many for one week" (Daniel 9:27). As the false Christ, Satan will "cause sacrifice and offering to cease" (Daniel 9:27). As the false Christ, Satan is the "one who makes desolate" and comes "upon the wing of abominations" (Daniel 9:27). Satan is "the desolator" (Daniel 9:27). Satan will reign for "half of the week" (Daniel 9:27) or three and one-half years. This dual application of Daniel 9 is shown on the graph at the end of this summary.

Daniel 11 also discusses last-day events, which relate to the abomination that makes desolate. Daniel 11 describes an attack on God's holy covenant (His Sabbath) followed by the abomination that makes desolate being "set up" (Daniel 11:28, 30, 31). This is consistent with the passage of the Sunday law prior to the reign of Satan as the "abomination that makes desolate" (Daniel 11:31). This false Christ will "take away the continual burnt offering" and "profane the temple" (Daniel 11:31). This will occur when Satan reigns in Jerusalem and ministers in the temple as the false Christ. Satan will attack God's people, described as "wise" (Daniel 11:32, 33) and many "shall fall by sword and flame, by captivity and plunder, for some days." These "wise shall fall, to refine and to cleanse them and to make them white, until the time of the end" (Daniel 11:35). This time of the end represents the close of probation when God's people will no longer fall or die. This is confirmed in Daniel 11:40 which shows that "the time of the end" is not the end of time, since several further battles occur after the time of the end. These events are shown on the graph at the end of this summary.

Daniel 12 begins by referring to Daniel 11 and connecting the time of trouble to "the time of the end" of Daniel 11:40. Daniel then describes this time of trouble "such as never has been" (Daniel 12:1). This is the same time period as the "great tribulation" Jesus described in Matthew 24:21. Daniel does not understand these events and wants to know "How long shall it be till the end of these wonders?" (Daniel 12:6). Daniel is told "that it would be for a time, two times, and half a time" (Daniel 12:7). This three and one-half times is 1260 days or three and one-half years. Daniel is also told that "when the shattering of the power of the holy people comes to an end all these things would be accomplished" (Daniel 12:7). This is Jesus' answer to Daniel's question. God's people's power will be shattered for 1260 days, then all "these wonders" will be accomplished (Daniel 12:6). The wonders that Daniel is referring to include the abomination he saw being set up, the profaning of God's temple by Satan as the false Christ, the cessation of offerings and sacrifice to the true God, the overthrow of Jerusalem by Satan, and the trampling of God's people. Jesus' answer is that the end of the overthrow of God's people's power will mark the end of these wonders. This will occur when Satan's reign ends in Jerusalem. In other words, when Satan's power is overthrown God's people's power will be restored. God's people's power will be shattered when Satan, as the false Christ, becomes the interpreter of God's Holy Word (the Old Testament and the New Testament). This will occur when the world accepts Satan as the Christ returned and Satan claims power to interpret God's Word, since he claims it is his book. This 1260-day period is the same time period as the one-half week of Daniel 9:27. It is also the three and one-half years when God's two witnesses are dead but not buried described in Revelation 11:9, 11.

Daniel still does not understand Jesus' answer and asks, "what shall be the issue of these things?" (Daniel 12:8). Jesus then answers that 1290 days will occur from the setting up of the abomination that makes desolate and the taking away of the continual burnt offering. Jesus does not separate these two events as some have suggested. Indeed, these two events are also linked together in Daniel 11:31, Daniel 8:13, and Daniel 9:27. Jesus is telling Daniel that time will extend beyond Satan's reign in Jerusalem for a short period. Daniel 12:12 confirms this by placing a blessing on those who wait for 1335 days. Jesus is telling Daniel that time will extend beyond this abomination for at least 75 days and the end will come shortly thereafter. These events are shown on the following graph.

Section I - The Abomination That Makes Desolate Summary Outline

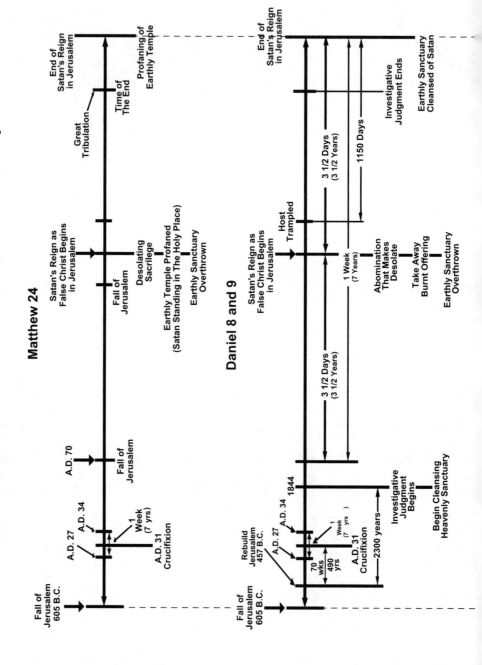

Matthew 24

Fall of Jerusalem 605 B.C.

A.D. 27
A.D. 34
A.D. 70 — Fall of Jerusalem

Week (7 yrs)
A.D. 31 Crucifixion

Fall of Jerusalem

Satan's Reign as False Christ Begins in Jerusalem

Desolating Sacrilege
Earthly Temple Profaned (Satan Standing in The Holy Place)
Earthly Sanctuary Overthrown

Great Tribulation
Time of The End

End of Satan's Reign in Jerusalem

Profaning of Earthly Temple

Daniel 8 and 9

Fall of Jerusalem 605 B.C.

Rebuild Jerusalem 457 B.C.
A.D. 27
A.D. 34
1844

Week (7 yrs)
70 wks
490 yrs
A.D. 31 Crucifixion

2300 years

Investigative Judgment Begins
Begin Cleansing Heavenly Sanctuary

Satan's Reign as False Christ Begins in Jerusalem

3 1/2 Days (3 1/2 Years)

1 Week (7 Years)

Abomination That Makes Desolate
Take Away Burnt Offering
Earthly Sanctuary Overthrown

Host Trampled

3 1/2 Days (3 1/2 Years)

1150 Days

End of Satan's Reign in Jerusalem

Investigative Judgment Ends

Earthly Sanctuary Cleansed of Satan

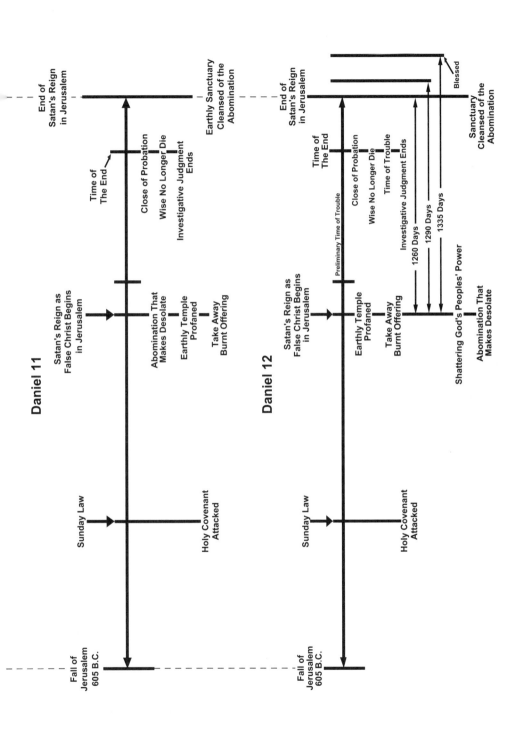

Section II

The Eighth King

Preface:
The Crowns and Their Meaning

Historically, crowns have been very important. A crown signified royalty. A crown signified power and authority. A crown signified ownership and sovereignty. A crown signified victory. In biblical prophecy, a crown is equally significant. In 1 Peter 5:4, God's people are promised a crown of glory. In Revelation 2:10, God's people are promised a crown of life. Crowns are also symbolic and are seen as part of the description of various beasts described in Daniel and Revelation. What is the significance of these crowns? Why do some horns have crowns and others do not? Why do some heads have crowns and others do not?

In Revelation 12:1, a crown is mentioned in connection with the woman: "on her head a crown of twelve stars." The Greek word used here is *stephanos,* which means a "victor's crown" or "wreath." This word was used in conjunction with winning something, for example, the wreath of victory for winning a race. In Revelation 12:3, the red dragon is described as having seven diadems upon his seven heads. Other Bible translations interpret diadems as crowns. Here the Greek word *diadimata* is translated as "diadems" or "crowns." This term is used to denote a king's crown or badge of royalty. We can see from these two texts in the same chapter that the same word crown can apply to different concepts. In one scripture it refers to victory and in another it refers to a symbol of rulership. The Greek meaning is important in determining the symbols' intended meaning.

When a crown is given to a king, it signifies that he has risen to his throne and is now the leader of that nation, tribe, or kingdom. A crown on a prophetic symbol has a similar meaning. The presence of a crown, when linked to a given kingdom means that the kingdom has been given power now or in the past. ***In biblical prophecy, a crown means that the entity with the crown has received its power.*** In other words, a horn uncrowned represents a kingdom that is to come, and a horn crowned represents a kingdom that has already arrived or existed. Understanding this principle helps us understand not only the prophecy but also the timing of the prophecy.

In Daniel 7:7, a fourth beast is described which is "terrible and dreadful and exceedingly strong" and this beast "had ten horns." In Daniel 7:8, "there came up among them another horn, a little one, before which three of the first horns were plucked up by the roots." In Daniel 7:23-25, we find God's explanation of these horns and the fourth beast.

> Daniel 7:23-25: *"Thus he said: 'As for the fourth beast,*
> *there shall be a fourth kingdom on earth, which shall be*
> *different from all the kingdoms, and it shall devour the*
> *whole earth, and trample it down, and break it to pieces.*
> *As for the ten horns, out of this kingdom ten kings shall*
> *arise, and another shall arise after them, he shall be*
> *different from the former ones, and shall put down three*

kings. He shall speak words against the Most High, and
shall wear out the saints of the Most High and shall think
to change the times and the law; and they shall be given
into his hand for a time, two times, and half a time.'"

It can be seen from the above text that the ten horns of the fourth beast are ten kings that represent ten kingdoms which would follow or arise out of this fourth beasts' kingdom. These are the same kingdoms as the ten toes of the fourth kingdom of Daniel 2:43. In Daniel 2:43, these kingdoms "will mix with one another in marriage, but they will not hold together." The four world kingdoms, which precede these ten kingdoms, are each described in Daniel 2 and also in Daniel 7. In Daniel 7:4, the lion kingdom is Babylon. This kingdom is followed by the bear kingdom in Daniel 7:5 which was Media-Persia. The next world kingdom was Greece described as a leopard kingdom in Daniel 7:6. The fourth world kingdom is pictured as a "terrible" beast (Daniel 7:7). This world kingdom was pagan Rome. Rome subsequently was divided into ten European kingdoms. Seven of those kingdoms still exist today: the Saxons (England); the Franks (France); the Alemani (Germany); the Burgundies (Sweden); the Lombard (Italy); the Visigoths (Spain) and the Suevi (Portugal). Three of the ten kingdoms were destroyed by Papal Rome or its agents. The three kingdoms that were destroyed were the Vandals, the Ostrogoths, and the Heruli. These three kingdoms disappeared at the rise of the Papacy. This fulfilled Daniel's prophecy in Daniel 7:8, 24 that the little horn would destroy or put down three kings. When Daniel was shown these ten horns, he was given a view of prophecy forward from his time to the end of time. ***He was looking forward into time and these ten kingdoms had not yet existed and therefore had no crowns.*** Crowns would indicate that they had received their power or status. These horns would receive their crowns in the future and come into existence in the future. The absence of crowns meant that this was yet to occur.

Revelation 13:1: *"And I saw a beast rising out of the sea,*
with ten horns and seven heads, with ten diadems upon its
horns and a blasphemous name on its heads."

Is this beast related to the beast of Daniel 7? Are these ten horns the same ten horns of Daniel 7:7 and 7:24? If these are the same ten horns or kingdoms of Daniel 7:24 then why do they have crowns? What do the seven heads represent? Why don't they have crowns? In order to understand Revelation 13:1, we must read the next verse.

Revelation 13:2: *"And the beast that I saw was like a*
leopard, its feet were like a bear's, and its mouth was like
a lion's mouth. And to it the dragon gave his power and his
throne and great authority."

The first thing we notice is that these are the same symbols Daniel used for his world kingdoms. The lion symbolizes Babylon, the bear symbolizes Media-Persia and the leopard symbolizes Greece (Daniel 7). The difference between John's list and Daniel's list is the order. John's list is backwards. Some authors suggest that John is looking back through time at the same kingdoms that Daniel had seen.[1] The important point to understand is that John's viewpoint is not from his time in the first century. He is describing the view from the beast's point in time backwards. We know this because John dies long before these ten horns come into existence, but these ten horns are crowned. These ten horns are seen as having already been in existence not only because of their crowns, but also because of the content of the rest of Revelation 13. This same beast that John sees "rising out of the sea" is described as having "a mortal wound" and healing that wound in Revelation 13:3. This mortal wound occurred in 1798 long after the ten European kingdoms existed. This same beast, in association with the lamb-like beast (Revelation 13:11) and the image of the beast (Revelation 13:14), will cause a mark "to be marked on the right hand or the forehead" (Revelation 13:16). This mark is part of the last-day events, which also occurs long after these ten kingdoms existed.

The crowns on the ten kingdoms mean that the ten European kingdoms have already existed prior to the events of Revelation 13. Indeed, Revelation 13 is actually describing events relating to the image of the beast and John is looking from these events backward through time. From this retrograde view of history the horns have been crowned and in existence long prior to the mark of the beast. John's retrospective view of world events is parallel to our current view backwards into history. In other words, Revelation 13 will apply shortly to all of us.

Revelation 13:1 also mentions "seven heads" but with no crowns. These same seven heads are seen in Revelation 12:3 but here these seven heads have crowns. These seven heads are also seen in Revelation 17:3, 7, but here again the seven heads do not have crowns. What are these seven heads and why do they not have crowns in Revelation 13 and Revelation 17 but they do have crowns in Revelation 12? The seven heads in Revelation 17:3 and Revelation 17:7 are described in Revelation 17:9-11.

> Revelation 17:9-11: *"This calls for a mind with wisdom; the seven heads are seven hills on which the woman is seated; they are also seven kings, five of whom have fallen, one is, the other has not yet come, and when he comes he must remain only a little while. As for the beast that was and is not, it is an eighth but it belongs to the seven, and it goes to perdition."*

These verses demonstrate that in Revelation 17 the viewpoint of history (the time frame of the scarlet beast and the scarlet woman) corresponds to the sixth king. This king is described as "one is" (Revelation 17:10). In other words, John is viewing history while standing in the time of the sixth king (the one who is). John is looking back over the prior five kings and forward to the seventh and eighth kings. The eighth king is the scarlet beast. The end of the world is described in Revelation 17:14 as "war on the Lamb, and the Lamb will conquer them." In the context of Revelation 17, these seven kings are related to the scarlet woman or Papal Rome as well as to the beast, which is Satan. The six kings are discussed in this book in the chapter on Revelation 17 (second part)—The Eighth King as well as in Dr. Robert Smith's book titled *The Sixth King*.[2] The scarlet woman is discussed in this book in Revelation 17 (first part)—The Scarlet Woman and Her Kings.

Thus, we can see that the crowns are not on the seven heads in Revelation 17 because all seven kings have not yet completed their reigns at the time of the vision. The vision occurs during the reign of the sixth king. This means that these same seven kings' reigns have not been completed at the time of the vision of Revelation 13, because the beast's seven heads in Revelation 13 do not have crowns. This is consistent with the concept that Revelation 13 is describing the beast during the time frame prior to the mark of the beast, and the seven kings have not yet completed their reign. The eighth king will be involved with the mark of the beast. Revelation 13 is describing events which involve one of the seven kings and therefore the seven heads are not crowned. The reign of the seven kings extends to the eighth king, which is Satan as the false Christ (discussed in Revelation 17 (second part)—The Eighth King).

Revelation 12 is describing events that occur after the reign of the seven kings, because in Revelation 12:3 we see that the dragon has seven heads that are crowned. This is the only description of a beast in the book of Revelation where the seven heads are crowned. This suggests that the time frame for this vision in Revelation 12 is after the time of the seven kings and after they have completed their reigns. This occurs during the reign of the eighth king who follows the seven kings (Revelation 17:11). The emphasis of Revelation 12 is on the dragon and who he is and what he does. In Revelation 17:11, the eighth king is the beast. The scarlet beast of Revelation 17 is the same beast as the red dragon of Revelation 12. This red dragon "is called the Devil and Satan" (Revelation 12:9), which is further discussed in Revelation 12—The Dragon and the Eighth King. The dragon pursues the woman, or the true church, and she flees into the wilderness "for a time, and times, and half a time" (Revelation 12:14). This is three and one-half years. Once the dragon reigns as the eighth king, the seven kings have completed their work. The timeframe of the vision of the red dragon beast in Revelation 12 is after the seven heads or kings have completed their reigns and given their power over to the dragon, the eighth king.

The final issue relating to the horns and their crowns in Revelation 12, 13, and 17 is whether the ten horns always represent the ten European countries Daniel described in Daniel 7:23-25. The ten horns of Revelation 13 are the same ten horns described in Daniel 7. John is looking back through history and they are crowned because these kingdoms have already existed. The ten horns of Revelation 17 and Revelation 12 do not have crowns. Who are these ten horns and why don't they have crowns? If they are the same as the ten European kingdoms then they should have crowns because Revelation 17 describes end-time events, as does Revelation 12. The ten European kingdoms existed long before these final events depicted in Revelation 12 and 17. The answer is found in Revelation 17:12-14.

> Revelation 17:12: *"And the ten horns that you saw are ten kings who have **not yet received royal power,** but they are to receive authority as kings for one hour, together with the beast. These are of one mind and give over their power and authority to the beast; they will make war on the Lamb, and the Lamb will conquer them, for he is Lord of lords and*

King of kings, and those with him are called and chosen and faithful" (emphasis supplied).

The ten horns are not crowned in Revelation 17:12 because they have "not yet received royal power." This is the key to understanding the presence or absence of their crowns. In Revelation 17, these ten kings will reign after the seventh king gives over his power to the eighth king. These ten kings will reign at the end of the eighth king's reign for only a short time described as "one hour." One prophetic hour is slightly over two weeks (one prophetic day equals one literal year and one twenty-fourth of a year equals approximately two weeks). These ten kings will serve the beast or eighth king who is Satan.

The dragon or beast of Revelation 12 is described with ten horns that do not have crowns. This means that they cannot refer to the ten European kingdoms that had already existed. These kingdoms have reigned long before the end of time when the remnant is pursued by the dragon. The ten horns of Revelation 12 are the same ten horns described in Revelation 17. These ten horns refer to the last ten kings which will exist at the very end of time when they will "make war on the Lamb" (Revelation 17:14). They do not have crowns because they reign just before Jesus returns as the Lamb. Revelation 12 does not extend to the Second Coming, but ends with the dragon still making "war on the rest of her offspring" (Revelation 12:17) and there-fore the dragon has not yet given the ten kings their power during the events described in Revelation 12. The absence of crowns on these ten horns is further proof that the focus of Revelation 12 is on the dragon, who will be the eighth king and who perse-cutes God's people for 1260 days (Revelation 12:14) just prior to the end of time (dis-cussed in Revelation 12—The Dragon and the Eighth King).

SUMMARY

The following table gives an overview of the beasts of Daniel 7 and Revelation 12, 13, and 17. The table includes the timeframe covered and the time in history from which the events are viewed (prophet's vantage point). To understand the table, one must realize that if there is no crown, that event is ongoing and incomplete or the event is in the future. In Revelation 17, which is seen during the reign of the sixth king, the seven heads are not crowned because the event is ongoing. The ten horns are in the future in Revelation 12 and 17, and, therefore, are not crowned. When a crown is placed on the symbol, it indicates that the event has occurred. This is demon-strated in Revelation 13 where John is looking back through history, and the horns are crowned. These horns are the ten European kingdoms that have already reigned at the time of John's vision. In Revelation 17, the seven heads represent seven kings who are replaced by the beast (Satan) as the eighth king.

The prophet's vantage point is the time during the vision when the prophet is viewing the event and is critical in order to understand the symbol. If the vision is seen as progressing into the future, then there will only be crowns on those symbols that have happened prior to the time of the vision. Thus, Daniel's ten horns have no crowns since prior to Daniel's vision none of the horns existed. On the other hand in Revelation 17, the time of the vision is the sixth king, which is during the seven kings' reigns that are ongoing; therefore, the heads are not crowned because their reigns have not been completed. If the event is not completed, they will not have crowns. In Revelation 13, the viewpoint of John's vision is backward through time from the time of the image to the beast, and thus, the ten horns existed previously and have crowns. In the table, the time frame emphasized by the visions relates only to the events symbolized in that vision pertinent to the beast. In Daniel 7, prior to the dragon beast (fourth beast), Daniel covers history from Babylon and Media-Persia through Greece.

Dragon Beasts of Daniel and Revelation

	Biblical Reference			
	Daniel 7	Revelation 13	Revelation 17	Revelation 12
Prophet's Vantage Point	Daniel's Time Forward	Time of Image of The Beast Looking Backward Through History	Reign of 6th King	Dragon as the False Christ
Beast's Time in History Emphasized	168 B.C.* to the 2nd Coming	End of 7th King's Reign backward to A.D. 538**	Lateran Treaty*** of 1929 to the 2nd Coming	Last 3-1/2 Years of Earth's History
Beast	Pagan Rome	Papacy	Satan (the 8th King)	Satan (the 8th King)
Ten Horns	Future 10 European Kingdoms	Prior 10 European Kingdoms	Last 10 Kings (Future)	Last 10 Kings (Future)
Little Horn	Papacy	--	--	--
Seven Heads	--	Last 7 Kings of Papacy	Last 7 Kings of Papacy	Last 7 Kings of Papacy

*Roman Empire Begins
**Papal Reign Begins
***Lateran Treaty (Papacy Restored as a Political Kingdom)

[1] Nichol, Francis D.(Ed.). *The Seventh-day Adventist Bible Commentary* (Review and Herald Publishing Association, Washington, D.C.) 1957, Vol. 7, p. 817.
[2] Smith, Robert N. Jr., *The Sixth King*, Copyright 1993, Robert N. Smith Jr., M.D., Fort Worth, Texas, pp. 99-150.

Revelation 13 (first part)
The Leopard-Like Beast Healed

Revelation 13 introduces another beast. This beast seems similar to the prior beasts of Daniel 7 and Revelation 12 but it is different in some of its characteristics. It is described as leopard-like but also has features of a bear and a lion. What is this beast? Where in earth's history does it exist? What does this beast have to do with last-day events?

> Revelation 13:1: *"And I saw a beast rising out of the sea, with ten horns and seven heads, with ten diadems upon its horns and a blasphemous name upon its heads."*

This beast which John saw "rising out of the sea" represents a kingdom, which would come up out of a populated area. The sea here represents "peoples and multitudes and nations and tongues" (Revelation 17:15). Waters and seas represent populated areas in biblical prophecy as opposed to coming up out of the earth, which represents arising from an unpopulated area (for example, Revelation 13:11).

This leopard-like beast (Revelation 13:2) has ten horns and seven heads. The ten horns have diadems on them. The seven heads do not have diadems or crowns on them. These crowns mean that the ten kingdoms have already existed but the seven heads have not completed their existence (discussed in the chapter Preface: The Crowns and Their Meaning). These ten horns represent the ten European kingdoms, which developed at the end of the Roman Empire. Seven of these kingdoms still exist today. Three of these kingdoms were overpowered by the little horn (Daniel 7:8, 24) (discussed in Revelation 13 (last part)—The Mark of the Beast). The little horn represents Papal Rome, which followed pagan Rome as the next world power. Papal Rome did overpower three of the original ten kingdoms. The three kingdoms, which no longer exist, are the Vandals, the Heruli and the Ostrogoths.

The seven heads represent seven kings: "the seven heads are seven hills on which the woman is seated; they are also seven kings" (Revelation 17:9, 10). These seven kings are related to the scarlet woman of Revelation 17 (discussed in Revelation 17 (first part)—The Scarlet Woman and Her Kings). These seven heads represent seven kings or rulers of the Papacy, not all of whom have been crowned. In other words, these seven kings have not completed their reigns when John sees this vision.

John's viewpoint, which is the time in history in which John views these events, is shown in Revelation 13:4. He is seeing history when both the dragon and the leopard beast are being worshiped. This can only occur during the reign of the seventh king, just prior to the eighth king's reign. The scarlet beast, as the eighth king, will take over from the seventh king (Revelation 17:11) (discussed in Revelation 17 (first part)—The Scarlet Woman and Her Kings). There is only one time in history when mankind will worship both the scarlet beast (the future eighth king) and the leopard-like beast (Papacy) at the same time. This will occur during the reign of the seventh king (discussed under Revelation 13:4).

John is looking back at prior history from this vantage point, which is the reign of the seventh king. It is important to recognize where John is standing in history when in vision in order to understand the events he is viewing. In Revelation 17, John is seeing history during the time of the sixth king since five kings have fallen and "one is" and the other "has not yet come"(Revelation 17:10). In other words John's viewpoint in Revelation 17 is actually prior to his viewpoint in Revelation 13. In Revelation 12, John's viewpoint is the time of the eighth king (the dragon), which occurs after the seventh king has reigned.

The "blasphemous name upon its heads" further connects this beast to a religious kingdom. It blasphemes God by taking God's attributes and applying them to itself (discussed in Revelation 13 (last part)—The Mark of the Beast). These seven heads would blaspheme God by claiming to be God on earth. Indeed, this is what the popes have claimed throughout history. They also blaspheme God by claiming power to forgive sins.

> Revelation 13:2: *"And the beast that I saw was like a leopard, its feet were like a bear's, and its mouth was like a lion's mouth. And to it the dragon gave his power and his throne and great authority."*

The description of this beast is similar to the four beasts of Daniel 7:3-8 except that the order of the four beasts is reversed. In Daniel 7:3-8, the lion is first, then the bear, then the leopard, and then finally the "terrible beast." These represent the kingdoms of Babylon, Media-Persia, Greece and finally Rome, first as pagan Rome and later as Papal Rome. In Daniel 7, these kingdoms are seen from Daniel's viewpoint in time looking forward. John is now looking backward in time and seeing these kingdoms in reverse order from Papal Rome through Pagan Rome through Greece then Media-Persia and finally Babylon (discussed in Preface: The Crowns and Their Meaning). This confirms that John is seeing the same world history that Daniel foretold, except that John is seeing it from a last-day perspective after it has occurred. Thus, John sees ten horns with crowns because they have already existed, whereas, Daniel's ten horns have no crowns because they are future kingdoms. It is important to note that the seven heads do not yet have crowns, since John is viewing history during the seventh king's existence.

The power behind this leopard-like beast is described as "the dragon" who gives the beast "his throne and great authority." The dragon is Satan (Revelation 12:9). Satan is clearly supporting this religious world power, which is attempting to be God on earth and is blaspheming the true God. Satan claims this earth as his own kingdom and by giving support to the Papal kingdom he is literally giving it his throne and great authority.

> Revelation 13:3: *"One of its heads seemed to have a mortal wound, but its mortal wound was healed, and the whole earth followed the beast with wonder."*

The leopard-like beast of Revelation 13 represents Papal Rome which followed pagan Rome and eliminated three horns or kingdoms when it first came into world power (Daniel 7:8, 24). This occurred in A.D. 538 when the Ostrogoths were overcome and Rome became the capital city of the Papal kingdom. The Vandals and Heruli had been overrun prior to A.D. 538. The Papal Empire existed in Rome for 1260 years. This was predicted in Daniel 7:25 where the little horn or Papal Rome was to have power over the saints "for a time, two times, and half a time." A prophetic time is equal to one year or 360 days (Jewish calendar year). Three and one-half times is three and one-half years or 1260 days. One prophetic day equals one literal year, therefore, 1260 days equals 1260 years. Exactly 1260 years after A.D. 538 in 1798 Napoleon's General Berthier captured Pope Pius VI in Rome and took over the city. The pope died in captivity. This was the "mortal wound." It is important to realize that the head that was wounded was the pope. This is consistent with the seven heads of Revelation 17, which are described as kings (Revelation 17:9, 10). The seven kings of Revelation 17 are also the seven popes who will exist just prior to the eighth king (Revelation 17:11) in the last days.

When the Papacy lost Pope Pius VI in 1798 it also lost its control over Rome. The Papacy continued as a religious entity but it no longer had temporal power as a separate kingdom. This "wound" was healed in 1929 when Mussolini signed the Lateran Treaty, which restored more than 108 acres to the Vatican and the Papacy became a church-state power once again. This church-state union restored the Papacy as a legitimate kingdom. Kingdoms have kings. These kings are described as the seven kings who will precede the eighth king or beast (Revelation 17:9, 10). Since 1929 the power and influence of Vatican City have become worldwide. The world truly has "followed the beast with wonder" since the Papacy's recovery of world leadership status. The pope is now considered by many to be the most influential spiritual leader in the world. The pope has an estimated one billion followers worldwide.

> Revelation 13:4: *"Men worshiped the dragon, for he had given his authority to the beast, and they worshiped the beast, saying, 'Who is like the beast, and who can fight against it?'"*

The content of Revelation 13 emphasizes last-day events. These events include an image to the beast and a mark of the beast as well as a death penalty (discussed in Revelation 13 (last part)—The Mark of the Beast). The other key event in this chapter is the healing of the mortal wound, which occurred in 1929.

John is viewing world history at the time when "men worshiped the dragon" and men "worshiped the beast." Historically, it has been taught that worshiping the dragon referred to spiritualism, which will become more prevalent toward the end of time.[1] However, another application of dragon worship will occur just prior to the end of time, and it will occur at the same time as the leopard-like beast and its image exists. The dragon is Satan (Revelation 12:9) and Satan will pretend to be Christ just prior to the end of the world (Matthew 24:15, 24). When Satan convinces the world that he is Christ, he will be worshiped by the world. This is the abomination that makes desolate (the reader is referred to the chapters on Daniel 8, 9, 11, and 12).

Once world Protestantism accepts him as Christ, then the leopard-like beast (Papacy) will also accept him as Christ. Once he becomes the leader of Catholicism he will take over power from the seventh king (pope) and will reign as the eighth king (Revelation 17:11).

There is only one time in history when the Papacy will be simultaneously worshiped by the world and also Satan (the dragon) will be worshiped by the world. This will occur during the reign of the seventh king or pope, just prior to the reign of Satan as the eighth king. At this time Satan will be increasing in popularity as the false Christ, while the world is still worshipping the leopard-like beast and its seventh king. This will occur during the existence of the image to the beast.

"Who is like the beast?" is a parody of several texts in the Old Testament: Exodus 15:11, Psalms 35:10, and Psalms 113:5, which ask who is like God? The world has now let the leopard-like beast take God's place and they are worshiping the leopard-like beast and the dragon instead of the true God.

> Revelation 13:5: *"And the beast was given a mouth uttering haughty and blasphemous words, and it was allowed to exercise authority for forty-two months."*

Historically, the leopard-like beast or Papacy has been uttering blasphemous words since its origin. In Daniel 7:25, it is described as speaking "words against the Most High" and it "shall think to change the times and the law." Because this leopard-like beast is the Papacy, it was thought that the 42 months of authority in this text referred to the 1260 years of its existence from A.D. 538 to 1798.[2] Certainly, this is one appropriate interpretation. However, there is another interpretation that also applies. The content of Revelation 13 emphasizes last-day events. The 42 months is brought up after the wound has healed (Revelation 13:3), which means after 1929. This description of the beast's characteristics occurs after the mortal wound has healed. This text is describing how the beast, that was mortally wounded, was given back its mouth after 1929 and began again to "utter blasphemous words."

In the last days this 42 months or 1260 days (42 months times thirty days equals 1260 days) correlates with the 1260 days of Revelation 11:3 when God's two witnesses are in sackcloth (discussed in Revelation 11 (first part)—The Two Witnesses). The two witnesses are God's Holy Word (the Old and New Testaments), which will be in sackcloth for 1260 days or 42 months (Revelation 11:3). They will then be killed and lie dead in the street for three and one-half days, which represents three and one-half years (Revelation 11:8, 9). The beast that ascends from the bottomless pit will kill them (Revelation 11:7). This beast is Satan who, as the false Christ, will reinterpret God's Word as his own and effectively kill it.

The leopard-like beast is given 42 months to exercise his authority. This time period occurs just prior to the dragon or Satan's reign. The dragon is also given 1260 days "a time, and times, and half a time" (Revelation 12:14). The leopard-like beast will reign during the 1260 days when the two witnesses are in sackcloth. The dragon will reign during the 1260 days when the two witnesses are dead but not buried (Revelation 11:9).

The event which triggers the sackcloth experience of God's two witnesses is described in the latter part of Revelation 13 (discussed in Revelation 13 (last part)—

The Mark of the Beast). This event is the passage of a mandatory universal Sunday law by the image to the beast. This event was also described in Daniel 11:28, 30 where Daniel describes this as an attack on the "holy covenant." This holy covenant is God's Sabbath.

This interpretation of the 42 months as a literal 1260-day time period during the last days is supported by the following facts.

> **First,** this time period occurs after 1929 when the leopard-like beast's wound was healed (Revelation 13:3).

> **Second,** this time period occurs when the world is worshiping the leopard-like beast and the dragon simultaneously, which is during the reign of the seventh king in the last days (Revelation 13:4).

> **Third,** it occurs in association with the lamb-like beast, which is a beast present in the last days (Revelation 13:11, 12) (discussed in Revelation 13 (last part)—The Mark of the Beast).

> **Fourth,** it occurs in association with the image of the beast, which develops in the last days (Revelation 13:14).

> **Fifth,** it occurs before the seventh king is crowned or all the heads on the beast would be crowned (Revelation 13:1).

Therefore, the 42 months of Revelation 13:5 can and does apply to last-day events.

> Revelation 13:6: *"it opened its mouth to utter blasphemies against God, blaspheming his name and his dwelling, that is, those who dwell in heaven."*

To blaspheme, in John's day, meant to claim to be God or to claim to be able to do things only God could do. For example, in Matthew 9:3, Jesus is accused of blasphemy because He forgave the sins of the paralytic. Again, Jesus is accused of blasphemy when He claims to be the Son of God (Mark 14:62-64). This leopard-like beast or Papacy will claim divine authority and assume divine titles, thus blaspheming God's name. This beast will set up its own temple on earth and pretend to forgive men's sins. This prophecy is fulfilled every time a priest claims to forgive someone's sins.

This beast, representing the Papacy, will also blaspheme "those who dwell in heaven." Those who dwell in heaven include God the Father, Jesus, the Holy Spirit and the angels. The Papacy has claimed to be God on earth. It has claimed the power to forgive sins, a right earned only by Jesus Christ, who died for our sins. The Papacy has claimed power over the angels of heaven. The Papacy has claimed the right to interpret scripture, which is the function of the Holy Spirit. The Papacy has elevated Jesus' mother Mary above her Son and has claimed the right to make men into saints who can be prayed to for assistance. Clearly, all those who "dwell in heaven" have been blasphemed by the Roman Catholic Church.[3]

> Revelation 13:7: *"Also it was allowed to make war on the saints and to conquer them. And authority was given it over every tribe and people and tongue and nation."*

Historically, this text has been applied to the persecution of the people of God during the years A.D. 538 to 1798 by the Roman Catholic Church. However, there is another application of this text in the last days. God's remnant will be persecuted again during the 42 months of Papal supremacy just prior to Satan's reign as the eighth king. Once Satan (the dragon) reigns in Jerusalem, he will continue the persecution for "a time, and times, and half a time" (Revelation 12:14). This persecution of God's remnant will then continue beyond Satan's reign in Jerusalem, right up to the return of Jesus in the clouds of heaven.

It will appear as if God's people are conquered, once the buy-sell legislation is passed and God's people have no economic support (this is discussed under Revelation 13:17 in the chapter on the Mark of the Beast). However, God will spiritually protect and sustain His people during this preliminary time of trouble. Unfortunately, many of God's people will not physically survive this persecution (Daniel 11:35) but their salvation will be secure.

This beast is described as having authority over "every tribe and people and tongue and nation." The Papacy will have worldwide influence in the last days just as it had during the Dark Ages. This audience is a subtle clue regarding the timing of this verse. This very same audience of tribes, peoples, tongues, and nations is the audience to which the three angels' messages are addressed. Revelation 14:6 states, "Then I saw another angel flying in mid heaven, with an eternal gospel to proclaim to those who dwell on earth, to every ***nation and tribe and tongue and people***" (emphasis supplied).

The three angels' messages are God's last day message because "the hour of his judgment has come" (Revelation 14:7). This message began to be proclaimed in the 1800s and is ongoing. The audience for this last day message is the same group over whom the leopard-like beast will have authority. This further connects these verses to the last days.

> Revelation 13:8: *"and all who dwell on earth will worship it, everyone whose name has not been written before the foundation of the world in the book of life of the Lamb that was slain."*

This text confirms that the world will be divided into two groups in the last days. The largest group will be those "whose name has not been written" in the book of life. The smaller group or remnant will be those whose names are written "in the book of life." Those, who worship or serve the beast, will not be saved. They will have his mark and his name (Revelation 13:16, 17).

The "book of life" contains the names of all God's people. This is one of the books, which Daniel described in Daniel 7:10: "the court sat in judgment, and the books were opened." This book is also described in Revelation 20:12 as one of the books involved in judgment. In Revelation 5:1, this same book is described as a "scroll written within and on the back, sealed with seven seals."

This book could only be opened by "the Lion of the tribe of Judah" (Revelation 5:5). This Lion is also the "Lamb standing, as though it had been slain" (Revelation 5:6). Only Jesus Christ, the Lamb Slain can open the book because He is the reason these names were placed in His book. Without His death as the Lamb Slain for our sins, we could not be saved. The book of life is God's list of those who have accepted His offer of salvation. The judgment scene of Revelation 4 and 5 is currently ongoing and the books are now being reviewed (discussed in Revelation 4 and 5—The Judgment Scene). Time is running out. The importance of having your name in the book of life is shown in Revelation 20:15 which states "and if any one's *name was not found written in the book of life, he was thrown into the lake of fire"* (emphasis supplied).

Revelation 13:9: *"if anyone has an ear, let him hear"*

This same phrase "He who has an ear, let him hear" is used with each of John's messages to the seven churches: Revelation 2:7, 11, 17, 29 and Revelation 3:6, 13, 22. This phrase is given to emphasize the importance of the message. It is given to emphasize the need to listen to the message and respond appropriately. When this message is given related to the seven churches, it is connected to the reward given for overcoming or conquering. The next verse suggests the reward for worshipping the beast.

> Revelation 13:10: *"If any one is to be taken captive, to captivity he goes; if any one slays with the sword, with the sword must he be slain. Here is a call for the endurance and faith of the saints."*

These rewards for worshipping the beast are the opposite of the rewards for overcoming. "He who conquers shall not be hurt by the second death" (Revelation 2:11). "He who conquers shall be clad thus in white garments, and I will not blot his name out of the book of life" (Revelation 3:5). The wicked are "judged by what was written in the books, *by what they had done"* (Revelation 20:12) (emphasis supplied). The rewards will match what was done.

"Here is a call for the endurance and faith of the saints." This phrase tells us that God's people will be undergoing persecution during these last-day events. This was described earlier as war "on the rest of her offspring" (Revelation 12:17). These saints are defined as those who "keep the commandments of God and the faith of Jesus" (Revelation 14:12). God's Law will become the test of their faith. They will need endurance and faith to remain connected to God. This phrase clearly is linked to Revelation 14:12 where God's people require the endurance of the saints and have the faith of Jesus. Revelation 14:12 is part of the third angel's message which will be given during the last days. The third angel's message is a warning for those who worship "the beast and its image, and receives a mark on his forehead or on his hand" (Revelation 14:9) (discussed in Revelation 14—The Three Angels' Messages). This "mark" of the beast occurs after the image to the beast is formed and enacts legislation enforcing the buy-sell law on God's people (Revelation 13:15-17). The second angel's message is fulfilled at the beginning of the 42-

month reign of the leopard-like beast (Papacy) when "all nations drink the wine of her impure passion" (Revelation 14:8). The second angel's message parallels the reign of the leopard-like beast. The "endurance and faith" required are referring to the same endurance and faith mentioned in Revelation 14:12.

SUMMARY

Revelation 13 introduces a leopard-like beast with ten horns that are crowned and seven heads that are uncrowned. This leopard-like beast is given its power and authority by the dragon (Satan). This leopard-like beast is seen before all of its seven kings have reigned because the seven heads are uncrowned. This leopard-like beast has all the characteristics of the little horn of Daniel 7 and does the same things. This leopard-like beast will blaspheme God and persecute God's people.

The timeframe of the vision of the leopard-like beast is during the reign of the seventh king since this leopard-like beast is being worshiped at the same time as the dragon is worshiped. This can only occur when the dragon is ascending in popularity and then replaces the already reigning seventh king. This leopard-like beast is seen after its mortal wound is healed. This healing occurred in 1929. The mortal wound was to its head, which was Pope Pius VI who was captured in 1798. The seven heads refer to the seven last popes beginning in 1929 after the wound was healed.

This leopard-like beast will coexist with the lamb-like beast who will support it (Revelation 13:12). It will coexist with the image to the beast formed by the lamb-like beast (Revelation 13:14). It will support the mark of the beast. The leopard-like beast is the Papacy after 1929.

The leopard-like beast or Papacy is seen in Revelation 13 after its wound has been healed. It is seen as a world power, which is being worshipped along with the dragon. It is seen as persecuting God's people. It is seen during the time of the second angel's message to the world. It is seen during the 42 two months or three and one-half years of its final supremacy on earth. It is seen just prior to yielding its authority to Satan who will reign as the eighth king. Satan, the eighth king, is the abomination that makes desolate and is the false Christ. The following graph outlines these events.

Revelation Chapter 13 - First Part

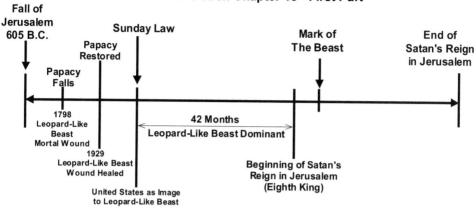

---

[1] Nichol, Francis D.(Ed.). *The Seventh-day Adventist Bible Commentary* (Review and Herald Publishing Association, Washington, D.C.) 1957, Vol. 7, p. 818.

[2] Ibid. pp. 809, 818.

[3] Ibid. p. 818.

Revelation 17 (first part)
The Scarlet Woman and Her Kings

Revelation 17 is an extremely important chapter for understanding last-day events. In this chapter, John is viewing history at the time of the sixth king. The reign of the sixth king has just ended. The sixth king was Pope John Paul II whose reign began in 1978 and ended in 2005. This makes Revelation 17 extremely important to those living at the current time! This chapter describes the scarlet woman who sits on a scarlet beast. This scarlet beast has ten uncrowned horns and seven heads, none of which are crowned. This scarlet beast will take over from the seventh king and subsequently turn against the scarlet woman. The imagery of this chapter will take us through the closing events of earth's history.

> Revelation 17:1: *"Then one of the seven angels who had the seven bowls came and said to me, 'Come, I will show you the judgment of the great harlot who is seated upon many waters'"*

This chapter opens with John being addressed by "one of the seven angels who had the seven bowls." This refers to the seven angels in Revelation 15:1, 7, 8 and Revelation 16:1. The seven angels are described as having "the seven bowls of the wrath of God" (Revelation 16:1). These seven bowls contain the seven last plagues (Revelation 15:1). The presence of this angel, who is involved in the very last-day events, suggests that John is going to be seeing last-day events in prophecy.

The angel is going to show John "the judgment of the great harlot." This judgment or verdict is described at the end of the prophecy in Revelation 17:16. This woman, described as a great harlot, represents apostate Christianity and specifically Babylon (Revelation 17:5). Pure women in prophecy represent God's true church, often portrayed as His bride (Revelation 19:7) (discussed in Revelation 12—The Dragon and the Eighth King). Harlots or prostitutes in prophecy represent those people or churches claiming to serve God but following false gods. These so-called Christians are actually apostate Christians who reject the true God. Those who reject God but claim to serve Him make up Babylon. During the Dark Ages the Papacy, representing apostate Christianity, killed millions of God's true believers.[1] This woman or harlot is called "Babylon, the great mother of harlots" (Revelation 17:5). This woman describes the Papacy, who was the mother of many subsequent apostate churches.

Also, this "woman that you saw is the great city which has dominion over the kings of the earth" (Revelation 17:18). This was true historically during the Dark Ages when the Papacy ruled the world and it will be true again in the last days. The city here described is the city with "seven hills" on which the scarlet woman or false church sits (Revelation 17:9). In John's day, as in our day, this city of seven hills was recognized as Rome. The scarlet woman of Revelation 17 is headquartered in Vatican

City, Rome. The "many waters," on which "the great harlot" sits, "are peoples and multitudes and nations and tongues" (Revelation 17:15). This refers to the many nations and peoples who are controlled or influenced by the Papacy.

> Revelation 17:2: *"with whom the kings of the earth have committed fornication, and with the wine of whose fornication the dwellers on earth have become drunk."*

The "kings of the earth" represent the world's political powers, as opposed to religious organizations. These political powers will commit fornication with the harlot by combining religion and politics. This church-state union will attempt to enforce the apostate church's belief system on the citizens of the nations who commit this fornication. God, in the Old Testament, described Israel's relationship with Him as a whore or harlot, because Israel worshipped false gods instead of remaining true to Him (the reader is referred to the book of Hosea). This "fornication" or intimate relationship between false religion and world powers will result in the world becoming "drunk" with her false teachings.

The "wine" represents the false teachings of this apostate church which will corrupt and destroy the world and its people. The "dwellers" represent the people of this earth who accept these false teachings. Drunkenness suggests impaired functioning, which is the result of accepting these false teachings.[2]

> Revelation 17:3: *"And he carried me away in the Spirit into a wilderness, and I saw a woman sitting on a scarlet beast which was full of blasphemous names, and it had seven heads and ten horns."*

John is now carried away "in the Spirit" to the wilderness. This means John was taken in vision to an empty or uninhabited place where he sees a "woman sitting on a scarlet beast." This "woman" is the same woman or great harlot described in Revelation 17:1 and Revelation 17:4-5. This "woman" is clothed in scarlet (Revelation 17:4). Scarlet is the symbol of sin: "though your sins are like scarlet, they shall be as white as snow" (Isaiah 1:18). The beast is covered with sin. The woman is covered with sin.

Historically, some have suggested that the "beast" described here represents the political powers under Satan's control and the "woman" represents the religious powers opposed to God's true church.[3] However, this "scarlet beast" is the same as the beast of Revelation 12 who was described as a "red dragon" (Revelation 12:3). Both of these beasts have ten horns and seven heads. The only difference is the beast in Revelation 12 has seven crowns on its heads. The beast (dragon) of Revelation 12 is Satan. "And the great dragon was thrown down, that ancient serpent, who is called the Devil and Satan" (Revelation 12:9). The scarlet beast of Revelation 17 is also Satan. This beast "was full of blasphemous names." Satan in the last days will claim to be Christ, the Lamb Slain, and the Savior of the world. He will claim to be God on earth. He will claim to forgive sins. The main difference between the red dragon of Revelation 12 and the scarlet beast of Revelation 17 is the absence of the crowns on the seven heads in Revelation 17:3 and Revelation 17:7. The presence of the crowns determines the time element of the prophecy. In Revelation 12, all seven heads are crowned; therefore, John is seeing history after the seven kings have finished their work. The time element of Revelation 12 is during the reign of the eighth king after the reign of the seven kings (discussed in Revelation 12—The Dragon and the Eighth King). In Revelation 17, the seven heads do not have crowns, which means John is seeing history before the seven kings have completed their reigns. This is shown in Revelation 17:10, which describes the seven heads and states "they are also seven kings five of whom have fallen, one is, the other has not yet come." John is seeing history during the "one is" reign of the sixth king (Revelation 17:10). This is why the seven heads have no crowns, since not all of them have completed their reigns (discussed in Preface: The Crowns and Their Meaning).

It is important to note that each of the prophecies regarding the beasts in Revelation 12, 13, and 17 all describe seven heads. These seven heads help us determine the prophetic viewpoint during which the vision is seen. If the crowns are present, then the seven kings have completed their reign. If the crowns are not present, then the seven kings have not completed their reign. These seven kings are not described in Daniel's prophecy of Daniel 7 because these seven kings relate specifically to last-day events. The seven kings are involved in events after the "mortal wound" of the beast is healed (Revelation 13:3, 12). The vision of Revelation 17 occurs during the reign of the sixth king. The vision of Revelation 13 occurs during the reign of the seventh king. The vision of Revelation 12 occurs during the reign of the eighth king.

> Revelation 17:4: *"The woman was arrayed in purple and*
> *scarlet, and bedecked with gold and jewels and pearls,*
> *holding in her hand a golden cup full of abominations*
> *and the impurities of her fornication."*

Historically, the woman in this verse has been interpreted as apostate Christianity. Apostate Christianity would include all those who claim to be Christians but serve false gods. More specifically, this can be applied to the Papacy as the leader of apostate Christianity. The purple raiment suggests royalty and the scarlet raiment suggests sin. This woman's scarlet color is contrasted to the pure color of the Bride's clothes: "his Bride has made herself ready; it was granted her to be clothed with *fine linen, bright and pure"* (Revelation 19:7, 8) (emphasis supplied). It is also contrasted with those who overcome: "He who conquers shall be clad thus in *white garments"* (Revelation 3:5) (emphasis supplied). The woman of Revelation 17 has royalty but is clothed in sin.

The "gold and jewels and pearls" are a symbol of economic success or wealth. However, her golden cup is "full of abominations." This false church or apostate religion will be economically rich but contain many abominations. Abomination as defined in Malachi 2:11 is profaning God's sanctuary. "Judah has been faithless, and abomination has been committed in Israel and in Jerusalem; for Judah has profaned the sanctuary of the Lord which he loves and has married the daughter of a foreign god" (Malachi 2:11). This "woman" or apostate church will profane God's sanctuary by setting up her own temple and false worship system. This "woman" will promote the worship of false gods by claiming to be God on earth and forgiving sins.

Abominations also represent unclean acts and specifically refer to the "impurities of her fornication." This fornication refers to this false church's use of political power to force its beliefs on the world. True religion changes the heart in response to God's love. Apostate religion uses force to coerce a change in behavior. This is an abomination in God's sight. This golden cup also contains the abominations of murder and persecution that this apostate church has done to God's people (Revelation 18:24).

> Revelation 17:5: *"and on her forehead was written a name of mystery: 'Babylon the great, mother of harlots and of earth's abominations.'"*

Names were given to reflect the character of the individual in biblical times. This name given to the woman reflects her character. The fact that the name is written on her forehead implies she has chosen this name or characteristic. God's people's names will be written on their foreheads (Revelation 9:4). The name is written on their foreheads because of a choice to serve Him. This woman's character was the result of her choices.[4] Her name was "Babylon the great, mother of harlots and of earth's abominations." This "name of mystery" was Babylon the great. The word mystery when used in Revelation means a symbol that is about to be explained, as opposed to an unexplainable symbol.[5]

Historically "Babylon the great" has been considered to represent the united apostate religious systems of the world including apostate Protestantism, Spiritualism and the Papacy.[6] The "harlots" in this verse were considered to represent apostate Protestant churches, which were the daughters of the original church which was the Papacy. The abominations represent all the immoral and unclean actions of this "mother of harlots."[7] The abominations also represent the profaning of God's sanctuary with a false worship system. However, in the last days, Babylon represents the Papacy which will again attack God's true followers because they refuse to accept its mark (discussed in Revelation 13 (last part)—The Mark of the Beast).

> Revelation 17:6: *"And I saw the woman, drunk with the blood of the saints and the blood of the martyrs of Jesus. When I saw her I marveled greatly."*

This "woman" or false church will be drunk or intoxicated with the blood of God's saints.[8] This false church has attacked God's people and many have been slain in the past. This "woman" will again attack God's saints in the future (Revelation 13:7). In the last days, these saints are the wise who "shall understand" (Daniel 12:11). Some of these "who are wise shall fall, to refine and to cleanse them and to make them white, ***until the time of the end"*** (Daniel 11:35) (emphasis supplied). These saints, who fall, will fall because of persecution initiated by the great harlot or Papacy and continued by the eighth king. This woman will be drunk on "the blood of the martyrs of Jesus." These martyrs or witnesses will be willing to die for their convictions. These people "who know their God shall stand firm and take action" (Daniel 11:32). Historically, the saints in this verse have been considered living and the martyrs considered dead. In this context, the woman is blamed for the death of the prior martyrs and counted as guilty for the saints she has not yet killed but is attempting to kill.[9] John is amazed at the power of this woman and her sins. This false church has:

1) seduced the world's leaders (Revelation 17:2)
2) committed fornication with the world (Revelation 17:2)
3) misled the world with false teachings (Revelation 17:2)
4) supported blasphemy (Revelation 17:3)
5) committed abominations (Revelation 17:4)
6) raised many daughter harlots (Revelation 17:5)
7) killed the saints (Revelation 17:6).

All of these things have been done by the Papacy in the past and most will be done again.

> Revelation 17:7: *"But the angel said to me, 'Why marvel? I will tell you the mystery of the woman, and of the beast with seven heads and ten horns that carries her.'"*

At this point, the angel is going to interpret the symbols of this vision to John. Historically, the "beast" has been interpreted as the political arm of the Papacy, which was lost in 1798 when General Berthier captured Pope Pius VI and imprisoned him.[10] At that time the papal kingdom, which was a church-state union, became a church only and no longer a kingdom or political entity. Mussolini reinstated its kingdom status in 1929 with the Lateran Treaty, which gave the Church of Rome the land on which Vatican City stands. This reinstated the Papacy as a political kingdom. During the time between 1798 and 1929, the Papacy was simply a world church.

However, there is another interpretation which is consistent with the prior description of the "beast" in Revelation 12. The "red dragon, with seven heads and ten horns" of Revelation 12:3, is explained in Revelation 12:9. "And the great dragon was thrown down, that ancient serpent, who is called the Devil and Satan" (Revelation 12:9). The scarlet "beast" of Revelation 17 is the red dragon of Revelation 12. They are both Satan. He will become the eighth king (Revelation 17:11). He will claim to be Christ returned in order to become the eighth king (discussed in Revelation 17 (last part)—The Eighth King).

This "beast" has "seven heads and ten horns." These seven heads represent the seven leaders of the false church or Papacy beginning with the time that its wound was healed. The wound occurred in its "head" (Revelation 13:3). The head represented the pope who was captured in 1798. From 1798 to 1929, this wound kept the false church from being a political kingdom. Since 1929, the Papacy has been restored as a political kingdom. The Papacy currently has political recognition from the United States Government with an embassy in Vatican City. Prior to 1929, the heads of the Papacy were religious leaders or popes. However, since 1929, they can be considered both pope and king since they reign over both a religious entity and a political kingdom.

The ten horns of this "beast" represent ten future kingdoms who will only reign for a short time (Revelation 17:12). These ten horns will be described in the discussion on Revelation 17:12. This scarlet beast is shown carrying the scarlet woman. This carrying implies that the beast, Satan, and the apostate church, the Papacy, will work together for the same purposes. The "beast" and the "woman" are two separate entities. One represents Satan and the other represents the Papacy. To divide the Papacy into two parts, political and religious, in order to represent these two symbols is not consistent with Revelation 12 where the beast is clearly Satan (Revelation 12:9). It is also not consistent with the beast destroying Babylon (Revelation 17:15, 16). It will be seen later in this chapter that this woman's kings will give over their reign to the beast as the eighth king.

> Revelation 17:8: *"The beast that you saw was, and is not, and is to ascend from the bottomless pit and go to perdition; and the dwellers on earth whose names have not been written in the book of life from the foundation of the world, will marvel to behold the beast, because it was and is not and is to come."*

Historically, this beast has been considered to represent the political power of the Papacy. This power was lost in 1798 and regained in 1929 (see comments on Revelation 17:7). The phrase "is to ascend" was applied to the healing of the wound in 1929. The "bottomless pit" was thought to refer to the beast when it was mortally wounded. The "dwellers on earth" represent the "waters" upon which the beast sits, which are the followers of the beast throughout the world. The phrase "it was and is not and is to come" was applied to the same wound of the beast in 1798 and its healing in 1929.[11] However, this is inconsistent with Revelation 17:10 because the sixth king is the vantage point of this vision and this beast "is to come." This beast is to follow the sixth and seventh kings as the eighth king (Revelation 17:11). The "is to come" cannot represent 1929 and the restoration of the Papacy because 1929 has already occurred prior to the sixth king who "is" existing when John sees this vision (Revelation 17:10).

This prophecy involves last-day events as shown by Revelation 17:14, which describes "war on the Lamb." This prophecy involves last-day events as shown by the vantage point of the prophecy during the reign of the sixth king. This prophecy involves last-day events because the beast who "is to ascend" is the same "beast that ascends" in Revelation 11:7, which is a last-day event. This prophecy is a last-days prophecy because it involves the "ten kings" who only exist at the time of the end (Revelation 17:12-14).

The last-day events include the final trumpets. The fifth trumpet describes the "star fallen from heaven to earth" as being given the key to "the shaft of the bottomless pit" (Revelation 9:1). This fallen star is described in Isaiah 14:12. This fallen star is Lucifer or Satan who said "I will make myself like the Most High" (Isaiah 14:14). Satan is bound in the "pit" of circumstances. This is the same type of "pit" he will be bound in during the 1000 year millennium of Revelation 20. Revelation 20:1, 2 states "Then I saw an angel coming down from heaven, holding in his hand the key of the bottomless pit and a great chain. And he seized the dragon, that ancient serpent, who is the Devil and Satan, and bound him for a thousand years."

Revelation 20:3 then explains the "pit." It states "and threw him into the pit, and shut it and sealed it over him, ***that he should deceive the nations no more,*** till the thousand years were ended. After that he must be loosed for a little while" (emphasis supplied). The pit is a pit of circumstances. Satan will be bound on earth with no one to deceive, since the wicked have all been killed at the Second Coming of Jesus Christ and the righteous have all been caught up in the clouds to be taken to heaven

(1 Thessalonians 5:17). This is confirmed in Revelation 20:7, 8 where Satan is "loosed from his prison" and comes "out to deceive the nations." These nations are the wicked who are raised to life just prior to Christ's Third Coming to earth when He brings the holy city New Jerusalem with Him (Revelation 21:2). Satan's pit is actually the circumstances or restrictions that God places on him. God has placed Satan under certain restrictions or rules of engagement. Satan cannot indiscriminately destroy mankind. If he could, all mankind already would be dead. When Satan is allowed to "ascend from the bottomless pit," God is removing certain restrictions or conditions under which Satan has had to operate.

We have seen how the beast of Revelation 17 is consistent with the dragon of Revelation 12 who is "the Devil and Satan" (Revelation 12:9). In the fifth trumpet, Satan is described as the "star fallen" who is released from the bottomless pit (Revelation 9:1). This beast who "ascends from the bottomless pit" (Revelation 11:7) is the beast who kills God's two witnesses or His Holy Scriptures. This "beast that ascends" (Revelation 11:7) is Satan as the false Christ, who kills God's Word by claiming to be its author (discussed in Revelation 11 (first part)—The Two Witnesses). This beast that ascends in Revelation 11:7 is the same beast "who was, and is not, and is to ascend from the bottomless pit" (Revelation 17:8). This beast is Satan who will become the eighth king when he ascends from the pit (Revelation 17:8, 11).

The phrase "who was" is referring to Satan as Lucifer prior to his fall from heaven. The phrase "who is not" describes Satan as he exists during the reign of the sixth king which is describing Satan as he now exists under God's current rules of engagement. These rules or circumstances control what Satan can or cannot do. This "pit" of circumstances will be released beginning with Satan's reign as the eighth king or the false Christ. Satan will be further released during the fifth trumpet and finally completely released during the sixth trumpet. When the four angels are released in the sixth trumpet, Satan will then be free to kill as many of the wicked as he wishes (Revelation 9:5).

The phrase "is to ascend from the bottomless pit" refers to Satan as the false Christ. As the false Christ, Satan will become the eighth king and the ruler of apostate Christianity. As the "beast that ascends," he will kill God's two witnesses, the Old Testament and the New Testament, because they testify about the true Christ. He will claim to be Christ returned. He will claim to interpret God's Word. This is the "abomination that makes desolate" of Daniel 8, 9, 11 and 12. This abomination will "profane the temple" (Daniel 11:31) and stand in "the holy place" (Matthew 24:15). This abomination will "magnify himself" above all gods (Daniel 11:36) and will take his place in God's temple "proclaiming himself to be God" (2 Thessalonians 2:4).

- *This means that the false Christ will reign in Jerusalem and minister in the temple just prior to Jesus return.*

Satan will reign as the eighth king or "beast that ascends" for three and one-half years (Revelation 11:9, 11) (discussed in Revelation 11 (first part)—The Two Witnesses). The beast "who is to ascend" has not yet ascended when John is viewing history during this vision, because this beast is the eighth king (Revelation 17:11). John is seeing history during the reign of the sixth king (Revelation 17:10) while the

Papacy is still dominant in the world's spiritual affairs. After the eighth king as the false Christ comes onto the world scene, then the seventh king or final pope will give his power over to the eighth king or beast (Revelation 17:11).

This beast or Satan truly will "go to perdition." Satan will be destroyed forever (Revelation 20:10). "The dwellers on earth" represent all those "whose names have not been written in the book of life." This clearly includes all those who have rejected God's salvation through His Son and have instead placed their faith in the false Christ or eighth king. The book of life is God's record of those who will be saved (Philippians 4:3, Revelation 20:14). This book has existed since the foundation of the world but could not be opened until the investigative judgment began in 1844 (discussed in Revelation 4 and 5—The Judgment Scene). This reference to the "book of life" further connects this prophecy to last-day events.

The phrase "marvel to behold the beast" refers to the world marveling after Satan's miracles and wonders which he will perform as the false Christ. Satan will present himself as an angel of light who will resemble the description of the Son of God in Revelation 1.[12] The phrases "it was, and is not and is to come" repeats the prior message. The repetition of this phrase reiterates the importance of understanding this issue. The beast or Satan "was" when he was in power as Lucifer. He "is not" currently in power because God has him held in the pit of circumstances under God's rules of engagement. He "is to come" into power after the seventh king turns over his kingdom to Satan as the eighth king. This is when Satan will finally begin his earthly reign.

SUMMARY

Revelation 17 introduces a scarlet woman who is seen riding a scarlet beast. This scarlet woman is described as a great harlot who leads the world and its political powers astray. The world commits fornication with this harlot by enforcing religion on its people. The world's kings will enforce her wine of falsehood on their people. The world will become intoxicated with her false teachings. This scarlet woman will blaspheme God. She is called Babylon the great. She is the mother of harlots or other false religions. She is seated on seven hills and is called a great city. This scarlet woman is known for her sins. This woman is the Papacy when it regains world domination after its mortal wound has healed. The woman is seated on a scarlet beast with seven heads and ten horns. The seven heads and the ten horns are not crowned, which means they have not yet completed their reigns. The seven heads represent the seven kings of Rome once the mortal wound has healed. These are the seven last popes of the Papacy beginning in 1929 when the Papacy became a kingdom again and the popes again became kings.

The scarlet beast of Revelation 17 is the same beast as the red dragon of Revelation 12. This beast is Satan who will become the eighth king. This beast was and is not and is to ascend. Satan was Lucifer, the highest angel in heaven; he is not currently in power because he is under God's restrictions; but he is to ascend when God removes those restrictions and Satan is allowed to reign as the eighth king. When John is viewing these events the sixth king is reigning because five "have fallen, one is, and the other has not yet come" (Revelation 17:10). The sixth king was the sixth leader of the Catholic Church since 1929. The sixth king was Pope John Paul II who has just died. The beast that "is not" is coexisting with the sixth king but is not yet reigning (Revelation 17:8). He will not reign until after all of the seven kings have reigned. This beast is yet "to come" (Revelation 17:8) and will reign or ascend as the eighth king (Revelation 17:11). These events are outlined on the graph, which follows Revelation 17 (third part)—The Ten Horns.

[1] Carroll, J. M., *The Trail of Blood*,(Electronic version). Retrieved May 31, 2004, from http://www.lovejesus.org/books/tob/tob7.htm

[2] Nichol, Francis D. (Ed.). *The Seventh-day Adventist Bible Commentary* (Review and Herald Publishing Association, Washington, D.C.) 1957, Vol. 7, p. 850.

[3] Ibid. p. 851.

[4] Ibid.

[5] Ibid. p. 740.

[6] Ibid. p. 852

[7] Ibid. p. 851

[8] Ibid. p. 852

[9] Ibid.

[10] Ibid. p. 851.

[11] Ibid. p. 853.

[12] White, Ellen G., *The Great Controversy* (Pacific Press Publishing Association, Nampa, Idaho) 1950, p. 624.

Revelation 17 (second part)
The Eighth King

The eighth king is introduced in Revelation 17:11. This is the only mention of this king in the book of Revelation. In order to understand who this king is, we must understand the symbols in Revelation 17. We must know who the seven kings are and who the scarlet woman is. Most importantly we have to identify the beast of Revelation 17.

The context of Revelation 17 involves last-day events. This is clear in the first verse. The angel that introduces this prophecy is one of the "angels who had the seven bowls" (Revelation 17:1). These seven bowls are the seven last plagues, which occur at the time of the end (Revelation 15:7, 8) (discussed in the chapter titled "Revelation 16—The Seven Last Plagues").

The message of Revelation 17 involves the time period just prior to the fulfillment of the second angel's message, which warns of Babylon who made "all nations drink the wine of her impure passion" (Revelation 14:8). Babylon has not fallen yet. The scarlet woman or great harlot of Revelation 17 is "Babylon, the great mother of harlots" (Revelation 17:5). This harlot makes the people on earth "drunk" with the wine of her "fornication" (Revelation 17:2). This message clearly connects this description of events to the second angel's message of Revelation 14:8 where Babylon makes "all nations drink the wine of her impure passion." Babylon is still "arrayed in purple and scarlet and bedecked with gold and jewels" (Revelation 17:4). These accouterments imply that Babylon is still reigning during this message. However, once Babylon falls, she will lose her riches and be naked (Revelation 17:16, Revelation 18:21).

The actual time frame during which John is viewing world history in Revelation 17 is seen in Revelation 17:10. John is describing seven kings, which are the seven heads of the scarlet beast. The scarlet beast is the same beast that John described in Revelation 12. In Revelation 12:3, John sees a "great red dragon, with seven heads and ten horns, and seven diadems upon his heads" (discussed in Preface: The Crowns and Their Meaning). This red dragon is Satan. This is confirmed in Revelation 12:9: ***"And the great dragon was thrown down, that ancient serpent, who is called the Devil and Satan,*** the deceiver of the whole world" (emphasis supplied). The scarlet beast of Revelation 17 is the red dragon of Revelation 12, who is Satan, but the timeframe of the two visions is different. The seven heads of the dragon in Revelation 17 are not crowned since they have not all reigned at the time of John's vision in Revelation 17 whereas, the seven heads are all crowned in Revelation 12 because they have completed their reigns and the eighth king is reigning,

> Revelation 17:9: *"This calls for a mind with wisdom: the seven heads are seven hills on which the woman is seated."*

The woman here is called "the great city which has dominion over the kings of the earth" (Revelation 17:18). In John's day, he would have recognized this great city as Rome, which ruled the earth during John's lifetime. Rome was also known as the city of seven hills, which further connects this scarlet woman to Rome. "It is within *the city of Rome, called the city of seven hills,* that the entire area of Vatican State proper is now located" (*The Catholic Encyclopedia*, s. v. "Rome") (emphasis supplied).[1]

The reference to a "mind with wisdom" suggests the "wise" of Daniel 11 and 12. These "wise shall understand" (Daniel 12:10). These wise will understand who the abomination that makes desolate is (Daniel 11:31). They will understand that Satan, pretending to be Christ, is the abomination that makes desolate.

This woman is called "Babylon the great, mother of harlots" (Revelation 17:5). In the book of Revelation, Babylon often represents false or apostate religions. A harlot represents religions that claim to know God in the intimate sense of a close relationship but instead prostitute themselves in a relationship with a false god. Thus, they are called harlots because they spiritually go after falsehood and ultimately are led by Satan, the father of lies.

In the context of Revelation 17, the scarlet woman, who rides the scarlet beast, is the Papacy, whose capital city is Rome. The Papacy is the "mother of harlots" since apostate Protestantism came from apostate Catholicism and apostate Protestantism continues to accept her false teachings. These false teachings are described as "wine" in Revelation 17:2. One of the most significant false teachings in the last days will be the false Sabbath (discussed in Revelation 13 (last part)—The Mark of the Beast). *The scarlet beast represents Satan, who is the dragon of Revelation 12.* This dragon will pursue God's people and make war on the remnant (Revelation 12:17). The remnant will refuse to disobey God's Commandments, specifically the fourth commandment regarding the Sabbath. They also will refuse to abandon faith in Jesus Christ in order to accept Satan, the dragon, as the false Christ.

> Revelation 17:10: *"they are also seven kings five of whom have fallen, one is, the other has not yet come, and when he comes he must remain only a little while."*

The seven heads of the scarlet beast are also seven kings. John is viewing history during the time of the sixth king: the one who "is." The first five kings have fallen or died. The seventh king is yet to come. Who are these seven kings?

The beast of Revelation 13 was wounded in "One of its heads" (Revelation 13:3). This wound appeared to be a mortal wound, "but its mortal wound was healed" (Revelation 13:3). The beast of Revelation 13 represents the Papacy and the head that was wounded was Pope Pius VI who was captured in 1798 by Napoleon's General Berthier (discussed in Revelation 13 (first part)—The Leopard-Like Beast Healed). The head of the beast represents the pope or leader of the Papacy. At the time of the wound, the Papacy lost its status as a world kingdom. In 1929, the wound to the Papacy was healed when Mussolini, gave the Papacy back the land on which Vatican City stands, by signing the Lateran Treaty. Prior to 1798 the Papacy was a world kingdom. After its mortal wound it lost its world kingdom status and became instead a world church. Since 1929, the Papacy has been reinstated as a kingdom: a church-state kingdom. Since 1929, the popes are truly kings of this church-state kingdom. The seven kings are the last seven popes prior to the eighth king.

- ***The seventh king will reign only for "a little while."***

The seventh king will give up his throne to the eighth king. The eighth king is the beast.

> Revelation 17:11: *"As for the beast that was and is not, it is an eighth but it belongs to the seven, and it goes to perdition."*

The beast "that was and is not" will become the eighth king. This verse tells us that the beast or Satan will be the final king. The seven kings represent the seven popes from the time the Papacy was restored as a kingdom, which occurred in 1929. The following is the list of popes who have reigned since 1929:

1—Pius XI (1922-1939)
2—Pius XII (1939-1958)
3—Blessed John XXIII (1958-1963)
4—Paul VI (1963-1978)
5—John Paul I (1978)
6—John Paul II (1978-2005).[2]
7—Benedict XVI (2005-present).

Dr. Robert Smith suggests we were living in the time of the sixth king, and I agree with his conclusion.[3] This means we are now living during the time in which the seventh king has begun to reign. This means we are living during the time of history that John was describing in Revelation 17.

- ***This means that the sixth king has already reigned.***

This text suggests that the eighth king will take over the rule of the Papacy as its last king or leader. The eighth king "belongs to the seven." The eighth king "belongs to the seven" because he has influenced them secretly for years. He "belongs to the seven" because he blasphemes God as they have and he will claim to be God just as they have. However, he will claim to be Christ returned. He "belongs to the seven" because he will claim to change God's Law as they have. He "belongs to the seven" because hc will persecute God's people on earth as they have. The only difference between the eighth king and the seven prior kings is that, instead of claiming to be the Vicar of Christ, he will claim to be Christ returned.

The eighth king is described in 2 Thessalonians 2:3, 4 as "the man of lawlessness" and the "son of perdition, who opposes and exalts himself against every so-called god or object of worship, so that he takes his seat in the temple of God, proclaiming himself to be God." The "lawless one" (man of sin) is linked to Satan in 2 Thessalonians 2:9. He will come "with all power and with pretended signs and wonders" (2 Thessalonians 2:9). He will also come "with all wicked deception for those ***who are to perish, because they refused to love the truth and so be saved"***

(2 Thessalonians 2:10) (emphasis supplied). Satan will deceive the world as the false Christ by working miracles and wonders. This deception will cause many to perish. This is the deception that Jesus warned His disciples about in Matthew 24:4, 15. The issue is whether people will accept the false Christ, who is the eighth king and the abomination that makes desolate, or whether they will "love the truth" and be saved. Jesus Christ is the truth (John 14:6).

This beast "that was and is not" is further identified in Revelation 17:8: "The beast that you saw was, and is not, and is to ascend from the bottomless pit and go to perdition; and the dwellers on earth whose names have not been written in the book of life from the foundation of the world, will marvel to behold the beast, *because it was and is not and is to come"* (emphasis supplied). This text tells us that the beast "is not" in power when John is viewing this history. This text tells us the beast had power before because "it was" and that it will have power again because it "is to come." The beast will gain power again when it becomes the eighth king and the world's spiritual leader as the false Christ.

This beast will "ascend from the bottomless pit." This clearly connects to Revelation 9:1, 2 and Revelation 11:7. Revelation 9:1 describes a "star fallen" which is given the "key of the shaft of the bottomless pit." This fallen star is Lucifer or Satan (Isaiah 14:12-14) (discussed in Revelation 9—The Seven Trumpets: The First and Second Woes). Revelation 11:7 describes "the beast that ascends from the bottomless pit" as the beast which kills God's two witnesses (the Old and New Testaments). This beast, which ascends from the pit of circumstances where God controls him, is Satan as the false Christ (discussed in Revelation 11 (first part)—The Two Witnesses). Satan is first given power to reign as the world's spiritual leader (Revelation 11:7-11) and later as the world's temporal leader (Revelation 9:2). This same Satan had previously lost his power when he was thrown out of heaven, described as the dragon thrown down (Revelation 12:8). He was the most powerful angel in heaven prior to his fall from grace. During the time of this prophecy in Revelation 17 Satan has not yet regained his power.

John's vantage point for this vision is during the reign of the sixth king (Revelation 17:10). John is viewing history during the time period when the scarlet woman or Papacy and her kings are dominant. This dominance will continue until the seventh king gives his power over to Satan. Then God will allow Satan to rule again. In the context of Revelation 17 Satan is the one who "was and is not and is to come" (Revelation 17:8). This beast or Satan will go "to perdition." When Satan as the eighth king is allowed "to ascend" (Revelation 11:7) he will do so by claiming to be Christ returned.

- ### *The eighth king is the false Christ.*

Then, as the false Christ, he will kill God's Holy Word (Revelation 11:7). Satan will reign for three and one-half years (Revelation 11:9, 11) prior to the end of world history. Subsequent events, which will follow, include the destruction of Babylon, the Battle of Armageddon and Christ's Second Coming.

Satan, as the eighth king, will be forced to give up some of his kingdom at the end of the three and one-half years because the world will turn against him. This rejection is seen in Revelation 11:13 when Satan's followers become afraid after

Jerusalem is struck by an earthquake and glorify "the God of heaven." These same people had previously been glorifying Satan as the false Christ. If Satan cannot protect them, then he must not be the god he claims to be. At this point, in order to maintain power, Satan will be forced to set up ten kings "who have not yet received royal power" (Revelation 17:12). These will reign for only "one hour" (Revelation 17:12), which represents a short time. This will be followed by Satan attacking Babylon with the help of the ten kings (Revelation 17:18), and then the final world battle called Armageddon (Revelation 16:16). This battle ends with Jesus' Second Coming.

SUMMARY

In summary, we can see that the eighth king will reign in the last days after the last seven kings of the Papacy have completed their work. We are now living in the time of the seventh king since the papal wound was healed in 1929.[4] Pope John Paul II was the sixth king. John in his vision of Revelation 17 was seeing the time in which we are now living! The eighth king will take over from the seventh king, Pope Benedict XVI. The eighth king is Satan pretending to be Christ. Once the false Christ is here, the world will determine that there is no longer a need for a Vicar of Christ. The eighth king will replace the last Vicar of Christ who is the seventh king Pope Benedict XVI.

The eighth king is the "red dragon" of Revelation 12, who will persecute God's remnant for three and one-half years (Revelation 12:14). The eighth king is the "beast that ascends from the bottomless pit" and kills God's Word (His two witnesses) for three and one-half years (Revelation 11:7, 9). The eighth king is "the man of lawlessness" or man of sin who takes over God's temple as the false Christ and claims to be God (2 Thessalonians 2:4). The eighth king is the "prince who is to come" of Daniel 9:26. The eighth king is the king who returns and comes "into the south" in Daniel 11:29 and sets up the abomination that makes desolate (Daniel 11:31). The eighth king is "the abomination that makes desolate," which is set up in Daniel 11:31. The eighth king is "the transgression that makes desolate" of Daniel 8:13. This eighth king is the false Christ, which Christ warned of in Matthew 24. The eighth king is the "desolating sacrilege" of Matthew 24:15. He is the false Christ who will deceive, if possible, the very elect (Matthew 24:24). These events are outlined on the graph following Revelation 17 (Third Part)—The Ten Horns.

---

[1] *The Catholic Encyclopedia,* Thomas Nelson, 1976, s. v. "Rome."

[2] Knight, K., (2003). *The Catholic Encyclopedia: List of Popes* (Electronic version). Copyright 2003, K. Knight, updated 15 September 2003. Retrieved May 31, 2004, from http://www.newadvent.org/cathen/12272b.htm

[3] Smith, Robert N. Jr., *The Sixth King,* Copyright 1993, Robert N. Smith Jr., M. D., Fort Worth, Texas, pp. 99-150.

[4] Knight, K., (2003). *The Catholic Encyclopedia: List of Popes* (Electronic version). Copyright 2003, K. Knight, updated 15 September 2003. Retrieved May 31, 2004, from http://www.newadvent.org/cathen/12272b.htm

Revelation 17 (third part)
The Ten Horns

The ten horns of Revelation 17 are initially introduced in Revelation 17:3. These ten horns are seen on the scarlet beast "which was full of blasphemous names" (Revelation 17:3). This scarlet beast is Satan (Revelation 12:9) as the false Christ (the eighth king). These are not the same ten horns which were seen in Revelation 13:1. The ten horns of Revelation 13 were crowned because they had already completed their reigns. The ten horns of Revelation 17 are not crowned because they have not yet reigned when John sees this vision during the reign of the sixth king. The ten horns will not reign until the end of the reign of the eighth king.

> Revelation 17:12: *"And the ten horns that you saw are ten kings who have not yet received royal power, but they are to receive authority as kings for one hour, together with the beast."*

The ten horns are found on the scarlet beast (Revelation 17:3, 7). These are the same ten horns seen on the dragon beast of Revelation 12:3. In both Revelation 12:3 and Revelation 17:3, 7 these ten horns are uncrowned. The absence of crowns indicates that these kingdoms have not yet come into existence (discussed in Preface: The Crowns and Their Meaning). John's view of history in Revelation 17 is during the reign of the sixth king, which is prior to the reign of the eighth king who will give power to these ten horns or ten kingdoms. Therefore, these ten horns have no crowns, because they do not yet exist during the time of John's vision.

In Revelation 12, these ten horns are the same ten kingdoms, which will follow the eighth king. In Revelation 12, John is viewing history during the time of the eighth king at the close of probation, and these ten kings have not yet existed. They will come into existence at the end of the reign of the eighth king when he is forced to divide up his kingdom.

The ten horns of Revelation 17:3, 7 are the same as the ten horns of Revelation 12:3. These ten horns are "ten kings who have not yet received royal power." These ten kings or kingdoms do not yet exist as shown by the absence of their crowns and will only exist for a very short time period. These ten horns are not the same ten horns seen in Daniel 7:7 and Revelation 13:1. The ten horns of Daniel 7:7 are ten kings which shall arise "out of this kingdom" (Daniel 7:24). This kingdom refers to the fourth kingdom which was pagan Rome (Daniel 7:23). These ten horns were the ten kingdoms of Europe, which appeared at the end of the Roman Empire.

The ten horns of Revelation 13:1 are the only ten horns which are crowned in these four chapters: Revelation 12, 13, 17 and Daniel 7. These ten horns are crowned because they represent the same ten kingdoms Daniel saw in vision. In Daniel 7, Daniel is looking forward toward those kingdoms and they have no crowns because they do not yet exist. Only kingdoms which have already existed have crowns. In Revelation 13:1, John is looking backward through history from the time of the seventh king to Daniel's day. It is clear in Revelation 13:1, 2 that John is looking backward through history because he begins with the leopard beast and moves in reverse order back toward the lion or Babylon. *It is very important to understand that the ten kingdoms of Daniel 7 and Revelation 13 are the same ten kingdoms. However, they are not the same ten kingdoms of Revelation 12 and 17, which have not yet come into existence.*

They "are to receive authority as kings for one hour, together with the beast." The beast or the eighth king will set up these ten kings at the end of his reign. They will receive power or authority for "one hour." This could indicate a short period of time or in prophetic time it could indicate approximately two weeks. Two weeks is based on one prophetic day equaling one literal year, therefore, one twenty-fourth of a day would equal one twenty-fourth of a year. A short time period is probably the better translation of "one hour" in this verse. These ten kings will reign together with the beast. This "one hour" of Revelation 17:12 is the same "one hour" of Revelation 18:19 during which Babylon is laid waste. This is shown in Revelation 17:16 because the ten horns "hate the harlot" and "they will make her desolate."

The reign of the ten kings will occur after the beast's reign of three and one-half years prophesied in Revelation 11:9-11. When God's two witnesses are resurrected (Revelation 11:11-13) an earthquake will fall on Jerusalem, Satan's capital city. The city will be terrified and will question Satan's claim to be God since he can not protect his own city. This is shown in Revelation 11:13: "the rest were terrified and gave glory to the God of heaven." Prior to this earthquake these same people were giving glory to Satan as the false Christ. After this earthquake they give glory to the God of heaven. The seven last plagues have also been falling, which have further eroded Satan's credibility. These ten kingdoms will come into existence as Satan's final attempt to control the world.

- *This division of the world into ten geographical divisions for future political control has already been formulated by the United Nations.*

When he realizes that he is losing control of the world Satan will be forced to share his power with the ten kings. Satan would never by choice share power with anyone unless he had no other options.

These ten kingdoms will come into existence as Satan's final attempt to protect his kingdom because he realizes that the world is about to attack him. Daniel 11:40-45 describe world events at the time of the end, which picture attacks on Jerusalem from the south and later from the north and finally simultaneously from the east and north. This final attack, which is described in Daniel 11:44 as coming from the east and the north, correlates with the sixth trumpet and the sixth plague.

> Revelation 17:13: *"These are of one mind and give over their power and authority to the beast."*

These ten kings are loyal to Satan as the eighth king. They will support him with their power and authority. They are "of one mind" meaning that they will carry out the beast or Satan's wishes. One of Satan's wishes will be to destroy all of God's true believers (Revelation 13:15). They will support him in his attempt to annihilate God's people. The death decree of Revelation 13:15 will be universal and will be enforced by these ten kings.

> Revelation 17:14: *"they will make war on the Lamb, and the Lamb will conquer them, for he is Lord of lords and King of kings, and those with him are called and chosen and faithful."*

The ten kings will exist when the final battle for this earth is fought. The final battle will involve the ten kings and Satan against the Lamb and His angels. This battle is described in Revelation 19. The Lamb, who is also called "Faithful and True" and "The Word of God," is seen with "the armies of heaven" (Revelation 19:11-14). "On his robe and on his thigh he has a name, inscribed, King of kings and Lord of lords" (Revelation 19:16). "And I saw the beast and the kings of the earth with their armies gathered to make war against him who sits upon the horse and against his army" (Revelation 19:19). The kings of the earth mentioned here are the ten kings of Revelation 17:14. The Lamb wins this battle: "and the Lamb will conquer them, for he is Lord of lords and King of kings."

"Those with him are called and chosen and faithful." Historically, this has been applied to God's people on earth, who are first called and then chosen and then become faithful. However, not all that are called are chosen and not all that are chosen are faithful.[1] This phrase can also be applied to Revelation 19:6-8, which describes the wedding feast of the Lamb. Many are called or invited but not all are chosen. Many are chosen but not all are faithful. Only the faithful will partake of the marriage feast of the Lamb.

> Revelation 17:15: *"And he said to me, 'The waters that you saw, where the harlot is seated, are peoples and multitudes and nations and tongues.'"*

This definition of waters or seas is important in understanding other texts in the book of Revelation. The scarlet woman or great harlot was seated on the world's population. In other words, this false church would control or influence many nations and tongues and peoples. Its influence would be worldwide. This concept of waters as representing populated areas is necessary in interpreting other texts and the opposite also applies: prophetic land or wilderness areas often refer to unpopulated regions. Specifically, this text tells us that the Papacy in the last days will control or influence many "peoples and multitudes and nations and tongues."

> Revelation 17:16: *"And the ten horns that you saw, they and the beast will hate the harlot; they will make her desolate and naked, and devour her flesh and burn her up with fire."*

This verse suggests that at the very end of time, after the ten kingdoms have been set up, these kingdoms along with Satan (the beast) will turn on the harlot or Babylon (Revelation 17:5). Babylon is the city on seven hills (Revelation 17:9 compare Revelation 17:4, 5). This city is Papal Rome. When Satan begins to lose political control of the world and is forced to share power with the ten kingdoms it is probable that there will be an attempt on the part of Rome to regain power as well. This will then bring about Satan's attack on Rome (Babylon) with the help of the ten kingdoms. This prophecy is further expanded in Revelation 18:17, 19, and 21 where Babylon is laid waste "in one hour." Babylon will be "burned with fire" (Revelation 18:8, 9, 18) and "shall be found no more" (Revelation 18:21).

Babylon the great harlot, or scarlet woman, will be destroyed "in one hour" (Revelation 18:10, 17, 19) by the ten kings who only exist for one hour (Revelation 17:12). This will occur at the end of the eighth king's reign as the false Christ or the abomination that makes desolate. This will occur during the time of the sixth trumpet and the sixth seal and the sixth plague. This one hour reflects a short time period, probably only a few weeks.

> Revelation 17:17: *"for God has put it into their hearts to carry out his purpose by being of one mind and giving over their royal power to the beast, until the words of God shall be fulfilled."*

The ten kings and the beast or Satan will actually carry out some of God's purposes in punishing the Papacy. They will be "of one mind" or unified in their attack on the scarlet woman. They will destroy Rome and "burn her up with fire" (Revelation 17:16). This will occur shortly before the Second Coming. These ten kings will support the beast for the length of time required to destroy the Papacy. This "authority as kings for one hour, together with the beast" (Revelation 17:12) will end shortly after the Papacy is destroyed. The destruction of the Papacy or Babylon will come "in one hour" (Revelation 18:17).

At the end of this short time period, the world's final battle will occur. It appears from Daniel 11:44, Revelation 9:14 and Revelation 16:12 that the final battle will involve the Middle East. This battle will center on Jerusalem, Satan's capital city. This battle of Armageddon will be terminated by the Lamb and His armies (discussed in Revelation 16—The Seven Last Plagues).

> Revelation 17:18: *"And the woman that you saw is the great city which has dominion over the kings of the earth."*

This scarlet woman or great harlot is called "Babylon the great" (Revelation 17:5). This woman sits on seven hills (Revelation 17:9). This woman has seven kings (Revelation 17:10) who are her final seven popes. These popes became kings when the "mortal wound was healed" (Revelation 13:3). This occurred when the scarlet woman or the leopard-like beast was reinstated as a church-state kingdom in 1929. This woman is "the great city which has dominion over the kings of the earth." This city in John's day was Rome and he would have recognized it as such. John is seeing this vision during the reign of the sixth king. This city at the time of the sixth king is still Rome. This city will be the center for apostate Christianity until the eighth king reigns.

SUMMARY

Revelation 17 introduces the scarlet woman and the scarlet beast. The woman represents the Papacy in the last days. The beast represents Satan, who will become the eighth king. As the false Christ he will claim to have returned to save mankind and fulfill the Old Testament prophecies. Satan will take over the spiritual rule of the world first by convincing the world's Christians and then the Papacy that he is the Christ returned.

John is viewing these events during the time of the sixth king (Pope John Paul II). The seventh king (Pope Benedict XVI) only has a short reign and is then followed by Satan as the eighth king, who is the false Christ and the abomination that makes desolate. The seven kings represent the seven last popes beginning when the Papacy became a kingdom again. This occurred with the healing of its mortal wound in 1929, when Mussolini reinstated the Papacy as a kingdom by giving it sovereignty over Vatican City. There have been seven kings over this city since this kingdom was re-established. *We are now living in the time of the seventh king.*[2]

Satan will reign as the eighth king or the beast "that ascends" for three and one-half years, which is described in Revelation 11:9, 11. He will then be forced to divide up his kingdom. The ten kings or ten horns will exist for only a short time and during that time they will destroy the woman or Papacy by attacking the city of Rome and destroying it.

These events will be followed by the last great battle, which will occur in the Middle East centered on Jerusalem, Satan's capital city. This final battle of Armageddon will be interrupted by the arrival of the Lamb who will destroy the wicked in order to save His people (Matthew 24:22). If God does not intervene, the entire world including His people would be destroyed. The following graph outlines the events described in Revelation 17.

Revelation Chapter 17

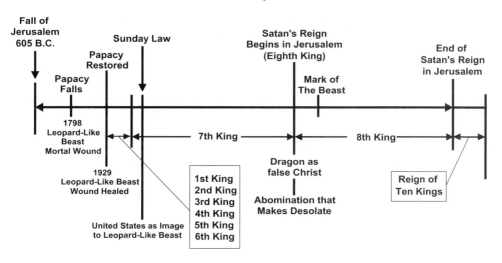

---

[1] Nichol, Francis D. (Ed.). *The Seventh-day Adventist Bible Commentary* (Review and Herald Publishing Association, Washington, D.C.) 1957, Vol. 7, p. 858.

[2] Knight, K., (2003). *The Catholic Encyclopedia: List of Popes* (electronic version). Copyright 2003, K. Knight, updated 15 September 2003. Retrieved May 31, 2004, from http://www.newadvent.org/cathen/12272b.htm

SUMMARY
Section II—The Eighth King

Revelation 13 begins by introducing a beast "with ten horns and seven heads" (Revelation 13:1) and with ten crowns upon the ten horns. This beast arises out of the sea and is described as leopard-like with bear's feet and a lion's mouth. This leopard-like beast is arising out of the world's population (the sea) after the ten horns have been crowned. This means that the timeframe of this vision is after the ten horns or ten kingdoms have existed. The ten horns of Revelation 13 represent the ten European kingdoms that Daniel described in Daniel 7:7, 8. The "little horn" of Daniel 7:7, 8, 24, 25 is the same beast as this leopard-like beast. In Revelation 13, John is looking backward through time as shown by the reverse progression of these symbols from beast to leopard to bear to lion as compared to the opposite order in Daniel 7, where Daniel was looking forward to these events.

The ten kingdoms of Daniel 7 came into existence when pagan Rome collapsed. Three of these kingdoms were overthrown (Daniel 7:24). These three kingdoms were overthrown by Papal Rome and disappeared. Papal Rome is the "little horn" of Daniel 7:8, 24 and is the leopard-like beast of Revelation 13.

The leopard-like beast had a mortal wound to its head, which healed. This mortal wound occurred in 1798 when General Berthier captured Pope Pius VI, who was the head of the beast. This wound was healed in 1929 with the signing of the Lateran Treaty, which restored the Papacy as a kingdom or church-state power. This kingdom would now have kings again. This healing resulted in the entire world following after the beast with wonder (Revelation 13:3). Following the restoration of the leopard-like beast, the world will again worship this beast and will also worship the dragon who is Satan (Revelation 13:4, 12:9).

This leopard-like beast is allowed to reign again after its wound is healed for another 42 months (Revelation 13:5) as a world power. After its wound is healed, it will be allowed to make war against God's people (Revelation 13:7). After its wound is healed, the leopard-like beast will reign along with the lamb-like beast (Revelation 13:12).

The lamb-like beast with two horns, which speaks like a dragon, represents the United States of America (discussed in Revelation 13 (last part)—The Mark of the Beast). The two horns represent religious and civil liberty. This lamb-like beast will form an image to the beast. This image will exist when the United States loses its first horn of religious liberty by forming a church-state union. This will occur with the passage of the universal Sunday law. This passage of the universal Sunday law represents the beginning of the 42 months or three and one-half years of world domination of the leopard-like beast with the support of the United States (discussed in Revelation 13 (first part)—The Leopard-Like Beast Healed). This also represents the second angel's message, which is fulfilled when all the "nations drink the wine of her impure passion" (Revelation 14:8). This image of the beast will then pass laws that will not allow anyone to buy or sell without the beast's mark. This mark of the beast is the third angel's message (Revelation 14:9-11). Those who refuse this mark will be threatened with death (Revelation 13:15). These events are outlined in the summary graph.

Revelation 17 is introduced by one of the seven angels with the seven last plagues, which connects this prophecy to last-day events. Revelation 17 describes a scarlet woman "seated upon many waters," which represents her control of the world (Revelation 17:15). This woman has seduced the world and made the world drunk with her falsehoods (wine). This woman is sitting on a scarlet beast with seven heads and ten horns. These seven heads and ten horns are uncrowned, which means that neither the heads nor the horns have completed their reigns at the time of this vision. The seven heads are seven kings (Revelation 17:10). The ten horns are ten kings (Revelation 17:12). This vision occurs during the reign of the sixth king of the seven kings (Revelation 17:10), which represents the reign of Pope John Paul II.

The scarlet woman is "Babylon the great, mother of harlots and of earth's abominations" (Revelation 17:5). She is "the great city which has dominion over the kings of the earth" (Revelation 17:18). This scarlet woman is "drunk with the blood of the saints" (Revelation 17:6). This scarlet woman is the leopard-like beast of Revelation 13. This scarlet woman is Papal Rome who will regain spiritual domination of the world during the reign of its seventh king.

The scarlet beast of Revelation 17 is the red dragon of Revelation 12. This scarlet beast or red dragon is Satan (Revelation 12:9). Satan will ascend "from the bottomless pit" (Revelation 17:8). This pit represents the rules of engagement under which Satan currently must operate. God will release these requirements in phases during the last days. Satan is the beast who "was" in power as Lucifer, who "is not" in power currently, but "is to come" into power when he ascends to his throne as the eighth king. When Satan ascends to his throne as the eighth king he will be ascending from the pit of circumstances with which God is currently controlling him.

The seven heads "are seven hills" (Revelation 17:9) and "are also seven kings" (Revelation 17:10). The seven hills link the seven kings to the "great city" (Revelation 17:18), which is Rome. The seven heads are seven kings of this city. One of this city's prior heads was mortally wounded (Revelation 13:3). These seven heads or kings are the seven last Popes of Rome. These seven Popes will reign once the mortal wound has healed (Revelation 13:3, 12). The vision of Revelation 17 occurs during the reign of the sixth king (Pope John Paul II), after five "have fallen" and one is yet "to come" (Revelation 17:10).

The eighth king is Satan as the false Christ or abomination that makes desolate (Daniel 11:31). The eighth king is the beast that is to ascend. The eighth king "belongs to the seven" (Revelation 17:11) because he will continue their agenda of persecution of God's people. The eighth king will be followed by ten kings who will reign "together with the beast" (Revelation 17:12). These ten kings will come into power in order for Satan to maintain control of the world. Satan will be losing world control because of the seven last plagues, which God is pouring out on the wicked. These ten kings will only reign for a short time. These ten kings will assist Satan in the destruction of Babylon (Revelation 17:16), which represents Papal Rome, and then will assist Satan in making "war on the Lamb"

(Revelation 17:14). This war on the Lamb represents the Second Coming when Jesus will conquer the wicked and save His people. These events are outlined in the following graph.

Section II - The Eighth King Summary Outline

Revelation Chapter 13 - First Part

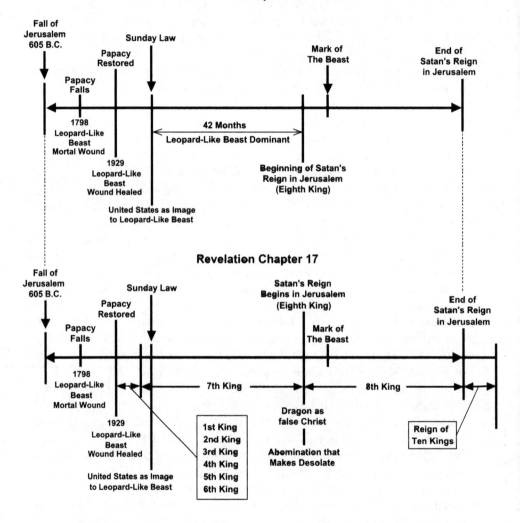

Revelation Chapter 17

The Judgment

Revelation 4
The Judgment Scene:
God's Throne Room

Revelation 4 introduces another vision. In this vision, John sees God's throne room involved in a judgment scene. This judgment scene was previously described by the prophet Daniel: "as I looked, thrones were placed and one that was ancient of days took his seat" (Daniel 7:9). Daniel continues, "the court sat in judgment, and the books were opened" (Daniel 7:10). This judgment scene would involve a jury with God as Judge, because "thrones were placed" (Daniel 7:9). In Revelation 4:5, there are 24 thrones that are placed around God's throne for this jury.

> Revelation 4:1: *"After this I looked, and lo, in heaven an*
> *open door! And the first voice, which I had heard speaking*
> *to me like a trumpet, said, 'Come up hither, and I will show*
> *you what must first take place after this'."*

"After this" is mentioned twice in this verse. Some authors suggest that this vision occurred after the first vision that related to the seven churches. However, they say that does not mean it is connected to the prior vision. They interpret the second "after this" as hereafter meaning after John's time.[1] However, many believe the church of Laodicea is God's last church and represents God's people after 1844. The year 1844 ends the 2300-year prophecy of Daniel 8:14, which is the longest time prophecy in Daniel. The time period from 1844 onward can be considered the last days. In this sense, the vision of Revelation 4 does occur "after" the beginning of the Laodicean time period, since it also relates to the time after 1844.

Since the investigative judgment began in 1844 and is currently ongoing, it is appropriate to consider this entire period from 1844 onward as the time period of the last-day events. When the investigative judgment ends, probation for this world also ends. It is important to recognize that Daniel specified a specific time as "the time of the end" (Daniel 11:35). This time specified by Daniel begins in Daniel 11:40 and includes the time of trouble. In Daniel 11:35, the "wise," which are God's people in the last days, will continue to fall "until the time of the end." This is consistent with the close of probation. God's people will no longer die once probation closes. This time of the end begins in Daniel 11:40 and extends to the Second Coming.

Revelation 15:8 states that "no one could enter the temple, until the seven plagues of the seven angels were ended." This suggests that the investigative judgment is completed at the beginning of the plagues, because no one can enter the heavenly temple once the plagues begin to fall. This means that the close of the investigative judgment, which marks the close of probation, is connected to the beginning of the plagues. These plagues will fall "in a single day" (Revelation 18:8), which is a prophetic day, and equals one literal year. In Daniel 11:35, 40, the "time of the end" correlates with the close of probation and represents approximately the last year of this world's history and the time of the seven last plagues.

The fact that Laodicea, the last church of God's true followers, began in the 1840s and the fact that Revelation 4 and 5 describe the judgment scene, which began in 1844, both suggest that "after this" can be taken literally. In other words, John is going to be shown scenes in heaven involving the judgment process, which begin after the church of Laodicea appears and continue during the time of the church of Laodicea. John is shown "in heaven an open door." This door opens into God's throne room.

God's throne room in heaven was symbolized in the Old Testament sanctuary as the most holy place. The most holy place contained the Ark of the Covenant, which symbolized God's throne in heaven. The most holy place, where God dwelt in the sanctuary on earth, was only entered once a year by the high priest. The most holy place was "open" only once a year in order to cleanse the sanctuary of the sins that had accumulated there throughout the year. During the year, a sinner would bring an unblemished lamb to the sanctuary and confess his sins over it. The lamb was slain and its blood sprinkled in the sanctuary. This process symbolically transferred the sins of the sinner to the lamb and then to the sanctuary.

Once a year at the Day of Atonement service, another lamb was slain and its blood was ministered by the high priest in the most holy place. The holy place, where the daily ministry was done, was separated by a veil (the "door" of Revelation 4:1) from the most holy place. This veil or "door" was opened only once a year and only by the high priest. This "open door" into God's throne room seen by John is represented as a veil in the Old Testament sanctuary service. The One "who opens" this door in the heavenly sanctuary is "the holy one" or the "true one" of Revelation 3:7. This Holy One is Jesus Christ. Jesus is the Lamb Slain and also the High Priest (Hebrews 4:14) ministering before God. This will be seen clearly in Revelation 5:5-7.

In other words, John is about to see the heavenly counterpart to the earthly cleansing of the sanctuary. John is going to see the actual events in heaven upon which the symbolic events in the earthly sanctuary were based. John is going to see the actual cleansing of the sanctuary in heaven which the Day of Atonement service symbolizes. John is going to see the actual restoring or cleansing of the sanctuary prophesied by Daniel to begin in 1844 (Daniel 8:14).

> Revelation 4:2: *"At once I was in the Spirit, and lo, a*
> *throne stood in heaven, with one seated on the throne!"*

John is now taken in vision, which he describes as being "in the Spirit." John sees the throne with "one seated." This "one seated" is God. John does not describe Him as human because He is not human.[2] The throne is God's throne in God's throne room. This is what Daniel saw in Daniel 7:9. This is the room where Daniel saw "the court sat in judgment" (Daniel 7:10).

> Revelation 4:3: *"And he who sat there appeared like jasper*
> *and carnelian, and round the throne was a rainbow that*
> *looked like an emerald."*

This is God the Creator of the universe. His beauty and brightness cannot be described. God is pictured as bright colors emanating from His throne. A rainbow, the color of emeralds, surrounds God's throne.

> Revelation 4:4: *"Round the throne were twenty-four thrones, and seated on the thrones were twenty-four elders, clad in white garments, with golden crowns upon their heads."*

These 24 thrones were described in Daniel 7:9 simply as "thrones were placed." These 24 elders are involved in this judgment process. They seem to represent the jury who is looking at the evidence. The evidence is contained in books which Daniel saw opened (Daniel 7:10). These 24 elders have been thought to represent many different things. Some have suggested they represent human beings who were saved previously and taken to heaven.[3] Others have suggested they represent Israel, 12 for literal Israel and 12 for spiritual Israel.[4] Some have suggested these are angels and some think they represent the 24 levels of the levitical priesthood.[5]

However, another possibility is that the 24 elders represent the unfallen worlds of God's universe. These unfallen worlds refused to accept Satan's lies and rejected Satan. These unfallen created beings might develop doubts regarding the fallen creatures that God is about to save. God has always gone to any length to save His creatures. God would also go to any length to keep sin from occurring again. God does not need to review the books in order to determine if He made the correct choice in saving us. He knows the end from the beginning. God's created creatures however, might have legitimate concerns over allowing sinners into their undefiled worlds and about the decision making process itself. In order to prevent doubt about God from ever arising again, God allows the unfallen worlds' representatives to review His decisions regarding those whose names are written in His book.

The 24 elders are robed in white. White is the symbol of purity. These unfallen beings would be pure, since they rejected Satan and have never sinned. Some have applied these white robes to the robes of white the righteous will wear, which represents Jesus' purity (Revelation 3:18).[6]

The 24 elders have "golden crowns upon their heads." The Greek word for crowns here suggests victory. These are crowns of victory. This could apply to humans, who were victorious through Christ, or to the unfallen leaders who were victorious through faith in God. However, it appears that the 24 elders represent unfallen leaders whom God is involving in the judgment process because He wants to eliminate all opportunity for doubt to arise.

> Revelation 4:5: *"From the throne issue flashes of lightning, and voices and peals of thunder, and before the throne burn seven torches of fire, which are the seven spirits of God."*

The picture of lightning, thunder, and voices that John sees coming from the throne suggests both power and majesty.[7] However, it can also suggest judgment. Similar scenes are described in Revelation 8:5 when the censer is cast down. The casting down of the censer is a time of judgment for the world. In Revelation 11:19, a similar description occurs during the seventh trumpet, which is the Second Coming and judgment of the world. Also in Revelation 16:18, which is the seventh plague, we find similar descriptions again relating to judgment on the world.

This courtroom scene is actually the beginning of the investigative judgment related to God's people. The investigative judgment will involve those people whose names are written in the book. This book is the book of life (Philippians 4:3). This does not involve the judgment of the wicked. The judgment of the wicked occurs for the living wicked at the Second Coming of Christ (Revelation 11:18) and for all the wicked at the post millennial return of Christ (Third Coming) (Revelation 20:11-15).

There are "seven torches of fire" which are before the throne of God. These seven torches "are the seven spirits of God." These "seven spirits of God" are also seen on the Lamb: "I saw a lamb standing, as though it had been slain, with seven horns and with seven eyes, which are the seven spirits of God sent out into all the earth" (Revelation 5:6). These same "seven spirits" are described in Revelation 1:4 as "the seven spirits who are before his throne." Some have attempted to connect the "seven torches" to the seven lampstands of Revelation 1:12. However, the seven lampstands "are the seven churches" (Revelation 1:20). These seven torches "are the seven spirits" and are clearly different from the seven churches.

These "seven spirits" are related to God and His throne and they are described as the seven horns and seven eyes of the Lamb. Horns suggest power or authority. The eyes suggest vision or knowledge. The torches suggest light. Light clearly is symbolic here because God's throne does not need extra light. The "seven spirits" represent the various activities of God's Holy Spirit. The "seven spirits" are connected to God, the Father on the throne and to His Son, the Lamb Slain. The seven horns suggest the power and authority of God's Spirit. The seven eyes suggest the Spirit's all-seeing vision and knowledge. The "seven torches" suggest the Holy Spirit in its roll as light of the world and as our Guide. One torch for each of the seven churches it guides thru history. God's Spirit is involved in the judgment scene just as God the Father and Jesus the Lamb are involved. The number seven here suggests completeness or perfection. The "seven spirits" represent all of the activities that God's Spirit does on our behalf.

> Revelation 4:6: "*and before the throne there is as it were a
> sea of glass, like crystal. And round the throne, on each side
> of the throne, are four living creatures, full of eyes in front
> and behind*"

God's throne is pictured as sitting above a "sea of glass" clear as crystal. Crystal is known for its transparency. This transparency suggests that nothing will be hidden during this judgment process. The New Jerusalem is described as having streets of "pure gold, transparent as glass" (Revelation 21:21). This sea of glass will reflect back God's glory just as we are to reflect His glory to others. Around God's throne are seen "four living creatures." These creatures will be described in the next verse. These four creatures are similar to the four creatures seen in Ezekiel 1 but different. In Ezekiel 1, these creatures "each had four faces" (Ezekiel 1:6) but in Revelation 4 and 5 they only have one face. Ezekiel calls his beings "cherubim" (Ezekiel 10:20) and they have four wings (Ezekiel 1:6). The four creatures in Revelation 4 and 5 have six wings (Revelation 4:8), which resemble the seraphim of Isaiah 6:2. These creatures have eyes "in front and behind." These eyes denote intelligence and vigilance.[8] The eyes in front and behind suggest that nothing goes unseen by these creatures. It also suggests looking forward and backward in time. This judgment process, in which they are involved, requires looking back into the past as well as up into the future.

> Revelation 4:7: *"the first living creature like a lion, the second living creature like an ox, the third living creature with the face of a man, and the fourth living creature like a flying eagle."*

These four creatures are each associated with events described later in the book of Revelation. The first creature or lion is associated with the first seal (Revelation 6:1, 2). This lion represents "the Lion of the tribe of Judah, the Root of David" who has conquered (Revelation 5:5) and will continue "to conquer" (Revelation 6:2). The "lion" is also the Lamb Slain (Revelation 6:6). This "lion" represents Jesus as victorious over sin. The first seal describes a white horse and rider who go out to conquer (Revelation 6:2). The "lion" introduces the first seal. This "lion" conquering is symbolic of the spread of Jesus gospel throughout the entire world after 1844. It especially applies to the worldwide reformations of the late 1800s and early 1900s (discussed in Revelation 6—The Seven Seals). The time period of the "lion" conquering extends from 1844 to the Second Coming.

The second creature is described as an "ox." The ox is known for strength.[9] The "ox" or second creature is associated with the second seal (Revelation 6:3). The second seal relates to warfare. The second seal involves the red horse and its rider, who are permitted "to take peace from the earth" (Revelation 6:4). This was fulfilled beginning in 1914 with World War I and later in 1939 with World War II (discussed in Revelation 6—The Seven Seals). The time period of the "ox" is from 1914 onward to the Second Coming. The "ox" is symbolic of Satan who will cause warfare, both spiritual and literal, which will continue to the Second Coming.

The third creature is described as a "man." This creature represents the "man of lawlessness" or "man of sin" (2 Thessalonians 2:3). This "man" of sin is called "the lawless one" who is "revealed" (2 Thessalonians 2:8). This "lawless one" will come with "all power and with pretended signs and wonders, and with all wicked deception for those who are to perish" (2 Thessalonians 2:9, 10). This "lawless one" is Satan. He is the one "who opposes and exalts himself against every so-called god or object of worship, *so that he takes his seat in the temple of God, proclaiming himself to be God"* (2 Thessalonians 2:4) (emphasis supplied).

This is Satan, as he will exist as the eighth king or false Christ. This is Satan as the abomination that makes desolate. When Satan returns as the false Christ he will claim to be God and will set up his throne in Jerusalem. He will claim that he has returned to fulfill the Old Testament prophecies regarding him. He will kill God's two witnesses, which are the Old Testament and the New Testament, by distorting their truths (discussed in Revelation 11 (first part)—The Two Witnesses). This "man" or third creature is connected to the third seal (Revelation 6:5). This seal depicts a black horse and rider with a balance or yoke held in his hand. This yoke is symbolic of the union of church and state, which will occur when the image to the beast is formed (discussed in Revelation 13 (last part)—Mark of the Beast). This union of church and state will eventually bring about the mark of the beast. The mark of the beast occurs once this church-state union enforces a law forbidding buying or selling without the mark (Revelation 13:17). The time period covered by the symbol of the "man" of sin begins with the church-state union or image to the beast and continues to the Second Coming. The "man" is symbolic of Satan and the famine, both spiritual and literal, which he will bring about. This famine will continue until the Second Coming.

The fourth creature is an "eagle." This "eagle" represents God's protection of His people. Exodus 19:4 states "You have seen what I did to the Egyptians, and how I bore you on eagles' wings and brought you to myself." The "eagle" represents how God carried Israel safely away from Egypt. In the book of Revelation the "eagle" is associated with last-day events. The "eagle" in Revelation 12:14 is pictured protecting God's church in the wilderness for three and a half years (discussed in Revelation 12—The Dragon and the Eighth King). In Revelation 8:13, the "eagle" is associated with the last three trumpets called "woes." These three woes will begin when Satan, as the fallen star, is released from the bottomless pit (Revelation 9:1). This will allow Satan to become world king (Revelation 9:11). The seven last plagues will begin at this time (discussed in Revelation 9—The Seven Trumpets: The First and Second Woes).

The "eagle" is also associated with the fourth seal (Revelation 6:7). The fourth seal pictures a pale horse whose "rider's name was Death" (Revelation 6:8). This seal depicts death from sword, famine, pestilence and wild beasts (discussed in Revelation 6—The Seven Seals). This time period of the world's history begins with the reign of the eighth king, when Satan is finally allowed to become the world's spiritual leader and is now able to further attack God's people. This seal is associated with the eagle's protection. The need for the eagle's protection will further increase when Satan becomes world king and the plagues begin to fall. The eagle is symbolic of God's protection, which continues to the Second Coming of Christ.

> Revelation 4:8: *"And the four living creatures, each of them with six wings, are full of eyes all round and within, and day and night they never cease to sing, 'Holy, holy, holy, is the Lord God Almighty, who was and is and is to come!'"*

These living creatures differ from Ezekiel's cherubim because they have six wings. Ezekiel's cherubim have only four wings (Ezekiel 1:6). In the matter of wings these four creatures are similar to the seraphim of Isaiah 6:2, which have six wings. The four creatures are full of eyes all around and within. The eyes represent the ability to see everything. This is critical in the judgment process in which they are involved. The eyes facing forward and backward also suggest the ability to see into the past and future.

These creatures are described as praising God endlessly: they "never cease" day and night to sing praise to God. The praise song is similar to the seraphim song in Isaiah 6:3 "Holy, holy, holy is the Lord of Host; the whole earth is full of his glory." Whenever created beings are allowed to enter God's presence they cannot keep from crying out His praises. True unending indescribable joy inhabits God's presence. These creatures are simply reflecting the joy that exists in God's presence and are unable and unwilling to stop their praises. Truly God inhabits praise and praise inhabits those who surround Him.

God is described as He "who was and is and is to come." This phrase suggests the eternal nature of God.[10] This phrase also points forward to the end of the investigative judgment when God "is to come" into His kingdom. This song of praise is completed in Revelation 12:10 when it states "Now the salvation and the power *and the kingdom of our God and the authority of his Christ have come"* (emphasis supplied).

In Revelation 4, we are viewing the beginning of the investigative judgment. In Revelation 12:10, we are seeing the end of the investigative judgment when God's kingdom has come. The end of the investigative judgment coincides with "the accuser of our brethren" being cast down (Revelation 12:10), because there is no one left to accuse; all of the righteous and all of the wicked have been accounted for. This is the close of probation when the "wise" will fall no more (Daniel 11:35) (discussed in Daniel 11—The Abomination and the Time of the End). This end of the investigative judgment is also the beginning of the seven last plagues when the temple will no longer be open and no one can enter (Revelation 15:8).

> Revelation 4:9: *"And whenever the living creatures give glory and honor and thanks to him who is seated on the throne, who lives forever and ever"*

The "living creatures" are the four creatures of Revelation 4:6-8. They are giving thanks to God, the Father, Who is "seated on the throne." The reason for their thanksgiving is related to the judgment process. As the court reviews each name and God's decisions are seen to be fair, just, and merciful beyond question, these creatures and elders fall down in praise to God. Special joy is brought fourth when one of the names is found to be saved for eternity. Eternity is what God is all about and it is what He is offering to the saved!

> Revelation 4:10: *"the twenty-four elders fall down before him who is seated on the throne and worship him who lives forever and ever; they cast their crowns before the throne, singing"*

The 24 elders join the four creatures in celebrating and worshiping God, the Father, for His justice and mercy and love in saving mankind. They praise Him as the Creator of all things, who did not need to risk Himself to save His creatures.

> Revelation 4:11: *"Worthy art thou, our Lord and God, to receive glory and honor and power, for thou didst create all things, and by thy will they existed and were created."*

The praise that is given to God the Father is in reference to His creatorship. He created all things including those who are being judged during this investigative judgment. As Creator, He had no obligation to restore His fallen created beings except the obligation of love. He is worthy of all honor and glory. This praise is different from the praise given to the Lamb Slain. The Lamb is praised for ransoming mankind and His work of salvation is emphasized (Revelation 5:9, 10).

SUMMARY

Revelation 4 describes God's throne room at the time of the investigative judgment, which was typified by the Day of Atonement service in the earthly sanctuary. The door is opened to the most holy place, or God's throne room, and the cleansing of sin from the heavenly sanctuary is about to begin. The only sins that are brought into the sanctuary are the sins of God's professed believers. These are typified in the Old Testament service as being placed on the sacrificial lamb. These are the sins of the penitent believers who bring their lamb to be sacrificed. They do not represent the sins of the unrepentant that do not bring a lamb to be slain. The blood of the lamb was then ministered in the sanctuary. The unrepentant wicked, who are lost; never bring their sins to the sanctuary to ask forgiveness. Therefore, their sins never contaminate the sanctuary. Only those who have claimed a relationship with God or Jesus Christ will have their sins symbolically brought into the heavenly sanctuary. These are the sins that will be cleansed or removed from the heavenly sanctuary. These are the sins that must be removed in order to restore God's heavenly sanctuary. This process of restoration or cleansing of the heavenly sanctuary is called the investigative judgment. This process involves the review of all the records of those who have ever claimed to believe in God or Jesus Christ. This judgment process involves a jury described as the 24 elders. God, the Father, is the Judge and Jesus as the Lamb Slain is our Advocate (John 2:1). Satan is the "accuser of our brethren" (Revelation 12:9, 10).

This process of restoring the heavenly sanctuary began in 1844 as prophesied by Daniel in Daniel 8:14: "And he said to him, 'For two thousand and three hundred evenings and mornings; then the sanctuary shall be restored to its rightful state.'" This 2300-year prophecy (one prophetic day equals one literal year) began in 457 B.C. and ended in 1844 (discussed in the chapters on Daniel 8 and 9). This investigative judgment process is ongoing now.

Each of the four creatures described correlates with different time periods involved in the last days. Each creature is connected to one of the first four seals of Revelation 6. The lion creature represents Jesus and His gospel, which will conquer and continue to conquer to the end. The lion is the Lion of Judah. This time period begins with a worldwide reformation.

The ox represents Satan and the warfare, both spiritual and literal, which will continue to the end. This time period begins with global warfare and is characterized by death and destruction to the end.

The man creature represents Satan and the famine both spiritual and literal which he causes to the end. This man creature is the dragon of Revelation 12 (discussed in Revelation 12—The Dragon and the Eighth King). He is the eighth king and the scarlet beast of Revelation 17 (discussed in Revelation 17 (second part)—The Eighth King). He is the beast that has ascended in Revelation 11 (discussed in Revelation 11 (first part)—The Two Witnesses). He is the dragon or Satan in Revelation 20:2. He is the fallen star of Revelation 9 (discussed in Revelation 9—The Seven Trumpets: The First and Second Woes). He is the lawless one or man of sin of 2 Thessalonians 2:3, 4.

The eagle represents God's protection of His people to the end. The eagle has two wings to carry them through the wilderness. The eagle or fourth creature is connected to the last-day events and represents God's protection of His church. The eagle is connected to the fourth seal and the last three trumpets or woes. The eagle is seen protecting God's people during Satan's reign as the eighth king (Revelation 12:14, 15). These events are outlined in the following graph.

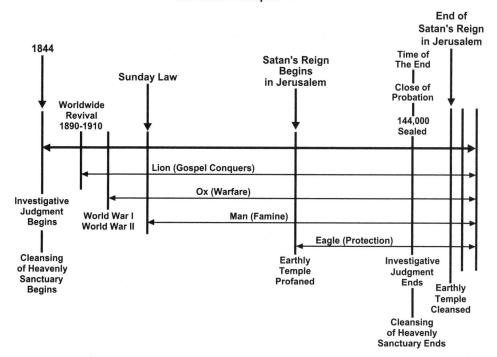

Revelation Chapter 4

---

[1] Nichol, Francis D. (Ed.). *The Seventh-day Adventist Bible Commentary* (Review and Herald Publishing Association, Washington, D.C.) 1957, Vol. 7, p. 766.

[2] Ibid. p. 767.

[3] Ibid. p. 767, 768.

[4] Ibid.

[5] Ibid.

[6] Ibid. p. 762.

[7] Ibid. p. 768.

[8] Ibid.

[9] Ibid. Vol. 4, p. 576.

[10] Ibid. Vol. 7, p. 732.

Revelation 5
The Judgment Scene: The Lamb Slain

"The fifth chapter of Revelation needs to be closely studied. It is of great importance to those who shall act a part in the work of God for these last days" (*Testimonies for the Church*, volume 9, page 267).[1] Revelation 5 continues the judgment scene, which John introduced in Revelation 4. In chapter 4, God's throne is seen surrounded by 24 thrones with 24 elders on these thrones. There are four living creatures that symbolize the time periods from the beginning of the investigative judgment to the end of time. The 24 elders and four living creatures are seen praising God for His work as our Creator and the salvation He provides. God is described as He "who was and is and is to come" (Revelation 4:8). This text points forward to the end of the investigative judgment at which time God's kingdom will come, which is described in Revelation 12:10.

> Revelation 5:1: *"And I saw in the right hand of him who was seated on the throne a scroll written within and on the back, sealed with seven seals"*

This verse continues the vision of the judgment scene with God seen "seated on the throne." This verse introduces a "scroll written." This "scroll" is held in God's right hand. This emphasizes the importance of this scroll or book. God is holding it Himself! This book is "written within and on the back." This means that it was written on both sides. This was often done in ancient times to fully utilize the scroll especially when there was much to record.[2] The scroll was sealed with "seven seals." The number seven suggests that the scroll was perfectly sealed or completely sealed.[3] These seals will be further explained in Revelation 6 and Revelation 8:1. These seals can only be opened by the Lion of Judah (Revelation 5:5). ***The seals are on the scroll and will be broken when the scroll is opened.*** This is important for determining the time periods the seals cover.

> Revelation 5:2: *"and I saw a strong angel proclaiming with a loud voice, 'Who is worthy to open the scroll and break its seals?'"*

This angel is described as strong and yet he is unable to open the "scroll." This angel proclaims "with a loud voice." When this phrase is used in the book of Revelation, it is almost always associated with the judgment process. In this throne room scene, this "scroll" is a key part of the investigative judgment. This "scroll" or book contains the names of all those who have claimed to serve God or Christ sometime during their lives. The question the angel asks is "Who is worthy to open the scroll?" The answer is found in Revelation 5:5. The phrase ***"open the scroll and break its seals"*** suggests that the seals will be broken at the time the scroll is opened (emphasis supplied). This in turn suggests that the time periods of the seals will begin with the scroll being opened and not prior to its opening.

> Revelation 5:3: *"And no one in heaven or on earth or under the earth was able to open the scroll or to look into it"*

This text confirms that no one on earth or in heaven can open this book or scroll. No one in the entire universe is qualified or capable of opening this book except the One who died in order for the names to be placed in this book.

> Revelation 5:4: *"and I wept much that no one was found worthy to open the scroll or to look into it."*

John was extremely upset because no one could open this book. John seemed to realize that this "scroll" was critical to the judgment process he was witnessing. John wept because he realized how important this book was and how important it was to open it. The issue is worthiness. Only Jesus Christ is worthy.

> Revelation 5:5: *"Then one of the elders said to me, 'Weep not; lo, the Lion of the tribe of Judah, the Root of David, has conquered, so that he can open the scroll and its seven seals.'"*

John is told to stop weeping because Someone can open the scroll. The One who can open the scroll is "the Lion of the tribe of Judah" and the "Root of David". Jesus was from the tribe of Judah (Matthew 1:2). In Isaiah 11:1, in a prophecy about Jesus, He is described as "a branch" out of the roots or stump of Jesse.[4] Jesse was David's father. Jesus is "the Lion of the tribe of Judah." The reason Jesus is worthy to open the scroll is because He "has conquered." Jesus "has conquered" Satan and sin. Jesus is the reason that each name can be put in the book. Without Jesus, no one can be saved and there would be no investigative judgment. The scroll exists only because of Jesus' death for the sinners who are recorded in it. Jesus is the only One worthy to open His scroll.

> Revelation 5:6: *"And between the throne and the four living creatures and among the elders, I saw a Lamb standing, as though it had been slain, with seven horns and with seven eyes, which are the seven spirits of God sent out into all the earth"*

John now sees a Lamb standing in the throne room. This Lamb stands "as though it had been slain." This is clearly a description of Jesus as "the Lamb of God, who takes away the sin of the world" (John 1:29). In the New Testament, only John calls Jesus "the Lamb" however, Philip and Peter apply the figure to Him (Acts 8:32, 1 Peter 1:19).

This Lamb is seen among the four creatures and the 24 elders. All of these creatures are involved in the judgment process and the Lamb is central to the entire process. The Lamb is our Advocate before the Father (1 John 2:1). The four creatures and the 24 elders are discussed in Revelation 4—The Judgment Scene: God's Throne Room. This Lamb has seven horns and seven eyes. The seven horns represent the seven spirits of God. The seven eyes represent the seven spirits of God. These seven spirits are "sent out into all the earth." These seven spirits represent the Holy Spirit and its work. In Revelation 4:5, they are described as "torches of fire." The horns represent strength and glory.[5] The torches represent how the Spirit is a light for the world. The eyes represent intelligence and wisdom.[6] The eyes also represent the Spirit's ability to see everything both in the past, present, and the future. This symbol of the seven spirits shows the close relationship between Jesus and the Holy Spirit.

> Revelation 5:7: *"and he went and took the scroll from the right hand of him who was seated on the throne."*

Jesus was the only One who could take the scroll and open it. Jesus went to the Father seated on the throne and took the scroll He had died to create. The Lamb Slain was the reason the book existed. Only God the Father and Jesus the Lamb Slain are described as holding this book. This again points out the value of this book.

> Revelation 5:8: *"And when he had taken the scroll, the four living creatures and the twenty-four elders fell down before the Lamb, each holding a harp, and with golden bowls full of incense, which are the prayers of the saints"*

When the Lamb took the scroll from His Father on the throne, the throne room erupted with praise to the Lamb. The four creatures and the 24 elders fell down and worshiped in adoration. They each hold harps or lyres. These "golden bowls" contain "incense" which represents "the prayers of the saints" or God's people. This demonstrates how important the prayers of the saints are, they are kept in God's presence.[7] These prayers are related to this judgment process. These prayers represent the plaintiff's pleas for mercy and forgiveness. This is the only part that we as sinners have in this process. We can only ask for forgiveness and accept God's grace. Jesus the Lamb Slain does all the rest.

> Revelation 5:9: *"and they sang a new song, saying, 'Worthy art thou to take the scroll and to open its seals, for thou wast slain and by thy blood didst ransom men for God from every tribe and tongue and people and nation'"*

This new song is a song of praise to the Lamb. This is a song celebrating redemption. This song will be sung by the redeemed.[8] This song celebrates the only One who is "worthy." He is worthy because He was slain and paid the ransom for our sins. He is worthy because "there is salvation in no one else, for there is no other name under heaven given among men by which we must be saved" (Acts 4:12). The description of the people from which the saved are ransomed is important. The saved are ransomed "from every tribe and tongue and people and nation." This is the same list of people to whom the three angels' messages are addressed (Revelation 14:6). This same list is found in Revelation 11:9, which describes the world during the eighth king's reign. This list of tribes and tongues and peoples and nations appears to be the targeted audience of the last-day events. The message of the investigative judgment will be aimed at this audience. In other words, the targeted audience for the three angels' messages is the same world audience as the audience for the message regarding the investigative judgment.

> Revelation 5:10: *"and hast made them a kingdom and priests to our God, and they shall reign on earth."*

This kingdom was described by Peter in 1 Peter 2:9: "But you are a chosen race, a royal priesthood, a holy nation, God's own people…" This kingdom includes all the ransomed throughout the history of the world. These ransomed will serve as "priests to our God." They will dwell in God's New Jerusalem where God Himself will dwell (Revelation 21:1-3). They will reign on earth: "He who conquers and who keeps my works until the end, I will give him power over the nations" (Revelation 2:26).

> Revelation 5:11: *"Then I looked, and I heard around the throne and the living creatures and the elders the voice of many angels, numbering myriads of myriads and thousands of thousands"*

The angels join in praising the Lamb for He alone is worthy. Heaven is filled with singing. John cannot count the number of angels he sees. He describes the scene as filled with "thousands of thousands" of angels. These millions of angels are singing praises to the Lamb.

> Revelation 5:12: *"saying with a loud voice, 'Worthy is the Lamb who was slain, to receive power and wealth and wisdom and might and honor and glory and blessing!'"*

This praise echoes the praise of the elders and the four creatures. This praise is for the Lamb who has saved His people and is the only One worthy to open the scroll. The Lamb (Jesus) is praised with seven praises. The number seven suggests completeness or perfect praise.[9] Not only is the Lamb worthy to open the scroll, He is worthy of perfect praise. The Lamb is worthy to receive "power and wealth and wisdom and might and honor and glory and blessing!" In actuality, Jesus already has all of these but the angels are restating His worthiness.

> Revelation 5:13: *"And I heard every creature in heaven and on earth and under the earth and in the sea, and all therein, saying, 'To him who sits upon the throne and to the Lamb be blessing and honor and glory and might for ever and ever!'"*

Not only do the angels break forth in praise to God and the Lamb but all creation also sings their praises. This verse demonstrates that every created being, wherever they may be, agrees with the angels. God the Father, who sits on the throne, and Jesus Christ the Lamb are truly worthy of all "blessing and honor and glory and might for ever and ever!"

> Revelation 5:14: *"And the four living creatures said, 'Amen!' and the elders fell down and worshiped."*

The four living creatures and the 24 elders, who had begun the praises, now end them. They end their praise with a simple "Amen." This word means "verily" or "sure."[10] All of the prior praises to God and the Lamb are true. These creatures and elders then fall down and worship their God.

SUMMARY

Revelation 5 continues the judgment scene that was introduced in Revelation 4. This investigative judgment will review the lives of all those who claimed to serve God. This process will restore or cleanse the heavenly sanctuary of the sins symbolically transferred there through the death of Christ as our Lamb Slain. Revelation 5 describes a scroll which no man can open. The only One worthy to open this book or scroll is the Lamb Slain. The reason He is the only One worthy is because His death is what made the book or scroll possible. His death allowed the names to be written therein. It is truly His book. This book is the book of life. Opening this book begins the process of judgment in heaven. This judgment involves only those written in this book. This investigative judgment began in 1844 when the 2300-year prophecy of Daniel 8:14 ended and the restoration or cleansing of the heavenly sanctuary began. The Lamb Slain is praised in Revelation 5 for His redemptive work just as the Father was praised for His creative work in Revelation 4. There are seven seals on the scroll. These seven seals will be broken when the scroll is opened. The seven seals will portray events that occur after the investigative judgment has begun, which means after 1844. Revelation 6 will continue by explaining the seven seals on this scroll. The following graph outlines the events of Revelation 5 in relation to Satan's reign as the false Christ and the Sunday law, both of which have been discussed previously in this book.

Revelation Chapter 5

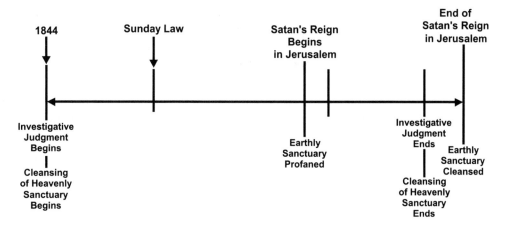

---

[1] Ibid. p. 773. White, Ellen G., *Testimonies for the Church* (Pacific Press Publishing Association, Mountain View, California) 1948, Vol. 9, p. 267.

[2] Nichol, Francis D. (Ed.). *The Seventh-day Adventist Bible Commentary* (Review and Herald Publishing Association, Washington, D.C.) 1957, Vol. 7, p. 770.

[3] Ibid.

[4] Ibid. p. 771.

[5] Ibid. p. 772.

[6] Ibid.

[7] Ibid.

[8] Ibid. p. 773

[9] Ibid. p. 772.

[10] Ibid. Vol. 5, p. 332.

Revelation 6
The Seven Seals

Revelation 6 is a continuation of the throne room scene depicted in Revelation 4 and 5. In Revelation 4, God the Father is seen sitting on the throne with 24 thrones set up around Him. This is the judgment scene of Daniel 7:9-10. This investigative judgment began in 1844 (discussed in Revelation 4 and 5—The Judgment Scene). In Revelation 5, a scroll or book is introduced that no one in the universe is worthy to open except the Lamb Slain. Jesus is the Lamb Slain, who died for mankind's sins and allowed man the opportunity to be saved. This book contains the list of all those who have ever attempted to serve God during their lives. Those who have never attempted to serve God do not get their names written in the book. Those who turned to God and then rejected Him will be part of this book but will not be saved, because they will be judged "by what they had done" (Revelation 20:13). This book is the book of life (Revelation 3:5).

On this scroll are seven seals (Revelation 5:1, 5). No one is worthy to open these seals except the Lamb Slain (Revelation 5:9). These seals and this book are involved in the investigative judgment. The scroll, with the names written in it, is necessary for the judgment process or John would not have been so concerned when he realized that no one could open it (Revelation 5:3-5). John was weeping because he realized how critical this book was to the judgment process. Indeed, if no one could open the book, then no one could be saved. The book was opened in 1844 when the investigative judgment began. This judgment was described by Daniel as the cleansing or restoring of the sanctuary (Daniel 8:14). This cleansing or restoration of the heavenly sanctuary began at the end of the 2300-year prophecy of Daniel 8:14. "And he said to him, 'For two thousand and three hundred evenings and mornings; then the sanctuary shall be restored to its rightful state'" (Daniel 8:14). This 2300-year prophecy began with the decree to restore Jerusalem (Daniel 9:25). This decree was given in 457 B.C. by King Artaxerxes of Media-Persia. Twenty-three hundred years later in 1844 the restoring of the sanctuary began in heaven with the investigative judgment of God's people.

The seven seals are attached to the scroll, which was opened in 1844. This scroll or book is part of the current ongoing investigative judgment. The seven seals are descriptions of events that will occur during the time of the investigative judgment. The seven seals are prophecies of world events that will occur from 1844 onward to the Second Coming of Christ. The seven seals are linear and progress through to the time of the end. The seventh seal in Revelation 8:1 describes "silence in heaven" because the Second Coming is happening and heaven is empty.

> Revelation 6:1: *"Now I saw when the Lamb opened one of the seven seals, and I heard one of the four living creatures say, as with a voice of thunder, 'Come!'"*

This chapter begins with the Lamb who is Jesus Christ opening one of the seven seals. Jesus is the only One who can open this scroll. He is the only One worthy. Jesus is seen opening "one of the seven seals." This is the first seal even though it is not specified as such. This is confirmed by reading the remainder of Revelation 6 and Revelation 8:1. All of the other six seals are listed by number, leaving only the first seal unlisted.

John initially sees the Lamb open this first seal and then he hears "one of the four living creatures" speak. This creature is one of the four creatures he had seen previously around God's throne (Revelation 4:6-8, Revelation 5:8, 11, 14). The exact creature is not stated in this verse but it can be deduced. It is the lion, which was the first of the four living creatures (Revelation 4:7). This deduction is based on the fact that the next three seals are each associated in order with the second, third and fourth creatures. This implies that the first seal is associated with the first creature or the lion. Each of the four creatures will be associated with a time period, which will relate to the corresponding seal. The lion represents the "Lion of the tribe of Judah" (Revelation 5:5). The "Lion of the tribe of Judah" is Jesus Christ. During the first seal, it will be apparent that the rider and horse will go forth conquering. This suggests victory. During the latter 1800s and early 1900s, there was a worldwide reformation and the gospel appeared to be conquering the world.

> Revelation 6:2: *"And I saw, and behold, a white horse, and its rider had a bow; and a crown was given to him, and he went out conquering and to conquer."*

Historically, this verse has been interpreted to represent the early apostolic church during the first century from A.D. 34 to A.D. 100. The "white horse" represented the purity of the early church. The "bow" represented warfare and the "crown" represented victory. Conquering represented the successful spread of the gospel.[1] This historical application is appropriate but there is at least one other application, which applies after 1844 and the beginning of the investigative judgment. In the context of last-day events, beginning with the investigative judgment, this prophecy was fulfilled again in the late 1800s. The success of the worldwide reformation that occurred in the late 1800s and early 1900s spread the gospel throughout the world. Truly, the gospel of Jesus Christ did appear to be "conquering" the world. The "bow" represents spiritual warfare and the "crown" represents the many victories won. The "white horse" represents God's people after 1844. The "rider" represents the gospel. The first seal represents the spread of the gospel of Jesus Christ (the Lion) beginning in the late 1800s. The creature is the lion. The lion is the Lion of Judah, which is Christ. The Lion represents Jesus whose gospel will continue to conquer to the end. The phrase "conquering and to conquer" can be interpreted as conquering and continuing to conquer, suggesting continued victory.[2]

> Revelation 6:3: *"When he opened the second seal, I heard the second living creature say, 'Come!'"*

Jesus the Lamb Slain is now seen opening the second seal. This is occurring in the throne room during the investigative judgment process. This second seal is associated with the second creature or the ox (Revelation 4:7). This ox is associated with the time period, which follows the lion. In last-day events, this would follow the reformation of the late 1800s and early 1900s. The ox will be associated with warfare, which will continue until the end of time.

> Revelation 6:4: *"And out came another horse bright red,*
> *its rider was permitted to take peace from the earth,*
> *so that men should slay one another; and he was given*
> *a great sword."*

Historically, this "red horse" has been thought to represent the time period from A.D. 100 to A.D. 313. This was a period of violent persecution of God's true church. The early church was persecuted by pagan Rome and its leaders. The "red" was thought to represent the contamination of the white or pure truth of the first seal with falsehood or heresies.[3] This application certainly fits that historical time period and is appropriate. However, there is another application, which is consistent with last-day events after 1844. This text states that its rider was "permitted to take peace from the earth, so that men should slay one another." Immediately following the reformation and spread of the gospel that occurred in the late 1800s and early 1900s, the world went to war. World War I, which began in 1914 and ended in 1919, was closely followed by World War II from 1939 to 1945. Truly peace was taken "from the earth." The second seal represents global warfare, both spiritual and literal beginning in 1914.

The rider "was given a great sword." This implies significant warfare or bloodshed. This certainly was fulfilled by the world wars. From 1914 thru 1975 it has been estimated that over 100 million people worldwide have died due to war and its consequences. World War I and World War II accounted for between 60 and 70 million of these deaths.[4] There have been more deaths due to warfare in the twentieth century than in any other century since John's day. Clearly, this prophecy was fulfilled beginning in 1914 and onward. The red horse represents warfare and bloodshed. The rider represents the countries involved in these wars. The ox represents Satan who will cause both spiritual and literal warfare to continue to the end.

> Revelation 6:5: *"When he opened the third seal, I heard the*
> *third living creature say 'come!' And I saw, and behold, a*
> *black horse, and its rider had a balance in his hands."*

Historically this verse has been applied to the time period A.D. 313 to A.D. 538. This time period reflected a union of pagan ideas and Christian teachings. During this time, the day of worship which was the Jewish Sabbath kept by the Christians, was changed to worship on Sunday. Sunday was the day the pagans worshipped the sun. The "black horse" represented falsehood, which was the opposite of the pure white truth of the early church. The "balance" represented the union of church with secular matters.[5]

However, there is another application, which applies in the last days. The man or third creature spiritually represents the man of sin or "the man of lawlessness" (2 Thessalonians 2:3). During the last days, God's Law will be attacked by Satan who is the man of lawlessness. During the last days there will be a union of church and state. During the last days there will be an attempt to change God's Sabbath to Sunday (discussed in Revelation 13 (last part)—The Mark of the Beast). When this law is passed to require Sunday worship, a church-state union will exist. The Greek term translated "balance" in this verse is "zugos" which means a yoke or the crossbar of a balance.[6] This yoking together of church and state will mark the beginning of the period of time covered by this seal. This yoking together of church and state will result in a Sunday law, which begins the time period of this seal. The third seal represents the church-state union which will change God's Law and the spiritual and literal famine during this time period (see Revelation 6:6).

The "black" color here suggests falsehood is dominant. Not only will the world be accepting a false Sabbath but the man of sin will appear and attempt to convince the world that he is Christ returned. Thus this seal is characterized by a dominance of falsehood culminating in a false Christ who will come "with all power and with pretended signs and wonders" (2 Thessalonians 2:9). He will come "with all wicked deception for those who are to perish" (2 Thessalonians 2:10). This time period begins with the union of church and state represented by the yoke or "balance." This union of church and state will be signaled by the passage of a universal Sunday law in the United States. The time period of this seal will end when the man of sin begins his reign as the world's spiritual leader.

> Revelation 6:6: *"and I heard what seemed to be a voice in the midst of the four living creatures saying, 'A quart of wheat for a denarius, and three quarts of barley for a denarius; but do not harm oil and wine!'"*

Historically, this verse has been applied to the time period of verse five which was from A.D. 313 to A.D. 538. The price for barley and wheat was extremely high. A "denarius," which is worth approximately eleven cents, was equal to one day's pay in John's day. To get only a quart of wheat or three quarts of barley was very expensive. These prices imply a famine in the land.[7] The oil and wine were thought to represent faith and love as opposed to the materialism of the time period.[8]

However, this text also has an application to last-day events. When the Sunday law is passed, it will occur because of economic collapse and global natural disasters. Famine will be occurring in the world's richest country, the United States of America. These ongoing calamities will cause the world to think that God is angry at them. This will bring about the union of church and state in this country in an attempt to appease God. This church-state union is described in Revelation 13 (discussed in Revelation 13 (last part)—The Mark of the Beast).

The phrase "do not harm oil and wine" also connects with the previous verse. This phrase suggests "harm" has already occurred. The "harm" was to God's Law, which was changed when the false Sabbath was instituted. The "oil and wine" which are not to be harmed represent God's Holy Spirit and Jesus' blood. God's Holy Spirit will be poured out during this time in preparation for the latter rain of Joel 2:28: "I will pour out my spirit on all flesh." This latter rain will be poured out during the preliminary time of trouble, which begins shortly after the false Christ ascends his throne.

The wine represents Jesus' blood spilled for each of us. During this time period, Jesus' blood will be under attack but the man of sin cannot harm it. God's message of salvation will be carried forward and souls will be saved, but the man of sin will be deceiving many with his "signs and wonders" (2 Thessalonians 2:9). Both spiritual and literal physical famine will dominate the world during this seal. The black horse represents falsehood, including the false Sabbath and the false Christ, which appear during this time period. The rider represents apostate Christianity, which will bring about a church-state union. The balance represents the church-state union or yoking of church and state, which will occur during this period.

> Revelation 6:7: *"When he opened the fourth seal, I heard the voice of the fourth living creature say, 'Come!'"*

Historically, the fourth seal was considered the time period from A.D. 538 to 1517. This was the time period during which Papal Rome dominated the world. This period ended with the onset of the Protestant Reformation.[9] The fourth creature is the eagle (Revelation 4:7). The eagle symbolically has been associated with God's protection. In Exodus 19:4, God states "You have seen what I did to the Egyptians, and *how I bore you on eagles' wings* and brought you to myself" (emphasis supplied). God is describing His care for Israel as bearing His people on eagles' wings. However, in the last days there will be an increased need for the eagle's protection beginning with the fourth seal. This is why the eagle creature is linked to the fourth seal.

This same eagle is also seen during the vision of the trumpets. Revelation 8:13 states "Then I looked, and I heard an eagle crying with a loud voice, as it flew in mid heaven, 'Woe, woe, woe to those who dwell on the earth, at the blasts of the other trumpets which the three angels are about to blow!'" Here the eagle is introducing the last three trumpets. These last three trumpets are different from the first four trumpets. The first four trumpets are warnings and are not universal. The last three trumpets are "woes" and are universal (discussed in Revelation 8 and 9—The Seven Trumpets). During these last three trumpets or woes God's people will require special protection. This is what the eagle represents in Revelation 8:13.

In Revelation 12:14, the eagle is also seen protecting God's people in the wilderness. Revelation 12:14 states "But the woman was given the two wings of the great eagle that she might fly from the serpent into the wilderness, to the place where she is to be nourished for a time, and times, and half a time." The woman represented here is God's true church. The church is seen being protected by God described as an eagle. The true church will be specially protected for three and one-half years in the last days (discussed in Revelation 12—The Dragon and the Eighth King). As will be shown later this three and one-half years of protection by the eagle described in Revelation 12:14 is the same period of protection covered by the eagle of Revelation 6:7.

> Revelation 6:8: *"And I saw, and behold, a pale horse, and its rider's name was Death, and Hades followed him; and they were given power over a fourth of the earth, to kill with sword and with famine and with pestilence and by wild beasts of the earth."*

Historically, this prophecy has been applied to the time period A.D. 538 to 1517. This time period covers the time of the supremacy of Papal Rome in world history. This time period was known for the persecution of God's true followers. Papal Rome killed millions of God's people during this time period. The color "pale" was thought to represent fear and death.[10]

The last-day application of this seal has been shown in the previous verse to involve God's protection as the eagle. This eagle is connected to the three and one-half years of the dragon's reign as the eighth king (Revelation 12:14), which is the same three and one-half years described in Revelation 11:9, 11. The eagle is also seen protecting God's people during the three "woes" (Revelation 8:13), which are the last three trumpets. The time period covered by the eagle begins after the man of sin is set up. This "man of lawlessness" is Satan (2 Thessalonians 2:9). Satan, represented by the scarlet beast of Revelation 17:3, becomes the eighth king (Revelation 17:11). This man of sin "takes his seat in the temple of God, proclaiming himself to be God" (2 Thessalonians 2:4). When Satan proclaims himself to be God and sets up his kingdom in Jerusalem as "the beast that ascends" (Revelation 11:7-8) then he will be the eighth king. As the eighth king he will take over the kingdom from the seventh king (Revelation 17:11). The "pale horse" represents death. The "rider" represents Satan once he is crowned the eighth king and becomes the spiritual ruler of Christianity.

"As the crowning act in the great drama of deception, Satan himself will personate Christ. The church has long professed to look to the Saviour's advent as the consummation of her hopes. Now the great deceiver will make it appear that Christ has come. In different parts of the earth, Satan will manifest himself among men as a majestic being of dazzling brightness, resembling the description of the Son of God given by John in Revelation 1:13-15. The glory that surrounds him is unsurpassed by anything that mortal eyes have yet beheld... In gentle, compassionate tones he presents some of the same gracious, heavenly truths which the Saviour uttered; he heals the diseases of the people, and then, in his assumed character of Christ, he claims to have changed the Sabbath to Sunday, and commands all to hallow the day he has blessed" (*The Great Controversy*, page 624).[11]

Satan can be considered the rider and death is his horse. His reign as spiritual leader will correspond to the third and fourth trumpets, after which he will become the world's temporal ruler. He is "given power over a fourth of the earth." Once Satan reigns as the eighth king and is spiritual leader of both Catholicism and Protestantism, he will have power over one "fourth of the earth." This represents approximately one-fourth of the world's population. This represents those people living in countries where Satan and his agents have total control. This will allow Satan to kill many of those who reject him as Christ. This will not include some democratic countries such as the United States, where Satan will not initially be in control. However, as the eighth king (the false Christ) Satan will have total power in many of the world's countries and be able to persecute God's people indiscriminately.

Ultimately, Satan will be allowed to kill as many of the wicked as he desires. This will occur during the second woe after the four angels are released, which occurs after the close of probation (discussed in Revelation 9—The Seven Trumpets: The First and Second Woes). He will not be able to kill God's people after the close of probation (Daniel 11:35) because of the protection of the eagle. In Daniel 11:35, the time of the end represents the close of probation after which God's people will not fall.

Satan will use many means to accomplish this destruction. This text lists death from the sword or warfare, from famine, from pestilence or illness and from wild beasts. Some have seen this as a natural progression; war leads to famine, which leads to illness, which leads to beasts dominating the environment.[12] Both spiritual and literal famine will dominate the world beginning with the third seal and will worsen during the fourth seal. Once Satan reigns as the eighth king, he will be able to kill many of God's people in the "fourth of the earth" that he has "power over." The fourth seal begins with Satan's reign as the eighth king. The rider is Satan as the eighth king. The pale horse represents the death of many righteous and wicked people during this time period. The fourth seal represents the reign of the false Christ as the eighth king.

> Revelation 6:9: *"When he opened the fifth seal, I saw under the altar the souls of those who had been slain for the word of God and for the witness they had borne."*

This text introduces the fifth seal. It is of note that the first four seals are depicted as four horsemen with their horses. The last three seals do not involve horsemen. The first four seals each involve one of the four creatures. The last three seals do not. Of the four creatures, two represent Satan and his attacks on the world in the last days. The other two creatures represent Christ's and God's work in the last days. Even though each creature introduces a time period, in a real sense the activities of that creature continue to the end of time. For example, the Lion and His gospel will continue to conquer spiritually all the way to the Second Coming. The ox will continue to cause war and physical destruction until the end. The man of sin will cause spiritual and physical famine until the end of time. The eagle will continue to protect God's people from spiritual destruction until the end of time. Thus, there is no need to reintroduce these creatures with the last three seals. The reader should note the parallel action and reaction portrayed by each of these creatures. Jesus spiritually conquers and then Satan attacks both spiritually and physically. Satan spiritually attacks and then God protects both spiritually and physically.

Historically, this text has been applied to the time period 1517 to 1755. This was the time of the Protestant Reformation. This verse is thought to represent God's people crying out for the vindication of God's name.[13] However, in the dual application for last-day events, this text represents those who shall fall "until the time of the end" (Daniel 11:35). Those saints who fall during the last days will be known for two things. Revelation 14:12 defines the saints as, "those who keep the commandments of God and the faith of Jesus." In the last days, when the eighth king reigns as the false Christ, there will be two major issues; a false Sabbath and a false Christ. The remnant, which Satan is trying to destroy, will refuse to accept the false Sabbath and will refuse to accept Satan as Christ. The saints will not break God's Law including the fourth (Sabbath) commandment and they will bear testimony to the true Jesus, keep faith in Him, and reject the false Christ.

In Revelation 6:9, "the word of God" represents God's Word spoken to man as His Ten Commandments and it can also represent Jesus who is "the Word" (John 1:14). "The witness they had borne" represents the saint's refusal to accept the false Christ, their "witness" about the true Christ, and their "witness" about God's true Sabbath. These verses will be fulfilled once Satan reigns as the eighth king, which was described in the prior seal (Revelation 6:7-8).

It is important to note that these souls who are crying out to God are symbolic. Revelation 6:9 is not a text on the state of the dead. These souls are symbolic, just as the Lamb Slain is symbolic.[14] *These souls are not living spirits up in heaven. They are symbolic of God's people who will be slain during the time period after the Sunday law is enforced up to the close of probation.* In Revelation 13:16, 17, the enforcement of the Sunday law is described as not being able to buy or sell without the mark. This enforcement will occur after Satan's reign as the eighth king and is not the same as the passage of the national Sunday law, which occurs under the third seal (discussed in Revelation 13 (last part)—The Mark of the Beast).

> Revelation 6:10: *"they cried out with a loud voice,*
> *'O sovereign Lord, holy and true, how long before thou*
> *wilt judge and avenge our blood on those who dwell upon*
> *the earth?'"*

Historically, this time period has been considered to be 1517 to 1755. This is the time period when many reformers were martyred. This verse pictures those martyrs crying out for judgment on the wicked who have slain them. However, when applied to the last days, *these martyrs represent all those who will be slain during the third angel's message* (discussed in Revelation 14—The Three Angels' Messages) prior to the time of the end when the wise will no longer "fall" (Daniel 11:35). This time of the end is the close of probation. The close of probation represents the time in history when all of the living have made their final choices for good or evil. This time correlates with the "time of the end" in Daniel 11:35 and in Daniel 11:40. This time also correlates with the "time of trouble" of Daniel 12:1. In Matthew 24:21, Jesus describes the "great tribulation, such as has not been from the beginning of the world until now, no, and never will be." This great tribulation is the same time period that Daniel describes as the "time of trouble, such as never has been since there was a nation till that time" (Daniel 12:1). In Revelation 7:14, 15, the 144,000 are described as: "These are they who have come out of the great tribulation." Thus, the 144,000 who are sealed (Revelation 7:4) are those who are involved in the great tribulation or the time of trouble. The close of probation occurs when the 144,000 are sealed. This occurs at the beginning of the time of trouble or the great tribulation.

Specifically, these martyrs who cry out represent those killed after the fourth seal and the "man of lawlessness" is set up in God's temple (2 Thessalonians 2:4). When the "man of lawlessness" is set up in God's temple as God, he will be the eighth king of Revelation 17:11. The eighth king is Satan, the beast, who claims to be Jesus Christ returned to save the world. This false Christ will set himself up "in the temple of God" and will claim to be God (2 Thessalonians 2:4). This is the "desolating sacrilege" Jesus saw "standing in the holy place" (Matthew 24:15). Once Satan as the eighth king reigns, he will then enforce his false Sabbath. The enforcement of this false Sabbath is the mark of the beast, which occurs with the buy-sell legislation (Revelation 13:16, 17). This buy-sell legislation will lead to the death of many of God's people. Those who are slain after this event are specifically seen here crying out to God asking "how long?" They are really asking "how long" the world will have to endure this eighth king. They are asking "how long" until God will end this "abomination that makes desolate" (Daniel 11:31). This is the same question that Daniel asked in Daniel 12:6, "How long shall it be till the end of these wonders?" The answer is found in Daniel 12:7, 11, 12 (discussed in Daniel 12—The Abomination and the Time of Trouble).

> Revelation 6:11: *"Then they were each given a white robe*
> *and told to rest a little longer, until the number of their*
> *fellow servants and their brethren should be complete,*
> *who were to be killed as they themselves had been."*

Historically this has been applied to the martyrs of the Protestant reformation.[15] However, in the last days, this will specifically apply to God's people who will be slain right up to the close of probation. These martyrs are told "to rest a little longer." This suggests a short time period and indeed the eighth king's reign will only be for about three and one-half years. During the last part of Satan's reign the plagues will begin to fall. When the plagues fall, the temple in heaven will be "filled with smoke" and "no one could enter the temple" (Revelation 15:8). This is the time when the investigative judgment has been completed. This is the time when probation is closed. This is the time when God's people who are called the wise "shall fall" no longer (Daniel 11:35).

The term "rest" is similar to Jesus' description of "sleep" when he described Lazarus after Lazarus had died (John 11:11-13). When God's people die they are asleep in Jesus. They will be raised at His Second Coming (1 Corinthians 15:51). The "dead know nothing" (Ecclesiastes 9:5, 6). These martyrs are symbolic of God's people who have died, but they are not spirits who can talk! These martyrs will be given a white robe, which is the robe of Christ's righteousness (Philippians 3:9).

This text states that these martyrs should rest "until the number of their fellow servants and their brethren should be complete, who were to be killed." This means that God knows exactly how many of His people will die. It also implies that once that number is filled, the end will come soon. ***This number of God's people killed will be complete at the close of probation.*** This text clearly connects to last-day events and the close of probation. These martyrs will know these "fellow servants" and "brethren" because they have worked together during the last days. Those who are left living after the number of martyrs is complete are called the 144,000 (Revelation 7:4). These are the living righteous at the time of the end and are sealed "upon their foreheads" with God's seal (Revelation 7:3, 4). The time period of this seal begins with the mark of the beast and ends at the close of probation.

> Revelation 6:12: *"When he opened the sixth seal, I looked,*
> *and behold, there was a great earthquake; and the sun*
> *became black as sackcloth, the full moon became like blood."*

Historically this seal has been applied to the time from 1755 to the end of time.[16] The "great earthquake" was considered the Lisbon earthquake in 1755. The sun and moon darkened were considered fulfilled on May 19, 1780 in the New England states of the United States of America.[17]

However, in the last days, the fourth seal refers to the reign of the eighth king and the fifth seal refers to the persecution of God's people under the eighth king, especially after the mark of the beast has occurred. This persecution leads up to the close of probation. The events of the sixth seal represent those events that occur after the close of probation and during the time of the seven last plagues. The seven last plagues will begin with the close of probation. The sun and moon darkened and the earthquake described here seem to be connected to the events of the next four verses and probably should not be separated out as single events but rather as part of the entire event pictured in verses twelve through seventeen. The event being described is the Second Coming. Jesus is seen as the "Lamb" and God is seen "seated on the throne" (Revelation 6:16). In Joel 2:31, these same events are connected to the Second Coming or "the terrible day of the Lord." The events described in Revelation 6:12, 13 will occur just prior to the Second Coming of Jesus Christ.

> Revelation 6:13: *"and the stars of the sky fell to the earth as the fig tree sheds its winter fruit when shaken by a gale."*

Historically, this event has been interpreted as the stars falling in New England in 1833.[18] However, the context of this verse suggests that the stars will fall along with the other events, which include the sky rolled up "like a scroll" (Revelation 6:14) and men crying out to the mountains to "fall on" them (Revelation 6:16). The stars will fall again at the end of time after the close of probation when Jesus returns for His people.

> Revelation 6:14: *"the sky vanished like a scroll that is rolled up, and every mountain and island was removed from its place."*

This event clearly has not happened yet. This event describes the entire world involved in a massive earthquake. This event occurs at Jesus' Second Coming. This earthquake is also seen in the seventh trumpet (Revelation 11:19) and in the seventh plague (Revelation 16:20). Revelation 16:20 states "every island fled away, and no mountains were to be found." Clearly, the seventh plague is describing the same event as the one described in this verse in the sixth seal.

> Revelation 6:15: *"Then the kings of the earth and the great men and the generals and the rich and the strong, and everyone, slave and free, hid in the caves and among the rocks of the mountains."*

This clearly connects this event to the entire world. Everyone "slave and free" is affected by this event. Money, power, position, social standing will mean nothing. All those who have rejected the Lamb will fear His coming: kings, slaves, rich and poor. All will cry out for protection from the Lord of the Universe.

> Revelation 6:16: *"calling to the mountains and rocks, 'Fall on us and hide us from the face of him who is seated on the throne, and from the wrath of the Lamb.'"*

The wicked will recognize God and His Son. They will run and hide but no one can hide from God. They will call for the rocks to "fall on us." They are filled with despair and want to die. They will do anything to get away from God's presence. The One "seated on the throne" is God the Father, who was described in Revelation 4:9 as Him "who is seated on the throne." This "wrath" represents the end of God's seven last plagues, which represent God's wrath (Revelation 15:1). This also represents the "wrath of the Lamb."

> Revelation 6:17: *"for the great day of their wrath has come, and who can stand before it?"*

The wicked recognize that this is the great day of "their wrath." "Their" refers to God the Father and to the Lamb. This is the "great and terrible day of the Lord" (Joel 2:31). This is the day the wicked finally meet their Creator face to face. This is the day that the false Christ is clearly revealed as he meets the Lamb in battle. This is the day the eighth king and his ten kings are overthrown. In Joel 2:10, 11, we see these same events outlined as a continuous event. The *"earth quakes before them, the heavens tremble. The sun and moon are darkened, and the stars withdraw their shining.* The Lord utters his voice before his army, for his host is exceedingly great; he that executes his word is powerful. *For the day of the Lord is great and very terrible;* who can endure it?" (Joel 2:10, 11) (Emphasis supplied).

The sixth seal is describing the events of Joel 2:10, 11, which occur together at the Second Coming of Jesus. The sixth seal ends with a question, the same question that Joel asked: "who can stand before it?" The answer is given in Revelation 7. The answer is the 144,000, represented as 12 tribes of 12,000 each (Revelation 7:4-8). These are the people of God who will "endure" (Joel 2:11). These are God's people who will be sealed "upon their foreheads" (Revelation 7:3). This sealing will be completed at the close of probation when the number "should be complete who were to be killed as they themselves had been" (Revelation 6:11).

> Revelation 8:1: *"When the Lamb opened the seventh seal, there was silence in heaven for about half an hour."*

Revelation 8 continues the seven seals. Revelation 7 answered the question "who can stand before it?" (Revelation 6:17) referring to the wrath of the Lamb (Revelation 6:16). Revelation 8 then completes the seven seals. The seventh seal is dramatically different from the prior seals. The prior seals have involved earthquakes, warfare and loud voices. This seal involves "silence." The "silence" is in heaven. This "silence" lasts for about a half an hour. This would be approximately one forty-eighth of a day or about one week (one prophetic day equals one literal year). This "silence" reflects the fact that heaven is empty. God and the Lamb and all their angels have gone to earth to collect the redeemed and to end the reign of the eighth king. This silence correlates with the Second Coming described in the sixth seal when the wicked are seen crying out to hide from the Lamb. The final battle between the Lamb and the eighth king will occur at this time (Revelation 17:14, Revelation 19:11, 19, 20). During this silence in heaven, the earth will be just the opposite. Thunder, lightning and the world's greatest earthquake will have just occurred (Revelation 16:18).

138

The seventh seal is a picture of heaven, empty and silent, because God and His Son are in the clouds above earth collecting their redeemed. Those "who are alive, who are left, shall be caught up together with them in the clouds to meet the Lord in the air; and so we shall always be with the Lord" (1 Thessalonians 4:17).

SUMMARY

The seven seals can be viewed as a historical overview from the Apostolic Age to the Second Coming or they can be seen as a description of last-day events beginning with the investigative judgment in 1844. The first four seals have both literal and symbolic applications. The gospel conquers both literally and spiritually. The warfare of the second seal is both literal and spiritual. Likewise, the famine of the third seal is both literal and spiritual. The protection God provides is also both literal and spiritual.

The first seal depicts the white horse and rider "conquering and to conquer" (Revelation 6:2). The "white horse" represents God's people after 1844. The "rider" represents the gospel. This seal is associated with the lion creature or the Lion of Judah. This seal represents the gospel of Jesus Christ spreading throughout the world in the late 1800s and early 1900s extending to the second seal. The lion represents Jesus and His gospel which will continue to conquer until the end. The second seal depicts a red horse and rider and is associated with the ox creature. The second seal represents global warfare. The second seal began in 1914 and extends to the third seal. The red horse represents warfare and bloodshed. The rider represents those countries involved in these wars. The creature is the ox which represents Satan, who will cause both spiritual and literal warfare to continue to the end. Satan is allowed to use these countries to take "peace from the earth" (Revelation 6:14). This was fulfilled from 1914 to 1945, during which World War I and World War II were fought.

The third seal depicts a black horse and is associated with a man creature. The black horse represents falsehood. The rider represents apostate Christianity which will bring about a church-state union and claim to change God's Law. The man creature represents the man of sin or Satan who is the antichrist who will cause both spiritual and literal famine to continue to the end. This seal involves a balance or yoke, which represents the church-state union, which will form in the United States in the last days. This union is called "the image of the beast" (Revelation 13:15). This church-state union will be the image of the original church-state union of the leopard-like beast of Revelation 13:2. The original leopard-like beast represents the Papacy. This church state image will pass a Sunday law, which will lead to the mark of the beast (discussed in Revelation 13 (last part)—The Mark of the Beast). The time period represented under the third seal begins with the Sunday law and extends to the reign of the eighth king. The third seal represents famine, both spiritual and literal, and the church-state union which will change God's Law.

The fourth seal depicts a pale horse and rider and is associated with the eagle creature. The eagle represents God's protection, both spiritual and literal, of His people during the reign of the eighth king and extending to the end. The pale horse represents death and the rider represents Satan as the eighth king or the abomination that makes desolate. When Satan reigns as the false Christ or eighth king, about one-fourth of the world will be under his power. This represents those countries where Satan as the eighth king rules and will include all those countries now ruled by Catholicism. The fourth seal represents the beginning of the reign of the false Christ as the eighth king and extends to the fifth seal.

The fifth seal depicts souls crying out to God for vengeance. These souls represent those souls killed during the reign of the eighth king. These saints will continue to die until their number "should be complete" (Revelation 6:11). This number is complete at the close of probation. This seal begins during the reign of the eighth king, after the mark of the beast (buy-sell legislation) is passed and continues to the close of probation. The close of probation represents the beginning of "the time of the end" (Daniel 11:35).

The sixth seal represents the last events of world's history, which include an earthquake "such as had never been since men were on the earth" (Revelation 16:18). The wicked see God the Father and His Son in the clouds and call for the rocks to fall on them. The seventh seal represents heaven silent and empty because Jesus, the Father, and the heavenly angels are in the clouds above earth redeeming the saved. The following graph depicts the last-day events of Revelation 6 and 7.

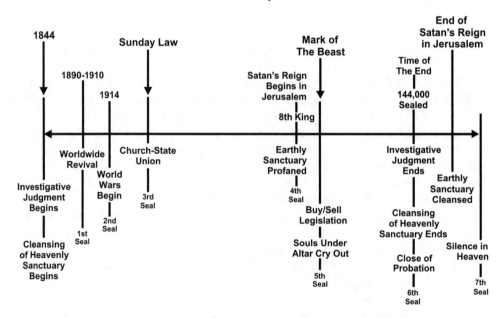

Revelation Chapters 6 & 7

Appendix (2)
Revelation 6

In the discussion on Revelation 6, the author has attempted to give both the historical approach as well as a dual application for the last days. In order to simplify these two approaches, the following table is provided for comparison purposes. It is important to understand that the book of Revelation shows a progressively more focused view of history. The broader outlines come first and overlap the later events. In other words, the seven churches cover the history of God's church from apostolic times to the Second Coming, while the seals cover only the time from 1844 to the Second Coming. This means the seals would correspond to the Laodicean church. Next, the trumpets cover the time from the Sunday law passage to the Second Coming and overlap the last five seals. The seven last plagues cover approximately the last year of time and would overlap the last three trumpets. In the historical approach, the seven churches and the seven seals and the seven trumpets all cover approximately the same time periods. The seven last plagues would occur at the time of the end. The following table (Appendix Table 1) outlines the historical approach to the seven churches and the seven seals. In the historical approach, the time periods are the same for the seven churches and the seven seals. However, in the dual application of these events to the last days, each group of seven symbols begins closer and closer to the Second Coming and therefore overlap only partially. The appendix time line at the end of this chapter (Appendix: Timeline (1)—7 Churches and 7 Seals) depicts these events as they occur in this dual application.

Appendix Table 1

Historical Application of Revelation Chapters 1-3 and 6

	Time Period	Seven Churches	Seven Seals
1st	A.D. 34 - A.D. 100	Ephesus	White Horse
2nd	A.D. 100 - A.D. 313	Smyrna	Red Horse
3rd	A.D. 313 - A.D. 538	Pergamum	Black Horse
4th	A.D. 538 - 1517	Thyatira	Pale Horse
5th	1517 - 1755	Sardis	Souls Cry Out
6th	1755 - 1844	Philadelphia	Sun, Moon and Stars Rocks Fall
7th	1844 - Second Coming	Laodicea	Silence in Heaven

Appendix: Timeline (1)

7 Churches and 7 Seals

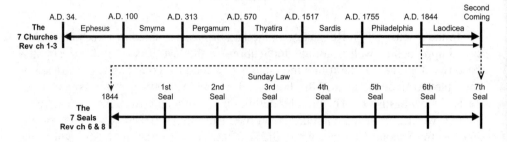

---

[1] Nichol, Francis D. (Ed.). *The Seventh-day Adventist Bible Commentary* (Review and Herald Publishing Association, Washington, D.C.) 1957, Vol. 7, p. 776.

[2] Ibid.

[3] Ibid.

[4] White, Matthew. *Source List and Detailed Death Tolls for the Twentieth Century Hemoclysm* (Electronic version). Copyright 2004, Matthew White, updated March 2004. Retrieved May 31, 2004, from http://users.erols.com/mwhite28/warstatl.htm

[5] Nichol, Francis D. (Ed.). *The Seventh-day Adventist Bible Commentary* (Review and Herald Publishing Association, Washington, D.C.) 1957, Vol. 7, p. 777.

[6] Ibid. p. 776.

[7] Ibid. p. 777.

[8] Ibid.

[9] *Revelation Seminars a Bible Prophecy Adventure* (copyright Review and Herald Publishing Association and Revelation Seminars, Keene, Texas) 1983, Teachers Manual, Section 9, p. 4.

[10] Nichol, Francis D. (Ed.). *The Seventh-day Adventist Bible Commentary* (Review and Herald Publishing Association, Washington, D.C.) 1957, Vol. 7, p. 777.

[11] White, Ellen G., *The Great Controversy* (Pacific Press Publishing Association, Nampa, Idaho) 1950, p. 624.

[12] Nichol, Francis D. (Ed.). *The Seventh-day Adventist Bible Commentary* (Review and Herald Publishing Association, Washington, D.C.) 1957, Vol. 7, p. 777.

[13] Ibid. p. 778.

[14] Ibid.

[15] Ibid.

[16] Ibid. p. 779

[17] Ibid.

[18] Ibid. Vol. 5, p. 502.

Revelation 8
The Seven Trumpets:
God's Final Warnings

Revelation 8 begins with the last of the seven seals. The seven seals are on the scroll, which is critical to the judgment process. The seven seals represent events that occur during the judgment process. The seven seals represent events from 1844 onward to the Second Coming. Revelation 8:1 is described with the seals (discussed in Revelation 6—The Seven Seals). The casting down of the censer and the trumpets of Revelation 8 are warnings to the world that "the hour of his judgment has come" (Revelation 14:7). These warnings have both a historical application as well as a last-day application for each event.

> Revelation 8:2: *"Then I saw the seven angels who stand before God, and seven trumpets were given to them."*

These seven angels are seen standing before God. The message of these angels will clearly come from God. These seven angels are given seven trumpets. Trumpets were used in the Bible in several situations. Trumpets were used to call to worship (Numbers 10:3). Trumpets were used for warning and to sound an alarm (Numbers 10:7). Trumpets were used to "go to war" (Numbers 10:9). Trumpets were used to celebrate (Numbers 10:10). In the context of Revelation 8, these trumpets are sounded as a warning. The first four trumpets differ from the last three. The last three are called "woes" (Revelation 8:13). The first four trumpets are warnings given prior to the last three woes. During the warnings, men can still change their minds. Once the woes begin, it will be too late to change your mind about salvation (discussed in Revelation 9—The Seven Trumpets: The First and Second Woes).

> Revelation 8:3: *"And another angel came and stood at the altar with a golden censer; and he was given much incense to mingle with the prayers of all the saints upon the golden altar before the throne."*

Historically, some have interpreted this verse as applying to Christ. They suggest that the casting down of the censer in Revelation 8:5 describes the end of Christ's ministry of intercession and the close of probation. This interpretation suggests that the angel described here is Christ. They interpret Revelation 8:5 with its thunder, lightning, noise and earthquake as the close of probation and link it to Revelation 11:19, which is the seventh trumpet.[1] Certainly, this interpretation could apply to these verses but there are several problems. The context of Revelation 8:3-5 is related to the trumpets. They are introduced in Revelation 8:2 and continued in Revelation 8:6. This suggests that the casting down of the censer is connected to the seven trumpets. If the close of probation occurs prior to the seven trumpets, then why give warnings at all? Also, the seven trumpets include the Second Coming as the seventh trumpet (discussed in Revelation 11 (last part)—The Seventh Trumpet: The Final Woe). Why would the seventh trumpet be given prior to the rest of the trumpets?

In last-day events, the casting down of the censer is symbolic of another event that will occur prior to the blowing of the seven trumpets. The angel described here appears to be an angel rather than Christ. Previously, Christ has been described as the Lamb in the book of Revelation (Revelation 4, 5, 6, and 7). He is described as the Lamb in Revelation 8:1. It seems improbable that John would not recognize Him as the Lamb in the remainder of this chapter. This angel has a specific duty to perform and then he is not mentioned again. The context of Revelation 8 is in the throne room where Jesus is consistently seen as the Lamb Slain and not as an angel.

The censer was used to burn incense before the Lord (Leviticus 10:1). The incense was special (Exodus 30:37, 38). The incense was a symbol of Jesus' intercession before the throne on behalf of His people.[2] Jesus' intercession is involved in the "prayers of all the saints."

> Revelation 8:4: *"and the smoke of the incense rose with the prayers of the saints from the hand of the angel before God."*

The smoke rising before God represents the prayers of God's people ascending to Him. This intermingling of Jesus' merits (incense) with His saints' prayers makes those prayers acceptable.[3] Jesus is the incense that changes the lives of His followers and turns their prayers into an acceptable fragrance before the Lord.

> Revelation 8:5: *"Then the angel took the censer and filled it with fire from the altar and threw it on the earth; and there were peals of thunder, loud noises, flashes of lightning, and an earthquake."*

Historically, this verse has been interpreted as the cessation of the investigative judgment and the close of probation.[4] However, the context of Revelation 8 suggests a second application. This event appears to occur in the context of the seven trumpets, since they are introduced before this event and then reintroduced after this event. The fire taken "from the altar" suggests judgment. The peals of thunder, loud noises, flashes of lightning and the earthquake also suggest judgment. However, this does not have to be the final judgment. Indeed, the earthquake is described as "an earthquake" as opposed to the earthquake described with the Second Coming. The earthquake described with the Second Coming is pictured as a "great earthquake such as had never been since men were on the earth, so great was that earthquake" (Revelation 16:18).

Some have suggested that the prayers of the saints refer to the martyrs' prayers for vengeance in the fifth seal. They interpret the throwing down of the censer as the end of Christ's ministry and the trumpets as God's wrath in answer to these prayers.[5] This approach interprets the trumpets as God's wrath, however, the first four trumpets are God's warnings as opposed to the woes of the last three trumpets. The seven last plagues are the wrath of God (Revelation 15:1). If the trumpets were God's wrath, this would place all the trumpets after the close of probation, because when God's wrath is poured out the temple is closed (Revelation 15:7, 8) which marks the end of the investigative judgment that occurs in the temple. The end of the investigative judgment marks the close of probation (discussed in Revelation 16—The Seven Last Plagues). This is inconsistent with the trumpets being warnings because it is too late for men to change their minds after the close of probation and any warnings would be useless. Also, the first four trumpets involve the sealing process, which is ongoing during these trumpets and is completed at the fifth trumpet (discussed in Revelation 9—The Seven Trumpets: The First and Second Woes). The sealing process is completed only at the close of probation, which means probation is not closed during the first four trumpets, since the sealing is completed at the fifth trumpet (Revelation 9:4).

The censer with its fire being cast down does represent judgment. Fire is clearly connected to judgment in the last days (Revelation 9:18, Revelation 14:10, Revelation 16:8, Revelation 18:8, Revelation 19:20, and Revelation 20:14). The question is: who is being judged at this time? The trumpets represent God's last warning to mankind to repent because "the hour of his judgment has come" (Revelation 14:7). The seven trumpets follow the casting down of the censer, which means the judgment the censer represents cannot refer to the final judgment of mankind.

A parallel situation occurred in the Old Testament. After Jesus came to earth, was crucified and then raised up from the dead, judgment occurred on God's favored nation. The special status of Israel as God's favored nation was lost, when that nation began to punish God's true believers for following Christ. This persecution of God's true people marked the end of literal Israel as God's favored nation. Literal Israel's probation closed in A.D. 34 when the gospel went to the Gentiles. This was prophesied in Daniel 9:24 when Israel was given 70 weeks or 490 years. This time period began in 457 B.C. with the rebuilding of Jerusalem and ended in A.D. 34. This did not close probation for individual Israelites but for the nation. This same scenario will happen again in the last days.

In Psalms 33:12 we read: "Blessed is the nation whose God is the Lord." In the last days of earth's history, one nation stands out as being favored by God. In the book of Revelation this nation is described as a lamb-like beast. It has "two horns like a lamb" but "spoke like a dragon" (Revelation 13:11). The two horns represent civil and religious liberty. The lamb-like beast is the United States of America (discussed in Revelation 13 (last part)—The Mark of the Beast). This lamb-like beast will make an image "for the beast which was wounded by the sword and yet lived" (Revelation 13:14). This wounded beast or leopard-like beast (Revelation 13:2) is the Papacy, which was mortally wounded in 1798 when Pope Pius VI was captured. This "mortal wound was healed" (Revelation 13:3) in 1929 when the Papal Kingdom was restored by Mussolini. This Papal Kingdom is a church-state union. When the United States passes a universal Sunday law, the United States will become an image to the leopard-like beast. In other words, the United States will become a church-state union just like the Papacy. This "image of the beast" will eventually pass a death penalty for failure to "worship the image of the beast" (Revelation 13:15).

God has protected and blessed the United States of America, since its founding, because this nation has provided religious freedom. Once this religious freedom is cast aside, this country will lose its protection from God. ***The casting down of the***

censer represents the close of probation for the United States as a favored nation under God. It represents the loss of God's protection for this country, just as literal Israel lost God's protection when it began to persecute His true church. This is a corporate judgment on a nation but not on its individuals. The close of probation for individuals will occur once the sealing of God's people is completed, which occurs prior to the fifth trumpet (Revelation 9:4).

The passage of the Sunday law will be a direct attack on God's Law. It will be instituted in the United States when the United States forms a church-state union. The passage of the Sunday law will signal the beginning of judgment on the United States. *The casting down of the censer is God's response to the Sunday law.* It will signal the beginning of the final warnings for the nations to repent. The seven trumpets will follow after the Sunday law. The Sunday law will eventually lead to the mark of the beast (discussed in Revelation 13 (last part)—The Mark of the Beast). The Sunday law will trigger the casting down of the censer and the beginning of the seven trumpets.

> Revelation 8:6: *"Now the seven angels who had the seven trumpets made ready to blow them."*

This text clearly connects the seven trumpets to the censer being cast down in the prior verse. "Now the seven angels...made ready to blow." In other words, the seven trumpets follow closely after the censer is cast down. Some suggest that the seven trumpets represent approximately the same time periods as the seven churches and the seven seals.[6] This approach begins the trumpets in the fourth century. However, the context of Revelation 8 suggests that these seven trumpets occur as part of the last-day events. They appear to begin after God has begun the judgment process discussed under the censer being cast down. Also, the trumpets are described as part of the throne room process (Revelation 8:2) which began after 1844. Furthermore, in the overall context of the book of Revelation, the trumpets occur after the investigative judgment begins described in Revelation 4 and 5 and after the seals have begun to be opened in Revelation 6.

> Revelation 8:7: *"The first angel blew his trumpet, and there followed hail and fire, mixed with blood, which fell on the earth; and a third of the earth was burnt up, and a third of the trees were burnt up, and all green grass was burnt up."*

Historically, some have interpreted this as the Roman Empire when it was invaded by the Visigoths in approximately A.D. 396.[7] However, with each of the trumpets, there are at least two other possible last-day applications. One application is to the spiritual world and the other is to the literal physical world. Many theories have been applied to the seven trumpets both spiritually and literally. However, the spiritual application is the most critical because the book of Revelation is primarily describing the spiritual battle between Satan and his followers and the Lamb and His people. There will also be literal applications that will become apparent as the events unfold.

If this verse is a literal description, then it appears to describe the destruction of a large part of the earth's vegetation by natural causes: hail, lightning and fire.

These natural causes are destructive agents seen in this world today. This picture of severe destruction of vegetation would lead to global famine. This would be consistent with the famine described under the third seal, which occurs just prior to this trumpet. These previous famines and natural disasters had brought about the formation of the image to the beast which led to the casting down of the censer. However, in the spiritual world, the "fire" and "blood" suggest spiritual warfare. This spiritual warfare will involve Satan, as the antichrist, who will be attempting to convince the world's Christians that he has returned as Christ to set up his kingdom. Satan, as the false Christ, will make his appearance in the world after the third seal (Sunday law), which is discussed in Revelation 17 (second part)—The Eighth King. He will work "with all power and with pretended signs and wonders" (2 Thessalonians 2:9).

The "third of the earth" can represent one third of the earth's land that is scorched with fire. This would result in massive famine worldwide. However, the Greek term for earth can also mean land in this text. If this is referring to one-third of the land, then it may be referring to the land of Israel, which would then suggest significant destruction of literal Israel. Some authors suggest that "trees" in the Old Testament refer to people (see Psalms 1:3).[8] If these trees represent people then the "third of the trees" may refer to literal Israel, which would imply significant destruction of Israel's people (see comments on Revelation 9:4).

Grass in the Old Testament was also applied to Israel (Isaiah 40:5-8).[9] If the "green grass" refers to literal Israel in Revelation 8:7 then this text is describing the destruction of the youth of literal Israel. This suggests warfare in the Middle East with significant loss of life (see comments on Revelation 8:8, 9). This is consistent with Daniel 11 which also describes war in the Middle East prior to the abomination that makes desolate being "set up" (Daniel 11:31).

There is one other spiritual application of this verse which must also be considered for the last days. During the time of the first trumpet after the censer is cast down, God's true believers will be persecuted by the leopard-like beast (Revelation 13:7) and many will die. It is possible that the "third of the trees" refers to God's people, which would then imply significant destruction of God's people (see comments on Revelation 9:4) During this time period, after the Sunday law is enacted, God's two witnesses are "clothed in sackcloth" (Revelation 11:3) (discussed in Revelation 11 (first part)—The Two Witnesses). God's two witnesses are His Old Testament and His New Testament. God's Word (His Old Testament and New Testament) will be in sackcloth because God's Law has been changed and a false Christ is now leading the world into falsehood. The two witnesses are described as having "power" to shut the sky that no rain may fall (Revelation 11:6). Also, if anyone would harm them, "fire pours from their mouth" (Revelation 11:5). Both of these powers are alluded to in this first trumpet.

Therefore, the first trumpet has a spiritual application to warfare involving the Christian world, which is described as an attack on one third of the earth (the one third that are Christians). The first trumpet portrays the persecution of God's people by the leopard-like beast during this time period (discussed in Revelation 13 (first part)— The Leopard Beast Healed). The spiritual warfare will lead to literal warfare which will then involve literal Israel leading to its overthrow.

> Revelation 8:8, 9: *"The second angel blew his trumpet,*
> *and something like a great mountain, burning with fire,*
> *was thrown into the sea; and a third of the sea became*
> *blood, a third of the living creatures in the sea died, and*
> *a third of the ships were destroyed."*

Historically, this text has been applied by some to the Vandals, whose navy attacked the coasts of Spain, Italy, and Greece and then invaded Rome in A.D. 455.[10] If this has a literal physical world application, then it could represent an asteroid striking one of the world's oceans or a volcano erupting and destroying the sea life and the merchant ships. However, this remains to be proven and must be considered speculative.

In the context of the last days, a spiritual application is much more likely. The two witnesses, who represent God's Holy Word, are under attack during this time period. This attack begins with the passage of the Sunday law and intensifies when Satan claims to be Christ returned. The two witnesses have "power over the waters to turn them into blood" (Revelation 11:6). Satan, as the false Christ, will attempt to convince the world that he belongs in Israel, which he claims is his kingdom. During this time period many of God's true believers will perish. This spiritual battle will lead to an overthrow of literal Israel. In Psalms 48:1, God's holy city is equated with His holy mountain. The burning "mountain," in this sense, would represent the destruction of Jerusalem. The sea would represent the populated world and the loss of life would be depicted by the blood. This war would involve a major portion of the Christian nations of the world and would involve some of those nations surrounding Israel. This scenario is described in Daniel 11:29, 30, where it describes a battle in the Middle East that occurs prior to the setting "up" of the "abomination that makes desolate" (Daniel 11:31). The abomination that makes desolate is Satan as the false Christ set up in Jerusalem. There must be a literal destruction of Israel in order for the abomination to be set up in Jerusalem. This destruction of literal Israel is described in Revelation 8:8 as a "mountain, burning with fire."

> Revelation 8:10: *"The third angel blew his trumpet, and a*
> *great star fell from heaven, blazing like a torch, and it fell*
> *on a third of the rivers and on the fountains of water."*

Historically, some have applied this trumpet to Attila the Hun who ravaged Europe and died in A.D. 458. He was known for his cruelty.[11] If this trumpet has a literal application, then it could suggest an asteroid striking a fresh water supply and poisoning it. However, this seems unrealistic and remains speculative. The spiritual application is far more significant. In Revelation 12:4, Satan's angels, who are thrown down with him (Revelation 12:9), are described as stars. The "great star" which falls from heaven represents Lucifer. In Isaiah 14:12 Lucifer (Satan) is described as the Day Star: "How you are fallen from heaven, O Day Star, son of Dawn! How you are cut down to the ground, you who laid the nations low!" Isaiah continues his description by saying, "You said in your heart, 'I will ascend to heaven; above the stars of God I will set my throne on high; I will sit on the mount of assembly in the far north;

I will ascend above the heights of the clouds, I will make myself like the Most High'" (Isaiah 14:13, 14).

This fallen star is also mentioned in the fifth trumpet where he is released from the bottomless pit (Revelation 9:1). This fallen star is seen "blazing like a torch" or lamp. When Satan reigns as the false Christ he will light the world up "like a torch." In this context, Satan is a false lamp or light for the world. This fallen star falls on a "third of the rivers and on the fountains of water." The rivers and fountains of water here represent the water of life and also the world's population, which claim to believe in Christ. Satan as the false Christ will poison the message of the true Christ, Who is the source of "a spring of water welling up to eternal life" (John 4:14). Satan will poison this water of life for one third of the world.

- *According to world population statistics approximately one third of the world's population was considered Christians in the year 2000.*[12]

This one "third" represents the Christian population of the world who will be misled by Satan in the last days.

> Revelation 8:11: *"The name of the star is Wormwood.*
> *A third of the waters became wormwood, and many men*
> *died of the water, because it was made bitter."*

Historically, this text has been applied to Attila the Hun when he ravaged Europe (see comments on Revelation 8:10). If there is a literal application to the physical world then this verse suggests a poisoning of the fresh water supply for a large part of the world. This remains speculative. However, there is a spiritual application, which is of far greater significance. The fallen angel or Satan is described as "Wormwood," which refers to bitterness or polluting of the water to make it undrinkable.[13] This is descriptive of how Satan as the eighth king will poison or change God's Word. The time frame described in the third trumpet corresponds to the ascension to the throne of the eighth king. When Satan claims the throne as the false Christ or the eighth king he will kill the two witnesses (Revelation 11:7, 8) (discussed in Revelation 11 (first part)—The Two Witnesses). When Satan reigns as the eighth king he will interpret God's Word, since he will claim authorship of the Holy Scriptures. When Satan interprets God's Word, which is Christianity's river of life, it will be poisoned and many men will die because they believe his lies. The Word of God, or God's truth, will "become wormwood" or bitter. The third trumpet is describing the Christian world once Satan, as the false Christ, has taken his throne.

> Revelation 8:12: *"The fourth angel blew his trumpet, and*
> *a third of the sun was struck, and a third of the moon and a*
> *third of the stars, so that a third of their light was darkened;*
> *a third of the day was kept from shining, and likewise a*
> *third of the night."*

Historically, this fourth trumpet has been applied to the gradual fall of the Roman Empire where first the emperors, then the senators and finally the counsels lost their power. This process began in A.D. 476.[14] If this trumpet is to have a literal fulfillment then it suggests partial darkening of the sun, moon and stars prior to the fifth trumpet. The spiritual application of this text is clearly connected to the prior trumpet. This trumpet portrays a spiritual darkening of the world. The "sun" represents Jesus and His gospel of light. The "moon" represents God's Word, which reflects the light of the Sun. The "stars" represent God's prophets and people, who reflect God's light to the world. When Satan reigns as the eighth king or the abomination that makes desolate, he will claim to be Christ returned. This will clearly obscure the view of the true Sun and His Word. Satan will convince the world he is Christ and Jesus' true believers will have difficulty convincing the world that Satan is not Christ. This trumpet symbolizes the spiritual darkness during the reign of the eighth king. When Satan reigns as the false Christ he will block the light of truth from Christ (the sun), His word (the moon), and His people (the stars). The one "third" reflects the portion of the world affected by this spiritual darkness. This one "third" represents the Christian population of the world.

> Revelation 8:13: *"Then I looked, and I heard an eagle crying*
> *with a loud voice, as it flew in midheaven, 'Woe, woe, woe*
> *to those who dwell on the earth, at the blasts of the other*
> *trumpets which the three angels are about to blow!"*

John now sees an eagle "crying with a loud voice." The eagle has been seen before in the throne room as the fourth creature (Revelation 4:7). The eagle was associated with the fourth seal (Revelation 6:7), which involved a rider named death. The fourth seal was connected to the eighth king, who would have power over one-fourth of the world (representing those countries Satan would totally dominate as the eighth king). The eagle represented God's protection of His people during the fourth seal and beyond. Now, the eagle is seen announcing with "a loud voice" as it "flew in midheaven" (Revelation 8:13). A loud or mighty voice is a call to judgment, as is seen in many other places in the book of Revelation: Revelation 14:7, Revelation 16:1, Revelation 18:2, and Revelation 19:17. Flying in mid heaven indicates a message to the entire world as is seen in Revelation 14:6. The following three trumpets are part of the judgment, which the world has earned by allowing Satan to be their king.

The first four trumpets were not worldwide. They affected only part of the world, which was described as one third. This one-third represents the Christian portion of the world, which will be involved in setting up the abomination that makes desolate in Jerusalem. The last three trumpets are worldwide. The first four trumpets are warnings to the world and the world can still choose to serve the true Christ. However, the last three trumpets are called "woes" and are part of the world's judgment. Once these "woes" begin it will be too late to change because God's people will have been sealed (discussed in Revelation 9—The Seven Trumpets: The First and Second Woes). The last three trumpets will occur after the close of probation and will coincide with the seven last plagues. When the seven last plagues fall, the temple in heaven will be closed because "no one could enter the temple until the seven plagues of the seven angels were ended" (Revelation 15:8). This closure of the temple confirms that the investigative judgment has been completed. This marks the close of probation. This is "the time of the end" prophesied in Daniel 11:35 when the wise will no longer fall. Satan will begin his reign as the eighth king or false Christ in the third trumpet. As the false Christ he has "power over" one-fourth of the world (Revelation 6:7) and poisons one third of the world (the world's Christians) (Revelation 8:10, 11). However, he still does not have total control of the world. During the fifth trumpet Satan will become world king. The beginning of the fifth trumpet marks the close of probation and the sealing of God's people.

SUMMARY

The seven trumpets are introduced with the casting down of the censer. The casting down of the censer represents the close of probation for the United States as a favored nation under God. The casting down of the censer represents judgment on the church-state union formed by the United States when it enacts the universal Sunday law. The seven trumpets begin after the Sunday law is enacted. The first two trumpets describe the spiritual and literal warfare, which goes on in the world prior to the setting up of the eighth king in Jerusalem. This eighth king or Satan as the false Christ is the abomination that makes desolate. The third trumpet describes the fallen star or Lucifer once he reigns as the eighth king, claiming to be Christ returned. As the false Christ he will poison God's truth. He will poison one third of the world's population (the Christians). This spiritual darkness is continued under the fourth trumpet where Satan is the interpreter of God's Holy Scriptures and hides the real Son of Righteousness from view. The fourth trumpet ends the time of warning. The next trumpet will begin the judgment or woes upon the wicked. Probation closes prior to or at the beginning of the fifth trumpet since God's people are described as sealed in this trumpet (Revelation 9:4). The events of Revelation 8 are outlined in the following graph.

Revelation Chapter 8

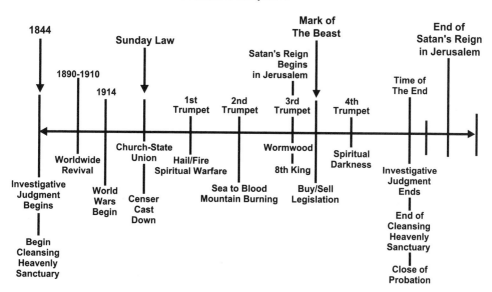

[1] Nichol, Francis D. (Ed.). *The Seventh-day Adventist Bible Commentary* (Review and Herald Publishing Association, Washington, D.C.) 1957, Vol. 7, p. 787.

[2] Ibid.

[3] Ibid.

[4] Ibid.

[5] Ibid. p. 788.

[6] Ibid.

[7] Ibid.

[8] Naden, Roy C., *The Lamb Among The Beasts* (Review and Herald Publishing Association, Hagerstown. Maryland) 1996, p. 143.

[9] Ibid.

[10] Nichol, Francis D. (Ed.). *The Seventh-day Adventist Bible Commentary* (Review and Herald Publishing Association, Washington, D.C.) 1957, Vol. 7, p. 789.

[11] Ibid.

[12] Gordan-Conwell Theological Seminary, South Hamilton, Massachusetts, World Christian Database (2004, March). *Largest Religion (by Country) in 2000.* Retrieved March 22, 2004 from the World Christian Database Web site: http://www.worldchristiandatabase.org/wed/esweb.asp?

[13] Nichol, Francis D. (Ed.). *The Seventh-day Adventist Bible Commentary* (Review and Herald Publishing Association, Washington, D.C.) 1957, Vol. 7, p. 789

[14] Ibid.

Revelation 9
The Seven Trumpets:
The First and Second Woes

Revelation 8 begins with the seventh seal and then describes the casting down of the censer. The casting down of the censer signals the beginning of the trumpets. The casting down of the censer represents the beginning of judgment on the image of the beast. This casting down of the censer represents the withdrawal of God's blessings on the lamb-like beast. The lamb-like beast will change into the image of the beast when it becomes a church-state union. The formation of the church-state union will be signaled by the passage of a universal Sunday law (discussed in Revelation 13 (last part)—The Mark of the Beast).

The first four trumpets are warnings and represent God's attempt to warn the world that probation is soon to close. The first trumpet represents both spiritual warfare as well as literal warfare. This warfare will precede the overthrow of literal Israel, which is described in the second trumpet. The third trumpet pictures the eighth king as a fallen star named Wormwood. This fallen star is Satan as the false Christ. Satan will poison truth and spiritual darkness will follow as described in the fourth trumpet (discussed in Revelation 8—The Seven Trumpets: God's Final Warnings).

The last three trumpets are introduced as "Woe, woe, woe" (Revelation 8:13). The last three trumpets are no longer warnings, but are judgments, which will fall on the earth. Each of these woes gets progressively worse. Each of these woes overlaps with some of the seven last plagues. Each of these woes occurs after the close of probation because God's people are sealed prior to the first woe (Revelation 9:4).

> Revelation 9:1: *"And the fifth angel blew his trumpet, and I saw a star fallen from heaven to earth, and he was given the key of the shaft of the bottomless pit."*

The fifth trumpet introduces the first "woe" of Revelation 8:13. Historically, this trumpet has been applied to the Saracens. The "key" was thought by some to represent the fall of Kohsrau in A.D. 628, which ended the Persian Empire. The "bottomless pit" represented the Arabian deserts.[1] If this trumpet has a literal physical world application, then there appears to be some type of insect, which spares the vegetation and attacks mankind. This is speculative.

There clearly is a spiritual application for this prophecy. This star, falling from heaven to earth, is described in Isaiah 14:12-14 and also in Revelation 12:4. In Isaiah 14:12-14, this "Day Star" is Lucifer. In Revelation 12:4, the "stars of heaven" are angels who "were thrown down with him" (Revelation 12:9), where "him" refers to the dragon or Satan (Revelation 12:9). Satan is the "star fallen from heaven to earth." Satan is also the "great star fell from heaven" in Revelation 8:10. That star's name "is Wormwood" (Revelation 8:11). Satan is described in the fifth trumpet as being given "the key of the shaft of the bottomless pit."

The "bottomless pit" is a pit of circumstances. Revelation 20:1 describes an angel with "the key of the bottomless pit and a great chain." In Revelation 20:2, 3, Satan is seized and bound for 1000 years and thrown "into the pit." The "pit" is shut and sealed over him. The reason he is chained in the "pit" is so he can "deceive the nations no more" (Revelation 20:3). However, he will be "loosed for a little while" after the 1000 years are ended (Revelation 20:3). In Revelation 20:7, 8, Satan is loosed from his "pit" and allowed to deceive the nations one last time. The "pit" that Satan is bound in is the "pit" of circumstances in which he exists during the 1000 years. Satan is bound by circumstances, since all the wicked people are dead and he has no one to tempt or deceive. This "pit" is removed when the dead are raised at the Third Coming of Christ (Revelation 20:7, 8).

The "pit" of circumstances referred to in Revelation 9:1 is simply a different set of circumstances. God has kept Satan bound by certain circumstances since the creation of the earth. Satan has never been free to become leader of the world. Satan has been controlled by God's rules of engagement. Satan's powers have been limited. If God had not done this, Satan would have long ago destroyed mankind. In Revelation 9:1, God is allowing Satan new freedom. God is now allowing Satan the right to rule the world as world king. However, he is not giving Satan full reign over mankind. He is told he can torture the wicked but not kill them (Revelation 9:5). He is not allowed to "harm" God's sealed people (Revelation 9:4). Satan will not be totally released to kill the wicked until the four angels are released, which will occur in the sixth trumpet.This first woe allows Satan, the fallen star, to rule the world. This truly will be a woe. The fact that he cannot kill the wicked (Revelation 9:5) indicates that Satan still has some restrictions. Those restrictions will be removed at the beginning of the next woe.

> Revelation 9:2: *"he opened the shaft of the bottomless pit,*
> *and from the shaft rose smoke like the smoke of a great*
> *furnace, and the sun and the air were darkened with the*
> *smoke from the shaft."*

Historically, this has been applied to the spread of Islam, which darkened the sun of Christianity.[2] The smoke was considered to be false teachings blocking the truth. If this trumpet has a literal physical application, then the smoke is the source of the locusts, which will torture mankind. This is speculative and can not be proven at this time.

The spiritual application relates to the fallen star or Satan. Satan has previously been "set up" in Jerusalem as the "abomination that makes desolate" (Daniel 11:31) or the eighth king (Revelation 17:11). He has claimed to be Christ returned and has done many "signs and wonders" (2 Thessalonians 2:9). Satan is now allowed to take over world domination. Satan would never be satisfied with ruling only a portion of the world. He would require total dominance and control. God has kept Satan from this position because God knows what will happen to the world when Satan is allowed to be king of the world.

The smoke from the shaft can be thought of as the falsehoods with which Satan as the false Christ has covered the world. The darkening of the sun and air can be considered the obscuring of all truth. Spiritually the world will be in darkness. This is a progression of the spiritual darkness, which affected only one third of the world in the fourth trumpet. In the fourth trumpet Satan's falsehoods affected mainly the world's Christian population (one-third of the world's people). Now his spiritual darkness will affect the entire world. This woe is universal and worldwide.

> Revelation 9:3: *"Then from the smoke came locusts on the earth, and they were given power like the power of scorpions of the earth."*

Historically, the locusts have been thought to represent the Moslem Arabian armies.[3] If there is a literal physical application, then these must represent some type of insect attack on mankind. Again, this must be considered speculative.

The spiritual application of this text is related to the falsehoods that come forth from Satan as the eighth king. The smoke represents prior false teachings. The "locusts" will arise out of these false teachings. These "locusts" will be empowered by Satan. Satan will convince the world that these "locusts" are his representatives, once he begins to reign as world king. These "locusts" will have the power of scorpions. These "locusts" will harm mankind but only those who believe them. God's people are already sealed and they will not accept their falsehoods and, therefore, will not be harmed (Revelation 9:4). These "locusts" represent Satan's messengers sent as angels of light to the world with "power" to rule.

> Revelation 9:4: *"they were told not to harm the grass of the earth or any green growth or any tree, but only those of mankind who have not the seal of God upon their foreheads."*

Historically, this text has been applied to the Saracens who protected the land and the conquered people.[4] If this is considered to have a literal application, then the vegetation will be spared and only mankind will be affected by this attack. This remains speculative.

The spiritual application of this text is consistent with the prior interpretation. The falsehoods that Satan pours "like a river out of his mouth" (Revelation 12:15) will not affect the "grass of the earth or any green growth or any tree." These falsehoods, which will be brought by Satan's messengers, will only harm those of mankind "who have not the seal of God upon their foreheads." Those who are not sealed by God are the wicked that have been sealed by Satan. Anyone who does not have God's seal upon his forehead will have Satan's seal on his "forehead or on his hand" (Revelation 14:9). Satan's seal or mark will ultimately lead to destruction (Revelation 14:10). This seal or mark of the beast is the Sunday law once the buy-sell penalty has been enforced (discussed in Revelation 13 (last part)—The Mark of the Beast). In the context of this verse, the grass of the earth and the green growth and the trees would represent God's sealed people who cannot be harmed by these falsehoods. This verse suggests that Revelation 8:7, which discusses "green grass" and "trees," is also describing God's people.

In the context of the last days, this text reveals that God's people will be sealed prior to the fifth trumpet since the fifth trumpet can only harm those *"who have not the seal of God"* (emphasis supplied). The sealed are called the 144,000 (Revelation 7:3, 4). These 144,000 are made up of 12 tribes of 12,000 each (Revelation 7:4-8).

These 144,000, who are sealed, are those who "can stand before it" (Revelation 6:17). This question in Revelation 6:17 was asked to find out who could stand the great day of the "wrath of the Lamb" (Revelation 6:16). These 144,000 are those who will be alive at Jesus' Second Coming and represent the faithful living at the end of time. The 144,000 are those alive at the close of probation who will live through Daniel's "time of trouble, such as never has been since there was a nation" (Daniel 12:1). The close of probation represents the time in history after which the "filthy" will "still be filthy" and the "holy" will "still be holy" (Revelation 22:11). The close of probation occurs when the investigative judgment ends. The seven last plagues begin to fall once the investigative judgment ends and the temple can no longer be entered, which is described in Revelation 15:8.

Thus, the fifth trumpet is marked by three important events. First, it cannot occur until God's people are sealed. This means it will occur after the close of probation. Second, this trumpet marks Satan's release from God's restrictions on his ability to rule the entire world. Satan will become world king. Third, the plagues will begin to fall since God's wrath is now going to be poured out and probation has closed.

> Revelation 9:5: *"they were allowed to torture them for five months, but not to kill them, and their torture was like the torture of a scorpion, when it stings a man."*

Historically, this verse has been applied to the Saracens or to the Turks. Josiah Litch interpreted the five months or 150 days as 150 years (one prophetic day equals one literal year). He applied this time period to 1299 to 1449 during which time the Turkish Empire was on the rise.[5]

If this verse has a literal application to natural events, then this torture will go on for 150 days or five months. This torture will be painful but not fatal. This parallels the first plague of Revelation 16:2 where those with the mark of the beast or Satan's seal suffer painful sores.

The spiritual application for last-day events suggests that God will control Satan for the first "five months" of his reign as world king. He will not be allowed to kill the wicked indiscriminately. His falsehoods will torture men but not kill them. This time span applied to last-day events is clearly not 150 years, since that would far exceed the other time prophecies related to Satan's end-time reign. It would also be inconsistent with a time of the end application.

> Revelation 9:6: *"And in those days men will seek death and will not find it; they will long to die, and death flies from them."*

Historically, Josiah Litch has applied this verse to the time period from 1299 to 1449. This 150 year period represents the time during which the Turkish Empire was expanding.[6] If this verse has a literal application to natural events, it suggests that mankind will be suffering terribly from this attack. This is consistent with the suffering described under the first plague where those with the mark of the beast "cursed the God of heaven for their pain and sores" (Revelation 16:11). It is important to note that only the people who have the mark of the beast have the plagues fall on them (Revelation 16:2). These are the same people who do not have God's seal on their foreheads. You can only have God's seal or Satan's seal but not both.

Spiritually, this text suggests that men will be suffering extremely. Men will want to die but death will not come. Men will be depressed to the point of suicide but death "flies from them." Satan's falsehoods will not give them any peace or joy. Satan's lies lead to further pain and suffering. His promises of peace and joy will be seen to be false.

> Revelation 9:7: *"In appearance the locusts were like horses arrayed for battle; on their heads were what looked like crowns of gold; their faces were like human faces."*

Historically, this verse has been applied to the Arabian military cavalry. The "human faces" suggested that human beings were involved.[7] If this verse applies directly to the physical events of the last days, these attacking locusts are unique in appearance.

Spiritually, the portrayal of the "locusts" that are "like horses" suggests power. This power was described in Revelation 9:3. These angels will have power over the earth to rule. These "locusts" or angels will be powerful and hard to defend against. These "locusts" or Satan's angels will wear crowns of gold. The crowns of gold suggest victory over the world. These angels will appear human and have human faces.

> Revelation 9:8: *"their hair like women's hair, and their teeth like lions' teeth."*

Historically, this text has been applied to the long hair of the Arabian troops and the lions' teeth have suggested strength.[8] Again, if these are literal insects then these locusts are unique.

Spiritually, the "hair like women's hair" suggests beauty. These angels or messengers from Satan will be beautiful to behold. The lions' teeth suggest the strength and power of these messengers as well as the danger involved.

> Revelation 9:9: *"they had scales like iron breastplates, and the noise of their wings was like the noise of many chariots with horses rushing into battle."*

Historically, this text has been applied to the attacking Turks during the 150 year period of 1299 to 1449.[9] If this has a literal or physical application, then it suggests that these locusts will be able to fly and will be easily heard in flight. Again this is speculative.

Spiritually, these symbols suggest that these angels will be extremely resistant to attack and will be overpowering in their onslaught. Men will not be able to resist them and God's help will no longer be available. The presence of "wings" is consistent with these locusts representing Satan's angels. The "noise" of these wings and the "horses" again suggest power. These will be powerful, awesome angels with an almost irresistible attraction. This will be the first time in earth's history that God has allowed Satan to reveal his angels to the world and it will be extremely convincing.

> Revelation 9:10: *"they have tails like scorpions, and sting, and their power of hurting men for five months lies in their tails."*

Historically, this verse has been applied by Josiah Litch from 1299 to 1449 as previously discussed.[10] If this has a literal application, it suggests that the poisonous effects of these insects are in their tails. This remains speculative. This verse suggests this plague of locusts will last for 150 days.

Spiritually, this verse reiterates that this attack on those who do not have "the seal of God upon their foreheads" (Revelation 9:4) will last for five months or 150 days. The sting or injury occurs because of the poison contained in the tail, which is like the scorpion. The poison represents the falsehoods which men will accept as truth in the hope that it will save them. The angels or messengers of Satan will be the ones providing this poison.

> Revelation 9:11: *"They have as king over them the angel of the bottomless pit; his name in Hebrew is Abad'don and in Greek he is called Apol'lyon (or Destroyer)."*

Historically, this king has been thought to represent the king of the Turks, Osman I, who founded the Ottoman Empire.[11] If this text has a literal application to the last days, then it suggests that the locusts are reigned over by "the angel of the bottomless pit."

Spiritually, this text confirms the connection of the locusts or Satan's angels to Satan their "king." These angels have an "angel" who reigns "over them." The "angel of the bottomless pit" is Satan as was described in the discussion under Revelation 9:1. Satan is the "fallen star" of Revelation 9:1. Here, he is confirmed as an "angel." The "bottomless pit" represents the circumstances that Satan is bound under on this earth. These circumstances are the rules of engagement, which God has imposed on Satan to keep him from destroying the world completely.

This verse further describes Satan as king. This is the only place in the book of Revelation where Satan is called king. This designation is significant. Satan will reign as king of the world during the fifth trumpet. Prior to this, in the third trumpet, he became the spiritual king of Christianity or the eighth king, and as the eighth king he poisoned one third of the world (Christianity). As the eighth king he took over Jerusalem as his capital city. Satan now becomes the world's king during the fifth trumpet. This is why it is described as the first woe. Satan is now able to rule the world. Satan, however, still has some restrictions on his activities. These will be released under the next trumpet. The exact time when Satan becomes world king during this trumpet is not given and therefore the close of probation, which precedes it, cannot be known.

The terms applied to this angel further confirm that this "angel" is Satan. His name is "Abad'don" in Hebrew and "Apol'lyon" in Greek. This name means "Destroyer" or destruction. What better name is there for Satan then the "Destroyer"? This is exactly what Satan is going to do under the next trumpet: destroy as many men and women as he can before time runs out.

Revelation 9:12: *"The first woe has passed; behold, two woes are still to come."*

This text confirms that the fifth trumpet is the first "woe." It is a "woe" or judgment because Satan has been released from God's restrictions against him ruling the world. Satan has been released from the pit of circumstances, in which God has held him. Satan has been allowed to reign as king of the world for the first time in earth's history even though Satan has claimed to be prince of this world since he deceived Adam and Eve. This truly is a "woe" for the wicked as well as the righteous. Satan will pursue the righteous in an attempt to annihilate them. The next two woes only get worse! The second "woe" or the sixth trumpet will release God's four angels allowing Satan to finally kill as many of the wicked as he wishes. The wicked he will kill are those who attempt to rebel against him. The third "woe" is the end of the world as we know it. It is the Second Coming of Jesus Christ.

Revelation 9:13: *"Then the sixth angel blew his trumpet, and I heard a voice from the four horns of the golden altar before God."*

Historically, the sixth trumpet has been applied by Josiah Litch to the Turkish Empire during its period of domination. Josiah Litch applied the fifth trumpet to the rise of the Turks to power.[12]

Spiritually, the sixth trumpet represents the last half of Satan's reign as the world's king. During the first five months of his reign, he could not kill the wicked who had "not the seal of God" (Revelation 9:5). During the sixth trumpet, Satan will be allowed freedom to become the "Destroyer" (Revelation 9:11).

John has seen this golden altar previously. The souls under this altar were crying out for vengeance (Revelation 6:9-10). They were told to wait "until the number of their fellow servants and their brethren should be complete, who were to be killed" (Revelation 6:11). This number was completed prior to the fifth trumpet (Revelation 9:4), when the last of the righteous died and probation closed. The fifth trumpet marked the completion of the sealing of God's righteous saved, represented by the 144,000 of Revelation 7:3, 4. The "voice" that is heard is God's voice of vengeance now releasing the four angels. This is God's continued response to the souls under the altar who were asking for vengeance. God's wrath (Revelation 16:1) had begun with the first plague (Revelation 16:2).

Revelation 9:14: *"saying to the sixth angel who had the trumpet, 'Release the four angels who are bound at the great river Euphrates.'"*

Historically, some have applied the "four angels" to the four Turkish sultans during the time of dominion of the Turkish Empire.[13] The Euphrates was considered the actual Euphrates River through which the Turks entered the Byzantine Empire.

If this trumpet has a literal application, then the river Euphrates must be considered the actual river involved. This suggests the possibility of massive warfare centered in the Middle East and focused on Jerusalem. This is consistent with Daniel 11:40-45 which covers the "time of the end" (Daniel 11:40) and describes warfare in the Middle East. This is also consistent with the fact that Satan will occupy his throne in the city "where their Lord was crucified" (Revelation 11:8) which is Jerusalem, Israel.

Spiritually, the sixth trumpet represents Satan's reign as the world's king in Jerusalem. His reign as world king began during the fifth trumpet. However, he previously had begun his reign as spiritual king during the third trumpet. This reign as world king will extend to the end of the 1290 day prophecy of Daniel 12:11.

The seven last plagues will fall in "a single day" (Revelation 18:8). This one day implies a one year period (one prophetic day equals one literal year). One literal day would be an unreasonably short time for the wicked to be repaid for their wickedness. Also, the torment suggested in the plagues would make little sense if it was over in one day. The plagues will fall after the close of probation, since they are God's wrath (Revelation 15:1) upon the wicked who have the mark of the beast (Revelation 16:1, 2) and the sealing of the wicked is completed only at the close of probation. The fifth trumpet, which begins after the close of probation, lasts 150 days. This also suggests that the plagues will continue for approximately one year rather than one day. Beginning with the fifth trumpet Satan will have the power worldwide to persecute the 144,000, who have been sealed. However, God will protect them. This is the time of trouble of Daniel 12:1. This is the "great tribulation" Jesus warned of in Matthew 24:21. The fifth trumpet also marks the beginning of "the time of the end" of Daniel 11:40. It will be shown later that the plagues overlap the fifth and sixth trumpets and lead into the seventh plague, which is the seventh trumpet or the Second Coming of Jesus Christ.

> Revelation 9:15: *"So the four angels were released, who had been held ready for the hour, the day, the month, and the year, to kill a third of mankind."*

Historically, this text has been interpreted by Josiah Litch as a time prophecy. One "year" equals 360 days; one "month" equals 30 days; one "day" equals one day; one "hour" equals one twenty-fourth of a day. Using one prophetic day equals one literal year; the total equals 391 years and two weeks. Josiah Litch predicted that the fall of the Turkish Empire would occur on August 11, 1840. This prediction came true.[14] This prediction apparently led to the conversion of many Moslems at that time. Certainly God used this interpretation to save souls. That does not however, preclude other applications, which may save additional souls prior to the time of the end.

Historically, the one-third has been interpreted as a significant or substantial part.[15] If this trumpet has a literal application, then the number of mankind killed is immense. A literal interpretation would suggest up to two billion people killed based on the current world population. However, at the time of the end, the world's population will probably be much smaller due to the natural disasters, wars and famine which precede this trumpet. Unfortunately, a literal application of this verse is probable.

Spiritually, this trumpet portrays God releasing His four angels who symbolize God's control over Satan's actions. This is also described in Revelation 7:1: "After this I saw four angels standing at the four corners of the earth, holding back the four winds of the earth, that no wind might blow on earth or sea or against any tree." These same four angels were told "Do not harm the earth or the sea or the trees, till we have sealed the servants of our God upon their foreheads" (Revelation 7:3). This attack on the earth, sea, and trees will involve the seven last plagues (Revelation 16:2, 3). This sealing was completed prior to the fifth trumpet (Revelation 9:4). God's four angels now being "released" in the sixth trumpet symbolize God's final release of the control He has exercised over Satan throughout the history of this earth. Once Satan is released, the world will experience the second woe.

> Revelation 9:16: *"The number of the troops of cavalry was twice ten thousand times ten thousand; I heard their number."*

Historically, this verse has been thought to represent a vast innumerable number.[16] If this has a literal application, then it represents the largest army ever assembled: "twice ten thousand times ten thousand" equals 200 million people.

Spiritually, the Euphrates can be considered a symbol of the world over which Babylon rules. Ancient Babylon sat upon the Euphrates. Spiritual Babylon represents apostate Christianity and particularly the union of apostate Protestantism and apostate Catholicism. This spiritual Babylon will be ruled over by Satan as the false Christ. The sixth trumpet pictures spiritual warfare with Satan's troops massed to attack. Spiritually, the troops can be considered Satan's angels who are now free to attack the earth and the sea. The earth represents the physical environment and the sea represents the world's population. The trees represent God's people. This is the continuation of the time of trouble for God's people (the great tribulation).

> Revelation 9:17: *"And this was how I saw the horses in my vision; the riders wore breast plates the color of fire and of sapphire and of sulphur, and the heads of the horses were like lions' heads, and fire and smoke and sulphur issued from their mouths."*

Historically, some have seen the color of fire, sapphire, and sulphur as symbols of the Turkish uniform of red, blue, and yellow. Others have suggested that fire, smoke and brimstone parallel the fire, sapphire and sulphur. Some have applied the use of gunpowder to the fire, smoke and sulphur described in this text, since the general use of gunpowder in warfare began during the Turkish Empire.[17] A literal application of this text would suggest the troops are cavalry who wear red, blue and yellow. It is possible that the horses here represent modern tanks, which issue smoke and fire from their guns.

Spiritually, the troops represent Satan's angels on the attack. The fire, smoke, and sulphur symbolize the end result of following Satan's lies or falsehoods (Revelation 20:10). The fire, smoke and sulphur also symbolize the fourth, fifth and sixth plagues occurring at this time. The lions' head suggests ferocity and the mouth is the source of the false teachings which Satan's angels spread.

> Revelation 9:18: *"By these three plagues a third of mankind was killed, by the fire and smoke and sulphur issuing from their mouths."*

Historically, this text was thought to be connected to the prior text representing either the Turkish uniform or the results of gunpowder.[18] Taking a literal approach would suggest that one-third of mankind will be killed by these three plagues using modern warfare techniques.

Spiritually, this verse clearly connects the events of the sixth trumpet to the seven last plagues. The fourth plague involves the sun and burning "men with fire" (Revelation 16:8). The fifth plague involves darkness: "and its kingdom was in darkness" (Revelation 16:10). This correlates with the smoke of the sixth trumpet. The sixth plague involves the final battle of Armageddon, which correlates with the sulphur. The spiritual warfare going on during this time is between Satan's angels who are attempting to destroy God's people and God's angels who are protecting the 144,000 from destruction. Simultaneously, the plagues are falling on the wicked as a manifestation of God's final wrath (Revelation 15:1). This text suggests that the plagues are what kill one-third of mankind. The sixth plague is a huge battle called Armageddon. This connection to the sixth plague makes a literal application probable, as well as a spiritual application. The "mouths" represent the source of the false teachings, which have led to the destruction of all these people.

> Revelation 9:19: *"For the power of the horses is in their mouths and in their tails; their tails are like serpents, with heads, and by means of them they wound."*

Historically, the horsetail was the Turkish standard.[19] This text has been applied to the Turkish dominion and subsequent fall predicted by Josiah Litch. A literal application of this verse, related to the previous global warfare, would suggest that this is a description of military tanks and weapons used in modern warfare. Horses here would represent tanks with guns in front and in back able to pour out fire and smoke and sulphur.

Spiritually, this power "in their mouths" represents the falsehoods that Satan and his agents use to control the world and deceive it. The serpent's head suggests deception, since the serpent was the one who originally deceived mankind. The end result of this deception will be the suffering and loss of life that will be experienced by those who "have not the seal of God upon their foreheads (Revelation 9:4).

> Revelation 9:20: *"The rest of mankind, who were not killed by these plagues, did not repent of the works of their hands nor give up worshiping demons and idols of gold and silver and bronze and stone and wood, which cannot either see or hear or walk."*

Historically, this verse has been interpreted to mean that the majority will survive but do not learn from the suffering of the others.[20] Using a literal application to time of the end events this verse suggests that the survivors continue to reject God. The survivors choose to follow after idols of their own making.

Spiritually, this verse confirms that the "plagues" are the real source of death and suffering. The "plagues" are what killed those "who bore the mark of the beast and worshiped its image" (Revelation 16:2). The "plagues" here referred to are the fourth, fifth, and sixth plagues of Revelation 16:8-16. These plagues involve fire, smoke, and brimstone. These plagues involve a global battle just prior to the Second Coming.

The "works of their hands" can be applied to idols the unrepentant made.[21] It can also describe their wicked behavior. A third application involves the mark "on his hand" of Revelation 14:9. The mark of the beast can be obtained by either a belief or commitment, which gives a mark in the forehead, or by actions with no belief or commitment, which gives a mark in the hand. The failure of these people to repent of the "works of their hands" could suggest their continued refusal to abandon this mark, which they obtained by their actions.

These unrepentant also refuse to give up worship of "demons and idols." In the context of the time of the end this demon worship refers specifically to the worship of the false Christ, which is Satan, the abomination that makes desolate. Those unrepentant worldwide, who do not accept Satan as their god, will continue to worship man-made idols or false gods. These "idols of gold and silver and bronze and stone and wood" represent anything that man puts between himself and God.[22]

> Revelation 9:21: *"nor did they repent of their murders or their sorceries or their immorality or their thefts."*

This list of sins, which the unrepentant refuse to abandon, is similar to the lists in Revelation 21:8 and Revelation 22:15, which describe the characteristics of the wicked, who are lost. The prostitution or immorality connects them to Babylon, the great mother of harlots (Revelation 17:5). The sorcerers also connects them to Babylon (Revelation 18:23).[23] These characteristics of the unrepentant are evidence that they are members of Babylon. In this context, Babylon represents all the apostate religions and those who refuse to "come out of her" will "share in her plagues" (Revelation 18:4).

SUMMARY

It can be seen that there are at least three possible applications of the seven trumpets. The first application is historical and the historical application was God ordained in order to save souls in the 1800s and early 1900s. The second application is a literal interpretation of these symbols applied to last-day events. Some of these events will be literal, but it is too early to ascertain which will be literal and which will remain symbolic. It appears speculative at this time to attempt a literal application to all the symbols of these trumpets. However, at least the sixth and seventh trumpets have a literal application. The third application of each of these trumpets is to apply them to the spiritual battle in the last days. There is clear support of this spiritual application in both Daniel and Revelation.

The spiritual end-of-time application of the fifth trumpet applies this trumpet to Satan. Satan is the fallen star, who is released from the pit of circumstances in which God has held him. Satan will now be allowed to become world king, something he has been denied since the fall of man. The fifth trumpet or first woe marks the beginning of the seven last plagues. The seven last plagues will fall on those with the mark of the beast or Satan's seal (Revelation 16:2). God's people are sealed prior to the fifth trumpet, since this trumpet can only harm those who are not sealed of God (Revelation 9:4).

The close of probation occurs once God's people are sealed. This means that the 144,000 are sealed and the close of probation has occurred prior to the fifth trumpet. The close of probation occurs when the investigative judgment has ended and the temple in heaven is no longer being entered (Revelation 15:8). The temple in heaven can no longer be entered when the seven plagues begin to fall (Revelation 15:8). Since the sealing is completed and probation has closed and the plagues are beginning to fall, this means that the fifth and sixth trumpets parallel the seven last plagues. This becomes apparent in the sixth trumpet when the fourth, fifth and sixth plagues are alluded to and blamed for the death of one-third of mankind. The fifth trumpet will last for five months. The seven last plagues will last for one year (Revelation 18:8). The fifth trumpet represents the first five months of the year of the plagues. The seven last plagues will end with the Second Coming (discussed in Revelation 16— The Seven Last Plagues). The locusts of the fifth trumpet represent Satan's angels, which Satan uses to deceive the world. Satan is called king in this trumpet but his real name is Apol'lyon or Destroyer.

The sixth trumpet represents the second woe. The three woes are God's judgments on the earth. The sixth trumpet occurs when God releases His four angels who are still restraining Satan. He was partially released during the third trumpet and allowed to be spiritual leader (eighth king). He was further released during the fifth trumpet and allowed to be world king. The sixth trumpet will mark Satan's final release from God's rules of engagement. The first three plagues will fall during the fifth trumpet. Then during the sixth trumpet (second woe) the next three plagues will fall and one-third of mankind will die. Satan will not be allowed to kill the wicked during the first woe but he will kill untold millions during the second woe. Satan will also be allowed to unveil his angels as described under the fifth trumpet. During this "time of the end" or "time of trouble" (Daniel 11:40, Daniel 12:1), Satan will attempt to destroy God's people but will not succeed because of God's protection (Revelation 12:14). The sixth plague will involve a great battle called Armageddon. This will occur in the Middle East (discussed in Revelation 16—The Seven Last Plagues). Those not killed by the first six plagues will be destroyed by the seventh, which is the Second Coming of Christ. The events of Revelation 8 and 9 are outlined on the following graph.

Revelation Chapters 8 & 9

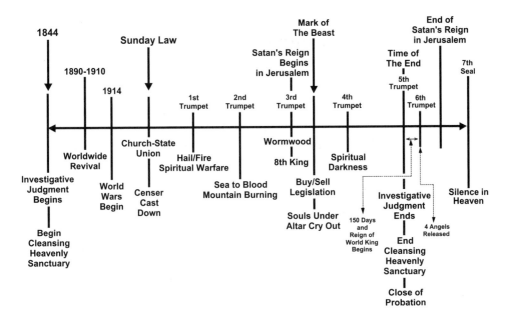

1   Nichol, Francis D. (Ed.). *The Seventh-day Adventist Bible Commentary* (Review and Herald Publishing Association, Washington, D.C.) 1957, Vol. 7, p. 791.
2   Ibid.
3   Ibid.
4   Ibid.
5   Ibid. p. 795.
6   Ibid.
7   Ibid. p. 792.
8   Ibid.
9   Ibid. p. 795.
10 Ibid.
11 Ibid. p. 792.
12 Ibid. p. 795.
13 Ibid. p. 793.
14 Ibid. p. 795.
15 Ibid. p. 788.
16 Ibid. p. 793.
17 Ibid. p. 794.
18 Ibid. p. 793, 794.
19 Ibid. p. 794.
20 Ibid.
21 Ibid.
22 Ibid.
23 Ibid. p. 866.

Revelation 11 (last part)
The Seventh Trumpet: The Final Woe

In order to understand the seventh trumpet, we must first understand why John wrote the book of Revelation. In the very first sentence of Revelation 1:1, John states that this is "The revelation of Jesus Christ." The focus of the entire book is on Jesus, His people, and His ultimate return to this world to save those who have accepted His gift of eternal life. Jesus is the only source of eternal life: "for there is no other name under heaven given among men by which we must be saved" (Acts 4:12). The Greek word *"apokalupsis,"* translated "revelation" means "unveiling" or "revealing." The book of Revelation can also be thought of as the apocalyptic book, which refers to the ultimate end of the story: the end of mankind's opportunity to choose God's salvation. Earth's history ends after mankind finally rejects God's truth and accepts falsehood in its place.

In this sense, the book of Revelation is describing the ultimate triumph of good over evil. This triumph of good over evil is represented as the final event in each series of seven in Revelation. For example, the seventh plague (Revelation 16:17-21) is describing the end of the judgment process in heaven and the Second Coming of Jesus Christ to save His people. In Revelation 3:14, we find a description of the last church of prophetic time, which is the church of Laodicea. This church will be in existence at Christ's Second Coming. This is the seventh church of that series. The seventh seal describes heaven as silent (Revelation 8:1) because heaven is empty and Jesus has gone to collect His people on earth. Each of these series of seven in the book of Revelation ends with the Second Coming. This is also true of the seven trumpets.

> Revelation 11:15: *"Then the seventh angel blew his trumpet, and there were loud voices in heaven, saying, 'The kingdom of the world has become the kingdom of our Lord and of his Christ, and he shall reign for ever and ever.'"*

Historically, this text has been applied to the time period after 1844. This is based on Revelation 11:19 where the temple is described as open. The open temple was interpreted to mean that the most holy place had been entered.[1] The most holy place is separated from the holy place in the earthly sanctuary by a veil between the two apartments. The most holy place was entered by the high priest only once a year to cleanse the sanctuary of sin. This Day of Atonement service was a type or symbol of the cleansing of the sanctuary in heaven. The sanctuary cleansing was foretold in Daniel 8:14. It was predicted to occur after "two thousand and three hundred evenings and mornings" (Daniel 8:14). If one evening and morning are considered one day, then this time period is symbolic of 2300 years (one prophetic day equals one literal year). The 2300-year prophecy of Daniel 8:14 was considered by many Christians in the early 1800s to be predictive of

Christ's Second Coming. This led to the Great Disappointment of 1844 when thousands of Christians believed that Jesus was to return during that year and He did not. However, this prophecy in Daniel 8:14 is actually referring to the sanctuary being cleansed or restored and not to the Second Coming of Christ. Daniel 8:14 states "For two thousand and three hundred evenings and mornings; then the sanctuary shall be restored to its rightful state." The beginning of this prophecy is found in Daniel 9:24 where the 70-week prophecy is explained. Daniel became ill, immediately after he was given the 2300-day prophecy, because he did not understand it. In Daniel 9:24, Daniel receives his explanation regarding the beginning of the 2300-day prophecy. He is told that "Seventy weeks of years are decreed" or cut off (Daniel 9:24) from the 2300-day prophecy.

The 70 weeks began with the "going forth of the word to restore and build Jerusalem" in Daniel 9:25. King Artaxeres in 457 B.C. gave this decree. This was the third decree to rebuild Jerusalem but the only one that restored Israel completely as a nation. Twenty-three hundred years later this prophecy timeline ended in 1844. The significance of 1844 in world history cannot be ignored. This prophecy stimulated many people to convert to Christianity and even though many fell away after the Great Disappointment many others remained firm and true to God. Clearly, God intended for this prophecy to be interpreted as it was in order to save many souls.

The cleansing of the sanctuary (Daniel 8:14), which began in 1844, represents the investigative judgment in heaven. This is described in Daniel 7:26 and Daniel 7:9, 10 where "the court sat in judgment, and the books were opened." This scene is also pictured in Revelation 4:2-4 and Revelation 5:6-10, where we see the courtroom pictured as God's throne room with 24 elders seated around Him and Jesus, as our Lamb slain, standing before the throne. Jesus is the only One who can open the book, which is sealed with seven seals (Revelation 5:1, 5). This book of life (Revelation 20:12, 15 and Revelation 3:5) contains the names of all those who have ever accepted Christ as their Savior or who have chosen to serve God. This judgment process began in 1844 and is now ongoing (discussed in Appendix (1)— The Investigative Judgment). The Second Coming of Christ occurs after this investigative judgment is complete and God's wrath has been poured out.

Revelation 11:15 states: "the kingdom of the world has become the kingdom of our Lord." This means that Christ has now been given His Kingdom. This event occurs when He receives it and not when the process of determining who will be in His kingdom begins. The beginning of the investigative judgment signifies the beginning of the last-day events but it is not the end of time. This verse appears to describe an event, which occurs at the end of time. This event is the Second Coming of Christ to receive His kingdom or His people.

The last-day events must be thought of as different from the time of the end events and from end-time events. Specifically, last-day events would include all events after 1844, which is the end of the 2300-year prophecy of Daniel 8:14 and the beginning of the investigative judgment in the heavenly throne room.

The time of the end applies to those events, which occur just prior to the end of time and also includes the end of time. This would include all of the plagues including the seventh. It would include the time of trouble in Daniel 12:1. The time of the end events would include the fifth, sixth, and seventh trumpets. The time of the end also includes the sixth and seventh seals. The time of the end includes all those events described in Daniel 11:40-45. The time of the end begins at the close of probation and extends through the Second Coming (discussed in Daniel 11—The Abomination and the Time of the End).

The end-time events refer to the Second Coming and its associated events. The end-time events include the sixth and seventh trumpets, the sixth and seventh plagues and the sixth and seventh seals. All of these events are involved in the final days of earth's history (discussed in Appendix (5)—The Last Days).

In Revelation, the phrase "loud voices" is generally associated with judgment. In this verse the judgment will come at the Second Coming when the human race will be destroyed, except for those saved by Jesus' blood. This is not the final judgment, which will occur at the end of the millennium (Revelation 20:9, 10, 14, 15).

Revelation 11:15 is introduced by the seventh angel who blows his trumpet. The seventh trumpet is the "third woe" (Revelation 11:14). The reason it is called a woe is not because it begins the investigative judgment. The investigative judgment is not a woe and does not begin at the end of the seven trumpets. The seventh trumpet is a woe because it represents Jesus' return to this world to collect His people, which will result in the total destruction of the world. This picture of total destruction is portrayed as "the great supper of God" in Revelation 19:17. The birds are invited to eat "the flesh of all men" (Revelation 19:18). This is the final and greatest woe for all mankind, when all the living who have rejected Christ as their Savior and Lord, will be forced to recognize Jesus as King. The penalty is death. Clearly, the seventh trumpet or third woe is the worst event for the wicked but the best event for the righteous. He "shall reign for ever and ever." This reign begins with the Second Coming when His kingdom is finally established by collecting all His saved. This involves the resurrection of His dead saints and the transformation of His living saints (1 Thessalonians 4:16, 17, 1 Corinthians 15:51-53).

> Revelation 11:16: *"And the twenty-four elders who sit on their thrones before God fell on their faces and worshiped God."*

These are the same 24 elders who are involved in the judgment scene. In Revelation 4:2, 3, John sees God's throne room in heaven with God seated on His throne and a rainbow around His throne. "Round the throne were twenty-four thrones, and seated on the thrones were twenty-four elders, clad in white garments, with golden crowns upon their heads" (Revelation 4:4). These thrones, set up around God's throne, are the same thrones Daniel saw "placed" in Daniel 7:9. These thrones were placed before "the court sat in judgment and the books were opened" Daniel 7:10. These 24 elders are dressed in white garments suggesting purity. These elders represent leaders of unfallen worlds involved in the investigative judgment process. These elders have golden crowns. The Greek word for crowns in Revelation 4:4 suggests victory over sin. These unfallen worlds were victorious over Satan because they rejected his lies.

This verse continues the theme began in Revelation 11:1, which introduced the investigative judgment. This judgment was symbolized by a measuring of

God's people in the temple. The investigative judgment is exactly that! The judges are going over the books related to God's people. This investigative judgment involves other judges reviewing God's decisions in God's holy temple in heaven. This process began in 1844 and is now ongoing. However, in Revelation 11:15 this process is complete and "the kingdom of the world has become the kingdom of our Lord." Revelation 11:15 is not describing the beginning of the investigative judgment but its ending. This investigative judgment has now ended and the 24 elders are seen celebrating with God. They are seen falling "on their faces" and worshipping God. The investigative judgment process is not for God's information. God already knows the end from the beginning. The investigative judgment process is God's answer to Satan's accusation that God is unfair (discussed in Appendix (1)—The Investigative Judgment). The investigative judgment proves beyond a shadow of a doubt that God is truly fair. The investigative judgment process allows the universe to affirm God's fairness and eliminate any future doubt, and once this process has been completed, the universe as represented by the 24 elders will celebrate and fall on their faces and worship God.

> Revelation 11:17: *"saying, 'We give thanks to thee, Lord God Almighty, who art and who wast, that thou hast taken thy great power and begun to reign.'"*

The 24 elders are now thanking God for finally beginning to reign. This has been interpreted by some to apply to 1844 at the beginning of the judgment process. However, this verse appears to be describing the end of the judgment process. The 24 elders in Revelation 4:11 praise God for creating all things. In Revelation 5:9, they praise the Lamb Slain for saving man saying, "by thy blood didst ransom men for God from every tribe and tongue and people and nation." Revelation 5:10 states "and hast made them a kingdom and priests to our God, and they shall reign on earth." Clearly in Revelation 5:10 the ransomed have not yet reigned because it states they "shall reign." This judgment is ongoing and the books are just being opened. However, in Revelation 11:17 God is being thanked because He has "begun to reign." God is already reigning in heaven and sitting on His throne when this statement is made so the statement must apply to that portion of God's kingdom, which He had temporarily lost to Satan. This kingdom has now been regained and God is now going to reign over the entire universe.

It is interesting to note that the audience of Revelation 5:9 is "every tribe and tongue and people and nation." This is the last-day's audience of Revelation 11:9 and Revelation 14:6. In other words, the investigative judgment involves the same audience as the message of the two witnesses and the three angels.

The title used for God in this verse also supports the idea that this is the end of the process of judgment. God is described as the "Lord God Almighty." This title is used to apply to God as victorious overall. In this verse the elders are celebrating God's victory over sin and Satan. God is finally going to reign over the earth again. God is going to take His rightful place as God of the entire universe.

> Revelation 11:18: *"The nations raged, but thy wrath came, and the time for the dead to be judged, for rewarding thy servants, the prophets and saints, and those who fear thy*

name, both small and great, and for destroying the destroyers of the earth."

This text clearly describes end-time events. At the end of time the nations will oppose God's message and also His return. The nations will "make war on the Lamb" (Revelation 17:14). The nations will rage: "I saw the beast and the kings of the earth with their armies gathered to make war against him who sits upon the horse and against his army" (Revelation 19:19).

This text also describes God's wrath which "came." This means that it has happened at the time of their celebration. God's wrath includes the seven last plagues. Revelation 15:1 states "Then I saw another portent in heaven, great and wonderful, seven angels with *seven plagues, which are the last, for with them the wrath of God is ended"* (emphasis supplied). Thus, if God's wrath has come then the seven plagues are ongoing. The seventh plague is God's return to this world to claim His people and destroy the wicked. The seven last plagues occur after the investigative judgment is ended and all of the world's people are sealed. They have either God's seal or Satan's mark.

The "time for the dead to be judged" has also arrived. The Greek word for time, *"Kairos,"* suggests a specific time with a definite purpose. A time of judgment and reward is consistent with this verse. A "time for the dead to be judged" can be translated "that they shall be judged." At the Second Coming the living wicked will be judged guilty and destroyed. At the Second Coming the righteous will be judged not guilty and given eternal life (1 Thessalonians 4:16, 17 and 1 Corinthians 15:51-53). The dead judged here includes God's people, since the next phrase lists God's servants, and it also includes the wicked described as the "destroyers of the earth." Judgment often has a negative connotation but when God's righteous receive their judgment it will be positive. They will receive eternal life.

Some have applied this "dead to be judged" to the destruction of the wicked after the 1000 year millennium (Revelation 20:13). However, it appears to better connect to Christ's Second Coming. The millennium is not part of the seventh trumpet but Jesus' Second Coming is.

This verse continues "for rewarding thy servants, the prophets and saints, and those who fear thy name, both small and great." This reward is eternal life through Jesus Christ (John 3:16, 17). This reward is based on believing and obedience. "He who believes in the Son has eternal life; he who does not obey the Son shall not see life, but the wrath of God rests upon him" (John 3:36). The reward will be related to what has been done. "Behold, I am coming soon, bringing my recompense, to repay every one *for what he has done"* (Revelation 22:12) (emphasis supplied). Also, Revelation 20:13 states "and all were judged by what they had done." We can only be saved by accepting Jesus Christ as our Savior and Lord. Accepting Him as Savior means accepting His sacrifice for our sins as all sufficient. There is nothing more we can do to save ourselves and nothing less we can do to be saved. However, if we truly accept Him as Savior then we must accept Him as Lord. When Jesus is Lord in our life then we will obey Him completely and our actions will reflect His Lordship in our lives. Then what we have done will be what He would have done.

There are three groups of "servants." These three groups are "the prophets," the "saints," and those "who fear thy name." The "prophets" are God's special servants who speak for Him. The "saints" are His holy ones representing the body of Christ or His true followers. The "saints" at the time of the end are defined as "those who keep the commandments of God and the faith of Jesus" (Revelation 14:12). The first characteristic of God's "saints" will be to keep God's Law or His Commandments (in other words obeying God and doing His will). The second characteristic of God's "saints" is having the faith of Jesus (accepting Jesus as their Savior and Lord) as opposed to accepting the false Christ. At the time of the end these two characteristics will be specifically challenged. God's Law will be attacked with a false Sabbath and faith in the true Jesus will be attacked by a false Christ. God's "saints" will reject both of these falsehoods.

Those "who fear thy name" represent those who do not fully know Christ but live up to all the truth they have. The Greek term used in this phrase is similar in Acts 10:2. Acts 10:2 describes people who worship the true God but who are not full proselytes to Israel. In the same sense those "who fear thy name" would include those who served God and lived up to the truth that they had regardless of their church affiliation or lack thereof. The critical issue here is that they live up to all the truth they are given.

"Destroying the destroyers of the earth" refers to the judgment of the wicked at the Second Coming. When Christ returns the second time He will save His people from the wicked who are attempting to destroy them. He will also destroy "the destroyers." This verse again is connected to the end of time. This is clearly an end-of-time event.

> Revelation 11:19: *"Then God's temple in heaven was opened, and the ark of his covenant was seen within his temple; and there were flashes of lightning, loud noises, peals of thunder, an earthquake, and heavy hail."*

Historically, this text has been interpreted to indicate that the work in the most holy place has begun because the ark is visible.[2] The ark was located in the most holy place in the earthly sanctuary. The work of cleansing the sanctuary occurred on the Day of Atonement. The high priest would enter the most holy place in order to minister the sacrificial blood of the lamb to cleanse the sanctuary. This cleansing of the sanctuary symbolized the investigative judgment in heaven, which cleanses God's heavenly sanctuary. In heaven, the "Lamb" slain is both the sacrifice and the High Priest, who is Jesus Christ (Revelation 5:6, Hebrews 8:1).

Since the Ark of the Covenant was visible only if the veil between the most holy place and the holy place was open, it was assumed that this indicated the beginning of the work in the most holy place. If this historical interpretation is correct then this verse spans from 1844 to the Second Coming, because the last half of this verse applies to the Second Coming.

It is clear that the veil is open; however, does that mean that the work is beginning or is it ending? The previous verses strongly suggest that God has completed His work and finished His wrath. He has judged the wicked and judged the righteous and is rewarding His people. All of these are consistent with the concept that the veil is open because the temple work is done.

This same event is described in the seventh seal: "When the Lamb opened the seventh seal, there was silence in heaven for about half an hour" (Revelation 8:1). God's temple is open and "the ark of his covenant was seen" because the temple is empty. God has left heaven to go and get His redeemed.

The Ten Commandments or God's Law is contained in the Ark of the Covenant (Exodus 40:20). God's Law will be critical in last-day events. God's Law will be changed just prior to His Second Coming. God's Law will become the basis for determining who God's people are at the end of time. God's saints are defined as "those who keep the commandments of God and the faith of Jesus" (Revelation 14:12). God's seal or mark is found in His Law. Satan's mark or seal will counterfeit God's seal (discussed in Revelation 13 (last part)—The Mark of the Beast).

Finally, Revelation 11:19 states "and there were flashes of lightning, loud noises, peals of thunder, an earthquake, and heavy hail." These events appear to be describing the same events that are recorded under the seventh plague. "The seventh angel poured his bowl into the air, and a great voice came out of the temple, from the throne, saying, 'It is done!'" (Revelation 16:17). The next verse continues "And there were flashes of lightning, loud noises, peals of thunder, and a great earthquake such as had never been since men were on the earth, so great was that earthquake" (Revelation 16:18). Heavy "hail" is described in Revelation 16:21 "and great hailstones, heavy as a hundredweight, dropped on men from heaven, till men cursed God for the plague of the hail, so fearful was that plague." This description is part of the seventh plague.

These events are clearly happening on earth at the time of the end. The description in Revelation 11:19 is describing the same global earthquake which is seen in Revelation 16:18 such as "had never been." The lightning, thunder, and noises will be terrifying. The plague of hail will flatten buildings and kill many of the wicked but God's people will be spared.

SUMMARY

The seventh trumpet is God's last woe. It follows the ascension of His two witnesses (His Holy Word) because their work is done. This trumpet describes the joy in heaven over God finally regaining His rightful sovereignty over the earth. This trumpet occurs after the investigative judgment has ended. This trumpet describes the end of the great tribulation when God's people will receive their reward. They are His saints who keep all of His Law. This trumpet describes the kingdom of this earth as becoming God's and Christ's Kingdom and no longer Satan's. This happens after Satan has reigned as the eighth king (spiritual leader of the world) and after he has reigned as the world's king (temporal leader of the world). This trumpet describes an empty heaven, where there is "silence" (Revelation 8:1). This trumpet describes an empty temple because God has left His throne to save His people and reign over the kingdom of this world. This trumpet describes the destruction of the destroyers and the reward of God's people, which occurs at the Second Coming. Finally, this trumpet describes the cataclysmic events associated with the Second Coming. The following graph outlines the last-day events described in Revelation 8, 9, and 11.

Revelation Chapters 8, 9 & 11

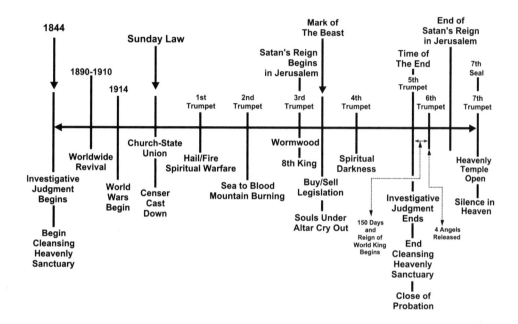

Appendix (3)
Revelation 8, 9, and 11

In the discussion on Revelation 8, 9, and 11 the author has attempted to portray both the historical approach as well as a dual application for the last days. In order to clarify these two approaches, the following table and timeline are provided for comparison purposes. In the historical approach, the seven churches and the seven seals and the seven trumpets all cover approximately the same time periods. The historical application of the seven churches and the seven seals is shown in Appendix Table 1. The historical application of the seven trumpets is shown in Appendix Table 2. The dual application of Revelation 8, 9, and 11 as it applies to the last days is shown in Appendix Timeline (2).

Appendix Table 1

Historical Application of Revelation Chapters 1-3 and 6

	Time Period	Seven Churches	Seven Seals
1st	A.D. 34 - A.D. 100	Ephesus	White Horse
2nd	A.D. 100 - A.D. 313	Smyrna	Red Horse
3rd	A.D. 313 - A.D. 538	Pergamum	Black Horse
4th	A.D. 538 - 1517	Thyatira	Pale Horse
5th	1517 - 1755	Sardis	Souls Cry Out
6th	1755 - 1844	Philadelphia	Sun, Moon and Stars Rocks Fall
7th	1844 - Second Coming	Laodicea	Silence in Heaven

Appendix Table 2

Historical Application of Seven Trumpets
Revelation Chapters 8, 9 and 11

Trumpets	Symbol	Historical Event	Time Period*
1st Trumpet	Hail - Fire - Blood	Visigoths Invade Roman Empire	A.D. 396 - A.D. 410
2nd Trumpet	Mountain Burning Sea to Blood	Vandals Overrun Europe	A.D. 410 - A.D. 455
3rd Trumpet	Wormwood Rivers and Lakes Poisoned	Attila and the Huns Invade Europe	A.D. 451 - A.D. 458
4th Trumpet	One-Third of Sun, Moon and Stars Darkened	Collapse of Roman Government	A.D. 476 - A.D. 538
5th Trumpet	Fallen Star/King Bottomless Pit Opened	Rise of Ottoman Turkish Empire	1299 - 1449
6th Trumpet	4 Angels Released One-Third Die	Domination of Ottoman Turkish Empire	1449 - 1840
7th Trumpet	God's Temple Open	Investigative Judgment	1844 - Second Coming

*Time Periods Approximate

Appendix: Timeline (2)

7 Churches, 7 Seals, and 7 Trumpets

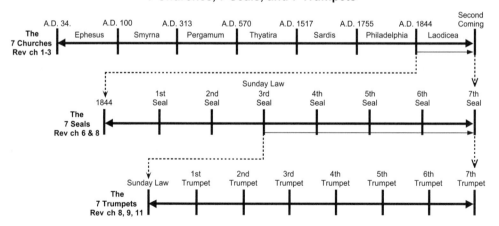

---

1   Nichol, Francis D. (Ed.). *The Seventh-day Adventist Bible Commentary* (Review and Herald
    Publishing Association, Washington, D.C.) 1957, Vol. 7, p. 805.
2   Ibid.

SUMMARY
Section III—The Judgment

Revelation 4 begins after John has been given the messages to the seven churches. The courtroom scene described in Revelation 4 occurs during the time of the Laodicean church. This courtroom scene occurs at the end of the 2300-year prophecy of Daniel 8:14, which began in 457 B.C. and ended in 1844. The Laodicean church represents the time period after 1844 and is the seventh and final church. The cleansing or restoring of the sanctuary "to its rightful state" (Daniel 8:14) refers to the cleansing of sin from the heavenly sanctuary. The cleansing process is called the investigative judgment. God's judgment process involves three phases: the investigative phase, the millennial phase, and the executive phase.[1] The investigative judgment is the initial phase in the judgment process. The investigative judgment was typified in the Old Testament by the Day of Atonement service. This service cleansed the earthly sanctuary of sin, just as the investigative judgment cleanses the heavenly sanctuary of sin. The Day of Atonement was the only day that the most holy place was entered. The most holy place represented God's throne room. The veil or door between the two earthly apartments was opened only once a year. Revelation 4 begins with this door "open" (Revelation 4:1) and God seated on His throne.

Revelation 4 and 5 are describing God's throne room and the judgment scene in heaven, which Daniel described in Daniel 7:10. This court scene involves a Judge (God the Father), a jury (the 24 elders) and an Advocate (the Lamb Slain). The list of defendants and the evidence are contained in the scroll described in Revelation 5:1. God's throne is surrounded by 24 thrones for the 24 elders and by four living creatures. These four living creatures are described as a lion, an ox, a man and an eagle. These four creatures are linked to the first four seals and the eagle is linked to the last three trumpets. The 24 elders and the four creatures praise God as the Creator of the universe and worthy "to receive glory and honor and power" (Revelation 4:11). Revelation 5 introduces a scroll, which no one can open. This scroll is critical to the judgment process, because John weeps over the fact that no one can open it. Only Jesus, the Lamb Slain, can open this scroll. Jesus died in order to place the names in this book. This book contains the names of all those who have chosen to serve God during their lifetimes. It does not contain the names of those who never attempted to serve God. This is typified in the Old Testament, because the Old Testament sanctuary was only contaminated with the blood of the sins of those who brought them there to be forgiven. In Revelation 5, Jesus is praised as the Lamb Slain because He ransomed men through His death and "made them a kingdom" (Revelation 5:10).

Revelation 6 introduces seven seals. The first four seals are described as four horses and riders. The first four seals are each associated with one of the four creatures and represent specific time periods. The four creatures also are associated with specific time periods. The seals are found on the scroll, which is involved in the investigative judgment. The seals will be opened as part of that judgment process and begin after 1844. The first seal (white horse and rider) represents the successful spread of the gospel throughout the world in the late 1800s and early 1900s. The white horse represents God's people after 1844 and the rider represents the gospel. The first creature (the lion) is the Lion of Judah and is linked to this seal. This Lion is Jesus and He and His gospel will conquer and will continue "to conquer" to the end (Revelation 6:2).

The second seal (red horse and rider) represents global warfare, both spiritual and literal. The red horse represents warfare and bloodshed and the rider represents those countries involved in these wars. This prophecy was fulfilled beginning with World War I and World War II, which began in 1914 and 1939 respectively. The second creature (the ox) represents Satan who is causing this warfare, both spiritual and literal, which will continue until the end of time.

The third seal (black horse and rider) represents the time period when the universal Sunday law will be enacted. The black horse represents falsehood. The rider represents apostate Christianity which will bring about a church-state union and attempt to change God's Law. The rider is carrying a balance or yoke. This yoking of church and state will occur during a time of global famine, represented by the high cost of food (Revelation 6:6). This yoking will occur because of natural disasters that will lead men to attempt to appease God in order to bring an end to these disasters. The third creature is the man, which represents the man of sin or Satan, who will cause both spiritual and literal famine to the end. This man is the cause of the famine described in this seal. The third seal represents worldwide famine, both spiritual and literal, and the changing of God's Law. This seal marks the beginning of the last prophetic week or seven years of earth's history described in Daniel 9:27. The Papal kingdom represented by the seventh king (Revelation 17:10) will be in control of the world during the first half of this last prophetic week of earth's history (Revelation 13:5). The passage of the Sunday law is the beginning of Satan's (the man's) increasing control of the world which will extend to the end of time. Satan's reign as the eighth king or false Christ will begin in the middle of this prophetic week.

The fourth seal (the pale horse and rider) represents the beginning of the reign of the eighth king or abomination that makes desolate. The pale horse represents death. The rider represents Satan as the eighth king and the abomination that makes desolate. This seal represents Satan when he ascends to the throne as the false Christ. When Satan reigns as the false Christ he will initially control approximately one fourth of the world's population, which represents the Christians in those countries where Satan has no effective opposition. Satan will cause the death of many of God's true believers during this time period. The fourth creature (eagle) is associated with this seal. The eagle represents God's special protection of His people from Satan's reign on to the end of time.

The fifth seal (the souls under the altar) represents the time of persecution of God's people which begins with the mark of the beast and extends to the close of probation, when the number "who were to be killed" will be complete (Revelation 6:11). The mark of the beast will begin with the enactment of the buy-sell legislation (Revelation 13:17). This mark of the beast is the Sunday law once penalties are attached. This Sunday law enforcement will occur after Satan has ascended to his throne. Many of God's people will be slain during this time period, but none of God's people will be slain after the close of probation occurs.

The sixth seal depicts events, which occur just prior to Jesus' Second Coming. These events include a great earthquake, the sun darkened, the moon turned to blood, and the stars falling from the sky. Every mountain and island will disappear and men will cry for the rocks to "Fall on us and hide us" from "the wrath of the Lamb" (Revelation 6:16).

Revelation 8 begins with the seventh seal, which is "silence in heaven" because Jesus has gone to earth to collect His people. The seventh seal is the Second Coming. Revelation 8 then introduces the seven trumpets and another angel with a golden censer. This censer is thrown down "on the earth" just prior to the beginning of the seven trumpets (Revelation 8:5). This throwing down of the censer represents judgment and the close of probation for God's favored nation. This favored nation is the United States of America. Its special protection by God will end with the throwing down of the censer. This will occur when this nation rejects God's Law and enacts a false Sabbath. This will occur at the passage of the Sunday law, when the United States becomes the image to the beast by forming a church-state union.

The seven trumpets will occur after the Sunday law is passed and the censer is cast down. The seven trumpets are divided into two groups. The first four trumpets are warnings and the last three trumpets are "woes" (Revelation 8:13). The last three trumpets will occur after God's people are sealed (Revelation 9:4) and after the close of probation. The first trumpet (hail, fire, and blood) represents both spiritual and literal warfare, which will occur once the Sunday law is passed. This trumpet involves God's people as well as literal Israel and many are slain.

The second trumpet (a great mountain burning) represents the attacks on both spiritual and literal Israel just prior to Satan's reign as the eighth king. This trumpet also involves the loss of many of God's people as well as the destruction of literal Israel. This trumpet will occur during the leopard-like beast's reign of 42 months.

The third trumpet (a great star fallen from heaven) represents Satan as the eighth king. This star is named Wormwood, which means poisoning. Satan will poison one-third of the world when he ascends to his throne. This one-third of the world poisoned represents the approximately two billion Christians out of a total world population of six billion.

The fourth trumpet (one-third of the sun, moon, and stars darkened) represents Satan's effect on Christianity once he can interpret the Bible. The sun represents Jesus, the moon represents the Holy Scriptures, and the stars represent God's people. The Christian world will be in darkness when Satan reigns as the false Christ.

Revelation 9 introduces the first woe. The fifth trumpet (the first woe) describes the "star fallen" given "the key of the shaft of the bottomless pit" (Revelation 9:1). This star is Satan who is already reigning as the eighth king or false Christ and is influencing one-third of the world (the Christians). In the fifth trumpet Satan is now further released from the pit of circumstances with which God has controlled him and now is allowed to become world king (Revelation 9:11). Satan can now harm those who do not have God's seal for five months, but he cannot kill them (Revelation 9:5). This trumpet occurs after the close of probation since God's people are sealed (Revelation 9:4). This trumpet correlates with the first three plagues of Revelation 16.

The sixth trumpet (the second woe) describes the release of "the four angels who are bound at the great river Euphrates" (Revelation 9:14). The three woes are judgments on the wicked and include the seven last plagues. The sixth trumpet includes the fourth, fifth, and sixth plagues. The four angels were protecting the world. Now Satan can kill the wicked in huge numbers, which he could not do during the fifth trumpet. This trumpet describes a massive battle and three plagues: fire, smoke, and sulphur. This massive battle is the Battle of Armageddon or the sixth plague, which will occur in the Middle East just prior to the Second Coming.

The seventh trumpet (the third woe) is described in Revelation 11:15-19. The seventh trumpet describes celebration in heaven over God rewarding His saints and "destroying the destroyers" (Revelation 11:18). The temple is open and empty because this is the Second Coming. The earthquake and hail are the same as those described under the seventh plague, which is also Jesus' Second Coming. These events are outlined in the following graph.

---

[1] *Seventh-day Adventists Believe* (Copyright Ministerial Association General Conference of Seventh-day Adventists, printed by Review and Herald Publishing Association, Hagerstown, Maryland) 1988, p. 319.

Section III - The Judgment Summary Outline

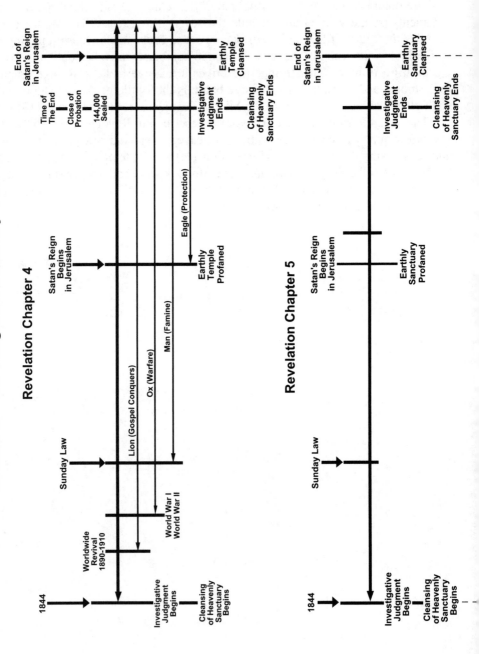

Revelation Chapter 4

End of Satan's Reign in Jerusalem

Time of The End
Close of Probation

144,000 Sealed

Investigative Judgment Ends

Cleansing of Heavenly Sanctuary Ends

Earthly Temple Cleansed

Eagle (Protection)

Satan's Reign Begins in Jerusalem

Earthly Temple Profaned

Lion (Gospel Conquers)

Ox (Warfare)

Man (Famine)

Sunday Law

Worldwide Revival 1890-1910

World War I
World War II

1844

Investigative Judgment Begins

Cleansing of Heavenly Sanctuary Begins

Revelation Chapter 5

End of Satan's Reign in Jerusalem

Investigative Judgment Ends

Cleansing of Heavenly Sanctuary Ends

Earthly Sanctuary Cleansed

Satan's Reign Begins in Jerusalem

Earthly Sanctuary Profaned

Sunday Law

1844

Investigative Judgment Begins

Cleansing of Heavenly Sanctuary Begins

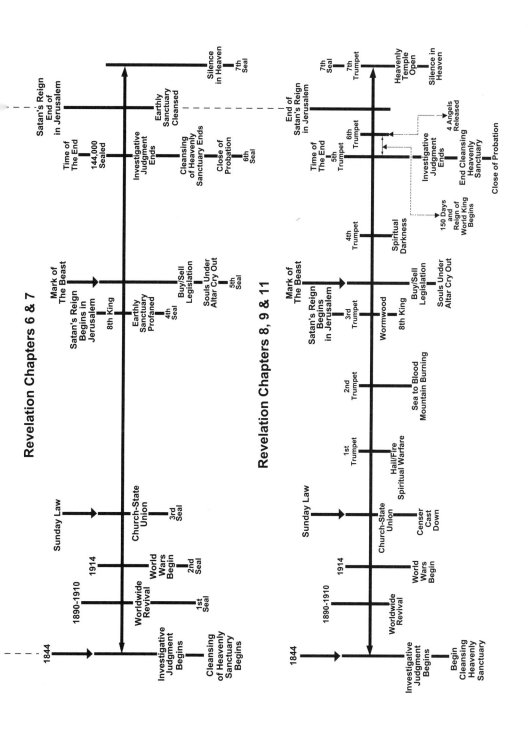

Revelation Chapters 6 & 7

1844 — Investigative Judgment Begins / Cleansing of Heavenly Sanctuary Begins

1890-1910 — Worldwide Revival

1914 — World Wars Begin / 2nd Seal

Sunday Law — Church-State Union / 3rd Seal

1st Seal

Mark of The Beast — Satan's Reign Begins in Jerusalem / 8th King / Earthly Sanctuary Profaned / 4th Seal / Buy/Sell Legislation / Souls Under Altar Cry Out / 5th Seal

Satan's Reign End of in Jerusalem — Time of The End / 144,000 Sealed / Investigative Judgment Ends / Earthly Sanctuary Cleansed / Cleansing of Heavenly Sanctuary Ends / Close of Probation / 6th Seal

Silence in Heaven / 7th Seal

Revelation Chapters 8, 9 & 11

1844 — Investigative Judgment Begins / Begin Cleansing Heavenly Sanctuary

1890-1910 — Worldwide Revival

1914 — World Wars Begin

Sunday Law — Church-State Union / Censer Cast Down

1st Trumpet — Hail/Fire / Spiritual Warfare

2nd Trumpet — Sea to Blood / Mountain Burning

3rd Trumpet — Wormwood / 8th King

Mark of The Beast — Satan's Reign Begins in Jerusalem / Buy/Sell Legislation / Souls Under Altar Cry Out

4th Trumpet — Spiritual Darkness

150 Days and Reign of World King Begins

End of Satan's Reign in Jerusalem — Time of The End / 5th Trumpet / 6th Trumpet / Investigative Judgment Ends / End Cleansing Heavenly Sanctuary / Close of Probation / 4 Angels Released

7th Seal / 7th Trumpet / Heavenly Temple Open / Silence in Heaven

The Time of The End

Revelation 14
The Three Angels' Messages

Revelation 14 begins with a description of the 144,000 who have the Lamb's name and His Father's name written on their foreheads. The apostle John has described these 144,000 earlier in Revelation 7. These are God's people who will be sealed prior to the four angels being released (Revelation 7:3, 4). These 144,000 represent God's people who will endure the final events of earth's history including the seven last plagues. These are the people who will "stand before it" (Revelation 6:17), which means they are the people who will still be standing after the wrath of the Lamb (Revelation 6:16). These are the people who will not accept the mark of the beast (Revelation 13:16) and are the living righteous at the Second Coming.

Revelation 13 ended with a description of those who have the mark of the beast. This mark could be on the forehead or on the hand (Revelation 13:16). This mark will signify worship of the beast or its image (Revelation 14:9). This mark is described in the chapter titled: Revelation 13 (last part)—The Mark of the Beast. Those who accept this mark will suffer the seven last plagues (Revelation 16:2). This mark is the seal of the beast. This mark seals the followers of the beast and guarantees their destruction. God's seal or mark guarantees His peoples' safety and salvation.

John was shown the 144,000 again at this point to reinforce the difference between God's people and the wicked. God's people are sealed with His mark on their foreheads and the wicked (described in Revelation 13:16) are sealed with Satan's mark on their right hand or their foreheads. It should be noted that God's people will only be sealed on the forehead. Sealing on the forehead means a conscious decision or choice to serve God. The wicked will be sealed on the forehead or the hand because whether they make a conscious decision to serve Satan or simply serve him for convenience by their actions, they still receive his mark. A conscious decision to serve Satan will give you a mark on the forehead. A decision to serve him out of convenience or to avoid penalties will give you a mark on the hand. You cannot fake a commitment to God by your actions and still be sealed. None of God's saints will be sealed on their hands. They will all be sealed on their foreheads because they all will be committed to serving Him.

> Revelation 14:1: *"then I looked, and lo, on Mount Zion stood the Lamb, and with him a hundred and forty-four thousand who had his name and his Father's name written on their foreheads."*

This verse begins another vision, which closely relates to the prior vision of Revelation 13. John now sees the victorious 144,000, who do not have Satan's mark or seal, but instead have the Lamb's name and the Father's name on their foreheads. These names signify they have overcome through the Lamb's blood and belong to the Father. These two characteristics will be further defined in Revelation 14:12. The saints are those "who keep the commandments of God and the faith of Jesus." God's Law reflects God's character and His name. The faith of Jesus reflects Jesus as their true Savior and His name. The 144,000 will reflect God's Law in their lives and will refuse to accept any false Christ for the true Jesus.

> Revelation 14:2: *"And I heard a voice from heaven like the sound of many waters and like the sound of loud thunder; the voice I heard was like the sound of harpers playing on their harps."*

John now hears a voice from heaven "like the sound of many waters" and like "the sound of loud thunder." This voice reminds us of Jesus' voice described in Revelation 1:15.[1] The voice is further described as "harpers playing on their harps." The next verse describes the sound of singers singing a new song. This song is the song of the 144,000, who are singing a song of redemption and praise that only they can sing. Only they have survived the worst time of tribulation the world has ever seen.

> Revelation 14:3: *"and they sing a new song before the throne and before the four living creatures and before the elders. No one could learn that song except the hundred and forty-four thousand who had been redeemed from the earth."*

The 144,000 are heard singing "a new song." They are seen singing this song before the throne where the Father reigns. The audience includes the four living creatures who introduced the first four seals and who are involved in last-day events. The audience also includes the 24 elders who sit in judgment during the investigative judgment. This "song" can only be sung by the 144,000, who are the living redeemed at the time of the Second Coming. They are the redeemed who live through the "time of trouble such as never has been" (Daniel 12:1). Their "song" is a song of experience unique to them. They are not the only ones redeemed from the earth but they are the only ones who lived through the time of the end and remained faithful.

> Revelation 14:4: *"It is these who have not defiled themselves with women, for they are chaste; it is these who follow the Lamb wherever he goes; these have been redeemed from mankind as first fruits for God and the Lamb."*

This text describes the 144,000 as "having not defiled themselves with women." This is not referring to physical sex.[2] This is referring to a spiritual defilement. The true church is seen in scripture as a "bride" and a pure woman (Revelation 19:7), as opposed to the apostate church which is portrayed as a prostitute or harlot (Revelation 17:5). Revelation 14:4 is describing the 144,000 during the time of the end who will refuse to defile themselves by joining to an apostate church. Some will come out of Babylon (Revelation 18:4) and will not go back. The "women" referred to in Revelation 14:4 refer to any apostate church or religion during the time of the end. The 144,000 are described as "chaste" or virgins because they will not violate their relationship with God by establishing a relationship with the false Christ, who is king of the world. The 144,000 will only "follow the Lamb" and will refuse to worship Satan as the false Christ.

Some have suggested that the 144,000 will have a special relationship with the Lamb throughout eternity.[3] This concept is described in Revelation 7:14-17. They are seen as "before the throne of God, and serve him day and night within his temple" (Revelation 7:15). This is consistent with Revelation 14:4, which states they will "follow the Lamb wherever he goes." The 144,000 are also described as "first fruits." This suggests they are a special gift or offering to God.[4] The 144,000 will be representatives of all the saved throughout eternity. At the time of the end (the close of probation), the 144,000 are technically the first saved. They are actually saved for eternity although they have not yet been taken to heaven and must endure the time of trouble. In that sense, they are the first fruits of those who will be raised at the time of the Second Coming.

> Revelation 14:5: *"and in their mouth no lie was found, for they are spotless."*

The Greek word for "was found" suggests at a certain point in time.[5] This does not mean they had never sinned or erred but that they had overcome at a certain point in time. The emphasis on lying is significant to the time of the end. There will be a false Sabbath, which will be a lie. There will be false Christ, which will be a lie. There will be false interpretations of scripture by the false Christ, which will all be lies. The 144,000 will not accept or follow any of these lies. The 144,000 will be "spotless" or "blameless" before God. They will keep His Commandments and never abandon faith in the true Jesus. These are the saints who are alive and serving God when probation closes. They remain faithful throughout the "time of trouble" of Daniel 12:1, which is called the "great tribulation" in Matthew 24:21. This time of trouble is the "time of the end" of Daniel 11:40.

> Revelation 14:6: *"Then I saw another angel flying in mid heaven, with an eternal gospel to proclaim to those who dwell on earth, to every nation and tribe and tongue and people;"*

John now sees "another angel flying in mid heaven." This angel represents God's people, who will carry this message that judgment has come.[6] This angel is seen "flying in mid heaven," which suggests a world wide message.[7] The world-wide nature of the message is confirmed by the audience. The message is "to those who dwell on earth." The audience is further identified as "every nation and tribe and tongue and people." Since this message is given to those who live in the last days, this audience (i.e., "every nation and tribe and tongue and people") is the last-day's audience. This message is given to all those who live during the "hour of his judgment" (Revelation 14:7).

The angel or messenger is carrying the "eternal gospel to proclaim" to the world. This eternal gospel is the good news about salvation through Jesus Christ. This gospel is eternal. This gospel will never change or be replaced. At the time of the end, this gospel will be challenged by a false Christ. However, this is the only true gospel. This gospel about the true Jesus is the only way to salvation: "for there is no other name under heaven given among men by which we must be saved" (Acts 4:12).

Revelation 14:7: *"and he said with a loud voice, 'fear God and give him glory, for the hour of his judgment has come; and worship him who made heaven and earth, the sea and the fountains of water.'"*

This angel speaks with a "loud voice." The "loud voice" suggests this message is important. The "loud voice" suggests this message will be heard by everyone.[8] Also, a "loud voice" in Revelation is often associated with judgment as is the case in this verse. This voice commands men worldwide to "fear God and give him glory." This concept of "fear" when applied to God in the Old and New Testaments refers to respect or reverence. The word "fear" also suggests loyalty and surrender to his will.[9] This call to "fear" or reverence the true God will become critical in the last days of earth's history. When Satan claims to be Christ returned, many will reverence Satan instead of the true God. Many will glorify the false Christ instead of the true God. In the presence of Satan as the false Christ, it will be very difficult to "fear" the true God.

The reason given to "fear God and give him glory" is because "the hour of his judgment has come." Historically, this text was fulfilled in 1844 when the investigative judgment began.[10] This judgment is the same judgment Daniel described in Daniel 7:9, 10. Daniel saw "thrones placed" and "the court sat in judgment" (Daniel 7:9, 10). This scene is portrayed in Revelation 4 and 5 where God's throne is surrounded by the 24 elders' thrones (Revelation 4:4). This judgment process began at the end of the 2300-year prophecy of Daniel 8:14. This prophecy ended in 1844 (discussed in Daniel 8—The Abomination and the Sanctuary). Thus, 1844 marks the beginning of the investigative judgment and also the beginning of the first angels' message. This message was initially preached from about 1830 to 1844 and is still being proclaimed today.[11]

The first angel's message is a call to worship the Creator God. This is confirmed by the call to "worship him who made heaven and earth, the sea and the fountains of water." This call to worship the true Creator was especially important in the 1800s because the theory of evolution became prevalent during that time period and it continues today.[12]

The call to worship the true Creator God is linked to Revelation 4 as well. In Revelation 4, we see God on His throne and the judgment scene unfolding. We then see the 24 elders and the four living creatures praising God because "thou didst create all things, and by thy will they existed and were created" (Revelation 4:11). It is the Creator God who is responsible for the judgment, which has come. The world is called to acknowledge that the Creator is their Judge.

This call to worship God as the Creator is also a reminder of His Sabbath day. In Exodus 20:8 we are told to "Remember the sabbath day, to keep it holy." The Sabbath day is the seventh day (Exodus 20:10). The reason given to keep the seventh day is recorded in Exodus 20:11: "for in six days the LORD made heaven and earth, the sea, and all that is in them, and rested the seventh day; therefore the LORD blessed the sabbath day and hallowed it." *The Sabbath day is to remind us that God created everything and deserves our worship.*

The Sabbath day will be under attack at the close of time. A false Sabbath will be substituted. This false Sabbath will be linked to the false Christ. The image of the beast will create this mark and will cause those "who will not worship the image of the beast to be slain" (Revelation 13:15, 16) (discussed in Revelation 13 (last part)—The Mark of the Beast). Thus, worship of the true God and Creator will be confirmed by worshipping on His true Sabbath and the worship of the beast will be confirmed by worshipping on his false Sabbath.

> Revelation 14:8: *"Another angel, a second, followed, saying, 'fallen, fallen is Babylon the great, she who made all nations drink the wine of her impure passion.'"*

This text introduces a second angel with a second message. This angel is described as following the first angel. The Greek word suggests either "to accompany" or "to follow." This angel's message will follow the first angel's message but will then accompany that message to the end of time.[13] The second angel's message will follow the first angel's message in time and it will occur at the close of time. The hour of judgment in the first angel's message began in 1844, this judgment is ongoing, and will continue to the end of time. Thus both messages will accompany each other to the end of time.

The second angel's message concerns "Babylon the great." This is the same "Babylon the great" described in Revelation 17:5. This "Babylon the great" is the scarlet woman of Revelation 17:3, 4. She is the "mother of harlots" in Revelation 17:5. She is the woman seated on "seven hills" (Revelation 17:9). This woman is also "the great city which has dominion over the kings of the earth" (Revelation 17:18). This scarlet woman represents apostate Christianity and specifically represents the Papacy in Revelation 17 (discussed in Revelation 17 (first part)—The Scarlet Woman and Her Kings). The city of seven hills, which had dominion over the world in John's day, was the city of Rome.[14] This city will have worldwide influence and dominion in the last days.

The second angel's message states that Babylon is "fallen" because she "made all nations drink the wine of her impure passion." This phrase connects to Revelation 17:2, which refers to the dwellers on earth who have become drunk with the wine of her "fornication." This wine of Babylon represents the false teachings, which the world has accepted. Drinking the wine and getting drunk indicates believing and acting on these false teachings. The state of drunkenness also suggests a certain lack of control and loss of the ability to think clearly. These falsehoods will cloud their minds and affect their actions. The acceptance of these falsehoods will limit their ability to recognize truth.

The "wine of her impure passion" or wine of her fornication means that the world has not only believed her false teachings but has established an adulterous relationship with Babylon. Instead of a pure relationship with the true God and Creator, the world has established an intimate relationship with the apostate or false church. This intimate relationship or fornication will result in a church-state union. This church-state union will then attempt to enforce its false religion on God's people through legislation. This is described in Revelation 13:15-17 when the image (the church-state union) passes laws, which threaten economic penalties or death, to force compliance on God's people (discussed in Revelation 13 (last part)—The Mark of the Beast).

The second angel's message will be fulfilled when "all nations drink" the wine

of her fornication. This will occur once the false Sabbath has been mandated as law in the United States of America and then accepted by other countries in the world. The use of "all nations" in this text does not mean every person will drink this wine. The universal or world audience in Revelation 14 is "every nation and tribe and tongue and people" (Revelation 14:6). In Revelation 14:8, "all nations" represents only a part of that audience and refers to those nations which claim a Christian heritage. These countries will also support this false Sabbath. This text does not mean that countries dominated by other types of non-Christian religions will accept this "wine." They have already accepted other falsehoods.

This text will be fulfilled after the image of the beast (described in Revelation 13:14, 15) is formed and has convinced the world that a false Sabbath or Sunday law is required. This passage of the universal Sunday law will confirm this church-state union. This Sunday law will occur as a result of natural disasters leading to economic collapse. These disasters will lead people to attempt to appease God by enacting legislation that will enforce religious dogma. This will eventually lead to the mark of the beast once the penalties are attached (Revelation 13:16, 17).

> Revelation 14:9: *"and another angel, a third, followed, saying with a loud voice, 'if anyone worships the beast and its image, and receives a mark on his forehead or on his hand.'"*

This "third" angel again announces his message "with a loud voice." This "loud voice" implies everyone will hear it and that it is important.[15] This "loud voice" also suggests judgment. The "third" angel's message is for those who worship "the beast and its image."

This beast:
1) Is described in Revelation 13:1-3, 5-8.
2) Has ten horns and seven heads (Revelation 13:1).
3) Had a mortal wound that healed (Revelation 13:3). This mortal wound to its head occurred in 1798, when General Berthier took Pope Pius VI captive. This wound healed in 1929 when Mussolini gave the Vatican City back the land on which it sits, which reinstated the Papacy as a church-state kingdom.
4) Will rule during the last days for 42 months or three and one-half years (Revelation 13:5)
5) Will exist at the same time as its image (Revelation 13:14).
6) Will exist at the same time as the lamb-like beast (Revelation 13:12).
7) Forms an image that will cause a mark to be created (Revelation 13:16).
8) Is the leopard-like beast of Revelation 13.
9) Is the Papacy (discussed in Revelation 13 (first part)—The Leopard-Like Beast Healed).

The image of this beast will be created by the lamb-like beast of Revelation 13:11. This lamb-like beast has been identified as the United States of America with its two horns of civil and religious liberty (discussed in Revelation 13 (last part)—The Mark of the Beast). This lamb-like beast will make "the earth and its inhabitants worship the first beast, whose mortal wound was healed" (Revelation 13:12). This lamb-like beast will make an image of the beast and "give breath to the image" (Revelation 13:15). The original leopard-like beast was a church-state union. The image of this beast will be the same. The United States of America will form the "image" of the beast when it becomes a church-state union.

The lamb-like beast will change into the image of the beast when it abandons its two horns. When the United States of America passes laws that abolish religious liberty and limit civil liberty, it will become the "image" of the original leopard-like beast. The leopard-like beast or Papacy, historically, was known for its lack of religious and civil liberty. The lamb-like beast will make the world "worship the first beast, whose mortal wound was healed" (Revelation 13:12). The image of the beast will come into existence with the passage of the universal Sunday law. *Once the Sunday law has been passed by the United States of America, the United States of America will become the image to the beast.* The initial passage of the universal Sunday law is not the "mark" of the beast. The "mark" of the beast is the keeping of the Sunday law once penalties have been attached. These penalties are described in Revelation 13:15, 17. The initial penalty will be the inability to buy or sell. The final penalty will be death. This "mark" will be on the forehead if it is a conscious commitment to and belief in the beast. This "mark" will be on the hand if the choice to serve the beast is not based on belief but on expediency. In other words, a real belief in falsehood will cause the "mark" to be in the forehead. An action to avoid the penalty of the "mark" will cause the "mark" to be in the hand. The hand here represents actions. The forehead represents commitment. Regardless, whether the Sunday law is kept out of real belief or to avoid the penalty, the person keeping the Sunday law will receive the "mark" after the penalties are enforced.

> Revelation 14:10: *"he also shall drink the wine of God's wrath, poured unmixed into the cup of his anger, and he shall be tormented with fire and brimstone in the presence of the holy angels and in the presence of the lamb."*

The third angel's message continues by describing what will happen to those who worship the beast or its image or receive its mark. Those who drink of the wine of the scarlet woman (Revelation 17:1, 2) will also get to drink "the wine of God's wrath." The wine of the scarlet woman is the false teachings of apostate Christianity. Those who believe these false teachings will, at the time of the end, get to drink God's wine. The wine of God's wrath in part refers to the seven last plagues: the "seven plagues, which are the last, for with them the wrath of God is ended." (Revelation 15:1). Clearly, the seven last plagues are part of God's wrath. The seven last plagues will fall on those "who bore the mark of the beast and worshiped its image" (Revelation 16:2). The temple is closed when the plagues fall (Revelation 15:8), which means that the investigative judgment is complete. Therefore, God's people (the 144,000) are sealed (Revelation 7:3, 4) prior to the onset of the plagues (discussed in Revelation 16—The Seven Last Plagues).

This wine of God's wrath will be "poured unmixed into the cup of his anger." This means that God's wrath will be undiluted.[16] God's wrath will be poured unmixed with His mercy. God's wrath will reflect His anger at how the wicked are treating His saints. The wicked will have slain many saints prior to the close of probation, which occurs at the "time of the end" referred to in Daniel 11:35. Once this time of the end begins, God will begin to repay the wicked for their sins. This repayment will involve the seven last plagues. The seven last plagues will begin to fall during the first woe or fifth trumpet (discussed in Revelation 9—The Seven Trumpets: The First and Second Woes).

As if drinking "the wine of God's wrath" is not enough, the worshipers of the beast are guaranteed more punishment. The third angel's message continues: "he shall be tormented with fire and brimstone in the presence of the holy angels and in the presence of the Lamb." This "fire and brimstone" suggests final destruction, since it is similar to the fire and brimstone which destroyed Sodom and Gomorrah (Genesis 19:24). This occurs in the presence of the holy angels and the Lamb, which also suggests the final destruction pictured in Revelation 20:10, 14, and 15. The seven last plagues will include the fiery destruction of the world at the Second Coming, but this separate mentioning of "fire and brimstone" suggests the final destruction of the wicked at the Third Coming of Christ after the 1,000 years of Revelation 20:3, 7. The wicked who are alive at the close or probation will get to experience God's wrath first with His plagues, and then again with their final destruction at the end of the millennium (1000 years).

> Revelation 14:11: *"And the smoke of their torment goes up for ever and ever; and they have no rest, day or night, these worshipers of the beast and its image, and whoever receives the mark of its name."*

This text has often been misinterpreted. The English translation seems to suggest endless torture or torment. The Greek phrase translated "forever and ever" actually means for a certain period until completed.[17] In other words, this should be translated the smoke of their torment goes up until they are completely destroyed. God will not torment sinners forever but He will torment them until they are consumed. Their destruction will be permanent or everlasting. The other phrase, which is often misinterpreted in this text, is: "they have no rest, day or night." The Greek word translated "rest" can also mean cessation or refreshment.[18] This phrase means that there will be no cessation of this continuous torment until it is complete.[19] In other words, both phrases, which have been interpreted to suggest eternal torture, actually mean to torment until destruction is complete. The remainder of this text simply reaffirms who will receive this punishment. This punishment is the eternal reward of those who worship "the beast and its image" and receive its "mark."

> Revelation 14:12: *"Here is a call for the endurance of the saints, those who keep the commandments of God and the faith of Jesus."*

This text is related to the prior three angel's messages. When Babylon has fallen, the world will have drunk the wine of her fornication or impure passion. This occurs when the image of the beast or church-state union is formed and the Sunday law is passed. This will then be followed by the mark of the beast, which occurs when the buy-sell penalty becomes law, which is described in Revelation 13:16, 17. This buy-sell penalty will force everyone to choose to accept or reject the false Sabbath. The reign of influence of the leopard-like beast (who was mortally wounded and subsequently healed) will begin again at the passage of the Sunday law. This reign will last for 42 months (Revelation 13:5). During the reign of the leopard-like beast and the subsequent reign of the dragon beast, God's saints will be persecuted and imprisoned. Once the buy-sell law has been enacted, God's people will not be able to buy or sell goods or services (Revelation 13:16, 17). Ultimately, a law will be passed that will "cause those who will not worship the image of the beast to be slain" (Revelation 13:15). Because of this persecution God's saints will need endurance and patience in order to survive.

This text also defines who God's saints are. God's saints are "those who keep the commandments of God and the faith of Jesus." In the context of the last days these two characteristics have special meanings. These two characteristics will be the characteristics of those that are sealed and make up the 144,000 (Revelation 7:3, 4). The "commandments of God" refers to the Ten Commandments of Exodus 20:3-17. God's people will keep all of His Commandments. In the last days, during the three angel's messages, one commandment is involved in all three messages. This commandment is the fourth commandment. The fourth commandment is the commandment to keep the seventh-day Sabbath. The fourth commandment is linked to the Creator God in the first angel's message. The fourth commandment is changed in the second angel's message with the passage of the Sunday law. The fourth commandment becomes God's seal or mark when the buy-sell law is enacted. This buy-sell law also creates Satan's seal or mark, which is the mark of the beast. In other words, the saints at the time of the end will keep God's true Sabbath, the seventh-day. They will do this regardless of man-made laws that require them to keep a false Sabbath or Sunday. God's saints will keep all of God's commandments. In the context of the last-day events God's saints will reject the false Sabbath.

God's saints will also be defined by "the faith of Jesus." This can be translated the faith of Jesus or faith in Jesus. Certainly, the saints will have faith in Jesus as their Savior and Lord. Our faith in Jesus is what saves us.[20] However, in the last days, there is a unique situation, which changes the emphasis of this phrase. Just before the time of the end, when probation closes, Satan will be reigning as the eighth king. As the eighth king, he will claim to be Christ returned. As the false Christ he will claim to interpret God's Law and he will support the false Sabbath as the real Sabbath.[21] Satan as the false Christ will claim the allegiance of the world's Christians. Any Christian who rejects Satan will be declared worthy of death. God's saints, in the last days, will reject the false Sabbath and also will reject the false Christ. God's saints will maintain a true faith in Jesus and reject the counterfeit false Christ. These two characteristics are the reasons why the dragon is "angry with the woman" (Revelation 12:17). The dragon is Satan, who is the eighth king or false Christ. The dragon will make war "on those who keep the commandments of God and bear testimony to Jesus" (Revelation 12:17). Revelation 12:17 is describing the same two characteristics as Revelation 14:12. *The saints at the end of time will be defined as those who refuse to accept Satan's false Sabbath and thereby break God's Law. The saints in the last days will be defined as those who reject the false Christ and keep faith in the true*

Jesus Christ, their Savior and Lord.

> Revelation 14:13: *"And I heard a voice from heaven saying,*
> *'write this: Blessed are the dead who die in the Lord*
> *henceforth.' 'Blessed indeed,' says the Spirit, 'that they*
> *may rest from their labors, for their deeds follow them!'"*

This text begins with another angel's voice heard from heaven. This is not one of the previous three angels but the message is clearly from God. This message begins with a blessing. This is one of the seven beatitudes or blessings found in the book of Revelation. These seven blessings are found in: Revelation 1:3, Revelation 14:15, Revelation 16:15, Revelation 19:9, Revelation 20:6, Revelation 22:7, and Revelation 22:14.[22]

This blessing states "blessed are the dead who die in the Lord henceforth." This blessing is placed on those who will die during the third angel's message up to the time of the end. This blessing is on the "wise" of Daniel 11:35, who fall prior to the time of the end. This time of the end, described again in Daniel 11:40, represents the close of probation and the beginning of the seven last plagues.

The "wise" of Daniel 11:33-35 are those who "shall understand" (Daniel 12:10). These wise will understand the last-day events and that the abomination that makes desolate is Satan reigning as the false Christ and the eighth king. Some of these wise will fall prior to the time of the end (Daniel 11:35). Those who fall or "die" are the ones who are "blessed indeed" in this beatitude. These are the ones who will die "henceforth," meaning after the third angels message. These are the ones who will be persecuted and slain because they refuse to accept the mark of the beast or worship the beast or its image (Revelation 13:15).

Death is described here as "rest from their labors." Jesus described death as a sleep (John 11:11-14). Those who die during the third angel's message are told to "rest from their labors, for their deeds follow them!" This is a reference to Revelation 20:12, 13 where the dead are judged "by what they had done." These saints do not need to worry because God will not forget their deeds. They are "blessed indeed." They are blessed in the sense that God is going to raise them to eternal life and they are blessed because they can rest through the time of trouble, such as has never been "since there was a nation" (Daniel 12:1).

> Revelation 14:14: *"Then I looked, and lo, a white cloud,*
> *and seated on the cloud one like a son of man, with a*
> *golden crown on his head, and a sharp sickle in his hand."*

Now John sees a new scene, which follows directly after the previous three angels' messages and is related to them. This text begins a vision of Jesus' Second Coming. The close connection of this vision to the prior three angels' messages shows their messages are God's last messages to the world prior to Jesus' Second Coming.[23] John sees "one like a son of man" seated on a white cloud. This Son of Man was previously described in Revelation 1:13 and is Jesus Christ. Jesus is wearing a crown of victory and holding a sharp sickle. Jesus is returning victorious to harvest His people. This harvest was described by Jesus in the parable of the good seed and the bad seed (Matthew 13:30). Jesus is returning to harvest the good seed or grain, which represents His true believers. These are those who have God's mark or seal in their foreheads. These are the saints who refused to accept a false Sabbath or a false Christ at the time of the end. These are the saints who have kept all of God's Commandments and kept faith in the true Jesus.

> Revelation 14:15: *"And another angel came out of the temple, calling with a loud voice to him who sat upon the cloud, 'Put in your sickle, and reap, for the hour to reap has come, for the harvest of the earth is fully ripe.'"*

This angel comes directly from the temple where God's throne is located. This temple is where the judgment process had been going on until the close of probation. Now God is telling Jesus it is time to reap the harvest. The righteous are symbolized by the ripened grain.[24] Jesus is pictured as the Harvester who will collect the ripened grain. Jesus is told "the hour to reap has come." This hour is the "day and hour no one knows, not even the angels of heaven, nor the Son" (Matthew 24:36). The hour to reap has come because "the earth is fully ripe." The harvest of the earth includes not only the grain but also the grapes. The grain has been ready since the close of probation but the wicked (grapes) have not yet completed their punishment. The world controlled by Satan and sin is almost ready to self destruct. God's wrath, or punishment, includes the seven last plagues. These plagues are now ending and the earth is "fully ripe." It is now time to harvest the earth. It is now time to harvest the grain and the grapes. It is now time to harvest the righteous and the wicked. It is now time to reward the righteous and to reward the wicked. It is now time to save the righteous and punish the wicked.

> Revelation 14:16: *"So he who sat upon the cloud swung his sickle on the earth, and the earth was reaped."*

Jesus is seen reaping the earth. This is the same scene John the Baptist described in Luke 3:17 where Jesus was seen gathering the wheat into His granary. Jesus is collecting His people at the end of time. This harvest number is complete at the close of probation, when the 144,000 are sealed and the investigative judgment ends. This reaping of the grain represents Jesus returning to earth to save His 144,000 who are sealed on their foreheads. The 144,000 represent all of God's people living at the time of the end. The 144,000 are the grain, which is harvested. The dead in Christ are also raised at this time and are caught up in the clouds with them (1 Thessalonians 4:16, 17).

> Revelation 14:17: *"And another angel came out of the temple in heaven, and he too had a sharp sickle."*

This is "another angel" and is different from the previous four angels. Just like the previous angel, this angel also has to do with judgment. This angel is seen coming out of the temple. The temple is where the throne of God is, and the temple is where God sits in judgment. Now judgment is about to fall on the wicked. This angel is described as carrying a "sharp sickle" just as the Son of Man carried a sickle. This "sickle" will be used to reap the wicked, who are represented as grapes.

> Revelation 14:18: *"Then another angel came out from the*

*altar, the angel who has power over fire, and he called with
a loud voice to him who had the sharp sickle, 'Put in your
sickle, and gather the clusters of the vine of the earth, for its
grapes are ripe.'"*

This is the sixth angel seen in Revelation 14. The first three angels give God's last message of warning to the world prior to the Second Coming of Christ. The next three are involved in the judgment of the righteous and the wicked. The judgment of the righteous will be a reward. The judgment of the wicked will be punishment. This sixth angel is seen coming from the altar. This angel can be understood to represent the angel of vengeance. The martyred saints were seen under the altar crying out for vengeance in the fifth seal (Revelation 6:9, 10). Now, God sends His angel from the altar in response to their cries.

This angel, who comes to avenge God's martyred saints, is described as the angel who has "power over fire." This is the fire that Peter described: "But the day of the Lord will come like a thief, and then the heavens will pass away with a loud noise, and the elements will be dissolved with fire and the earth and the works that are upon it will be burned up" (2 Peter 3:10). Peter goes on to say, "Since all these things are thus to be dissolved, what sort of persons ought you to be in lives of holiness and godliness, waiting for and hastening the coming of the day of God, because of which the heavens will be kindled and dissolved, and the elements will melt with fire!" (2 Peter 3:11, 12). This angel calls with a "loud voice." This loud voice is a voice of judgment that will be heard worldwide. This angel tells the angel with a sickle to "gather the clusters of the vine of the earth, for its grapes are ripe."

The "grapes" represent the wicked, who "bore the mark of the beast and worshipped its image" (Revelation 16:2). These are the same men and women who have already endured God's wrath in the form of His last plagues (Revelation 15:1). These "grapes" represent those who worship "the beast and its image" and receive "a mark on his forehead or on his hand" (Revelation 14:9). These "grapes" will drink of "the wine of God's wrath" (Revelation 14:10) and they will be crushed. These "grapes" are those who drank of Babylon's "wine of her impure passion" (Revelation 14:8). These are the wicked who accepted the false Sabbath and received the mark of the beast. They also worshiped the false Christ, who is the eighth king and the abomination that makes desolate. These "grapes" are now ripe. God has completed the first five plagues. Satan's rule in Jerusalem has now ended and the final plagues are about to occur.

Revelation 14:19: *"So the angel swung his sickle on the
earth and gathered the vintage of the earth, and threw it
into the great wine press of the wrath of God;"*

This angel is now pictured as harvesting the grapes. His sickle is swung "on the earth," which means that this judgment will fall worldwide. This judgment will involve the entire earth. The angel is seen gathering "the vintage." This gathering of the wicked correlates with Revelation 16:16: "And they assembled them at the place which is called in Hebrew Armageddon." The wicked will be gathered together for one final battle (Revelation 16:14). This battle will occur "outside the city" (Revelation 14:20). This battle will occur outside Jerusalem since Jerusalem will be

Satan's capital city. This battle is also described in Daniel 11:44, 45. This will be the final battle on earth just prior to Jesus' arrival in the clouds of heaven. This same battle is described in Revelation 9:14-16 where the four angels at the river Euphrates are released and "a third of mankind" is killed. This battle of Armageddon is the sixth plague and is part of the wrath of God. The angel is seen throwing the "vintage" or grapes into "the great wine press of the wrath of God." The wicked are gathered or assembled and then God's sixth plague occurs. The wicked are slain in God's wine press "outside the city" (Revelation 14:20).

> Revelation 14:20: *"and the wine press was trodden outside the city, and blood flowed from the wine press, as high as a horse's bridle, for one thousand six hundred stadia."*

This text completes this description of the punishment of the wicked. The wicked are described as grapes and are "trodden outside the city." This phrase is symbolic of the destruction of the wicked, which will occur outside Jerusalem at the end of time. This is the final battle described as the battle of Armageddon (Revelation 16:16). This same battle is described in Joel 3:2: "I will gather all the nations and bring them down to the valley of Jehoshasphat, and I will enter into judgment with them there." Joel further states, "Hasten and come, all you nations round about, gather yourselves there. Bring down thy warriors, O Lord. Let the nations bestir themselves, and come up to the valley of Jehoshaphat; for there I will sit to judge all the nations round about" (Joel 3:11, 12). If there is any question regarding the connection between Joel's prophecy and Revelation 14:16, Joel's next verse clearly links them together. "Put in the sickle, for the harvest is ripe. Go in, tread, for the wine press is full. The vats overflow, for their wickedness is great" (Joel 3:13).

The prophet Joel foresaw the same events that John saw portrayed in Revelation 14:17-20. This outpouring of God's wrath or sixth plague will occur "outside the city" of Jerusalem in the valley of Jehoshaphat. This is the final battle of Armageddon. This is the" wine press" of God's wrath after the wicked are "gathered" (Revelation 14:19). The harvest is ripe because the wicked have gone as far as God will allow them to go. Indeed, without God's intervention it is likely the entire world would be destroyed including God's people. This final battle will involve large population centers because of the large numbers who will be killed: "a third of mankind" (Revelation 9:15, 18).

Joel continues: "Multitudes, multitudes, in the valley of decision! For the day of the Lord is near in the valley of decision. The sun and the moon are darkened, and the stars withdraw their shining. And the Lord roars from Zion, and utters his voice from Jerusalem, and the heavens and the earth shake. But the Lord is a refuge to his people, a stronghold to the people of Israel" (Joel 3:14-16). Joel follows this battle scene with a description of the Second Coming of Christ. Joel's description of events includes the sun and moon darkened and the stars failing to shine. Joel had previously described these same three events associated with the great and terrible "day of the Lord" (Joel 2:10, 11). Joel had also described the sun and moon darkened in Joel 2:31 linked to this same "day of the Lord." Clearly, Joel is describing end-of-time events in all three of these situations. These descriptions parallel the sixth seal events which occur just prior to Jesus' Second Coming:

"the sun became black as sackcloth, the full moon became like blood, and the stars of the sky fell to the earth" (Revelation 6:12, 13).

Joel also states "the heavens and the earth shake" (Joel 3:16). This also parallels the events of the Second Coming as described in Revelation 16:18: "and a great earthquake such as had never been since men were on the earth, so great was that earthquake." This battle being described by Joel is followed by the Second Coming of Christ, which is "the great and terrible day of the Lord" (Joel 2:31).

Revelation 14:20 closes with "blood flowed from the wine press, as high as a horses bridle, for one thousand six hundred stadia." This description is symbolic of massive loss of life. This same battle in Revelation 9:15 is described as killing one-third of mankind. If this is a literal number this would represent between one and two billion people destroyed. Sixteen hundred stadia is about 184 miles.[25] This is the area involved in the final battle of Armageddon, which will be covered with the wicked dead. However, God's people will be spared.

SUMMARY

Revelation 14 begins with a description of God's people who will not accept the mark of the beast described in Revelation 13. These 144,000 will be unstained by the beast or its false churches. They will reject the false Sabbath and the false Christ or the eighth king. The 144,000 are the righteous believers who have the endurance of the saints. They will keep all of God's commandments including the seventh-day Sabbath. They will maintain faith in the true Jesus in the presence of Satan as the false Christ.

Next, following this description of God's people who will overcome Satan, the three angel's messages are described. The first angel warns that the hour of God's judgment has come. Men are told to fear God, who is the Creator. They are reminded that true Sabbath worship was established because God is our Creator. This hour of judgment began in 1844, when the cleansing of the heavenly sanctuary began. This investigative judgment is still ongoing.

The second angel's message warns that Babylon has fallen because she made all nations drink of her impure passion. This impure passion or fornication symbolizes the church-state union, which apostate Christianity will bring about in the last days. This church-state union will be instrumental in passing a mandatory day of worship, which will be the Sunday law. When this law is passed the nations will have drunk of her impure passion. This Sunday law will mark the beginning of spiritual control of the world by the leopard-like beast. This control will last 42 months (Revelation 13:5).

The third angel's message warns of a mark of the beast that will lead to God's wrath. This mark of the beast will be enforced by the image to the beast. The image to the beast is the United States of America after it becomes a church-state union and enacts the Sunday law. The enactment of the Sunday law is not the mark of the beast. The enforcement of the Sunday law is the mark of the beast. The mark of the beast will occur when the buy-sell law is passed enforcing Sunday observance under the threat of economic penalties (Revelation 13:16, 17). This law will enforce observance of Sunday, the false Sabbath, with the penalty of the loss of all economic power.

The saints are described as those who keep God's Law and have the faith of Jesus. In the last days this means they reject the false Sabbath and reject the false Christ. The false Christ will begin his reign as the eighth king after the Sunday law has been passed but before the mark of the beast has been enacted. Satan's reign as the false Christ is described as follows: "As the crowning act in the great drama of deception, Satan himself will personate Christ . . . In different parts of the earth, Satan will manifest himself among men as a majestic being of dazzling brightness, resembling the description of the Son of God given by John in the Revelation. Revelation 1:13-15. The glory that surrounds him is unsurpassed by anything that mortal eyes have yet beheld . . . he heals the diseases of the people, and then, in his assumed character of Christ, he claims to have changed the Sabbath to Sunday, and commands all to hallow the day which he has blessed. He declares that those who persist in keeping holy the seventh day are blaspheming his name by refusing to listen to his angels sent to them with light and truth. This is the strong, almost overmastering delusion" (*The Great Controversy*, page 624).[26] Satan appears as the false Christ prior to the enactment of the penalties to enforce Sunday keeping or he would not have to command the keeping of his Sunday law.

Revelation 14 closes with a description of God's redeemed just as the chapter began. Jesus is seen harvesting the 144,000 represented as grain. This harvest appears to occur prior to the wrath of God falling on the wicked, suggesting that once probation closes God's people are secure. This chapter ends with a description of a massive destruction of the wicked, which occurs at the battle of Armageddon "outside the city." This city is Jerusalem, Israel in the Middle East. This parallels Joel's description of the same battle, and also parallels the sixth trumpet and the sixth plague. This event will be followed by Jesus' Second Coming, which is the seventh trumpet and the seventh plague. The following chart summarizes the events described in Revelation 14.

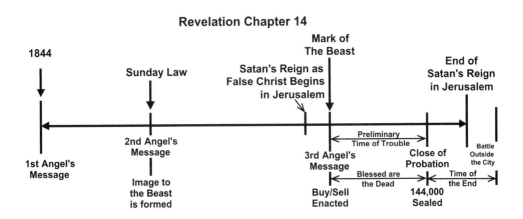

Revelation Chapter 14

[1] Nichol, Francis D. (Ed.) *The Seventh-day Adventist Bible Commentary* (Review and Herald Publishing Association, Washington D. C.) 1957, Vol. 7, p. 825.

[2] Ibid. p. 826.

[3] Ibid.

[4] Ibid. p. 827.

[5] Ibid.

[6] Ibid.

[7] Ibid.

[8] Ibid.

[9] Ibid.

[10] Ibid. p. 828.

[11] Ibid.

[12] Ibid.

[13] Ibid.

[14] *The Catholic Encyclopedia*, Thomas Nelson, 1976, s. v. "Rome."

[15] Nichol, Francis D. (Ed.) *The Seventh-day Adventist Bible Commentary* (Review and Herald Publishing Association, Washington D. C.) 1957, Vol. 7, p. 827.

[16] Ibid. p. 831.

[17] Ibid. p. 832.

[18] Ibid.

[19] Ibid.

[20] Ibid. p. 833.

[21] White, Ellen G., *The Great Controversy* (Pacific Press Publishing Association, Nampa, Idaho) 1950, p. 624.

[22] Nichol, Francis D. (Ed.) *The Seventh-day Adventist Bible Commentary* (Review and Herald Publishing Association, Washington D. C.) 1957, Vol. 7, p. 833.

[23] Ibid. p. 834.

[24] Ibid.

[25] Ibid. p. 835.

[26] White, Ellen G., *The Great Controversy* (Pacific Press Publishing Association, Nampa, Idaho) 1950, p. 624.

Revelation 13 (last part)
The Mark of the Beast

The mark of the beast is introduced in Revelation 13:16. This is the first mention of this mark or sign found in Revelation. This mark or sign is clearly linked to the beast of Revelation 13. It is also linked to the image of the beast and to the lamb-like beast. Who are these beasts? What is the image? What is the mark? Who receives the mark? Why is the mark important? When does the mark occur?

The timing of when the mark occurs is critical to understanding what the mark is and who will receive it. In order to understand the timing, we must examine Revelation 13 closely. Revelation 13 is introduced by describing a beast "rising out of the sea" (Revelation 13:1). This beast has ten horns and seven heads and the ten horns are crowned (discussed in Preface: The Crowns and Their Meaning). Revelation 13:2 shows that John is looking backward through time, since the order of Daniel's symbols is reversed. Daniel described a lion, a bear, a leopard and a beast in that order (Daniel 7:4-7). Daniel's beast had ten horns with no crowns, because they did not yet exist as kingdoms. John's beast has ten horns with crowns because these horns have already become kingdoms and already existed prior to the other events described in this vision (Revelation 13). John's viewpoint in Revelation 13 is looking back in history from the time of the image of the beast. This image of the beast occurs after the beast's wound has healed (Revelation 13:3, 12). This image of the beast occurs after the lamb-like beast exists (Revelation 13:11, 12) and is formed by the lamb-like beast (Revelation 13:14, 15).

Who is the beast of Revelation 13:1? The answer is found in Daniel 7, which John is referring to in Revelation 13:2. In Daniel 7:7, the fourth beast is introduced, which was "terrible and dreadful and exceedingly strong; and it had great iron teeth." This beast had ten horns. This beast also had a little horn described in Daniel 7:8, which "came up" among the ten horns and devoured three of these horns. In Daniel 7:23-25, we find the explanation: "As for the fourth beast, there shall be a fourth kingdom on earth, which shall be different from all the kingdoms, and it shall devour the whole earth, and trample it down, and break it to pieces. As for the ten horns, out of this kingdom ten kings shall arise, and another shall arise after them; he shall be different from the former ones, and shall put down three kings. He shall speak words against the Most High, and shall wear out the saints of the Most High, and shall think to change the times and the law; and they shall be given into his hand for a time, two times, and half a time."

This beast with "great iron teeth" (Daniel 7:7) that ruled the world was the fourth world kingdom. The iron refers to Daniel 2:40: "And there shall be a fourth kingdom, strong as iron." The first world kingdom was Babylon (Daniel 2:37-38). The second world kingdom was Media-Persia, which was followed by Greece as the third world kingdom. These kingdoms are described in Daniel 8:20, 21 as the ram that followed Babylon and the "he-goat," which overcame the ram. The fourth world kingdom was

Rome, which conquered Greece. Rome was known for its "iron teeth." Pagan Rome overran Greece and the rest of the world to become the fourth world kingdom.

The ten horns represent "ten kings" which come "out of this kingdom" (Daniel 7:24). These ten kingdoms would rise out of pagan Rome and would occupy Europe. Three of these kingdoms would be put down by the little horn, which is described as "different from the former ones" (Daniel 7:24). There were ten kingdoms that arose from the ashes of pagan Rome. Seven of these kingdoms still exist today. Three of the ten kingdoms were overthrown or incorporated into the Papal kingdom. The Papacy or Roman Catholic Church took over the kingdoms of the Vandals, the Ostrogoths, and the Heruli and they no longer exist today. The "little horn" of Daniel 7 and 8 represents the Papacy.

Daniel 7:24 states: "he shall be different from the former ones." This verse was totally accurate. The little horn or Papacy was a church run kingdom. The "former ones," referring to the ten kingdoms, were temporal kingdoms and were not church controlled.

Daniel 7:25 states: "He shall speak words against the Most High, and shall wear out the saints of the Most High, and shall think to change the times and the law." The Papacy fulfills each of these prophecies. The Pope has effectively claimed to be God on earth.[1] The Roman Catholic Church persecuted millions of other Christians during the Dark Ages and clearly wore "out the saints." The Roman Catholic Church claims it has changed the Sabbath to Sunday, changing God's Law in the process.[2]

The final portion of Daniel 7:25 refers to a time prophecy: "a time, two times, and half a time." This is 1260 days. A" time" equals one year or 360 days (Jewish calendar year), "two times" equals 2 times 360 days or 720 days, a "half a time" equals 180 days, and the total is: 360 plus 720 plus 180 equals 1260 days. In prophecy, one prophetic day equals one literal year. Thus, the Papacy would rule for 1260 years. The Papacy began its rule in A.D. 538 and its rule ended in 1798. Exactly 1260 years after A.D. 538, Pope Pius VI was captured by Napoleon's General Berthier and imprisoned. This ended the world dominance of the Papacy and ended the Papal kingdom as a world power. This was the mortal wound of the leopard-like beast. This wound changed the Papacy from a worldwide kingdom into a worldwide church.

This "mortal wound" is described in Revelation 13:3, 12. Revelation 13:3 states: "One of its heads seemed to have a mortal wound, but its mortal wound was healed." The head referred to here is Pope Pius VI, who was captured by General Berthier. This helps us identify the seven heads of Revelation 17. The seven heads are seven leaders or Popes of the Catholic Church. This mortal wound was healed in 1929 when Mussolini gave the approximately 108 acres that was occupied by Vatican City to the Catholic Church. This re-established the church-state status of the Roman Catholic Church and it became a kingdom again. A kingdom is a political entity and kingdoms have kings. A church is a spiritual entity and typically does not have kings. The seven heads of Revelation 17 are seven kings (Revelation 17:10), who will reign after this kingdom is re-established.

The beast of Daniel 7, which continued as the little horn, represented pagan and then Papal Rome. The leopard-like beast in Revelation 13:1 is the same beast as the little horn in Daniel 7. John is simply looking back in time at the same events. The leopard-like beast in Revelation 13 represents the Papacy. The head mortally wounded, described in Revelation 13:3, 12, is the Pope who was captured in 1798. The healing of this mortal wound occurred in 1929 when Vatican City was restored to the Papacy.

If the beast is the Papacy, then what is the mark of the beast? The term "mark" can also be thought of as the sign or seal of the beast. In order to understand what this sign or seal is, we must first identify God's sign or seal. A seal must include three elements in order to qualify as a legitimate seal: the name of the owner, his title and his territory.

In Exodus 20:8-11 we read "Remember the sabbath day, to keep it holy. Six days you shall labor, and do all your work; but the seventh day is a sabbath to the Lord your God; in it you shall not do any work, you, or your son, or your daughter, your manservant, or your maidservant, or your cattle, or the sojourner who is within your gates; for in six days the Lord made heaven and earth, the sea, and all that is in them, and rested the seventh day; therefore the Lord blessed the sabbath day and hallowed it." This is the fourth commandment of God's Ten Commandments. It contains God's seal:

1) God's name: "the Lord your God."
2) God's title as Creator: He who "made heaven and earth."
3) God's territory: "heaven and earth."

The fourth commandment is God's seal or sign. It contains all the required elements for a seal. It commands that mankind "Remember the sabbath day, to keep it holy."

Exodus 31:16, 17 states: "Wherefore the people of Israel shall keep the sabbath, observing the sabbath throughout their generations, *as a perpetual covenant. It is a sign for ever between me and the people of Israel that in six days the Lord made heaven and earth, and on the seventh day he rested, and was refreshed"* (emphasis supplied). God intended for the seventh-day Sabbath to be His perpetual covenant with His people. God intends for His Sabbath to extend into the eternal ages. The Sabbath "is a sign for ever" between God and His people.

Exodus 31:13 states: "You shall keep my sabbaths, for this is a sign between me and you throughout your generations, that you may know that I, the Lord, sanctify you." Not only is the Sabbath God's sign of His creation (Exodus 31:17) but it is also a sign of sanctification: "that you may know that I, the Lord, sanctify you." In other words, God's seventh-day Sabbath is a sign of God's creation or ownership of each of us and also His re-creation and purchase of each of us through Christ's death and resurrection. *The seventh-day Sabbath is God's mark or sign that we are God's people and He is our God.* This sign is perpetual or eternal and will not change throughout eternity. This sign is God's promise of our salvation: "that you may know that I, the Lord, sanctify you."

If God's sign or mark or seal is the seventh-day Sabbath, then what is the mark or seal of the beast? The beast has been shown to be the Papacy. Does the Papacy keep God's Sabbath? The answer is no. Referring to the little horn, Daniel 7:25 states "and shall think to change the times and the law." This prophecy about the Papacy was fulfilled when the Papacy took credit for changing God's Law. God's Law or His Ten Commandments clearly states that the seventh day is the Sabbath. Peter Geiermann's *The Convert's Catechism of Catholic Doctrine,* page 50 states:

> Question: Which is the Sabbath Day?
> Answer: Saturday is the Sabbath Day.
>
> Question: Why do we observe Sunday instead of Saturday?
> Answer: We observe Sunday instead of Saturday because the Catholic Church, in the Council of Laodicea (A.D. 364), transferred the solemnity from Saturday to Sunday." [3]

This confirms that the Papacy or Catholic Church has changed God's Law. It is extremely important to realize that the portion of God's Law that was changed is also God's mark or sign or seal for His people. Satan, as the world's final spiritual leader, will insist that he has changed the day of worship and his day must be kept. The leopard-like beast (the Papacy) of Revelation 13 will be involved in originating this false Sabbath as a sign or mark of allegiance.

Revelation 13:4 states: "Men worshipped the dragon, for he had given his authority to the beast, and they worshipped the beast." The dragon is Satan and the beast is the Papacy. The only time both will be worshipped by large numbers of the world and exist visibly as world leaders simultaneously will be during the reign of the seventh king just prior to the reign of the eighth king. John's viewpoint in Revelation 13 is during the reign of the seventh king. The image of the beast will be created during the reign of the seventh king.

When the universal Sunday law is enacted, the world will have accepted the false Sabbath of the Papacy as the solution to the world's catastrophes. This acceptance of the Papacy's false Sabbath will be a form of worship of the beast or Papacy. While this process is ongoing, the false Christ will appear and deceive, "if possible, even the elect" (Matthew 24:24). This false Christ is the beast or eighth king who will take over from the seventh king (Revelation 17:10, 11). During this time period, just prior to the rise of the eighth king (depicted as "the beast that ascends" in Revelation 11:7 and the beast who "is to ascend" in Revelation 17:8), both the Papacy and the dragon will be worshipped. The Papacy will then turn over its rule and authority to the dragon (Satan) as the eighth king (discussed in Revelation 17 (first part)—The Scarlet Woman and Her Kings).

> Revelation 13:11, 12: *"Then I saw another beast which rose out of the earth; it had two horns like a lamb and it spoke like a dragon. It exercises all the authority of the first beast in its presence, and makes the earth and its inhabitants worship the first beast, whose mortal wound was healed."*

These two verses introduce a new power who will assist the first beast. This power or kingdom exists simultaneously with the first beast because it "exercises all the authority of the first beast in its presence." The time frame is after 1929 because the first beast's "mortal wound was healed." This lamb-like beast "makes the earth and its inhabitants worship the first beast." This phrase suggests that this lamb-like beast has worldwide influence and power. Also the phrase "spoke like a dragon" suggests great power, since dragons are symbolic of power. This beast has "two horns like a lamb." The lamb-like nature of this beast suggests a country that prefers peaceful negotiations to war-like activity. The two horns of Revelation 13:11, which dominate the lamb-like beast, represent two characteristics of this lamb-like nation. These two horns are symbolic of civil and religious freedom, which make the United States unique in the world. The United States clearly speaks "like a dragon," since it is now the world's greatest superpower. The United States has always been lamb-like in its approach to other countries compared to most prior world powers. The United States has become involved in world conflicts but usually only after diplomatic attempts to avoid involvement have failed.

This beast "rose out of the earth." In Bible prophecy "waters" (or the sea) refers to populated areas (Revelation 17:15) and the earth refers to unpopulated areas. This beast arising "out of the earth" means it arose from an unpopulated area. The United States of America arose "out of the earth" because it arose in North America, which was only sparsely populated. The United States of America has not yet made the earth or its inhabitants "worship the first beast" (Revelation 13:12) however, this will happen in the near future. The "first beast" refers to the leopard-like beast or Papacy, which will encourage the development of the image to the beast.

> Revelation 13:13: *"It works great signs, even making fire*
> *come down from heaven to earth in the site of men."*

Historically, this text has been applied to miracles done that would convince men to believe in Satan.[4] Bringing "fire down" from heaven brings to mind Elijah on Mount Carmel (1 Kings 18:17-39) where only God could bring fire down. Some see this as a reference to spiritualism: Satan claiming to be God and working miracles.[5] However, the context here strongly suggests that the lamb-like beast is the cause of the fire coming down and the great signs. In this case, the lamb-like beast would be the one performing these wonders. One present day fulfillment of "making fire come down from heaven" was seen at the end of World War II when the United States of America destroyed Hiroshima and Nagasaki with the atomic bomb. Certainly, the United States of America has done many other "great signs" since World War II. Great "signs" or wonders could include such things as: putting a man on the moon, supersonic travel and unbelievable technological advances.

> Revelation 13:14: *"and by the signs which it is allowed to*
> *work in the presence of the beast, it deceives those who*
> *dwell on earth bidding them make an image for the beast*
> *which was wounded by the sword and yet lived."*

Historically, Revelation 13:14 has been applied to Satan who is the great deceiver.[6] Satan does fulfill some of the characteristics described in Revelation 13:13, 14. However, in the context of this verse, "it" refers to the lamb-like beast, which is not Satan. Satan is the "dragon" of Revelation 13:2, 4. The "beast" referred to here represents the Papacy. This is clear from the latter part of this verse. This is the "beast," which "was wounded by the sword and yet lived." This wound was previously described in Revelation 13:3 as a "mortal wound." Revelation 13:3 states:

"One of its heads seemed to have a mortal wound, but its mortal wound was healed, and the whole earth followed the beast with wonder" (emphasis supplied). This mortal wound occurred in 1798 when Napoleon's General Berthier took Pope Pius VI into captivity and captured Rome. Pope Pius VI died in captivity and this appeared to be a fatal wound for the Papacy. This wound was healed when Mussolini signed the Lateran Treaty in 1929. This treaty gave Vatican City back its land and reestablished the Papacy as an official church-state kingdom. Clearly, the head of this beast was one of the Popes. These same heads are described as seven kings in Revelation 17:9, 10 and the seven kings of Revelation 17 are the last seven Popes (discussed in Revelation 17 (first part)—The Scarlet Woman and Her Kings) which will reign after the mortal wound is healed. However, Revelation 13:14 is describing the working of "signs" by the lamb-like beast. This verse suggests that the United States of America will work "signs . . . in the presence of the beast and these signs will occur after the beast's wound is healed." It also means that they will work together to deceive those who dwell on earth. This deception will convince those who dwell on earth to "make an image for the beast."

As political kingdoms one of the major differences between the United States of America and the Papacy is that the Papacy is a church-state union, whereas the United States of America separates church and state. One of the "two horns" (Revelation 13:11) of the lamb-like beast, which is the United States of America, is religious liberty. The United States of America was formed by people who fled Europe because of religious persecution. It seems impossible that this country could ever rescind its position on religious freedom but it will! *Once this horn has been removed, the United States of America will have become an "image" of the beast.* The Greek word *"Eikon"* translated "image" in this verse means "a likeness." Once the United States of America abandons religious liberty it will become like the Papacy. The United States of America will have formed an "image" or likeness to the beast. The United States of America will then enforce religious beliefs on its people. This will only occur because the United States citizens ask for it. They will ask for it once they are convinced it is the only way to stop the natural disasters that have been increasing in number. They seem to be occurring because of the loss of God's favor. These natural disasters are considered "acts of God" in common terminology. These natural disasters will trigger huge economic losses in this country, which will then lead to worldwide economic collapse. This will in turn trigger the loss of religious freedom in this country resulting in the formation of the "image." The "image" represents the union of church and state with the loss of religious freedom. This church-state union will then attempt to enforce religious laws on its people. *The "image of the beast" in Revelation 13 is formed when the United States of America becomes a church-state union.*

> Revelation 13:15: *"and it was allowed to give breath to the image of the beast so that the image of the beast should even speak, and to cause those who will not worship the image of the beast to be slain."*

The lamb-like beast (the United States of America) will "give breath to the image." This image or church-state union will come to life in the United States of

America. This image's birth will come as a result of a repudiation of religious liberty. This repudiation of religious liberty will come as a result of natural disasters and economic collapse, which will be blamed on God. It will be thought that this country has wandered too far from God and must do something to restore His favor. In an attempt to gain God's favor, the United States will sacrifice religious freedom in order to achieve nationwide compliance. This legislation will lead to the church-state union and the enforcement of religious dogma.

The image will "speak" by passing laws that will impact every American. These laws will restrict activities and enforce a religious holy day. This religious holy day will be the day chosen by the leopard-beast (Papacy) and the dragon (Satan) and it will become their sign of allegiance. This sign of allegiance will ultimately become the mark of the beast and its image. Revelation 13:15 predicts a death penalty for the uncooperative. The "image" will "cause those who will not worship the beast *to be slain"* (emphasis supplied). ***The church-state union will become so powerful that it will be able to enforce a death penalty.*** Clearly, religious freedom is dead. The image to the leopard-like beast will be formed by the lamb-like beast when the United States of America abandons religious liberty in favor of enforced religion. The image to the beast is formed when the lamb-like beast sheds its first horn (i.e. religious liberty).

> Revelation 13:16: *"Also it causes all, both small and great, both rich and poor, both free and slave, to be marked on the right hand or the forehead."*

The image will cause every American, regardless of economic status or social position, "to be marked." This universal requirement for everyone "to be marked" has not yet occurred. This marking will be linked to a penalty (Revelation 13:17). This event will occur during the reign of the eighth king (discussed in Revelation 17 (second part)—The Eighth King). The eighth king is Satan as the false Christ or abomination that makes desolate.

This "image" of the Papacy is formed in the United States of America when apostate Protestantism unites with Catholicism. This union will cause the United States of America to form a church-state union which will be the image to the beast. This "image" will seek to enforce the Papacy's sign of allegiance or mark, which is Sunday observance. The universal Sunday law will become the test of faith. Those who keep Sunday will be considered law keepers. Those who refuse to observe Sunday as their Sabbath will be lawbreakers. Those who refuse to keep Sunday will eventually be threatened with the death penalty (Revelation 13:15). This same situation is described in Daniel 11:30. In Daniel 11:30, the "holy covenant," which represents God's true Sabbath, will be attacked. Satan, as the false Christ, will "give heed to those who forsake the holy covenant" and will then "set up the abomination that makes desolate" (Daniel 11:30, 31). However, God's people will not accept this false Sabbath. The holy covenant is God's true Sabbath (Exodus 31:16, 17). In Daniel 11:32, 33, "the people who know their God shall stand firm and take action. And those among the people who are wise shall make many understand, though they shall fall by sword and flame, by captivity and plunder, for some days." This prophecy suggests that some of God's people will die prior to His return, because they reject this false Christ and his false Sabbath.

The image will cause everyone "to be marked on the right hand or the forehead." The "hand" is a symbol for labor or work. In this situation, the "hand" symbolizes actions. When the Sunday law is kept out of expediency, then the mark will be on the hand. In other words, if someone keeps the Sunday law in order to avoid the penalty, even though they do not believe in the Sunday law, they will still receive its mark. If someone keeps the Sunday law because they actually believe it is true and are convinced of that truth, then they will receive the mark on their forehead. Whether you accept it as truth or don't accept it as truth, if you keep it once the buy-sell law is enacted (Revelation 13:17), you will receive the mark of the beast. This occurs because by accepting this mark or seal you have rejected God's mark or seal. At the end of time, only God's sealed people will be saved from death.It is noteworthy to realize that God's mark or seal can only be obtained on the forehead. Revelation 9:4 describes those "who have not the seal of God upon their foreheads." God's seal can only be obtained on the forehead. God's seal can only be obtained through commitment to His truth and acceptance of His truth. You cannot fake an acceptance of God's seal by keeping His Sabbath. God's seal does not involve a mark on the hand, only the beast's seal does. God knows our hearts and will only accept those hearts given to Him in allegiance. Satan and his false church will accept actions or beliefs as long as you do their wishes.

> Revelation 13:17: *"so that no one can buy or sell unless he has the mark, that is, the name of the beast or the number of its name."*

This is the first penalty that will be used to enforce the Sunday law. The second penalty will be the death decree mentioned in Revelation 13:15. This buy-sell sanction will attempt to enforce the Sunday law through economic pressure. Those who refuse to accept this Sunday law will lose their ability to buy or sell anything. This will effectively remove the other horn from the lamb-like beast. The horn representing civil liberty will be destroyed when people can no longer work or purchase goods. The two horns of the lamb-like beast represent religious and civil liberty. **When the United States loses both horns, it will have established the "mark" of the beast.** The image of the beast is formed when the first horn (religious liberty) is lost, which also signals the beginning of the second angel's message (Revelation 14:8). *The "mark" of the beast occurs when the second horn (civil liberty) is lost, which signals the beginning of the third angel's message (Revelation 14:9-11).*

Once the buy-sell sanction is enacted and the mark of the beast occurs, the preliminary time of trouble for God's people will begin. This preliminary time of trouble will precede the "time of trouble" (Daniel 12:1) or "great tribulation" (Matthew 24:21). The preliminary time of trouble will extend to the close of probation and the end of the investigative judgment. The time of trouble begins at the close of probation. The preliminary time of trouble will end at the "time of the end" (Daniel 11:35) when God's people will no longer die. This preliminary time of trouble begins at the beginning of the 2300 evenings and mornings described in Daniel 8:14. This time period covers the time when God's people will be under increased attack by Satan. This time period is when the "host" or God's people are "trampled under foot" (Daniel 8:13). This time period will end when the sanctuary is no longer "trampled under foot" (Daniel 8:13). This time period ends when the "continual burnt offering" and "the transgression that makes desolate" are ended (Daniel 8:13, 14). This time period is 2300 "evenings and mornings" (Daniel 8:14) which represents 1150 days of Satan's reign in Jerusalem during which he carries out his persecution of God's people by enforcing the mark of the beast. This 1150-day time period will include the preliminary time of trouble and part of the time of trouble and will end with the destruction of the temple in Jerusalem, which occurs shortly prior to the end of time.

The preliminary time of trouble will correspond to the sealing time of God's people. This final sealing will begin with the third angel's message and the mark of the beast. This sealing will end prior to the release of the "four angels standing at the four corners of the earth, holding back the four winds of the earth" (Revelation 7:1). These four angels are not to "harm the earth or the sea or the trees" until "we have sealed the servants of God upon their foreheads" (Revelation 7:3). This sealing process ends at the close of the investigative judgment. This sealing process is completed prior to the fifth trumpet since God's sealed people are protected during this trumpet (Revelation 9:4). Since God's people are sealed, the fifth trumpet marks the release of the four angels described in Revelation 7:1-4: to "harm the earth and the sea." However, they are not released to harm the trees. This release to harm the earth and sea refers to the first three plagues, which are poured out on the "earth" and the "sea" and "the rivers and the fountains of water." These first three plagues will occur during the fifth trumpet. The sealing of God's people is completed prior to the outpouring of the seven last plagues.

This preliminary time of trouble also parallels the outpouring of God's Spirit in the last days. This outpouring is called the latter rain. This "latter rain" (Joel 2:23) is further described in Joel 2:28: "And it shall come to pass afterwards, that I will pour out my spirit on all flesh." This latter rain will precede the Second Coming which is described in Joel 2:30-32. This special outpouring of God's Spirit will begin with the enactment of the buy-sell legislation and will extend until the end of time. This outpouring can only occur when God's people are willing to empty themselves, in order to be filled with His Spirit. Once this buy-sell law goes into effect, God's people will be forced to choose either to depend on themselves and abandon God or choose to totally depend on Him. Once the buy-sell law is enacted, God's true followers will lose their jobs and even their ability to buy food unless they comply. The choice to serve God will mean they must now depend totally on Him. This total dependence on God is a prerequisite for the filling of the Holy Spirit. We must be empty of self in order to be filled with his Spirit. This filling with His Spirit is the latter rain. The latter rain will occur at this time and will lead to many souls saved. Many of those saved at this time will be those who respond to the call to "Come out of her, my people, lest you take part in her sins, lest you share in her plagues" (Revelation 18:4). The plagues will begin to fall at the end of this preliminary time of trouble.

The "mark" of the beast is connected to the beast's name and its number, which is discussed in the next verse. By accepting the "mark" of the beast, you accept his name. You become part of the beast's church and fellowship. You become one of those "who have not the seal of God" (Revelation 9:4).

Revelation 13:18: *"This calls for wisdom; let him who has understanding reckon the number of the beast, for it is a human number, its number is six hundred and sixty-six."*

This verse means that both wisdom and understanding will be required to determine or reckon the beast's number. In Daniel 11:33, 35 and Daniel 12:3, 10, we find that the "wise" are mentioned in relationship to the "time of the end." These wise will understand that God's Law has not been changed, that the true Sabbath is the seventh-day and that Satan is not Christ as he claims to be. They will recognize the leopard-like beast of Revelation 13:2, 3, 11 as the Papacy and will not accept its mark in their foreheads or in their hands.

Historically, the number of the beast has been interpreted from the Pope's claim to be the "Vicar of the Son of God." This phrase in Latin is "Vicarius Filii Dei" which contains the number 666 (Vicarius = 112; Filii = 53; Dei = 501; and the total = 666). This is based on the Latin numerals contained in this phrase. This number is thought to further connect the Papacy to the beast.[7]

There have been many other applications of this number to historical figures, however, the important point is not to accept the beast's mark. Some will ask if keeping Sunday now implies they have accepted the mark of the beast. The answer is not necessarily. The mark of the beast occurs when one consciously rejects God's true Sabbath and accepts Satan's false Sabbath. The choice to accept or reject God's true Sabbath versus Satan's counterfeit Sunday will determine if you are going to receive God's seal or mark or accept Satan's seal or mark. For most of the world this will occur at the time when the buy-sell sanctions are enforced.

SUMMARY

Revelation 13 introduces a leopard-like beast that is given its authority by the dragon. This leopard-like beast represents the Papacy. The dragon represents Satan. This leopard-like beast will be worshipped by the world together with the dragon. This will occur during the reign of the seventh king or seventh pope counting from 1929, who is Pope Benedict XVI. General Berthier mortally wounded this leopard-like beast in its head (the pope) in 1798 and its wound was healed in 1929 when Mussolini restored Vatican City to the Papacy.

This leopard-like beast will rise to power after 1929 and will be supported by the lamb-like beast. The lamb-like beast has two horns, which represent religious and civil liberty. The lamb-like beast will arise out of the earth, representing unpopulated areas. The lamb-like beast will speak like a dragon: representing world dominance. The lamb-like beast will work signs and wonders: representing scientific and technological advances. The lamb-like beast is the United States of America. The lamb-like beast will work with the leopard-like beast and deceive the world. This deception involves creating an image to the leopard-like beast. This image will be formed when the lamb-like beast forms a likeness to the leopard-like beast by becoming a church-state kingdom. This union of church and state will occur in the United States after natural disasters and economic collapse force the government to abandon religious liberty. This image occurs when the false Sabbath is made law. This image of the beast is created when the Sunday law is enacted. This Sunday law signals the loss of the lamb-like beast's first horn: religious liberty. This Sunday law signals the beginning of the second angel's message.

Once this image or church-state union is formed and the world is deceived, the image will speak by passing further laws restricting religious and civil liberty. The image will eventually pass laws forbidding the buying or selling of anything unless you keep its false Sabbath. This law will ultimately be followed by a death penalty for failure to have the mark of the beast. The mark of the beast will occur when the buy-sell law is enacted. This buy-sell law enforcing the Sunday law will signal the loss of the lamb-like beast's second horn: civil liberty. This buy-sell law will signal the beginning of the third angel's message. When the United States of America loses its first horn (religious liberty) it will become the image to the beast. When the United States of America loses its second horn (civil liberty) it will have established the mark of the beast. The following graph outlines these events described in Revelation 13.

Revelation Chapter 13 - Last Part

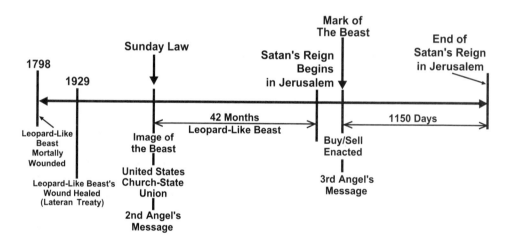

1 Nichol, Francis D. (Ed.) *The Seventh-day Adventist Bible Commentary* (Review and Herald Publishing Association, Washington D. C.) 1957, Vol. 4, p. 831.
2 Geiermann, Peter, *The Convert's Catechism of Catholic Doctrine* (1930), p. 50.
3 Ibid.
4 Nichol, Francis D. (Ed.) *The Seventh-day Adventist Bible Commentary* (Review and Herald Publishing Association, Washington D. C.) 1957, Vol. 7, p. 821.
5 Ibid.
6 Ibid.
7 Ibid. p. 823.

Revelation 11 (first part)
The Two Witnesses

Revelation 11 is divided into two main sections. Revelation 11:1-14 describes the two witnesses and the end of the second woe. Revelation 11:15-19 describes the third woe, which is the Second Coming of Christ. The story of the two witnesses is connected to last-day events, since the second woe ends with this story. The three woes are part of God's judgment at the time of the end. As will be shown in the following discussion, the two witnesses actually involve these last-day events.

The first part of Revelation 11 is mainly a vision about the two witnesses. The chapter begins with a temple scene and ends with another temple scene. The story of the two witnesses is described between the two temple scenes because it occurs between these two events in history. As will be shown later, the first temple scene represents the investigative judgment and the final temple scene represents events at the Second Coming. The experience of the two witnesses will occur shortly before the Second Coming of Christ.

> Revelation 11:1: *"Then I was given a measuring rod like a staff, and I was told: 'Rise and measure the temple of God and the altar and those who worship there.'"*

John is given a "measuring rod" and told to "measure the temple of God and the altar and those who worship there." However, he is told not to measure the outside court because it is "given over to the nations" (Revelation 11:2). This process of measuring is linked to the restoration of Jerusalem and the restoration of God's people in Zechariah 2:1-4. This "measuring" of God's people is described in Daniel 7:9-10 as a courtroom set up for judgment; God, "the Ancient of Days," is seated on His throne and other "thrones were placed" around Him. In Revelation 4:4, there are 24 thrones set up for the 24 elders, which are placed around God's throne. These are the thrones that Daniel refers to in Daniel 7:9. These were set up prior to the Ancient of Days taking a seat.

This placement of the thrones marks the beginning of a judgment scene in heaven. This is confirmed in Daniel 7:10, which states: "the court sat in judgment, and the books were opened." One of the books that is opened is further described in Revelation 5:1 as "a scroll written within and on the back, sealed with seven seals." This book or scroll no man could open except "the Lion of the tribe of Judah" who "can open the scroll and its seven seals" (Revelation 5:5) (discussed in Revelation 4 and 5—the Judgment Scene).

John's vision of the "measuring" of God's people is symbolic of the ongoing judgment of God's people. This investigative judgment involves those whose names are written in "the book of life" (Revelation 3:5). These names include all those who have accepted Jesus as their Savior or worship the true God. The "temple of God" described here is God's throne room set up for judgment and "the altar" is a symbol of Jesus' sacrificial work as the Lamb of God. Jesus as our "Lamb who was slain" is also pictured in Revelation 5:6, 9, and 12, where He is involved in opening the book which is sealed. Only Jesus can open this book because it contains the names of those saved by Jesus alone. No other being has the right or the power to open this book except the One who died for mankind.

This investigative judgment involves God's people, since only their names go into the book of life. In Revelation 20:12, we find other "books." In these books, the dead were judged "by what was written in the books, by what they had done" (Revelation 20:12). The dead referred to in Revelation 20:12 are the wicked dead who will be cast into "the lake of fire" (Revelation 20:14). The fact that John's "measuring" refers to the investigative judgment of God's people is further supported by his instructions in Revelation 11:2. He is told not to measure those in the courtyard. The courtyard was the place where Gentiles, or nonbelievers, were allowed. They could not go into the temple because only true believers were allowed inside. Thus, there is a distinction being made between believers and nonbelievers. "Those who worship there" are believers in God. The believers are represented by God's people inside who worship at the altar of Jesus' sacrifice. These believers are the people whose names are in the book, which is involved in the investigative judgment. This book is the book of life (Revelation 3:5). The nonbelievers represent those who are lost, because they failed to accept Jesus as their Lord and Savior. These nonbelievers are not involved in the investigative judgment and therefore are not being measured or counted at this time. These nonbelievers are described as being in the courtyard.

Thus, the opening verse of Revelation 11 sets the time frame for the rest of the chapter. The time frame involves the investigative judgment and it must be ongoing since the "measuring" occurs prior to or during the subsequent events. The context of Revelation 11 is related to last-day events, since it is part of the sixth trumpet or second woe. The beginning of the investigative judgment was in 1844 when the 2300-year prophecy of Daniel 8:14 ended (discussed in Daniel 8—The Abomination and the Sanctuary). Since John is describing the investigative judgment, he is describing events which will occur after 1844. In the context of Revelation 11 John is describing events that occur during the sixth trumpet, which occurs immediately prior to Jesus' Second Coming. The third woe or seventh trumpet describes the Second Coming, which follows shortly after the two witness's resurrection (Revelation 11: 12-19).

> Revelation 11:2: *"but do not measure the court outside the temple; leave that out, for it is given over to the nations, and they will trample over the holy city for forty-two months."*

Revelation 11:2 now introduces a time prophecy and a location: "and they will trample over the holy city for forty-two months." The word "they" refers to those outside the temple or "the nations," which represent the nonbelievers. This is compared to the believers, who are God's people, "who worship there" described in Revelation 11:1.

To John there was only one "holy city" and that was Jerusalem. In the book of Revelation, John does refer to the New Jerusalem on many occasions, however, in this verse the nations are trampling "over the holy city." Therefore, this cannot refer to the New Jerusalem.

Some suggest that "the holy city" refers to God's people.[1] However, God's people are called "those who worship there" in the previous verse (Revelation 11:1). Why would God change to symbols in the next verse? More importantly, John further describes this city in Revelation 11:8 as "the city where their Lord was crucified." The "city" where their Lord was crucified was Jerusalem. The "city" is mentioned again in Revelation 11:13 where "a tenth of the city fell." Is John referring to God's people as "those who worship there" in verse one and then to the "holy city" as God's people in verse two? It seems unlikely.

Some suggest that "the great city" in Revelation 11:8 is France and John's phrase "where their Lord was crucified" refers to France.[2] However, historically the phrase "a tenth of the city" in Revelation 11:13 was also considered France, as one of the ten kingdoms of Europe, but this would then suggest the "city" represents Europe. Is the "city" in Revelation 11:2 God's people, and the "city" in Revelation 11:8 France, and the "city" in Revelation 11:13 Europe? It seems more reasonable to conclude that John was referring to his holy city Jerusalem, where his "Lord was crucified" (Revelation 11:8), in all three of these texts.

Revelation 11:2 also introduces a time prophecy: "they will trample over the holy city for forty-two months." This 42 months can be literal or prophetic. If literal, it would equal 1260 days, since the Jewish calendar has 30 days in each month and 42 times 30 equals 1260. If this is 42 prophetic months, then it represents 1260 years since one prophetic day equals one literal year (Numbers 14:34). Historically, this time period has been interpreted by many authors as prophetic time representing 1260 years. Since Daniel also described a similar period of 1260 years, this was thought to be the same time period.[3] In Daniel, we see a similar time period described as: "a time, two times, and half a time" (Daniel 7:26, Daniel 12:7). A "time" is equal to a year or 360 days on the Jewish calendar. Thus, "a time, two times, and half a time" is three and one-half years or 42 months or 1260 days. However, closer inspection of these verses in Daniel 7:26 and Daniel 12:7 suggests that these two time periods in Daniel may not be the same time periods at all (discussed in Daniel 12—The Abomination and the Time of Trouble).

Those who link Revelation 11:2 to Daniel 7:26 suggest that this 1260 year period (one prophetic day equals one literal year) is the time period which dates from A.D. 538 to 1798. This time period began with the establishment of Papal Rome as a world power and ended with the capture of Pope Pius VI in 1798 by Napoleon's General Berthier. This concept is consistent with the interpretation of the "little horn" of Daniel 7:8, 24, and 25 as representing Papal Rome. However, just because the number can be derived in Daniel 7:26 and equals 1260 days does not necessarily mean that it is the same prophetic time period as in Revelation 11:2.

Those who connect Revelation 11:2 with Daniel 12:7 also assume that since 1260 days is mentioned in Daniel 12:7, it must be the same time period as Daniel 7:26. However, the context of Daniel 12 is significantly different from that of Daniel 7. Daniel 12 clearly relates to the time of trouble, the time of the end, and to the last-day events. Daniel 12:1 is a time of the end event and not an event which occurred from A.D. 538 to 1798. Daniel 12:7, which contains 1260 days inferred from "a time, two times, and a half a time," is the response to Daniel's question in Daniel 12:6. Daniel is asking "How long shall it be till the end of these wonders?" He is referring to the "wonders" described relating to the abomination that makes desolate (Daniel 11:31) and the time of trouble (Daniel 12:1). The context of Daniel 12 suggests this time prophecy relates to last-day events and not to the Dark Ages of world's history. Also, the "shattering" of God's peoples' power is the end point. The end point of the 1260 years, A.D. 538 to 1798 was the shattering of the Pope's power. The reader is referred to Dr. Robert Smith's book, *The Sixth King,* for an excellent discussion on Daniel 12 and its relationship to this issue.[4] This author agrees with Dr. Smith's assessment that the time period of Daniel 12:7 is not the same time period as that of Daniel 7:26 (discussed in Daniel 12—The Abomination and the Time of Trouble).

If the 42 months of Revelation 11:2 is not symbolic of 1260 years, then it must be a literal 1260-day period. It should be remembered that the context of Revelation 11 is the sixth trumpet or second woe of last-day events. Revelation 11:1 suggests that it occurs after 1844 and during the investigative judgment. It is inconceivable that this judgment will go on for 1260 years. This leads to only one conclusion. There is at least one 1260-day period in the last-day events. This conclusion is consistent with Daniel 12:7, which also suggests a 1260-day time period centered around the time of trouble (Daniel 12:1).

The "nations" represent the non-believers who are not measured in the investigative judgment, which is why they are seen in "the court outside the temple." The "nations" represent those who "will trample over the holy city" during this 1260-day period. The "nations" represent the non-believers who will trample over Jerusalem in the last days.

> Revelation 11:3: *"And I will grant my two witnesses power to prophesy for one thousand two hundred and sixty days, clothed in sackcloth."*

Revelation 11:3 introduces the subject matter of the first half of Revelation 11. The focus of attention in the first half of Revelation 11 is the two witnesses. Who are the two witnesses? What power do they have? Is this 1260-day time period related to the prior 42-month time period? Why are they clothed in sackcloth? The two witnesses are further described in verse four as "two olive trees" and "the two lampstands which stand before the Lord of the earth." In Zechariah 4:14 we see these two olive trees are "the two anointed who stand by the Lord of the whole earth." The olive trees are the source of oil and the oil represents the Holy Spirit.[5] The two witnesses represent God's Holy Word, the Old Testament and the New Testament.[6] The Holy Spirit flows through God's Word to us. In Zechariah 4:11-14 we see the connection between the olive trees, the oil, and the lampstands. The oil, which represents God's Holy Spirit, flows through His two olive trees (the two witnesses) into the lampstands. The lampstands represent God's churches (Revelation 1:20). God's churches guided by the two witnesses will then shed their light to the world. The two witnesses represent the Old Testament and the New Testament, which is God's Holy Word. The power of the two witnesses will be described in comments on Revelation 11:5, 6.

Many prior scholars have concluded that the two witnesses are the Old and the

New Testaments. It can be found as a footnote in the discussion on Revelation 11 in some Bibles. In John 5:39, Jesus describes the Scriptures as "they that bear witness to me." Here Jesus was referring to the Old Testament because the New Testament scriptures had not yet been written. The New Testament is clearly a witness about Jesus. Therefore, it is reasonable to conclude that the Old Testament and the New Testament are the two witnesses John is referring to in Revelation 11. They are also the two olive trees referred to by Zechariah (Zechariah 4:14).

What is the relationship between the 42 months of Revelation 11:2 and the 1260 days of Revelation 11:3? If the 42 months or 1260 days of verse two is literal and relates to last-day events, which occur around the time of trouble, then what does the 1260 days of verse three refer to? It cannot refer to 1260 years because then it could not be a last-day event. Therefore, it must be a literal 1260 days. The context suggests that it is related to the prior verse, since it is connected to the prior verse with "and." The 1260 days of Revelation 11:3 are related to last-day events and are a literal 1260 days. However, this 1260-day period is not the same as the 1260 days of Revelation 11:2. These represent two distinct time periods during the last days. This will be further discussed later in this chapter. Previous interpretations have applied both of these time periods to the same time period and have applied both of them to A.D. 538 to 1798.[7] This interpretation, however, does not fit with the context, which is last-day events.

Why are the two witnesses "clothed in sackcloth"? The two witnesses are God's Word (the Old and the New Testaments), which are in mourning. Sackcloth was used in biblical times to denote mourning, as would occur when someone mourned the loss of a loved one. This symbol suggests God's Word is suffering. Previous authors have suggested that during the Dark Ages the Bible (God's Word) was overruled by human traditions.[8] When human traditions or laws take ascendancy over scripture, then God's two witnesses are not as effective in bringing people to Christ. This occurred during the Dark Ages when the Catholic Church was the sole interpreter of God's Word.

However, in the last days God's Word will be under attack again. God's Word, particularly God's Law, will be changed and replaced by human traditions. The most significant last-day event, as it relates to God's Word, will be the passage of the Sunday law. This law will initiate the closing events of earth's history (discussed in Revelation 13 (last part)—The Mark of the Beast).

The reason that the two witnesses are in mourning is because the universal Sunday law has been passed. Furthermore it appears that they will be in mourning for 1260 days. During this time period, God's people will still be able to witness to others. It has been suggested that people should not violate this Sunday law by deliberately working but that they should use this time to witness to others as to why they keep the seventh-day Sabbath.[9] During this time period, people can still accept Christ. God's Word is not dead but in mourning. Human traditions will clearly be in ascendancy over God's Word, which is what the "sackcloth" implies in this verse.

> Revelation 11:4: *"These are the two olive trees and the two lampstands which stand before the Lord of the earth."*

These olive trees are described in Zechariah 4:11 as standing "on the right and the left of the lampstand." These two olive trees are called "the two anointed who stand by the Lord of the whole earth" (Zechariah 4:14). These two olive trees are the two witnesses. In Zechariah, the two olive trees are connected to the golden pipes out of which flows the oil. The oil is in turn used to light the lamps on the lampstand. This is a graphic illustration of how God's two witnesses, which are the Old and the New Testaments, provide light to the world. This light is provided through the function of the oil, which represents the Holy Spirit. When God's churches or His people allow His Spirit to fill them, they can then shed the light of truth about His Son to the world. Jesus is the Truth (John 14:6) and also the Light of the World (John 8:12).

The function of the two olive trees, the two lampstands and the two witnesses are identical, since they are identical. Their function is to spread the light of truth about Jesus as our Savior and Lord. When man changes God's Law and makes man's rules supersede God's rules, then God's two witnesses will be weakened and in mourning. It is important to note, however, that the two witnesses are still effective and not dead yet. The application of the two witnesses to the Dark Ages is consistent with the concept that God's Word was in mourning, because during the Dark Ages God's Word was overruled by church traditions and by church authority. However, this application also applies in the last days and is consistent with the overall content of Revelation 11. In the last days God's two witnesses will be in mourning because God's Law will have been changed.

> Revelation 11:5: *"And if anyone would harm them, fire pours from their mouth and consumes their foes; if anyone would harm them, thus he is doomed to be killed."*

Historically, this "fire" has been applied to the death of the wicked in the final cleansing fire of Revelation 20:13-14, which describes the second death or the eternal death, from which there is no resurrection.[10] However, here in Revelation 11:5, the wicked are described as enemies of God's Word or as those who "would harm them." In this text "them" refers to the two witnesses or God's Word. The context of this verse suggests God's Word is alive and prophesying in sackcloth when it is harmed.

The phrase "fire pours from their mouth" refers to God's response to the attack on His two witnesses. The next phrase confirms that those who would harm God's Word are still alive (as opposed to being dead as described in Revelation 20:13) because it states they will be "doomed to be killed." Therefore, it appears that the threatened punishment for harming God's Word, His two witnesses, is going to occur at the time of the injury to God's Word. This suggests that God's two witnesses have power to punish those who are harming them. This also suggests that the punishments being described in this verse are actually ongoing during the time of the two witnesses being in sackcloth. This means that some of God's response to the attack on His two witnesses will occur during the 1260 days in which God's Word is in mourning. God's two witnesses are still living, have not yet been killed, and have not yet been raised to ascend to heaven.

If this "fire" is not the final judgment fire, what is it? There are two end-time events that involve "fire" prior to the Second Coming of Christ. The first is found in Revelation 8:7: "The first angel blew his trumpet, and there followed hail and fire, mixed with blood, which fell on the earth." This is the first trumpet of the seven trumpets discussed in Revelation 8, 9, and 11. The second event that involves "fire," which occurs prior to the Second Coming, is found in Revelation 16:8: "The fourth angel poured his bowl on the sun, and it was allowed to scorch men with fire." This is the fourth plague of the seven last plagues.

The overall content of Revelation 11 suggests a connection to the first trumpet (Revelation 8:7) because Revelation 11 is actually describing events prior to and including the sixth trumpet. This is confirmed in Revelation 11:14 where it states "The second woe has passed." The second woe is the sixth trumpet (see Revelation 8:13). The sixth trumpet was introduced in Revelation 9:13 and continues through until Revelation 11:14. The apparent diversion by John in Revelation 10 to describe the bittersweet experience may not be a diversion at all. There will be a more contemporary application of Revelation 10's bittersweet experience to the time of the trumpets. This will occur when the Sunday law is passed and many believers assume that the end is near only to be disappointed. Regardless of Revelation 10, the content of the end of Revelation 9 is the sixth trumpet and the end of Revelation 11 is the seventh trumpet. *The story of the two witnesses explains the events that occur during the trumpets,* which lead up to and include the time of the sixth trumpet, ending just prior to the seventh trumpet.

God's Word appears to have power to afflict its enemies. This affliction will be God ordained and God controlled. Revelation 11:5 suggests that God will defend His Word against its enemies. One of the trials His enemies will suffer appears to involve fire and death. These trials will begin to occur during the 1260 days when God's witnesses are prophesying in sackcloth. This "fire" correlates with the first trumpet, which comes from God and involves "hail and fire, mixed with blood."

> Revelation 11:6: *"They have power to shut the sky, that no rain may fall during the days of their prophesying, and they have power over the waters to turn them into blood, and to smite the earth with every plague, as often as they desire."*

This text also connects this time period to the earlier trumpets. Notice that the power or authority to "shut the sky" is given during the "days of their prophesying." The "days of their prophesying" refers to the 1260 days of Revelation 11:3 when the two witnesses are in sackcloth.

Historically, this text has been thought to allude to Elijah's experience when he prophesied that there would be no rain in Israel (1 Kings 17:1).[11] However, the last-day application of this text connects it to the first trumpet in Revelation 8:7. This trumpet describes "a third of the earth was burnt up, and a third of the trees were burnt up, and all the green grass was burnt up" (Revelation 8:7). This text in Revelation 8:7 certainly is describing a world without rain, which parallels Elijah's day. This is a literal application of this trumpet but there is also a spiritual application (see comments on Revelation 8:7). The three and one-half years or 1260 days will involve untold suffering, famine and death.

The power over turning water "to blood" has historically been connected to the first plague in Egypt where Moses turned water into blood (Exodus 7:17, 18). However, it also connects to Revelation 8:9: "and a third of the sea became blood," which is the second trumpet. It could also connect to the second and third plagues in Revelation 16:3, 4 which describe waters turned to blood. However, these plagues occur after the two witnesses are dead and not while they are living (discussed in Revelation 16—The Seven Last Plagues).

The two witnesses also have power "to smite the earth with every plague, as often as they desire" (Revelation 11:6). This phrase suggests that when God's Word is attacked by His enemies, He will counterattack, not only with fire and heat (the sun) and no rain (drought) and water to blood but also with the plagues. All these are last-day events which relate to the seven trumpets and the seven last plagues. This further connects the two witnesses to the last-day events.

> Revelation 11:7: *"And when they have finished their testimony, the beast that ascends from the bottomless pit will make war upon them and conquer them and kill them."*

Historically, this event has been thought to represent the end of the 1260 year period of A.D. 538 to 1798 at which time France, which was considered to be the "beast," killed God's Word by destroying the French Bibles.[12] It should be noted that historically, France has also been applied to the "city" in Revelation 11:8 and to the "one tenth" in Revelation 11:13 (see comments on Revelation 11:2). The "bottomless pit" was thought to represent atheism which had no foundation.[13] The "war" represented the attempt to destroy God's Word.[14]

The last-day application suggests that "the beast that ascends" is the same beast that descends into the bottomless pit (Revelation 20:1, 2). This beast is the "star fallen" who is given the "key of the shaft of the bottomless pit" (Revelation 9:1). This beast is also called the dragon "who is the devil and Satan" (Revelation 20:2). He will be bound for 1000 years, the millennium, described in Revelation 20:2. That he is bound by circumstances is shown in Revelation 20:3 because he can "deceive the nation's no more." This same dragon or Satan is described in Revelation 12:9, where he is called "the Devil and Satan, the deceiver of the whole world." He is "thrown down to the earth, and his angels were thrown down with him" (Revelation 12:9). Satan is the "star fallen" of Revelation 9:1 who is given the key to the bottomless pit.

In Isaiah 14:12-15, Satan is also described as a star "fallen from heaven." This fallen star is bound on earth because of circumstances. On this earth, God has placed restrictions on Satan's power. If God had not restriced Satan, then Satan would have long ago destroyed all of God's people. These restrictions on Satan can be thought of as God's rules of engagement. Prayer is an example of one of God's rules of engagement. Prayer empowers God's people and limits Satan's power.

In Revelation 9:1, 2, the fallen star is given "the key of the shaft of the bottomless pit" and is allowed to open the shaft. This fallen star is now allowed to do something God has never allowed him to do. This release from the pit represents God's loosening the rules of engagement, which restrict the beast's (Satan's) power. Satan will now be allowed to reign as the king of the world. However, some restrictions will continue as described in Revelation 9:4, which states that he can only harm those of mankind "who have not the seal of God upon their foreheads." In Revelation 9:11, Satan is described as "king over them, the angel of the bottomless pit."

However, prior to Satan reigning as king of the world, he will reveal himself as the Messiah, Christ. Ellen G. White states that "this is the strong, almost overmastering delusion" *(The Great Controversy,* page 624).[15] Satan, as the false Christ, will initially come to power as the eighth king. He will reign in Jerusalem. He will claim to be God on earth. This event is described in the third trumpet. Satan is described as "a great star fell from heaven" (Revelation 8:10). This fallen star will first reign as the eighth king and poison the world. The "name of the star is Wormwood" (Revelation 8:11). The name Wormwood implies poisoning or bitterness. This fallen star will subsequently be given "the key of the shaft of the bottomless pit" (Revelation 9:1). Once Satan has claimed spiritual leadership of the world as the eighth king, he will then seek world domination as the world's king.

Revelation 11:7 describes Satan, "the beast that ascends," as overpowering God's Word and killing his two witnesses. When Satan reigns as the false Christ who has returned to save mankind, he will then be able to reinterpret God's Word as his own. When Satan reigns as the false Christ and becomes the interpreter of God's Word, for all practical purposes God's Word is dead. Satan will reinterpret God's Law in order to allow sin to be in control. Truly the two witnesses will be dead to all those who believe Satan's lies.

> Revelation 11:8: *"and their dead bodies will lie in the street*
> *of the great city which is allegorically (spiritually) called*
> *Sodom and Egypt, where their Lord was crucified."*

Historically this text has been applied to France, which through atheism attacked God's Word and killed it.[16] The "city" was thought to represent France.[17] The fact that the dead bodies were not buried represented indignity and mistreatment of God's Word.[18] "Sodom" represented the moral degradation of France and "Egypt" represented France's denial of the existence of the true God.[19]

The Greek word translated "allegorically" means "spiritually." Thus, Sodom and Egypt are spiritually like this "great city." Sodom and Gomorrah have been representative of moral degradation since their existence (Genesis 19:1-11). Egypt was known for worshiping many false gods and rejecting the true God of Israel. Thus, this "great city" will be known for its moral degradation, its rejection of the true God, and worship of a false god. This will occur when Satan becomes king of this "city."

The "city" here mentioned is further described as the city "where their Lord was crucified." The two witnesses' "Lord" is Jesus Christ. He is the subject matter of both the Old Testament and the New Testament and He is their Author. The city where Jesus Christ was crucified still exists today and it is Jerusalem, located in Israel in the Middle East. This is the same "city" John refers to as "the holy city" in Revelation 11:2. This city will be trampled over for 42 months.

When Satan becomes ruler of this world spiritually, he will take over as the eighth king (Revelation 17:11). He is "the beast that ascends from the bottomless pit" (Revelation 17:8). When Satan takes over as the eighth king, he will then control the Christian world, with the exception of those remnant believers who have not accepted him as Christ (discussed in Revelation 17 (second part)—The Eighth King).When Satan reigns as the eighth king, he will have control of world Catholicism. He will also have control of the world's Protestants who have accepted him because of his miracles, signs and wonders. The Protestant world is currently looking for a Messiah to come and reign in Jerusalem and establish a 1000 years of peace. Satan will establish his world reign in Jerusalem, which is the birthplace for both Catholic and Protestant religions. However, it is also an important center of worship for Islam and is the center of the Jewish religion. In order for Satan to establish his kingdom in Jerusalem and fulfill Old Testament prophecy, he will have to convince both Israel and the Moslem world to agree to let him reign in Jerusalem. This will be extremely difficult.According to some Islamic teachings, Jesus Christ was considered to be a prophet. Therefore, when Satan comes as the false Christ (Messiah), Islam will be willing to listen to Him. According to one Islamic tradition,

- ***the Moslems claim that Jesus will return as Messiah for the Moslems and destroy the Jewish nation.***[20]

If the Jewish nation rejects Satan, then the Moslems could accept him as their Messiah and assist Satan in removing the Jewish nation. In order for Satan to establish his kingdom in Jerusalem, he must resolve the Jewish-Moslem conflict. Another possible solution would be for the Jewish nation to accept Satan as their Messiah. This would, however, lead to further conflict between Israel and its Arabian neighbors, since Satan will occupy the temple in Jerusalem, which will certainly anger the surrounding countries.

The most likely scenario to occur in the Middle East will be the destruction of the Jewish kingdom. This scenario is based on the events described in Daniel 11:28-31. These events suggest a battle centered on Israel prior to the reign of the abomination that makes desolate, which is Satan as the eighth king. It is unlikely that the Jewish nation will give up its sovereignty voluntarily. It is more likely that Satan will invade Israel against their wishes.

The "city where their Lord was crucified" (Revelation11:8) is Jerusalem, Israel. Daniel 11:28-31 describes the events just prior to the abomination that makes desolate being "set up." One of these events is an attack on God's holy covenant. God's holy covenant is His Sabbath. The attack on His Sabbath will replace it with a false Sabbath or Sunday. The Sunday law will be enacted prior to the abomination being "set up" (Daniel 11:31). Once Satan becomes king of this city as Christ returned, he will interpret God's Word. At this point, two things have occurred. First, the abomination that makes desolate has been set up. Second, God's two witnesses (His Holy Word) are now dead because Satan has now replaced Christ and is reinterpreting God's Word. The world does not realize the Bible is dead because they accept Satan's interpretation as Christ's. Therefore, the two witnesses are dead but not buried.

With Satan reigning in Jerusalem, the city will become truly Sodom and Egypt. It will become known for its moral degradation like Sodom and because it is ruled by Satan, it will reject the true God. In this sense, it will be Egypt restored.

> Revelation 11:9: *"for three days and a half men from the peoples and tribes and tongues and nations gaze at their dead bodies and refuse to let them be placed in a tomb."*

This verse suggests the time period during which the two witnesses (Old Testament and New Testament) will be dead but not buried. The men who refuse "to let them be placed in a tomb" are described as "peoples and tribes and tongues and nations." This description is used in Revelation 14:6 as the audience for the first angel's message "to every nation and tribe and tongue and people." Since both of these messages have the same audience, this suggests that the last day message of Revelation 14:6 coexists with these events.

The time period is described as three and one-half days. This time period could be a literal three and one-half days or symbolic of three and one-half years. If it is symbolic of three and one-half years, it would equal 1260 days (30 days x 12 x 3½ = 1260 days). The content of Revelation 9:1-6, which describes the events related to this same beast that ascends from the "bottomless pit," suggests that this beast is in ascendancy for much longer than three and one-half days. In Revelation 9:5, this beast will torture its victims for five months. The content of Revelation 11 also suggests that this event, the death of the two witnesses, is followed shortly by the Second Coming of Christ (see the discussion on Revelation 11:15-19). The seven last plagues also fall just before the Second Coming. Therefore, the seven last plagues will fall when the two witnesses are dead just prior to the Second Coming. These plagues will fall over a one year time period (Revelation 18:8): "so shall her plagues come in a single day" (one prophetic day equals one literal year). This suggests that the three and one-half days are symbolic of three and one-half years or 1260 literal days. This time period would begin when the beast (Satan) ascends to his throne as the false Christ.

This ascending to the throne is allowed by God and is the first time Satan will be able to rule over mankind. When Satan becomes the eighth king of Revelation 17:11 and pretends to be Christ who has returned to this world, he will become the interpreter of the Old and New Testaments. Satan will claim that authority, since as Christ, he claims the Bible to be his book. Satan will now be the one determining what the Bible says! At this point the Bible (the Old Testament and the New Testament) will be dead to those who accept Satan as Christ. The purpose of the Word of God is to reveal Jesus Christ to us in order to save us from sin and restore our relationship with God. The Old Testament pointed forward to Christ on the cross and the New Testament points back to Him on the cross. Now Satan can distort any Bible truth he desires since he claims to be Christ returned.

Revelation 11:9 also states that the world (nations, tongues, peoples, and tribes) will "gaze at their dead bodies and refuse to let them be placed in a tomb." The world will not realize that God's Word is dead. They will think that Satan as Christ returned is now making the Scriptures clearer than before. They will accept these false doctrines and lies as truth. These false truths are "poured water like a river out of his mouth" (Revelation 12:15). These false doctrines will seek to drown the true church. The dragon of Revelation 12 will try "to sweep her away with the flood" (Revelation 12:15), where "her" refers to the woman who represents God's true believers. This flood of false doctrines will totally mislead the majority of the world.

> Revelation 11:10: *"and those who dwell on the earth will rejoice over them and make merry and exchange presents, because these two prophets had been a torment to those who dwell on the earth."*

The "two prophets" represent the two witnesses. Those "who dwell on the earth" represent the wicked who will be lost for eternity. This verse describes how the wicked react to Satan's new interpretation of the Bible. The world will no longer have to worry about the burdens of the Ten Commandments in the Old Testament or Jesus' explanation of the Ten Commandments in the New Testament. Satan will now explain away these truths and turn them into falsehoods. The wicked will now be free from the condemnation of God's Word and the conviction of His two witnesses on their hearts. The wicked will rejoice in their new freedom from God's troublesome requirements. The Bible will no longer be a torment to men's souls because Satan as the false Christ will explain how men had misunderstood its requirements.

> Revelation 11:11: *"But after the three and a half days a breath of life from God entered them, and they stood up on their feet, and great fear fell on those who saw them."*

This verse begins by reiterating the time period during which the Old and the New Testaments are effectively dead but not buried. This is the time period when the Bible is being explained by Satan but the world thinks he is Christ. The Bible is dead to Satan's listeners but not buried because they think it is alive! At the end of "three and a half days," which represents three and one-half years, God restores life to His two witnesses. This means that the world will once again recognize God's Word as truth. Since God's Word is about the true Christ who is "the truth, and the life" (John 14:6), it appears that the world will finally realize they have been misled by Satan. God's Word will be vindicated. This occurs at the end of time just shortly before Christ's return, which is described under the seventh trumpet (Revelation 11:15-19). This resurrection of God's two witnesses will occur just prior to the last few weeks of earth's existence described in Revelation 17:12-14. During this last time period Satan, as the eighth king, will share power with the ten horns or ten kingdoms. These ten kingdoms will subsequently make "war on the Lamb" (Revelation 17:14). Satan would not voluntarily give up any of his power, but he will be forced to do this after the world realizes he is not who he claims to be!

The two witnesses are able to stand up "on their feet," which suggests that they have regained their status as God's Word. This idea is further supported by the fact that "fear fell on those who saw them." The world will not only recognize that they have been misled by Satan, but will realize that God's requirements are still in effect. This will strike fear into them because God's Word has always warned of judgment to come (Revelation 14:6). This realization that Satan has misled the world will bring about the breakdown of Satan's kingdom and his forced establishment of the final ten kingdoms of Revelation 17:12. These kingdoms will exist for only "one hour" (Revelation 17:12). One hour is best interpreted as a short period of time. God's two witnesses being raised to "life" suggests that the world will recognize God's truth as opposed to Satan's lies. This recognition, that the world has been misled, will not lead to a change of heart. Probation has already closed and the wicked will "still do evil" (Revelation 22:11).

> Revelation 11:12: *"Then they heard a loud voice from heaven saying to them, 'Come up hither!' And in the sight of their foes they went up to heaven in a cloud."*

This text shows that the two witnesses, who were raised at the end of the three and one-half years, do not continue to witness but are called home to heaven. Clearly, the same God who raised them up also calls them home to Him. The loud voice is God calling them home because their work is completed. Since no one can any longer accept Christ as their Savior, the work of the two witnesses is over. Probation has already closed. The resurrection of the two witnesses occurs just prior to the seventh trumpet, which is Christ's Second Coming. This is described in Revelation 11:15-19. This resurrection of the two witnesses occurs at the end of the sixth trumpet or second woe (Revelation 11:14). During the sixth trumpet, the fourth, the fifth, and the sixth plagues will occur (see the discussion on Revelation 9:17-18). The close of probation also occurs at the beginning of the seven last plagues. Since the close of probation occurs at the beginning of the seven last plagues and the two witnesses are resurrected just prior to the seventh plague, it will be too late for anyone to accept Christ at this time (discussed in Revelation 16—The Seven Last Plagues). Thus, the two witnesses work is complete.

It is time for them to go home! The phrase "went up to heaven in a cloud" is similar to Acts 1:9-11, where Jesus ascends to heaven in a cloud. Jesus' work on earth was completed and He ascended in "a cloud" (Acts 1:9). The work of God's two witnesses, the Old Testament and the New Testament, is now completed, which is symbolized by them ascending "in a cloud." There is no one left to save; all decisions for eternity have been made. "Let the evildoer still do evil, and the filthy still be filthy, and the righteous still do right, and the holy still be holy" (Revelation 22:11).

> Revelation 11:13: *"And at that hour there was a great earthquake, and a tenth of the city fell; seven thousand people were killed in the earthquake, and the rest were terrified and gave glory to the God of heaven."*

This text predicts that at the time when God takes His Word, the two witnesses, to heaven, a great earthquake will fall on the "city." The "city" here is described as the "holy city" in Revelation 11:2 and the "great city" where "their Lord was crucified" in Revelation 11:8. This "city" is Jerusalem, Satan's capital city. This is not the final earthquake associated with the Second Coming but a smaller earthquake, which will destroy "a tenth of the city" and "seven thousand" people will be killed. This earthquake demonstrates that God is in control. It proves that Satan is not in control and is not who he claims to be. This earthquake proves Satan to be a liar who cannot protect his own city. The inhabitants response will be terror, because not only is the earthquake terrible but it proves they are serving a false god. Because they recognize that this earthquake comes from the true God they glorify Him instead of Satan, but it is now too late for any of them to change their lives (Revelation 22:11). The "tenth of the city" suggests God's portion of the city. In the Old Testament God's portion was one tenth and was called a "tithe." This earthquake will destroy God's portion of Jerusalem including the temple. This earthquake will destroy the temple in Jerusalem and end Satan's ministry in the temple. This earthquake will end the profaning "of the temple" described in Daniel 11:31. This earthquake will end Satan's ministry as the false Christ in the temple. This earthquake will end the three and one-half year reign of Satan in Jerusalem.

Revelation 11:14: *"The second woe has passed; behold, the third woe is soon to come."*

This verse shows that some of the events related to the two witnesses occur during the sixth trumpet, which ends just prior to the seventh trumpet (the third woe). This verse helps identify the time frame for the story of the two witnesses. The two witness's story spans 1260 days of "sackcloth" or mourning (Revelation 11:3) and then the two witnesses are "dead" but not buried for three and one-half days symbolizing three and one-half years (Revelation 11:9). The total time covered by this story is seven years. This seven year time period includes a portion of the reign of the seventh king as well as the entire reign of the eighth king. This seven year time period includes the 42 month reign of the leopard-like beast (Revelation 13:5). This seven year time period includes the 1260-day reign of the beast that ascends (the eighth king). This time period includes the close of probation and the seven last plagues and ends with the resurrection of the two witnesses and their ascension to heaven. Their resurrection occurs just prior to the Second Coming of Christ, which is described in the next few verses as the seventh trumpet (discussed in Revelation 11 (last part)— The Seventh Trumpet: The Final Woe).

This seven year period will begin with God's Law being changed and His two witnesses in mourning. This will occur when the universal Sunday law is enacted. The death of the two witnesses occurs when Satan masquerades as Christ and sets himself up as the eighth king (Revelation 17:11). In Matthew 24:15, Jesus applies the "desolating sacrilege" to the last days. The "desolating sacrilege" is Satan as the "abomination that makes desolate" (Daniel 9:27 and Daniel 11:31). Daniel 9:27 has a dual application and in the last days can be understood to refer to "the prince who is to come" that destroys the city (Daniel 9:26). That prince will have seven years or one week at the time of the end (Daniel 9:27). That prince will cause "sacrifice and offerings to cease" in the midst of that week. This correlates with Satan reigning as the false Christ. Satan is the abomination that makes desolate or the "desolator" who will be destroyed at the "decreed end" (Daniel 9:27).

This verse ends the "second woe." The first woe occurred when Satan was allowed to become king of the world (Revelation 9:1-12) but was still under some of God's rules of engagement. The second woe occurred when the four angels were released, which freed Satan to kill mankind, leading to the battle of Armageddon (Revelation 9:12-21 and Revelation 16:12-16). The story of the two witnesses overlaps these two woes and ends just prior to the Second Coming of Jesus Christ. The second woe will result in the death of one third of the world's population (Revelation 9:15). This is the same battle described in Revelation 16:14-16 as Armageddon. This battle is interrupted by the third woe, which is the Second Coming of Jesus Christ.

It is important to recognize that the presence of a dual application of Revelation 11 does not negate the historical application. The historical application of this chapter to the Dark Ages and the French Revolution is not incorrect, just because another application of this prophecy exists. The presence of another application simply confirms that God is the Author of the Bible. God wrote prophecies, which have multiple applications.

To suggest that God would only be concerned about those generations of believers who lived in the 1800s and not be concerned about those who live in the last days is to misunderstand God's love for all mankind. God intended this prophecy to be applied to the Dark Ages in order to save many who lived in the 1800s. The presence of a dual application for Revelation 11 does not harm or negate the historical application. The two applications are not in competition for supremacy. The two applications both serve to help prepare God's people for His soon coming. God intended for this prophecy to have more than one application. The historical application was not incorrect. It was God ordained to encourage those who lived in the 1800s and 1900s and to help prepare them for His soon coming. The fact that church leaders throughout the past several generations have accepted the historical approach does not mean that they were wrong. It was always part of God's plan.

SUMMARY

Revelation 11 begins with a temple scene representing the investigative judgment. Only God's people are being measured. The court outside the temple is not being measured, since the investigative judgment only involves God's people. Revelation 11:2 next describes the holy city as being trampled over by the nations for 42 months. This holy city is Jerusalem and it will be trampled over for three and one-half years once Satan begins his reign as the eighth king. This city is called the city "where their Lord was crucified" (Revelation 11:8).

In Revelation 11:3, the two witnesses are introduced. These two witnesses represent God's Holy Word (the Old and the New Testaments). These two witnesses are in "sackcloth" because God's Law has been changed. This change in God's Law is the universal Sunday law enacted by the United States of America when it became the image to the beast. God's two witnesses are in mourning or "sackcloth" for 1260 days or three and one-half years. During these three and one-half years the trumpets begin to blow. These trumpets are referred to as power over fire, rainfall, and turning water to blood.

The plagues are also connected to the two witnesses in Revelation 11:6. In Revelation 11:7, the two witnesses are killed by "the beast that ascends." This beast is Satan ascending to his throne as the eighth king. Satan will claim to be Christ returned and will claim the right to interpret the Bible that he says he wrote. Thus God's two witnesses will be dead to those who believe Satan's lies. However, they are not "buried" because those who listen to Satan will believe they now understand the Scriptures better than before.

The wicked will rejoice at the death of the two witnesses because they will no longer torment their consciences. The two witnesses will be dead for three and one-half days, representing the three and one-half years of Satan's reign in Jerusalem. At the end of the three and one-half years the two witnesses are resurrected and taken to heaven because their work is done. There is no one left to save. All decisions for Christ have been made and probation has long since closed. God will then destroy one tenth of Jerusalem, which represents God's portion. God will destroy the temple in Jerusalem and end Satan's reign as the false Christ. This will be followed by the reign of the ten kings, the battle of Armageddon, and the Second Coming of Jesus Christ.

We are now living in the last days. It is time for us to wake up and open our eyes. God is about to begin the final chapter of earth's history. He has given us ample warning and has revealed these last-day events in Daniel and Revelation. The story of the two witnesses is part of His last-day warning to our generation. The following graph outlines the events described in Revelation 11.

Revelation Chapter 11

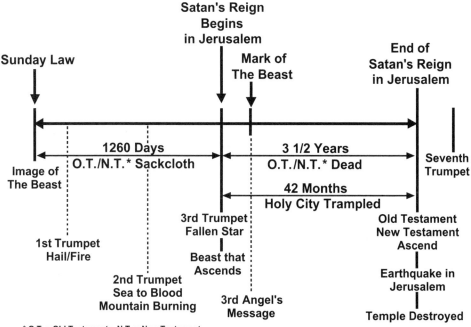

[1] Nichol, Francis D. (Ed.) *The Seventh-day Adventist Bible Commentary* (Review and Herald Publishing Association, Washington D. C.) 1957, Vol. 7, p. 801.

[2] Ibid. p. 803.

[3] Ibid. p. 801.

[4] Smith, Robert N. Jr., *The Sixth King*, Copyright 1993, Robert N. Smith Jr., M. D., Fort Worth, Texas, pp. 26-37.

[5] Nichol, Francis D. (Ed.) *The Seventh-day Adventist Bible Commentary* (Review and Herald Publishing Association, Washington D. C.) 1957, Vol. 7, p. 801.

[6] Ibid.

[7] Ibid. p. 802.

[8] Ibid.

[9] White, Ellen G., *Testimonies for the Church* (Pacific Press Publishing Association, Mountain View, California) 1948, Vol. 9, p. 232.

[10] Nichol, Francis D. (Ed.) *The Seventh-day Adventist Bible Commentary* (Review and Herald Publishing Association, Washington D. C.) 1957, Vol. 7, p. 802.

[11] Ibid.

[12] Ibid.

[13] Ibid.

[14] Ibid.

[15] White, Ellen G., *The Great Controversy* (Pacific Press Publishing Association, Nampa, Idaho) 1950, p. 624.

[16] Nichol, Francis D. (Ed.) *The Seventh-day Adventist Bible Commentary* (Review and Herald Publishing Association, Washington D. C.) 1957, Vol. 7, p. 803.

[17] Ibid.

[18] Ibid.

[19] Ibid.

[20] Rast, Jennifer. *Muslin, Jewish, and Christian End-Times Prophecy Comparison* (electronic version). Retrieved June 8, 2004, from http://www.contenderministries.org/prophecy/eschatology.php

Appendix (4)
Revelation 11
A Last Day's Application

The historical approach to the interpretation of Revelation 11 has been focused on the Dark Ages. The "forty-two months" and "one thousand two hundred and sixty days" in Revelation 11:2, 3 have been interpreted as the same time period from A.D. 538 to 1798 and applied to the two witnesses in sackcloth. The three and one-half days of Revelation 11:9, 11 have been interpreted as 1793 to 1797 when France rejected the Bible at the time of the French Revolution. This represented the three and one-half years during which the two witnesses (God's Old and New Testaments) were dead. The ascension of God's two witnesses to heaven was not completely explained.

If a dual application of Revelation 11 to last-day events applies, then the context and content of this chapter must support it. There should be contextual clues supporting this additional interpretation. The first contextual clue is in the overall setting of the story of the two witnesses. The story is introduced between the sixth trumpet (the second woe), which is found at the end of Revelation 9, and the seventh trumpet (the third woe), which completes Revelation 11. Both the sixth trumpet and the seventh trumpet are last-day events.

Next, the story of the two witnesses ends with the announcement that the second woe (sixth trumpet) has passed and is complete (Revelation 11:14). John further connects the two witnesses with the immediate last-day events by stating that the "third woe is *soon to come"* (Revelation 11:14) (emphasis supplied). These facts suggest that the story of the two witnesses overlaps the sixth trumpet. The sixth trumpet occurs just prior to the return of Christ, which is the seventh trumpet or third woe.

In Revelation 11:9, we find another connection to the last-day events. Here we see that the participants addressed are "peoples and tribes and tongues and nations." This is the same group to whom the message of Revelation 14:6 is addressed. Revelation 14:6-11 includes the three angel's messages to be given to the world during the last days. The three angel's messages are not the messages of the Dark Ages.

Several other time clues are contained within the story. In Revelation 11:5, 6, there is a description of the power of the two witnesses. They control the sky with "no rain" and "fire pours from their mouth" and they have power to turn waters "into blood." These same events are suggested in the first and second trumpets, which describe one-third of the earth "burnt up," "fire" from heaven, and water turned to "blood" (Revelation 8:7, 8). The historical approach places these trumpets in the late fourth and early fifth centuries when the barbarians overran Rome. However, there is a last day application of the trumpets, which places them as part of the last-day events just prior to the Second Coming and after the investigative judgment has begun (discussed in Revelation 8, 9, and 11—The Seven Trumpets).

In Revelation 11:6, we find a connection between the two witnesses and the plagues. The "plagues" mentioned in Revelation 11:6 can connect to the previous water to blood, fire, and absence of rain described in Revelation 11:5, 6 or could also

229

be referring to the same plagues described in Revelation 16:3, 4. In Revelation 16:3, 4, water is turned to blood and in Revelation 16:8, the sun scorches men "with fire." If Revelation 11:6 refers to Revelation 16, which describes the seven last plagues, then this is a last-day application. The seven last plagues fall just prior to Christ's Second Coming.

In Revelation 11:7, we find that the "beast that ascends from the bottomless pit" is the one who kills the two witnesses. This beast is described in Revelation 20:2 as "the dragon" and "the Devil and Satan" who will be later bound in the same pit for 1000 years. This pit refers to a binding of circumstances. In the case of the 1000 years Satan will be bound on earth since the earth will be empty of any living humans. He has no one to deceive and is bound by the circumstances. This is confirmed, in Revelation 20:7, 8 where he is "loosed from his prison" and will "come out to deceive." The prison or bottomless pit is his inability to deceive anyone. He is "loosed" in Revelation 20:7 because the wicked are raised and he can now deceive them again.

This same beast (Satan) is described as a "star fallen from heaven" in Revelation 9:1. In Revelation 12:4, Satan's angels are described as "stars" and in Revelation 12:9, Satan is thrown down to the earth with his angels. In Revelation 8:10, Satan is the "great star" fallen from heaven who poisons the rivers and fountains of water and one third of the waters were affected. This poisoning of one third of the world occurs when Satan begins to reign as the eighth king. This reign as the eighth king is described as "the beast that ascends" (Revelation 11:7). Satan ascending refers to the change in circumstances, which God now permits. God has never allowed Satan to have complete freedom to harm mankind but He will at the end of time. If Satan had complete freedom he would have long ago destroyed all of God's people and there would have been no need for God's angels to protect us or hold "back the four winds of the earth" (Revelation 7:1).

Revelation 11:7 connects "the beast that ascends from the bottomless pit" to the two witnesses. This beast will ascend in the last days to reign as king. This beast that ascends is Satan as the eighth king. This reign of the eighth king is a last-day event and involves the two witnesses.

Revelation 11:2 describes a measurement of God's temple and "those who worship there." This measurement or accounting began in 1844 when the investigative judgment began (Daniel 7:9, 10 and Daniel 8:14). This measurement or accounting is clearly a last-day event, which ends in Revelation 12:10 when the "kingdom of our God and the authority of his Christ have come" and the "accuser of our brethren" is thrown down. This measuring process is ongoing during the events discussed in the story of the two witnesses and that is why the story begins with the measuring of God's people. Revelation 11 begins with the investigative judgment being described (Revelation 11:1) and the chapter ends with the Second Coming (Revelation 11:18). The investigative judgment is a last-day event, as is the Second Coming.

In Revelation 11:12, we see that the two witness's work is complete. In Revelation 11:11, they are resurrected from the dead and in Revelation 11:12 they are called up to heaven and ascend "in a cloud." This parallels Acts 1:9, 11 where Jesus ascends into heaven in a cloud. Just as Jesus had completed His earthly ministry and would no longer be seen on earth in the flesh so the two witnesses were to ascend to heaven symbolizing the completion of their work. Jesus' ascension signified the end of His earthly ministry and this ascension of the two witnesses signifies the end of their work on earth. This is a time of the end event that will occur after the close of probation, since probation has closed and the presence of God's two witnesses can no longer bring about the salvation of the wicked. Therefore, God's two witnesses are no longer of any use to the wicked.

The final clue is found in the last half of Revelation 11. Once the two witnesses have completed their work and have ascended to heaven the kingdom is given to Christ. Revelation 11:15 states "The kingdom of the world has become the kingdom of our Lord and of his Christ, and he shall reign for ever and ever." This is the ultimate end-time event. Now Jesus can come and reward His children (Revelation 11:18).

In summary, the following points can be made for a last-day application of the story of the two witnesses.

1) The two witnesses' story overlaps and completes the sixth trumpet.
2) The two witnesses' story ends at the beginning of the third woe (seventh trumpet).
3) The audience of this story is the last-day audience of Revelation 14:6.
4) The sackcloth time period overlaps the first and second trumpets, which are last-day events.
5) The two witnesses' story overlaps the plagues.
6) The two witnesses are killed when Satan is released from the bottomless pit and ascends to his throne as the eighth king during the third trumpet.
7) The two witnesses' story occurs during the investigative judgment.
8) The two witnesses' story ends with God's Word ascending to heaven because its work is complete.
9) The two witnesses' story is followed by the Second Coming of Christ, and the rewarding of His servants.

Revelation 12
The Dragon and the Eighth King

Revelation 12 has been considered a general outline of the great controversy between good and evil. Revelation 12 covers earth's history from before creation to the time of the end. John describes the conflict in heaven between Satan and his angels and Christ (Michael) and His angels. Satan is shown attempting to destroy Jesus, "the child" (Revelation 12:4), and the church, "the woman" (Revelation 12:5). Satan, the dragon, is described making war on "the rest of her offspring" or the remnant of the church (Revelation 12:17). Satan is seen "in great wrath" because "his time is short" (Revelation 12:12). It has been taught by some that Revelation 12:7-11 simply repeats the story outlined in Revelation 12:1-6. The time period of Revelation 12:6 was thought to be the same as the time period of Revelation 12:14. Both time periods have been applied to the 1260 years from A.D. 538 to 1798.[1] The above historical interpretation of Revelation 12 is correct. However, there is a dual application, which applies to last-day events. The emphasis in Revelation 12 is on the dragon: Revelation 12 attempts to identify who the dragon is, who he is fighting against, who his wrath is aimed at, and how long he will be in control. All of these issues can be applied to both historical as well as last-day events.

> Revelation 12:1: *"And a great portent appeared in heaven, a woman clothed with the sun, with the moon under her feet, and on her head a crown of twelve stars."*

This chapter begins by introducing a symbol of a woman. A pure woman in Bible prophecy often symbolizes God's true church. "For your Maker is your husband, the Lord of hosts is his name; and the Holy One of Israel is your Redeemer, the God of the whole earth he is called. For the Lord has called you *like a wife* forsaken and grieved in spirit, *like a wife* of youth when she is cast off, says your God" (Isaiah 54:5-6) (emphasis supplied). Here in Isaiah God is called the "husband" and Israel His true church is called the "wife."

In Bible prophecy, a corrupt woman, prostitute, whore, or harlot is often used to describe an apostate church. "Surely, as a *faithless wife leaves her husband,* so have you been faithless to me, O house of Israel, says the Lord" (Jeremiah 3:20) (emphasis supplied). Here Israel is a "faithless wife," often called an adulteress, because she has left her husband the Lord. Israel can be a pure woman, when she is faithful, or a corrupt woman (prostitute) when she is apostate or unfaithful.

This "woman" in Revelation 12:1 represents God's true church throughout history.[2] It includes all those who have served God both before and after Jesus' life and death for our sins. This church includes every true believer from Adam to the end of time. In the context of the first few verses, it specifically represents God's true believers prior to Jesus' birth; however, later in this chapter it represents those true believers who have accepted Christ up to the end of time.

This "woman" is "clothed with the sun." This "sun" represents the glory of God as revealed in His Son. This "sun" also can represent the gospel or good news about God as seen in Jesus Christ. Jesus is the Light of the World and will be our Sun in the New Jerusalem (Revelation 21:23).

This "woman" is standing on the "moon." Historically, some have interpreted the "moon" to represent the ceremonial laws of the Old Testament, which reflected Jesus' work and were replaced by Him.[3] However, in the last days the "moon" represents the Word of God or the Holy Bible. The "moon" reflects the sun's light. The Bible reflects Jesus' love to man, both in the Old and the New Testaments. In the last days God's church (the woman) will stand on God's Word (the moon) (see discussion under Revelation 8:12).

The woman is wearing a crown. The Greek word "*Stephanos*" in this text means a victor's crown or wreath. This symbolizes the church as the ultimate victor in the fight with Satan. This crown has "twelve stars." These "twelve stars" have been applied to the 12 patriarchs of Israel in the Old Testament.[4] They have also been applied to the 12 apostles in the New Testament.[5] However, in the context of Revelation 12 with its emphasis on the dragon and the last-day events, the "twelve stars" represent the 12 tribes of Revelation 7.

The "twelve tribes" of Revelation 7 make up the 144,000 who are able to "stand before it" (Revelation 6:17). They will be able to stand before the wrath of the Lamb (Revelation 6:16). The 144,000 represents God's true church, which will endure all the trials of the time of the end and will be alive at Jesus' Second Coming. The 144,000 are those who are sealed with God's seal at the time of the end (Revelation 7:3, 4). These are the "saints" described in Revelation 14:12: "those who keep the commandments of God and the faith of Jesus." It should be noted that the "twelve tribes" of Revelation 7 are not the same as the 12 patriarchs or the 12 tribes of Israel. Each list of 12 tribes is different.

The "twelve tribes" of Revelation 7 are unique in that they will be honored for all eternity. They are "before the throne of God, and serve him day and night within his temple" (Revelation 7:15). It seems appropriate that this group, who will be honored for enduring "a time of trouble such as never has been" (Daniel 12:1), would be symbolized in the crown of victory. If any group will be known for overcoming or for victory, it will be these 12 tribes who "stand firm and take action" for their God at the time of the end (Daniel 11:32).

Thus, in Revelation 12:1, we see a description of the "woman" or God's true church as victorious. The "crown" is one of victory not royalty. The "crown" includes those who will overcome in the final great tribulation (Matthew 24:21). The "twelve stars" connect this symbol to the time of the end and God's remnant (Revelation 12:17). These "twelve stars" will only be victorious after the close of probation when God's people are sealed. Therefore, the "twelve stars" suggest that this vision is related to the time after the close of probation, which occurs at the time of the end. The symbols on the dragon will also connect this prophecy to the time of the end.

> Revelation 12:2: *"she was with child and she cried out in her pangs of birth, in anguish for delivery."*

The woman, who represents God's true church or His true believers, is pictured as "with child." This "child" represents Jesus who came to this world as a baby "wrapped in swaddling cloths and lying in a manger" (Luke 2:12). Jesus Christ, the Son of God, Lord of the Universe and Creator of the World, lowered Himself to our level: "And the Word became flesh and dwelt among us" (John 1:14). God's true believers had been under constant attack by Satan prior to Christ's birth, but the intensity of the attack was to increase as Satan attempted to destroy the Savior of mankind. Satan would attempt to kill Jesus by using political power. Initially, he used King Herod "to search for the child, to destroy him" (Matthew 2:13). This attempt failed. However, ultimately Satan would appear to win when Pilate ordered Jesus crucified. This victory was short lived because Jesus rose triumphant from the grave (John 20:14-17).

> Revelation 12:3: *"And another portent appeared in heaven; behold a great red dragon, with seven heads and ten horns, and seven diadems upon his heads."*

John now sees another "portent" or wonder in heaven. This beast is described as a "great red dragon." This dragon will become the focus of Revelation 12. This dragon is identified in Revelation 12:9: ***"And the great dragon was thrown down, that ancient serpent, who is called the Devil and Satan,*** the deceiver of the whole world" (emphasis supplied). This red dragon is Satan. In the Bible the color red often is used to symbolize sin. Satan is the dragon pictured as having ten horns and seven heads. The seven heads have seven crowns (see Preface: The Crowns and Their Meaning for a discussion on the symbolic meaning of being crowned).

Historically, the 1260 days of Revelation 12:6 has been applied to the time from A.D. 538 to 1798 and then connected to these "ten horns."[6] However, applying these ten horns to the ten European kingdoms is not consistent with the symbols. The ten horns on this beast are not crowned, which means that at the time that John sees this beast in vision, these kingdoms have not yet existed. This means that these horns cannot represent the ten European kingdoms, since they all have reigned and three have disappeared prior to the rise of the Papacy in A.D. 538. The absence of crowns indicates that these ten kingdoms do not yet exist.

If these "ten horns" do not represent the ten horns of Daniel 7:24 or Revelation 13:1, which do represent the ten European kingdoms, then what ten kingdoms do they represent? The answer is found in Revelation 17:12 which states: "And the ten horns that you saw are ten kings *who have not yet received royal power,* but they are to receive authority as kings for one hour, together with the beast" (emphasis supplied). They do not have crowns because they have not yet received power. The crowns are placed on the symbol after they receive power and rule. The "ten horns" of the beast in Revelation 12 are the same as the ten horns on the beast in Revelation 17. In each case, they represent the same ten kingdoms, which exist only at the end of time for a very short time period. This time period is described as one hour, which prophetically can either represent approximately two weeks or it can simply represent a short period of time (Revelation 17:12). The "red dragon" of Revelation 12 is the same beast as the "scarlet beast" of Revelation 17. Both represent Satan in his final role as world leader.

The seven heads are crowned, which means they have completed their reign prior to the time of John's vision. The seven heads are "seven kings" (Revelation 17:10). The seven heads represent the seven last popes, who will lead the Papacy, after the mortal wound is healed. The Papacy's mortal wound (Revelation 13:3) was healed in 1929 when Mussolini gave the Vatican the land on which it exists today. This restored the Vatican to a church-state status and restored it as a kingdom. The six popes since 1929 are truly kings since they now reign over a church-state union, which is a kingdom. The wound that the Papacy sustained in 1798 was to "One of its heads" (Revelation 13:3) and the head that was wounded was Pope Pius VI, who was captured in 1798 by Napoleon's General Berthier and died in captivity. The head in Revelation 13:3 represented the pope. The seven heads in Revelation 12 represent the seven heads or kings of Vatican City since 1929 (discussed in Revelation 17 (first part)—The Scarlet Woman and Her Kings).

The seven heads or popes have been crowned, which means that the time period that John is seeing in vision in Revelation 12 occurs after all seven kings have finished their reign. This is the time period of the reign of the eighth king. In Revelation 13, the seven heads are not crowned, and John is actually seeing events during the reign of the seventh king, just prior to the eighth king's reign (discussed in Revelation 13 (first part)—The Leopard Beast Healed). In Revelation 17, the seven heads are not crowned and John is viewing history during the reign of the sixth king. The sixth king is described as "one is" (Revelation 17:10), meaning that the sixth king is reigning at that time.

The beast or Satan in Revelation 12 is seen by John after all seven kings or popes have finished their reigns. The time period of emphasis during Revelation 12 is during the reign of the eighth king, who follows the seventh king and "belongs to the seven" (Revelation 17:11). This time period corresponds to the three and one-half year time period described in Revelation 11:7-9. "The beast that ascends" in Revelation 11:7 is the same beast as the dragon of Revelation 12 and the scarlet beast of Revelation 17. This beast is Satan who claims to be Christ returned to the world to save mankind. This beast is "the transgression that makes desolate" of Daniel 8:13 and "the desolater" of Daniel 9:27. This beast is "the abomination that makes desolate" in Daniel 11:31 and Daniel 12:11.

It should be noted that John's visions in chapters 17, 13, and 12 each focus on one of the reigns of the last three of the eight kings. John's vision in Revelation 17 is focused on the time of the sixth king. Revelation 13 is focused on the time of the seventh king, when the Sunday law is passed and the image to the beast will occur. Revelation 12 is focused on the time after the Papacy and its kings have finished their work and turned over their kingdom to Satan as the false Christ. He will then reign as the eighth king. This same time period, when the dragon is depicted as the eighth king, is depicted in Revelation 11 as the time period when the beast "ascends" and kills God's two witnesses, who are dead for three and one-half years. *Therefore, the first three verses of Revelation 12 connect this chapter to last-day events and particularly to the time when Satan will reign as the eighth king.*

> Revelation 12:4: *"His tail swept down a third of the stars of heaven, and cast them to the earth. And the dragon stood before the woman who was about to bear a child, that he might devour her child when she brought it forth."*

The "stars of heaven" represent angels. The dragon, or Satan, who was called Lucifer in heaven, took about one-third of the heavenly angels with him when he was cast out. These angels chose to believe Satan's lies and were cast out of heaven because they rejected the true God and chose to follow the deceiver. Satan won the earth from Adam in the Garden of Eden, when Adam and Eve first sinned. From that time on, Satan has claimed the earth as his own. This is clearly seen when he offers to give Christ all the kingdoms on earth if Christ will worship him (Matthew 4:8). Once Christ was born, Satan made every effort to destroy Him. The "child" in Revelation 12:4 refers to Jesus Christ.

> Revelation 12:5: *"she brought forth a male child, one who is to rule all the nations with a rod of iron, but her child was caught up to God and his throne."*

The woman or God's true believers "brought forth a male child." This "male child" is Jesus Christ, who was "to rule all the nations with a rod of iron." This alludes to Psalms 2:8, 9, which is a prophecy about the Messiah.[7] Jesus was "caught up" in the clouds and then into heaven (Acts 1:11) where He sits "at the right hand of the Majesty on high" (Hebrews 1:3).

> Revelation 12:6: *"and the woman fled into the wilderness, where she has a place prepared by God, in which to be nourished for one thousand two hundred and sixty days."*

Historically, this text has been applied to the persecution of God's people during the Dark Ages. During the Dark Ages, the woman or God's true church fled from persecution by the apostate church or Papacy. The Greek word translated "wilderness" also can be interpreted as "empty places" or "unpopulated areas."[8] The "wilderness" represents those unpopulated areas. These areas were where God's people could safely survive the persecution of Papal Rome. Historians estimate that Papal Rome killed millions of Christians during this time period.

The "one thousand two hundred and sixty days" represent 1260 years (one prophetic day equals one literal year: Numbers 14:34 and Ezekiel 4:6). This 1260-year time period exactly coincides with the rule of Papal Rome, which began in A.D. 538 and ended in 1798 with its "mortal wound" (Revelation 13:3) (see comments on Revelation 12:3).[9] Revelation 12:6 is best understood as a historical reference to the 1260 years of Papal reign, including the Dark Ages. This wilderness experience is linked to God's protection, whereas, the second wilderness experience in Revelation 12:14 is linked to the eagle's protection. The eagle is clearly connected to last-day events as will be discussed later. Revelation 12:6 was fulfilled when God protected millions during the persecution of the Christians in the Dark Ages. The Huguenots and Waldensees are examples of God's protective hand during this time.

> Revelation 12:7: *"Now war arose in heaven, Michael and his angels fighting against the dragon; and the dragon and his angels fought."*

This verse begins the explanation of Revelation 12:1-6 and also gives an overview of the plan of salvation and the great controversy between God and Satan.

Revelation 12:7 explains who the combatants are in this great controversy. Michael, who is Jesus Christ (compare Daniel 10:13, Daniel 12:1, and Jude 9), is seen fighting against the dragon or Satan.[10] This battle occurs in heaven and involves Jesus and His angels versus Satan and his angels.

> Revelation 12:8: *"but they were defeated and there was no longer any place for them in heaven."*

Satan's angels were defeated by Jesus and His angels and "a third of the stars of heaven" were cast down (Revelation 12:4). In Revelation 12:4, the angels are referred to as stars. These angels lost their home in heaven near God's throne. Satan took approximately one-third of the heavenly angels with him when he was thrown down (Revelation 12:4).

> Revelation 12:9: *"And the great dragon was thrown down, that ancient serpent, who is called the Devil and Satan, the deceiver of the whole world—he was thrown down to the earth, and his angels were thrown down with him."*

This text completes the explanation of the war in heaven. This text tells us whom the dragon represents. The dragon is Satan. This text describes Satan's most important characteristic. Satan is called "the deceiver of the whole world." This characteristic will become more significant in the last days when he masquerades as the false Christ and the world worships him (Revelation 13:4).

Satan is "thrown down" to the earth along with his angels. Since Satan overcame Adam he has claimed the right to be prince of this world (Job 1:6, Matthew 4:8, 9). Historically, this verse has been applied to Satan's original downfall from heaven, which is consistent with the context.[11] However, some have suggested that after Christ's death and ascension to heaven, Satan was banned from heaven or permanently kept out.[12] They connect this application to the next few verses which emphasize the Lamb Slain. Either interpretation will fit this verse; however, the historical interpretation linking this verse to the war in heaven is most consistent with the prior eight verses.

> Revelation 12:10: *"And I heard a loud voice in heaven, saying, 'Now the salvation and the power and the kingdom of our God and the authority of his Christ have come, for the accuser of our brethren has been thrown down, who accuses them day and night before our God.'"*

Historically, this text has been applied to Jesus' victory over Satan at the cross. This interpretation suggests that Revelation 12:10-12 describes the celebration in heaven when Jesus overcame sin forever.[13] Certainly, this application is appropriate. However, the remainder of Revelation 12 is closely connected to these verses. Revelation 12:12 suggests that Satan's "time is short." Revelation 12:13-17 relates to last-day events and God's faithful people at the time of the end (His remnant church). These connections to the last days suggest a dual application for the remainder of this chapter, which relates to last-day events.

"And I heard a loud voice in heaven." Historically, this has been thought to represent rejoicing in heaven.[14] This interpretation is appropriate. However, when you evaluate the term "loud" in the book of Revelation, it is almost always associated with judgment events. For example, the "loud voice" of Revelation 14:6 states "the hour of his judgment has come." The "loud voice" of Revelation 14:9 relates to the judgment of "God's wrath" on those who have the mark of the beast. The "loud voice" of Revelation 8:13 is associated with the last three trumpets, which are called "woes" because of the terrible judgments included in each woe. In Revelation 16:1, the "loud voice" announces the beginning of the seven last plagues, which are God's judgments on the world. Other examples include Revelation 11:15, Revelation 14:15 and Revelation 14:17, where each "loud voice" relates to the Second Coming and the punishment of the wicked and the salvation of the righteous.

Judgment is not negative for everyone. For the righteous, judgment is positive. It means they will finally receive their rewards. This "loud voice" is announcing the completion of the judgment process in heaven. This process began in 1844 with the investigative judgment pictured in Daniel 7:10, when "the court sat in judgment and the books were opened." This same judgment scene is pictured in Revelation 4:3-9 and Revelation 5:6-10. Revelation 5:10 states "and hast made them a kingdom and priests to our God." The "new song" of Revelation 5:9 is sung to the Lamb before He opens the book, which has seven seals. This book contains the names and actions of all those who have accepted God or Jesus as their Lord during their lives. This is the book of life mentioned in Revelation 20:12-15. This book is what is reviewed during the investigative judgment. This process involves the 24 elders and the four creatures around the throne. This process allows the universe, through its representatives, to reaffirm God's decisions prior to the righteous and wicked receiving their rewards. This process is not to educate or to change God's mind but to make certain that the entire universe has the opportunity to affirm that God is fair and just. This process will guarantee that doubt will never again arise in God's creatures, as it did when Lucifer sinned.

The "new song" states that God has "made them a kingdom" (Revelation 5:9, 10). This refers to God's kingdom of the saved from the earth. Christ's death as our Lamb Slain is what makes this kingdom possible (Revelation 5:9). This statement at the beginning of the investigative judgment confirms that God has a special kingdom whose names are in the book.

Revelation 12:10 states: "Now the salvation and the power and the **kingdom of our God** and the authority of his Christ have come" (emphasis supplied). This statement suggests that the kingdom being investigated in Daniel 7:10 and in Revelation 4:3-9 and Revelation 5:6-10 has now been completed. The "kingdom of our God" has come. This statement also suggests that salvation has come and that God's power and Christ's authority have been re-established. There is only one point in time prior to the Second Coming when this can occur. Clearly, this verse does not refer to the Second Coming of Christ, since Satan is thrown down to the earth to continue his evil activities after this kingdom has come (Revelation 12:10, 12, 13). Satan still has time left to make war on God's remnant (Revelation 12:17).

The only time when God's kingdom is complete, prior to the Second Coming, occurs at the end of the investigative judgment and the close of probation. The investigative judgment involves a review of the books on all of God's people, including those who later rejected God. This review will be completed at the close of probation. Once probation closes no one else will choose for or against God. This is the point in time when God lets the holy "still be holy" and the "filthy still be filthy" (Revelation 22:11). Daniel describes this same time period in Daniel 11:35 when he states "some of those who are wise shall fall, to refine and to cleanse them and to make them white, until the time of the end." Daniel is describing the point in time when God's people no longer die, which occurs at the close of probation. These "wise" are those who "shall understand" (Daniel 12:10). They understand what Daniel did not understand (Daniel 12:6, 8). They understand that Satan is the eighth king and is not Christ and they also refuse to accept Satan's change in the holy covenant (Daniel 11:30-32).

Revelation 12:10 is announcing the end of the investigative judgment, which will occur at the close of probation. The living righteous will now endure the time of trouble "such as never has been" (Daniel 12:1). Revelation 15:7-8 states, "And one of the four living creatures gave the seven angels seven golden bowls full of the wrath of God, who lives for ever and ever, and the temple was filled with smoke from the glory of God and from his power, and *no one could enter the temple until the seven plagues of the seven angels were ended"* (emphasis supplied). This text implies that during the seven last plagues the investigative judgment has been completed, since no one is able to enter the temple during the time of the plagues. The investigative judgment has ended and God's wrath has begun.

Thus, Revelation 12:10 can be interpreted as a celebration in heaven, relating to the end of the investigative judgment and the close of probation, which signifies that God's kingdom is complete. Since the investigative judgment is completed, Satan can finally be cast down. Satan has no one else to accuse except those living on earth. God cannot be seen as unfair, since He has allowed Satan to accuse everyone prior to being "cast down." Satan is now banned from heaven. It could be argued that God is taking a risk by accepting the 144,000 as sealed at this time. However, God knows that none of these will fail Him. Satan will be enraged at the idea that none of these can be lost and this will further increase his anger at those who are sealed.

Revelation 12:10 continues "for the accuser of our brethren has been thrown down, who accuses them day and night before our God." Satan is the "accuser of our brethren." Satan has accused each of us of being unworthy to be saved. He accuses our God of being unfair if He saves us. These accusations are involved in the investigative judgment. God's answer is to point to the Lamb Slain. Jesus' blood is our only hope. Jesus' blood is the answer to Satan's accusations. Satan claims God is not fair or merciful. Jesus' blood proves He is.

Historically, it has been argued that Jesus' death on the cross assured the success of God's kingdom.[15] However, Satan's accusations regarding each of the saved will not disappear until the close of probation, when every person's fate has been resolved. "Let the evildoer still do evil, and the filthy still be filthy, and the righteous still do right, and the holy still be holy" (Revelation 22:11). Revelation 15:8 states that the temple is filled with smoke during the seven last plagues and no one can enter, this is consistent with the close of probation. This is consistent with Satan the accuser having been cast down and the end of the courtroom proceedings in heaven.

Revelation 12:11: *"And they have conquered him by the blood of the Lamb and by the word of their testimony, for they loved not their lives even unto death."*

Historically, this text has been applied to all Christians throughout the ages who have conquered or overcome Satan. They have conquered through Jesus' blood and their witness to others about His love for them. Many of these conquerors have died for their faith rather than accept Satan's lies. In the context of the last-day events, the statement "loved not their lives even unto death" will apply up until the close of probation. After "the time of the end," the wise shall not fall (Daniel 11:35). Daniel's time of the end represents the close of probation.

Revelation 12:12: *"Rejoice then, O heaven and you that dwell therein! But woe to you, O earth and sea for the devil has come down to you in great wrath, because he knows that his **time is short**"* (emphasis supplied).

Historically, this rejoicing was thought to represent the joy in heaven when Jesus was raised triumphant over sin.[16] When applied to the time of the end, heaven is rejoicing because no more of God's people will die and God's kingdom is completed. Probation has closed and the investigative judgment is finished. All the saved have been accounted for and the 144,000 are sealed. God's temple is filled with His glory, Satan is cast down, and no one can enter the temple. The "earth and sea" represent the entire world, both unpopulated and populated areas. It can also be thought of as the physical planet earth and its people. The earth as a planet and the earth's people are being warned. Both the physical earth and its inhabitants are about to suffer Satan's wrath as well as God's wrath. The "woe" mentioned here reminds us of the woes of Revelation 8:13. The woes of Revelation 8:13 will fall during the time of the end. The first woe falls after God's people are sealed (Revelation 9:4, 12). The first woe (the fifth trumpet) occurs with the seven last plagues (discussed in Revelation 16—The Seven Last Plagues). The seven last plagues are God's wrath on the wicked (Revelation 15:1). All three woes will occur after the close of probation because God's people are sealed prior to the first woe (Revelation 9:4). The Devil is described as coming down in "great wrath" because he knows his "time is short." Historically, this has been interpreted as meaning the Devil only had approximately two thousand years left after the cross.[17] It was suggested that Lucifer had existed for unknown ages prior to his fall and two thousand years would be a short time for him.

However, if one interprets these verses as relating to last-day events, then truly, Satan has only a very short time. The content of Revelation 12 suggests the focus should be on the dragon (the eighth king). The eighth king will only reign for about three and one-half years (discussed in Revelation 11 (first part)—The Two Witnesses). Satan will be cast down at the close of probation, which occurs during the latter portion of his reign as the eighth king.

The description of Satan being thrown down (Revelation 12:10, 12, 13) helps identify the fallen "star" of the third trumpet in Revelation 8:10. In Revelation 8:10, the third angel blew his trumpet "and a great star fell from heaven, blazing like a torch." We have seen previously in this chapter how stars represent angels. The fallen star of Revelation 8:10 is Satan. The same "star fallen from heaven" will be released from the "pit" in Revelation 9:1, 2 and will be called "king" (Revelation 9:11). The "star fallen" of Revelation 9:1 is also Satan. Each of these texts is describing Satan once he becomes the world's leader, first as the world's spiritual leader (the eighth king) (Revelation 8:10) and then later as the world's temporal leader (world king) (Revelation 9:1, 11).

This vision, which shows Satan being thrown down to earth in Revelation 12:10, 12, represents the end of the investigative judgment. There is no longer a judgment process ongoing. It has ended. Satan has no one else to accuse and is thrown out of heaven forever. This end of the investigative judgment marks the completion of the sealing of God's people, who are the 144,000 of Revelation 7:3, 4. The completion of this sealing marks the close of probation: no more names will be added or subtracted from the list of those saved for eternity. The temple will be closed and filled with smoke (Revelation 15:8): no one can enter it. The seven last plagues will begin to fall and the first of the three woes will occur.

The presence of the 12 stars on the woman's crown of victory suggests a connection to the time of the end. This victory crown can only be worn once victory has occurred. Victory can only occur at the time of the end, which begins with the close of probation. The 12 tribes described in Revelation 7 are the 12 stars on this victory crown. The 12 tribes represent the 144,000 (Revelation 7:4-8), which means that the victory that this crown represents relates to the 144,000. This victory crown can only exist after the close of probation. The 144,000 represent God's sealed righteous who have overcome. This sealing is accomplished prior to the fifth trumpet or first woe (Revelation 9:4). This sealing is completed prior to the close of probation. The 12 stars would be victorious and part of the victory crown only if the sealing were finished.

Thus, the victory crown with 12 stars suggests that John is viewing time during the end of the dragon's reign, after the sealing is completed. The sealing of the 12 tribes or 144,000 is completed prior to the fifth trumpet, because the locusts are told to harm "only those of mankind *who have not the seal of God upon their foreheads*" (Revelation 9:4) (emphasis supplied). Revelation 9:4 shows that God's people have been sealed by the time of the fifth trumpet. Therefore, John is viewing time after the fifth trumpet in Revelation 12:10-13 and during the latter part of the eighth king's reign.

> Revelation 12:13: *"And when the dragon saw that he had been thrown down to the earth, he pursued the woman who had borne the male child."*

Historically, this text has been applied to the time from the cross onward.[18] It was taught that Satan was overcome at the cross and cast out of heaven. However, being "thrown down" may have another application. Satan is described as our accuser in heaven[19] and once the investigative judgment is completed, Satan will be cast down forever since there is no one left to accuse. The dragon (Satan) will recognize his time is short. He understands time of the end prophecies. He understands that as God allows him to do more, his time becomes shorter and the end of time nearer. He will now have only a very short time to capture and kill God's people before the Second Coming of Christ. He will only have a very short time to prove God was wrong in sealing His 144,000 prior to the Second Coming. This represents Satan's last chance to prove that God is unfair. If Satan can make even one of these saints fail he can claim victory, because he can claim that God was unfair in sealing that saint. This is why this will be the most severe test of God's people ever (Daniel 12:1). The dragon will pursue God's people in an attempt to destroy them because he knows his time is short.

> Revelation 12:14: *"But the woman was given the two wings of the great eagle that she might fly from the serpent into the wilderness, to the place where she is to be nourished for a time, and times, and half a time."*

The "woman," who represents God's people, is going to receive help. This help comes in the form of an "eagle" with two wings. Historically, this verse has been applied to the 1260 years of persecution from A.D. 538 to 1798.[20] A "time, and times, and half a time" equals 1260 days. 1260 days equals 1260 years (one prophetic day equals one literal year: Numbers 14:34, Ezekiel 4:6). The "eagle" was thought to represent God's protective care and the two wings were interpreted as deliverance and haste.[21]

There is, however, another last-day application, which applies to this verse. The "eagle" is clearly related to last-day events. The "eagle" is first seen in Revelation 4:7. It is the fourth in the series of the "four living creatures" (Revelation 4:6, 7). This "eagle" is later involved in opening the fourth seal (Revelation 6:7). This "eagle" is next seen introducing the three woes or the last three trumpets (Revelation 8:13).

In Revelation 4 and 5, the "eagle" is related to the investigative judgment, which began in 1844. Each of the four living creatures represents a time period since 1844, and the "eagle" represents the last time period, which occurs just prior to the Second Coming (discussed in Revelation 6—The Seven Seals).

The eagle is also related to the fourth seal. The fourth seal describes the reign of Satan as the eighth king and his attacks on God's people. The fourth seal occurs after the union of church and state has been formed during the third seal, which is described as a yoke or "balance" in Revelation 6:5 (discussed in Revelation 6—The Seven Seals). Both of these seals involve last-day events.

The "eagle" is related to the trumpets. The seven last trumpets relate to last-day events. These trumpets come on the scene after the investigative judgment is ongoing and begin to blow "after the censer" is cast down. The trumpets occur during the last days of earth's history, after the United States forms the "image" to the beast (discussed in Revelation 13 (last part)—The Mark of the Beast). The eagle introduces the last three trumpets or woes (Revelation 8:13). These woes are clearly involved in time of the end events. The last woe (the seventh trumpet) is the Second Coming of Christ. The second woe is the final battle of Armageddon and the release of God's four angels holding back the winds of strife. The first woe is Satan after he is released from God's restrictions and is allowed to rule the world (discussed in Revelation 9—The Seven Trumpets: The First and Second Woes). Thus, the "eagle" is related to the time period after the image of the beast occurs and during the final three trumpets or woes.

The eagle itself has been thought to represent God's protection (Exodus 19:4). Clearly, whether this text is applied to the Dark Ages time period of A.D. 538 to 1798 or it is applied to the last three and one-half years of earth's history, the eagle does represent God's protection.

The "two wings" of the eagle have been described as haste and deliverance. The "two wings," however, can also represent the two characteristics for which God's people at the time of the end will be known. These characteristics are described in Revelation 12:17. In Revelation 12:17, God's remnant is described as "those who keep the commandments of God and bear testimony to Jesus." These same two characteristics are the definition of the "saints" in Revelation 14:12: "those who keep the commandments of God and the faith of Jesus." In the circumstances of the last days, God's Law will be under attack. A false Sabbath will be forced on the world. Also, the false Christ, the dragon or Satan, will be attacking anyone who keeps faith in the true Jesus or bears testimony to Him and rejects the false Christ. These "two wings" will be what sustain God's people during the time of trouble. These "two wings" can be considered keeping God's Commandments, especially the true Sabbath, and keeping faith in the true Christ.

God's people are told to "flee to the mountains" in Matthew 24:16, when they see the "desolating sacrilege" standing in the holy place (Matthew 24:15). This desolating sacrilege or abomination that makes desolate (Daniel 11:31) is Satan as the false Christ. He is the "desolating sacrilege spoken of by the prophet Daniel" (Matthew 24:15, see Daniel 9:27) (discussed in Daniel 9—The Abomination and the Final Week). When Satan reigns in Jerusalem as the false Christ, God's people will be under attack and God's people will truly be in "the wilderness." However, God will sustain them and they will "be nourished for a time, and times, and half a time."

This "time, and times, and half a time" is 1260 days or three and one-half years. This three and one-half year time period is the time of the reign of the dragon as the false Christ or the abomination that makes desolate. This is the time of the eighth king. This time period is the same three and one-half years described in Revelation 11:9, 11. This is the time when God's two witnesses are dead but not buried. This is the time when the two witnesses, the Old Testament and the New Testament, are interpreted by the false Christ. They are dead but they are not buried. The world thinks Jesus is interpreting scripture for them but actually they are listening to Satan. This three and one-half-year period is the same period described in Revelation 11:2 as "forty-two months." During this 42-month period, Satan, as the false Christ or eighth king (Revelation 17:11), and the nations he represents "will trample over the holy city" (Revelation 11:2). This same time period is described in Daniel 12:7. In Daniel 12:7, the "time, two times, and half a time," which is 1260 days, will end when "the shattering of the power of the holy people comes to an end." This shattering of God's peoples' power occurs when God's Holy Word is taken over by the false Christ and ends when God's Word is resurrected (Revelation 17:11) (discussed in Revelation 11 (first part)—The Two Witnesses). God's two witnesses, the Old Testament and the New Testament, are resurrected just prior to the seventh trumpet, which is

Jesus' Second Coming (Revelation 11:15).

> Revelation 12:15: *"The serpent poured water like a river*
> *out of his mouth after the woman, to sweep her away with*
> *the flood."*

Historically, this has been interpreted to represent Satan's attacks on God's people during the Dark Ages.[22] These attacks included attempts to destroy God's people with persecution and to mislead them with falsehood. The "river out of his mouth" represented false doctrines Satan tried to impose on God's church.

In the last days, Satan will also do the same thing. He will attempt to destroy God's people with persecution. This persecution will be the worst persecution the world has ever seen. This persecution will worsen once Satan rules as the eighth king. During these last three and one-half years, Satan will attempt to kill every true believer. God's Word is the fountain of life. Satan will now interpret God's Word and change it into a flood of falsehood. Satan will poison God's Word and "a third of the waters became Wormwood" (Revelation 8:11). Wormwood refers to being made bitter or poisoned. Satan wins if you accept his lies. God's people will not accept his lies. The "water like a river" that Satan pours out upon God's people represents the false doctrines he claims to be truth. The "water like a river" can also represent the large number of people Satan sends after God's children.

> Revelation 12:16: *"But the earth came to the help of the*
> *woman, and the earth opened its mouth and swallowed the*
> *river which the dragon had poured from his mouth."*

Historically, some have interpreted "the earth" as the true doctrines of the Reformation, which swallowed up the false doctrines of the Dark Ages period.[23] Others have interpreted this as a symbol of North America, which was unpopulated and served as a haven for the religiously persecuted.[24]

In the context of the last days, "the earth" can be seen as truth or God's Word. John 17:17 states "thy word is truth." God's Word is dead for the world (the two witnesses killed by the beast) during the last three and one-half years of time but not dead for God's people. God's truth will reflect and absorb the false teachings of the false Christ (the eighth king). God's truth will truly swallow up falsehood. God's truth will swallow "the river which the dragon had poured from his mouth." The "earth" can also represent the unpopulated areas, which will protect God's people from Satan's followers who are persecuting them.

> Revelation 12:17: *"Then the dragon was angry with the*
> *woman, and went off to make war on the rest of her offspring,*
> *on those who keep the commandments of God and bear*
> *testimony to Jesus. And he stood on the sand of the sea."*

Historically, this text has been interpreted as representing Satan who is enraged at God's people and attempts to destroy the remnant or remaining ones.[25] God's people are defined as "those who keep the commandments of God and bear testimony to Jesus." The testimony to Jesus has been interpreted as either testimony about Jesus or having the spirit of prophecy (Revelation 19:10). Using this historical approach, the remnant represents God's true believers at the end of time.

In the context of last-day events, Satan as the eighth king will be angry or enraged, because God's people are the only people on earth who refuse to bow down to him as Christ returned. Also, God's people will be the only people on earth who refuse to accept his counterfeit Sabbath. They will refuse to violate the holy covenant (Daniel 11:32). They will refuse to accept the mark of the beast (Revelation 13:16, 17). After the close of probation, God's sealed people are Satan's last chance for him to prove that God is wrong. If Satan can make them lose faith he can claim God was unfair in closing probation and sealing them. The "rest of her offspring" suggests that some of God's church will be killed during this time of persecution. These will "fall" up to "the time of the end" (Daniel 11:35). The "time of the end" is not the end of time as is shown in Daniel 11:40-45, which describes events that occur at "the time of the end." Daniel's "time of the end" is a specific time period, which includes the "time of trouble" of Daniel 12:1. Daniel's time of the end represents the close of probation.

The "rest of her offspring" or the remnant can be considered God's people, who are alive during the third angel's message. This includes the 144,000, who will be sealed at the close of probation. The 144,000 are represented by the 12 stars on the woman's crown (Revelation 12:1). Those "who keep the commandments of God and bear testimony to Jesus" are the remnant. They are also called "saints" in Revelation 14:12. This is God's definition of the last-day's saint. The last-day's saint will keep all of God's Commandments and reject Satan's false Sabbath or mark. The last-day's saint will bear testimony to Jesus and reject Satan as the false Christ. This is why Satan (the dragon) is enraged. As the world's spiritual leader (the eighth king), he will require obedience or severe penalties will be imposed (Revelation 13:17).

The phrase "bear testimony to Jesus' also suggests that God's remnant will accept His spirit of prophecy. Revelation 19:10 states "for the testimony of Jesus is the spirit of prophecy." God's end-time people will know the end-time events. They will study God's Word and will be wise. They will have the spirit of prophecy and trust in it. They will be called "wise" because they "understand" (Daniel 12:10). They understand God's final prophecies and are prepared to stand firm on His Word. In this sense, the testimony of Jesus has a dual application both as the spirit of prophecy and as testimony about the true Jesus.

"And he stood on the sand of the sea." Historically, this final phrase has been thought to belong with Revelation 13:1, which begins a new vision about the leopard-like beast who is seen "rising out of the sea."[26] However, Satan is the beast of Revelation 12 and at the time of the end, he will truly stand "on the sand of the sea." Sand is used to describe a large number of people. In Genesis 32:12, Jacob quotes God's promise "and make your descendants as the sand of the sea." At the time of the end, the dragon will stand on the world's population, initially, as its spiritual leader, and finally as the world's king.

SUMMARY

In Revelation 12, we can see that there are two applications of this prophecy, which apply equally well. The historical application was of value for previous generations but the last-day application is of value now. It can be seen that Revelation 12 is describing the dragon (Satan) from his fall from heaven to his final reign on earth.

Revelation 12 begins by describing a woman wearing a crown of victory with 12 stars. These 12 stars represent the 144,000 who are victorious at the close of probation. The close of probation is described in this chapter when "the kingdom of our God" has come (Revelation 12:10). The great controversy between God and Satan is explained in Revelation 12:1-9. The dragon is seen with seven heads and ten horns. The seven heads are crowned, which means that John is seeing this vision after the time of the seven kings. This means that John is viewing history at the time of the eighth king. Since the 12 stars are on the woman's victory crown, John is actually viewing history at the end of the eighth king's reign after the close of probation.

John describes the events in heaven which coincide with the close of probation: God's kingdom has come, God's power and salvation have come, and Jesus' authority to save all his people has come. The investigative judgment has ended. The close of probation has occurred. God's people, the 144,000, have been sealed. Satan has no one left to accuse and is cast down to earth. Satan is enraged because his time is short. God's court is no longer in session and the plagues are beginning to fall (Revelation 15:8). The woes (Revelation 8:13) are also beginning (Revelation 12:12).

John also describes the events on earth, which precede the close of probation. The three and one-half years of Revelation 12 refers to Satan's reign as the false Christ (the eighth king), which marks his ascension to the throne in Jerusalem. This is also described in Daniel 12 and Revelation 11. This three and one-half year period is when Jerusalem, or the "holy city," is trampled on for 42 months (Revelation 11:2), and God's Old Testament and New Testament are dead but not buried (Revelation 11:8). God's remnant, at whom Satan is enraged, are those who refuse to accept Satan's false Sabbath and worship him. They keep God's Commandments and refuse to accept Satan as the Christ. They bear testimony to the true Jesus. The remnant will be protected by the eagle, which represents God's protection of His people. The following two charts outline these events. The first chart outlines the historical approach described in Revelation 12:1-9, which still applies. The second chart outlines the last-day application of Revelation 12:10-17. Both applications are valid.

Revelation Chapter 12
Verses 1-9

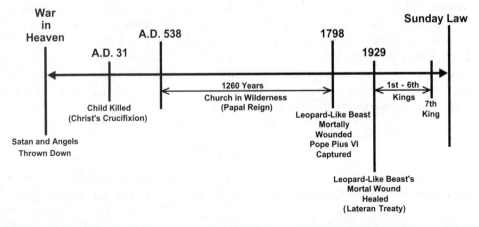

246

Revelation Chapter 12
Verses 10-17

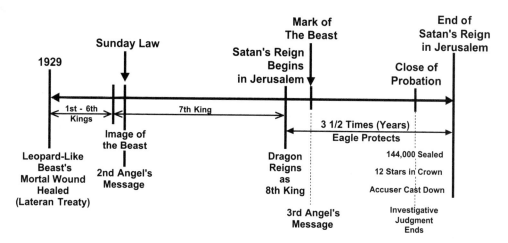

1   Nichol, Francis D. (Ed.) *The Seventh-day Adventist Bible Commentary* (Review and Herald Publishing Association, Washington D. C.) 1957, Vol. 7, p. 809.

2   Ibid. p. 807.

3   Ibid.

4   Ibid.

5   Ibid.

6   Ibid. pp. 808, 809.

7   Ibid. p. 808.

8   Ibid.

9   Ibid. p. 809.

10   Ibid.

11   Ibid.

12   Ibid. p. 810.

13   Ibid.

14   Ibid.

15   Ibid. p. 811.

16   Ibid.

17   Ibid. pp. 811, 812.

18   Ibid. p. 811.

19   White, Ellen G., *Testimonies for the Church* (Pacific Press Publishing Association, Mountain View, California) 1948, Vol. 5, p. 473.

20   Nichol, Francis D. (Ed.) *The Seventh-day Adventist Bible Commentary* (Review and Herald Publishing Association, Washington D. C.) 1957, Vol. 7, p. 809.

21   Ibid. p. 812.

22   Ibid.

23   Ibid.

24   Ibid.

25   Ibid.

26   Ibid. p. 816.

Revelation 16
The Seven Last Plagues

Revelation 15 introduces the seven plagues, which are called "the last" plagues (Revelation 15:1). They also are said to represent God's wrath (Revelation 15:1). These seven last plagues will represent the end of God's wrath (Revelation 15:1). This means that the seven last plagues occur at the end of this world's history. In Revelation 15, immediately after the seven last plagues are introduced, John sees "those who had conquered the beast and its image and the number of its name" (Revelation 15:2). This group had been described earlier in Revelation 7:3-4. At the time of the end, this group of overcomers is called the 144,000 and they will have God's seal "upon their foreheads" (Revelation 7:3). They have conquered the beast and its image by refusing its mark or seal (Revelation 13:15-17).

Revelation 15 first introduces the seven last plagues; it then introduces God's people who are victorious at the time of the seven last plagues. They are victorious and they are sealed prior to the seven last plagues being poured out. They "sing the song of Moses, the servant of God, and the song of the Lamb." This is a song of victory. They sing a song praising God because He alone is holy and also praising Him for revealing His judgments. They praise Him as the only Holy One as opposed to the false Christ who claims holiness. They praise God for beginning His judgments, which are the seven last plagues. Thus, God's 144,000 are sealed and are seen as victorious prior to the seven last plagues. This sealing occurs prior to the fifth trumpet, since this "woe" can only fall on those "who have not the seal of God on their foreheads" (Revelation 9:4, 12). The fifth trumpet marks the first woe and also the beginning of the seven last plagues. The seven angels are given "seven golden bowls full of the wrath of God who lives for ever and ever" (Revelation 15:7). These bowls will be emptied as the plagues are poured out.

> Revelation 15:5: *"After this I looked, and the temple of the tent of witness in heaven was opened."*

This opening of the temple shows that the temple business has been completed. The temple had previously been involved in the investigative judgment process, which is now finished. One of the four living creatures who were previously involved in the investigative judgment is now seen giving the seven angels their "bowls full of the wrath of God" (Revelation 15:7). This shows that the investigative judgment is over, because the pouring out of the plagues begins God's punishment phase of judgment. Also the 144,000 are praising God for finally revealing His judgment (Revelation 15:4). Revelation 15:8 confirms that the investigative judgment has ended.

> Revelation 15:8: *"and the temple was filled with smoke from the glory of God and his power, **and no one could enter the temple until the seven plagues of the seven angels were ended"** (emphasis supplied).*

God's holy temple, where the investigative judgment had been ongoing since 1844, is now closed. His executive judgment on the wicked is now beginning and smoke fills His temple. No further arguments will be heard. No additional saints will be added to the list of those who will be saved. All have made their choices. Probation has closed. The plagues are about to fall. No more righteous will die (Daniel 11:35). The 144,000 have been sealed. This occurs at the beginning of the fifth trumpet (Revelation 9:4).

Thus, Revelation 15 introduces the seven last plagues and gives the historical setting for these plagues. These plagues represent God's final wrath (Revelation 15:1). These plagues involve the time of history when the beast, its image, and its number are in existence. Those who endure these plagues and conquer are those who have overcome the beast and its image. These plagues will fall after the investigative judgment is complete because "the temple of the tent of witness" is open (Revelation 15:5) and "no one could enter" the temple because it is "filled with smoke" (Revelation 15:8).

At the time of the plagues, God's people are victorious because they are seen singing the "song of Moses" and the "song of the Lamb," which is a song of victory (Revelation 15:3). This means that probation has closed, because God's people are victorious only after probation closes. Finally, God is seen revealing His judgments on the wicked, which means the executive phase of judgment has begun, and the investigative phase of judgment has ended. The close of probation occurs when the investigative judgment has ended and the 144,000 are sealed. The close of probation marks the beginning of the seven last plagues.

> Revelation 16:1: *"Then I heard a loud voice from the temple telling the seven angels, 'Go and pour out on the earth the seven bowls of the wrath of God.'"*

A loud voice is usually associated with judgment. In this case, the voice is coming from God's throne. God's throne room is no longer involved in the investigative judgment. The executive judgment is about to begin and no one can enter the temple (Revelation 15:8). This command marks the beginning of the wrath of God being poured out on the wicked. These plagues are not given to change man or bring repentance.[1] Mankind can no longer choose salvation because God's people have been sealed and probation has closed.

> Revelation 16:2: *"So the first angel went and poured his bowl on the earth and foul and evil sores came upon the men who bore the mark of the beast and worshiped its image."*

The plagues of Egypt were literal plagues described in Exodus 7:17 through Exodus 12:39. The last day plagues will also be literal. These plagues will fall on those who have rejected God's seal upon their forehead and have chosen the mark or seal of the beast and its image (discussed in Revelation 13 (last part)—The Mark of the Beast). The mark of the beast occurs after the enactment of laws enforcing penalties for failure to keep Sunday holy. The mark of the beast is rejecting God's true Sabbath once these laws are enforced. The mark of the beast is observance of Sunday as the Sabbath, after the buy-sell penalties have been enacted, which is described in Revelation 13:17. The mark of the beast occurs once economic sanctions are applied to the Sunday law.

The first plague is a physical disease characterized by painful open sores on the skin. These sores will persist, because they still exist unhealed during the fifth plague (Revelation 16:11). These sores are not curable by Satan or his demons, which demonstrates they are from God. Indeed, God is cursed because of them (Revelation 16:11). These sores remind us of Job's suffering under Satan's attack (Job 2:7).[2] These sores mark the beginning of God's judgment "revealed" (Revelation 15:4). Beginning with this plague and continuing with each subsequent plague, God will demonstrate His power over His creation as opposed to Satan's claimed power as the false Christ. Each of the seven last plagues will demonstrate that Satan is a liar and is not the god that he claims to be. The seven last plagues will demonstrate that Satan is not Christ and that he cannot do what he claims. This will lead the world to conclude that Satan is vulnerable, which will lead to the final world battle.

> Revelation 16:3: *"The second angel poured his bowl into the sea, and it became like the blood of a dead man, and every living thing died that was in the sea."*

This plague is poured "into the sea." The previous plague was poured on the earth. Specifically, those of mankind on the earth, "who bore the mark of the beast and worshiped its image" (Revelation 16:2). The fact that the plagues fall on those who have the mark of the beast means that God's people are spared.

Many have noted that the trumpets and the plagues seem to parallel each other. The order, however, is different. The trumpets begin with hail and fire in the first trumpet, where as the plagues introduce fire in the fourth plague and hail in the seventh. Both the trumpets and the plagues involve turning the sea into blood, however, only the plagues turn the fountains of water into blood. In the trumpets, the rivers and fountains are turned bitter or poisoned. Both the sixth trumpet and the sixth plague involve warfare and the Euphrates River. The fourth trumpet involves the sun, moon and stars, while the fifth plague, involves darkness on the seat of the beast. Clearly, there is overlap, however, they appear to represent distinct events, most of which occur at different times. The first four trumpets are warnings to the world while the world still has time to choose salvation. Beginning with the fifth trumpet (the first woe), probationary time has expired and probation has closed. This is confirmed by the sealing of God's people (Revelation 9:4). The first three plagues will fall during the fifth trumpet. The fourth, fifth, and sixth plagues will fall during the sixth trumpet. Since they overlap, the events of the sixth trumpet and the sixth plague will directly parallel each other, as will the seventh trumpet and the seventh plague.

Another comparison can be made between the days of creation and the plagues. God first created light, then the atmosphere, then vegetation, then the sun, then the sea, then humanity and finally rested. The plagues will attack the light with darkness. The sea will be turned to blood. The vegetation will be burned with fire and crushed with hail. The atmosphere will be choked with smoke. The sun will become man's enemy instead of his friend. Humanity will be tortured with sores. There will be no rest for the wicked.[3]

The sea will become "like the blood of a dead man." This plague parallels the first plague of Egypt (Exodus 7:20-21). In Egypt the river Nile was turned to blood and all the fish died. Egypt was known for rejecting the true God and worshiping false gods. At the time of the end, almost the entire world will have rejected the true Christ and accepted the false Christ, Satan, as the world's king. It is fitting that the end-time wicked would receive similar punishments for similar sins. These plagues will be literal just as they were literal in Egypt's time. The impact on the world of poisoning the sea will be immense. The death of "every living thing" in the sea will greatly affect the world's food supply and economy. Large parts of the world will be afflicted with famine. This famine will be made worse because of the many natural disasters that have preceded these final plagues. This plague will not be universal or mankind would not survive.

> Revelation 16:4: *"The third angel poured his bowl into the rivers and the fountains of water, and they became blood."*

The third plague will affect the drinking water of the world. This plague will poison the rivers and fountains of water. This plague will make the water undrinkable. If this plague were worldwide, humanity would not survive. Ellen G. White states that this plague will not be universal.[4] In order to survive, men will have to drill new wells just as the Egyptians "dug round about the Nile for water to drink, for they could not drink the water of the Nile" (Exodus 7:24).

> Revelation 16:5: *"And I heard the angel of water say, 'Just art thou in these thy judgments, thou who art and wast, O Holy One.'"*

The angel is now heard praising God for His judgments. The angel is saying that God is "just" in His judgment. The wicked are reaping what they have sown. These judgments are what the souls under the altar had "cried out" for in Revelation 6:10. These judgments are part of the final wrath of God described in Revelation 15:1. These judgments are part of the plagues, which will fall on Babylon (Revelation 18:4, 8). These judgments are coming from the eternal Holy One. These are God's judgments on those who have rejected Him.

> Revelation 16:6: *"For men have shed the blood of saints and prophets, and thou hast given them blood to drink. It is their due!"*

The reason that this plague and the one prior to it are just is because the wicked, upon whom these plagues are falling, have shed the blood of innocent people. The angel states it is fitting that they should have to drink blood, since they have shed so much blood in the past. The "saints" here referred to are the "saints" described in Revelation 14:12: "those who keep the commandments of God and the faith of Jesus." These are the "saints" who were killed during the time of the second and third angel's messages by these living wicked. These are the "saints" who refused to accept the mark of the beast and thereby break God's Law. They refused to accept a false Sabbath for the true seventh-day Sabbath of God's Law. These are the "saints" who refused to worship Satan as the eighth king: the king who claimed to be Jesus Christ, the Savior of the world. These are the "saints" who rejected the false Christ and kept faith in the true Jesus.

The "prophets" mentioned here are clearly end-time prophets, just as the "saints" are end-time saints, because those are the only ones that these living wicked could have slain. This text confirms that God will have end-time "prophets" who will explain His Word to the world. He will have end-time "prophets" who will be willing to die for their beliefs just as the "saints" are willing to die for theirs. God will have end-time prophets living during these last-day events and some will be slain for their beliefs. Truly God's judgment of turning the wicked's water to blood is their due.

> Revelation 16:7: *"And I heard the altar cry, 'Yea, Lord God the Almighty, true and just are thy judgments!'"*

This voice is agreeing with the prior angel's praise. This voice comes from the altar. This voice represents the souls who were crying out for vengeance during the fifth seal (Revelation 6:10). This further connects the fifth seal to last-day events. God is finally beginning to avenge His righteous slain. God's judgments are proclaimed to be "true and just." These plagues are God's judgments on the wicked.

> Revelation 16:8: *"The fourth angel poured his bowl on the sun, and it was allowed to scorch men with fire."*

The fourth plague involves the sun. This plague will affect both man and beast through drought and famine.[5] This plague will bring about the worst famine this world has ever seen. This plague will increase the misery of the wicked. Their sores have not healed and now the heat is intense. This plague is not universal.[6] This plague will cause extensive drought and fires will result. The wicked will be scorched with fire. The sun has been the source of life for mankind. It will now be turned into a source of death. The sun has been worshiped as a god in the past but now it will be cursed. Satan has claimed to be Christ, the Son of God on earth. Each of these plagues will further weaken his claim to have control over nature and to be able to heal men miraculously. Satan will have no power to heal the sores. Satan will have no power to change the water back to life-giving fluid. Satan cannot restore the sea animals to life. Now Satan will be unable to stop the horrible heat of the sun or the famine, drought, and fires that result. The world will be losing confidence in Satan as the god that he claims to be. Through these plagues God is demonstrating that He alone is the Creator and that Satan is a false god.

> Revelation 16:9: *"men were scorched by the fierce heat, and they cursed the name of God who had power over these plagues, and they did not repent and give him glory."*

The wicked will refuse to repent. The heat of the sun will be fierce. Men will be scorched by the sun. The wicked will recognize that these plagues are the result of God's power but they will not repent of their wickedness. The wicked will recognize that God is the Creator and has control and that Satan is not the Creator and is not in control. The wicked will recognize that these plagues are God's judgments on them, but they will refuse to glorify Him. In other words, these judgments will not lead the wicked toward salvation, but will simply reinforce their wickedness.

This is consistent with the close of probation having already occurred at the beginning of the plagues. All of those who have chosen to serve God have already done so and are part of the sealed (the 144,000) (Revelation 7:3-4). These plagues are part of the "harm" predicted in Revelation 7:1, 3. The four angels are held back from harming "the earth or the sea or the trees" (Revelation 7:3) until God's servants are sealed "upon their foreheads." The sealing occurs prior to the harming of "the earth or the sea or the trees" (Revelation 7:3). The harming of the earth was described under the first plague when the angel "poured his bowl on the earth" (Revelation 16:2). The harming of the sea began when the second angel "poured his bowl into the sea" (Revelation 16:3). The harming of the trees began with the third angel who "poured his bowl into the rivers and fountains of water." This began the poisoning of the vegetation. The harming of the trees was continued with the fourth angel who "poured his bowl on the sun." This fierce heat caused further drought and loss of vegetation. This plague also represents the control the Creator has over His creation.

As has been seen earlier, God's creation week is symbolized by seven things; light, atmosphere, vegetation, sun, sea, humanity, and God's day of rest. Satan had changed God's day of rest. The plagues will attack all of the other symbols. In a sense, God is showing how He created all of these and that they are still under His control. *The plagues can be seen as God's testimony that He is, and always will be, the Creator.* He created this world and He still controls it, regardless of Satan's lies. Not only will the wicked recognize that God is the source of these plagues but they will also curse "the name of God." These wicked will recognize God is all-powerful, but will refuse to repent and instead will curse Him. Truly God's judgments are "true and just" (Revelation 16:7).

> Revelation 16:10: *"The fifth angel poured his bowl on the throne of the beast, and its kingdom was in darkness; men gnawed their tongues in anguish."*

Historically, this plague has been thought to apply to the Papacy.[7] Since the Papal kingdom is worldwide, it has been suggested that this darkness may be worldwide.[8] The critical question in evaluating this plague is determining whom the beast represents. In the context of the time of the end in which the plagues fall, what beast is reigning? Revelation 17 contains the answer. The scarlet beast, which represents Satan, is the eighth king. The scarlet woman, who represents the Papacy, has seven kings. The seventh king of the Papacy gives his kingdom over to the eighth king. The eighth king (Satan), who is the scarlet beast, is the final spiritual leader of the world. Satan subsequently sets up his kingdom in Jerusalem, where he is the abomination that makes desolate. Satan then begins to minister in the rebuilt temple. At the time of the seven last plagues, Satan is reigning in Jerusalem and is king of the world. This is further demonstrated in Revelation 17:16, 17. These verses describe the beast (Satan) and his ten kings doing God's work by destroying Babylon (the Papacy). This destruction is described in Revelation 18.

The beast, who is put in darkness, is Satan who claims to be Christ. His throne is in Jerusalem and his kingdom will be put "in darkness." When God turns out the lights in Satan's capital city by darkening the sun, it will cause the world to further doubt Satan's claim to be God. This plague will make Satan appear vulnerable for attack by the world, which will occur shortly thereafter. This plague will also serve as a reminder of Who created light in the first place. Since Satan's kingdom is worldwide beginning with the fifth trumpet, this plague will be universal in application. Mankind's response will be to gnaw "their tongues in anguish." Men will be "in anguish" and will be afraid but will not repent.

> Revelation 16:11: *"and cursed the God of heaven for their pain and sores, and did not repent of their deeds."*

Even though God has now demonstrated His power over the sea and fountains of water, over men's bodies, and over light and darkness, men still refuse to bow down. The wicked refuse to "repent of their deeds" and instead they curse God for their pain and sores. The sores are the result of the first plague, which proves that the plagues are sequential.[9] The sores have not responded to any of Satan's miracles and have persisted into the fifth plague.

The "deeds" that the wicked have refused to "repent of" will become the basis of their final judgment. "And I saw the dead, great and small, standing before the throne, and books were opened. Also another book was opened, which is the book of life. *And the dead were judged by what was written in the books, by what they had done"* (Revelation 20:12) (emphasis supplied). These very "deeds" that the wicked refuse to repent of will be the basis of their final judgment. These "deeds" will lead to their eternal loss.

> Revelation 16:12: *"The sixth angel poured his bowl on the great river Euphrates, and its water was dried up, to prepare the way for the kings from the east."*

Historically, there have been several theories to explain this plague. One theory suggests that there are both literal-geographic as well as figurative applications. Another theory suggests that this plague is entirely symbolic or figurative.[10] The literal theory suggests a battle between the west and the east at Megiddo. This would take place after the Ottoman Empire shrinks represented by the drying of the Euphrates.[11] The symbolic theory suggests that mystical Babylon loses its world support, represented by the drying up of the Euphrates.[12] The world then unites to destroy God's people on the entire earth but there is no literal battle.[13]

In the context of the time-of-the-end events, a literal interpretation is suggested. Satan is occupying Jerusalem in the Middle East. Satan is claiming control of the world. However, God has demonstrated that Satan is not in control. God has poisoned the water. God has caused non-healing sores. God has turned out the lights by darkening the sun. Satan appears to be vulnerable. The world will now appear to see a weakness and will attempt to overthrow Satan.

Daniel foretold these events beginning in Daniel 11:40 with the phrase "at the time of the end," which refers to the time of the plagues. The time of the end is linked to the close of probation when the wise will no longer "fall" or die (Daniel 11:35). In Daniel 11:40, the king of the south (Egypt) will attack Satan first, but Satan will overthrow Egypt and temporarily succeed. However, in Daniel 11:44, "tidings from the east and the north shall alarm him." The "tidings from the east and north," which alarm Satan, are what John is describing in this verse. The river Euphrates runs through Iraq, which is east of Israel. The kings of the east represent the Arabian countries to the east of Israel who will attempt to overthrow Satan's kingdom. The drying "up" of the Euphrates can be seen as either literal, providing a highway to the east or as symbolic. If symbolic, it represents Satan's loss of influence over these kingdoms. Either way, there appears to be ample evidence to suggest a literal battle in the Middle East in the region of Megiddo. This same battle is described in Joel 3:2, 11.

The sixth trumpet is also connected to this event, as has been shown earlier. The sixth trumpet includes the fourth, fifth, and sixth plagues. The sixth trumpet describes this same event as a battle in which one-third of mankind is killed. The sixth trumpet also is connected to the river Euphrates. In the sixth trumpet, the four angels who are "bound at the great river Euphrates" are released (Revelation 9:14). This connects the release of the four angels to the final battle as well. The release represented in the sixth trumpet is the release of God's control on Satan, who is now allowed to kill the wicked (Revelation 9:5) and God's release of the wicked who will ultimately attack Satan triggering the Battle of Armageddon.

Thus we can see that Daniel foresaw a battle at the time of the end involving Jerusalem and the kings of the north and east. John saw this same battle in the sixth trumpet and in the sixth plague. Joel also foresaw this battle in the valley of Jehoshaphat. This battle is literal and will be fought in the Middle East.

> Revelation 16:13: *"And I saw, issuing from the mouth of the dragon and from the mouth of the beast and from the mouth of the false prophet, three foul spirits like frogs."*

Historically, these "three foul spirits" have been thought to represent the three types of false religions that exist at the end of time.[14] These three false religions are represented by "the dragon," "the beast," and "the false prophet." The "dragon" represents Satan and he is worshipped through paganism or spiritualism. This would include most of the world's false religions that involve worship of any god other than the true God. The "beast" in this text would represent the Papacy and Catholicism.[15] The "false prophet" represents apostate Protestantism.[16] These "three foul spirits" would then represent all those who belong to Babylon.[17] In this sense, Babylon represents all apostate religions. These "demonic spirits" (Revelation 16:14) are described as "like frogs." This suggests their repulsiveness.[18] These spirits are issuing "from the mouth" of the dragon, the beast, and the false prophet. This means that these spirits are under the control of their corresponding parent. These foul spirits are doing the will of Satan and his false churches. At the time of the end, the dragon, the beast, and the false prophet control these "three foul spirits." At the time of the end the dragon is Satan as world king, the beast is the Papacy, and the false prophet is apostate Protestantism. All of these had been under Satan's control until this plague. These three powers will be involved in this final battle.

> Revelation 16:14: *"for they are demonic spirits, performing signs, who go abroad to the kings of the whole world, to assemble them for battle on the great day of God the Almighty."*

Historically, this verse has been applied to the previously discussed two theories (see discussion under Revelation 16:12). According to these two theories, the world is either being gathered for a battle between the east and the west or the world is being prepared to destroy God's people.[19]

Daniel 11:40-45 supports a battle involving Satan as "the abomination that makes desolate" and the kings of the north and east. The sixth trumpet suggests a huge battle in the Middle East involving the countries around the river Euphrates. The sixth plague appears to be describing the same event. Satan will recognize he is under attack and he will endeavor to enlist the support of the world by sending out his demons to work miracles and convince the world's kings to support him. The world's armies will meet in the valley of Megiddo and untold millions will die. This battle is called "the great day of God the Almighty" (Revelation 16:14). This battle is the battle that will "kill a third of mankind" (Revelation 9:15). This will account for a huge loss of life. This is the second "woe" (Revelation 9:12). This is the same battle Joel describes in the valley of Jehoshaphat (Joel 3:2, 9-16).

> Revelation 16:15: *"('Lo, I am coming like a thief! Blessed is he who is awake, keeping his garments that he may not go naked and be seen exposed!')"*

This statement is similar to 1 Thessalonians 5:2: "For you yourselves know well that the day of the Lord will come like a thief in the night." Jesus' Second Coming will surprise the wicked because they thought Jesus was here already. Revelation 16:15 is a reminder that Jesus' return will surprise the world and it is a warning not to be found unprepared. This is one of the seven "blessings" found in the book of Revelation.[20] This blessing is for those who are ready for Jesus' Second Coming. These "garments" represent the garments Jesus provides to protect His saints. These "garments" represent the Law of God and faith in Jesus (see the discussion under Revelation 14:12). The faithful will ultimately be clothed in Christ's righteousness described in Revelation 3:18 as "white garments to clothe you and to keep the shame of your nakedness from being seen." This blessing on those who are ready for Jesus' return is similar to Daniel 12:12. Daniel states "Blessed is he who waits and comes to the thousand three hundred and thirty-five days." Both John and Daniel are describing the same people at the time of the end. The ones who wait are those who understand: they are the "wise" of Daniel 12:10. They are wise because they understand the last-day events and prophecies and are prepared for them. They are clothed with God's truth for the time of the end. They are "awake" keeping their "garments."

> Revelation 16:16: *"And they assembled them at the place which is called in Hebrew Armageddon."*

Historically, the first theory suggests that this is a literal place, Megiddo.[21] The second theory suggests that this is a frame of mind into which the world's kings are gathered prior to their attacking God's people throughout the world.[22] The second theory would apply Armageddon ultimately to the place where Satan and Christ meet in battle.[23]

Since the plagues appear to be literal and Daniel and John appear to be focused on the Middle East at the time of the end, it appears that Armageddon is a literal place. Also, since Satan will be reigning in Jerusalem and he is the target of this last attack (Daniel 11:44), Megiddo is most likely a literal location. However, no actual geographical site has ever been identified in the Old Testament or the New Testament. The Greek word translated "Armageddon" can be translated the "mount of the congregation" or the "mount of assembly." In either case, whether Armageddon is referring to Megiddo or to the mount of assembly, both of these sites refer to locations in the Middle East. Armageddon's battle will be real, will be deadly, and will be located in the Middle East.

The Battle of Armageddon is described in Revelation 9:15, 18 as the day Satan is allowed to kill "a third of mankind." This is the sixth trumpet, which corresponds to the sixth plague of Revelation 16:12-16. This final battle is also described in Joel 3:2: "I will gather all the nations and bring them down to the valley of Jehoshaphat, and I will enter into judgment with them there." At the end of time, there will be one final great battle centered in Israel. The world will attack Satan and his supporters. This final battle will most likely involve nuclear war, because of the large numbers killed. This battle will demonstrate to the universe that once sin is allowed to reign it will self destruct. Satan has only been freed from God's rules of engagement for a few months (see the discussion on Revelation 9:13-18) and now the world is about to totally destroy itself. If God does not intervene with the Second Coming, the entire world including God's people will be destroyed and God will not allow that to happen (Matthew 24:22). The Battle of Armageddon proves to the universe that sin is totally self destructive. The Battle of Armageddon is interrupted by the third woe (the seventh trumpet). The Battle of Armageddon is terminated by the Lamb seen in the clouds of heaven. The Battle of Armageddon is ended to save God's people.

> Revelation 16:17: *"The seventh angel poured his bowl into the air, and a great voice came out of the temple, from the throne, saying 'It is done!'"*

The seventh angel represents the last plague. This plague is universal.[24] This bowl is emptied into the air. This plague will correspond to the Second Coming of Jesus Christ. This plague corresponds to the seventh trumpet (Revelation 11:15-19). This seventh plague corresponds to the seventh seal (Revelation 8:1) where heaven is silent because heaven is empty.

This plague is poured out into the air because that is where this battle will occur. Jesus will not descend onto the earth. He and His angels will be seen above the earth in the air. Jesus will call forth His saints who will meet Him "in the air" (1 Thessalonians 4:17). This plague will involve the destruction of the earth and its inhabitants. This is the third "woe" (Revelation 11:14-19).

The voice "from the throne" is God's voice. The plan of salvation is complete. It is time to go to earth and get God's faithful people. The reign of sin is over. It is time to begin Satan's punishment. It is time for the wicked to reap their reward. The rebellion of the wicked is complete. "It is done."

> Revelation 16:18: *"And there were flashes of lightning, loud noises, peals of thunder, and a great earthquake such as had never been since men were on the earth, so great was that earthquake."*

This description of events parallels the seventh trumpet. Revelation 11:19 states: "Then God's temple in heaven was opened, and the ark of his covenant was seen within his temple; and there were flashes of lightning, loud noises, peals of thunder, an earthquake, and heavy hail." The seventh plague is describing the same events as the seventh trumpet. These events will occur when Jesus returns to reclaim His people. This is described in Revelation 11:18 as the time "for rewarding thy servants."

Matthew 24:29-31 states: "Immediately after the tribulation of those days the sun will be darkened, and the moon will not give its light, and the stars will fall from heaven, and the powers of the heavens will be shaken; then will appear the sign of the Son of man in heaven and then all the tribes of the earth will mourn, and they will see the Son of man coming on the clouds of heaven with power and great glory; and he will send out his angels with a loud trumpet call, and they will gather his elect from the four winds, from one end of heaven to the other."

After the "great tribulation," referred to in Matthew 24:21, the sun will be darkened (Matthew 24:29). This tribulation occurs after the abomination that makes desolate or the "desolating sacrilege" is set up in the "holy place" (Matthew 24:15). In other words, the events Jesus described in Matthew 24:29 occur after Satan's reign as the eighth king and they occur after the time of trouble of Daniel 12:1. The time of trouble of Daniel 12:1 is the same as the "great tribulation" that Jesus described in Matthew 24:21. Just prior to Jesus' return there will be signs in the heavens to include the sun, moon, and stars. There will be thunder and lightning and the world's worst earthquake. Similar signs in the sun, moon, and stars are described in Joel 2:30-32 and Joel 3:15, 16, which occur just prior to the "great and terrible day of the Lord."

> Revelation 16:19: *"The great city was split into three parts, and the cities of the nations fell, and God remembered great Babylon, to make her drain the cup of the fury of his wrath."*

Historically, "the great city" has been applied to mystical Babylon.[25] One great city is described in Revelation 17:18: "And the woman that you saw is the great city which has dominion over the kings of the earth." The woman in Revelation 17 is the scarlet woman who is called "Babylon the great" (Revelation 17:4-5). Thus, the great city and Babylon were considered the same and thought to represent apostate religions in general and the Papacy in particular.

Some have suggested that "split" in this text represents the splitting up of the three part union of mystical Babylon.[26] This union was described in Revelation 16:13 as the dragon, the beast, and the false prophet. Certainly, this does occur because the dragon beast (Satan) in Revelation 17 does turn against Babylon (the Papacy) (Revelation 17:16-17).

However, this verse has both literal and symbolic applications at the end of time. Certainly, the great city will be destroyed both literally and symbolically. Also, other cities will be destroyed demonstrating how huge this earthquake will be. The real issue is which city is "the great city." In Revelation 11:8, another "great city" is described. Revelation 11:8 states "and their dead bodies will lie in the street of *the great city* which is allegorically called Sodom and Egypt, where their Lord was crucified" (emphasis supplied). This city is Jerusalem, where Satan will reign as the false Christ at the time of the end. Jerusalem is "the great city" referred to in Revelation

16:19, because this is the world's capitol city at the end of time. It should be noted that Babylon ("the great city" of Revelation 17:18) has already been destroyed previously by Satan (the eighth king) and his ten kings (Revelation 17:16).

Babylon's destruction or judgment is the subject of Revelation 17 and 18. Babylon in Revelation 17 is the Papacy in Rome (discussed in Revelation 17 (first part)—The Scarlet Woman and Her Kings). This is shown in Revelation 17:5 where Babylon is described as the "mother of harlots" and in Revelation 17:4 where Babylon sits on seven hills. It is also shown in Revelation 17:18 where Babylon is described as "the great city which has dominion over the kings of the earth." Finally, Vatican City in Rome is where the seven kings reign.

Revelation 17:1 introduces Babylon's judgment, which is described in Revelation 17:16. This destruction of Babylon is God's will (Revelation 17:17) and is carried out by the ten kings during their reign of "one hour" (Revelation 17:12). This same destruction of Babylon is again described in Revelation 18. This destruction occurs in "one hour" (Revelation 18:10, 17, 19). This destruction occurs prior to the Second Coming because the earth's kings are able to see it and mourn (Revelation 18:9). They are described as standing "afar off" in Revelation 18:10. The world's merchants and seafarers observe this complete destruction and mourn over it, which also suggests this occurs prior to the Second Coming and not as part of the seventh plague (Second Coming). Babylon (the Papacy) is destroyed prior to the seventh plague.

Finally, Revelation 16:19 differentiates "the great city" from the "cities of the nations" and from "great Babylon." This also suggests that "the great city" is not the same as "Babylon." The "great city" at the Second Coming is Jerusalem. "Babylon" in Revelation 16:19 at the Second Coming is spiritual Babylon (apostate Christianity).

Spiritual Babylon is the particular target of God's wrath because through spiritual Babylon "all nations were deceived" (Revelation 18:23). Babylon is the recipient of God's wrath because "in her was found the blood of prophets and of saints, and of all who have been slain on earth" (Revelation 18:24). God will make Babylon "drain the cup of the fury of his wrath." In other words, Babylon will drink it all. Babylon will get no further mercy. "Babylon" here represents all apostate religions, all of which will be destroyed.

> Revelation 16:20: *"And every island fled away, and no mountains were to be found."*

This verse simply confirms that this is the greatest earthquake of all time. No mountain will be left standing. No island will be left intact. There will be nowhere to hide. Those who survive the earthquake will be left to face the King of Kings. This is described in the sixth seal. The sun is darkened, the moon is turned to blood, the stars fall and there is a great earthquake (Revelation 6:12). The sixth seal continues with the same description: "every mountain and island was removed from its place" (Revelation 6:14). The sixth seal continues with the wicked "calling to the mountains and rocks, 'Fall on us and hide us from the face of him who is seated on the throne, and from the wrath of the Lamb'" (Revelation 6:16). The sixth seal parallels Matthew 24:29. The sixth seal is describing the events of the seventh plague just as Jesus described the same events in Matthew 24:29, which were to occur prior to His Second Coming.

> Revelation 16:21: *"and great hailstones, heavy as a hundred-weight, dropped on men from heaven, till men cursed God for the plague of the hail, so fearful was that plague."*

This final plague of hail will destroy what remains of earth. This is the hail that God told Job He had reserved for the time of trouble. God asked Job, "have you seen the storehouses of the hail, which I have reserved for the time of trouble, for the day of battle and war?" (Job 38:22-23). These "hailstones" probably weigh about 66 pounds.[27] These "hailstones" will kill many people and will destroy buildings as if they were made of paper. This final plague will not bring about repentance. Instead the wicked will curse God.

SUMMARY

Revelation 15 introduces the time period of the seven last plagues. These plagues will occur at the time of the end, since they are the last plagues and will end God's wrath (Revelation 15:1). These plagues occur after God's people are victorious, since they are seen singing the victory song of Moses (Revelation 15:3). These plagues occur after the beast and its image exist, since God's people have overcome the beast and its image (Revelation 15:2). These plagues represent the beginning of God's executive judgment (Revelation 15:4). These plagues occur when God's temple is opened, full of smoke, and no one can enter it (Revelation 15:5, 8). The fact that God's temple cannot be entered means that the investigative judgment is complete and probation has closed. Wicked men can no longer access divine mercy.

The seven last plagues represent God's wrath, which will fall on the wicked that have the mark of the beast and worship its image (Revelation 16:2). The plagues will demonstrate that Satan is not the creator he claims to be. Each of the plagues will demonstrate God's power over His creation. Each of the plagues correlates with God's original creation week. The plagues will fall after the temple work is completed and the investigative judgment is finished. The plagues will occur at the time of the end. At that time, the wise will no longer fall (Daniel 11:35), since probation has now closed. The close of probation marks the sealing of God's people. The sealing will occur prior to the harming of the earth, the sea, and the trees (Revelation 7:3). The harming of the earth, the sea, and the trees occurs during the seven last plagues. God's people are sealed, prior to the fifth trumpet (Revelation 9:4), which marks the beginning of the fall of the plagues. The plagues will fall during the fifth and sixth trumpets.

The first plague will fall on the earth, and mankind will have non-healing sores, which Satan as the false Christ cannot heal. This plague demonstrates Satan's inability to cure mankind's afflictions as he previously claimed.

The second plague will poison the sea and turn it to blood. The third plague will poison the drinking water by turning it to blood. These plagues are partial payment for the saints' blood that the wicked have spilled, especially, those saints who were killed during the second and third angels' messages. These plagues also demonstrate God's power over the sea and the drinking waters, which He created.

The fourth plague will allow the sun to burn mankind. This plague demonstrates Satan's inability to protect his kingdom. This plague again demonstrates God's power over the sun, which He created. This plague also reminds the world that God still exists and is the actual Creator. The world's cursing of God shows they recognize who God is but refuse to repent.

The fifth plague will put Satan's kingdom in darkness. This plague is poured on the throne of the beast. During the fifth plague, the beast on the throne is Satan and Satan's throne is located in Jerusalem. This plague will demonstrate that Satan is not who he claims to be: he is not God. This plague will make Satan vulnerable to be attacked by the world, especially by his Moslem neighbors. The sixth plague describes a global war, which will begin in the Middle East, as an attempt to overthrow Satan's rule in Jerusalem. This was prophesied in Daniel 11:44, Revelation 9:14-15, and in Joel 3:2, 12.

The seventh plague pictures the final events just prior to Jesus' Second Coming. These events are described in Revelation 6:12-17, in Joel 2:10, 11, and in Matthew 24:29-31. These events include signs in the heavens, the world's worst earthquake, and then massive destructive hail. This is followed by Jesus' Second Coming to gather His saints "in the air" (1 Thessalonians 4:17). Jesus' Second Coming will interrupt the Battle of Armageddon; otherwise all of mankind, including God's living saints would be destroyed. The following two graphs outline these events. The first graph demonstrates the timeline relationship between the seven seals, the seven trumpets, and the seven last plagues: Appendix Timeline (3). The second graph outlines the seven last plagues in relationship to time of the end events: Timeline-Seven Last Plagues.

Appendix: Timeline (3)

7 Churches, 7 Seals, 7 Trumpets and 7 Plagues

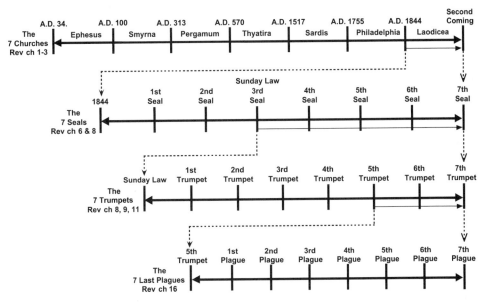

261

Timeline - Seven Last Plagues

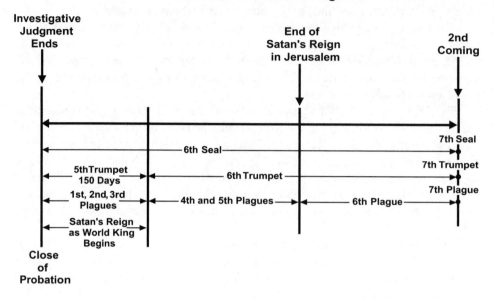

---

[1] Nichol, Francis D. (Ed.) *The Seventh-day Adventist Bible Commentary* (Review and Herald Publishing Association, Washington D. C.) 1957, Vol. 7, p. 839.

[2] Ibid.

[3] Naden, Roy C., *The Lamb Among The Beasts* (Review and Herald Publishing Association, Hagerstown. Maryland) 1996, p. 141,142.

[4] White, Ellen G., *The Great Controversy* (Pacific Press Publishing Association, Nampa, Idaho) 1950, p. 628.

[5] Nichol, Francis D. (Ed.) *The Seventh-day Adventist Bible Commentary* (Review and Herald Publishing Association, Washington D. C.) 1957, Vol. 7, p. 841.

[6] Ibid.

[7] Ibid. p. 841, 842.

[8] Ibid. p. 842.

[9] Ibid.

[10] Ibid. p. 843.

[11] Ibid. p. 842.

[12] Ibid. p. 843.

[13] Ibid. p. 845.

[14] Ibid. p. 844.

[15] Ibid.

[16] Ibid.

[17] Ibid.

[18] Ibid.

[19] Ibid. p. 845.

[20] Ibid. p. 833.

[21] Ibid. p. 845.

[22] Ibid.

[23] Ibid. p. 846.

[24] Ibid.

[25] Ibid. p. 847.

[26] Ibid.

[27] Ibid. p. 848.

SUMMARY
Section IV—The Time of the End

Revelation 14 begins by introducing those who will overcome the beast, its image and its mark. These are God's people, who are called the 144,000, and have God's seal on their foreheads. God's seal is His true Sabbath. Satan's seal or mark is his false Sabbath. Next, Revelation 14 describes three angels with messages for the entire world in the last days. The timing is shown by the fact that these messages describe God's judgment and are followed by Jesus' Second Coming (Revelation 14:14-20).

The first angel's message tells the world to worship the Creator God because the hour of His judgment has come. This judgment began in 1844 when the heavenly court began to review the names listed in the scroll (Daniel 7:10, Revelation 5:1). This investigative judgment was to restore or to cleanse the heavenly sanctuary (Daniel 8:14) and began at the end of the 2300-year prophecy. The 2300-year prophecy began in 457 B.C. and ended in 1844. This emphasis on the true Creator God, which His Sabbath is a reminder of, will become more significant when the false god (Satan) is dominant in the world. This emphasis on the Creator God will become even more apparent during the executive phase of God's judgment when the plagues begin to fall.

The second angel's message describes the fall of Babylon because she "made all nations drink" of her falsehoods (Revelation 14:8). Babylon is the "mother of harlots" (Revelation 17:5) and "the great city which has dominion over the kings of the earth" (Revelation 17:18). Babylon here represents the Papal kingdom once it is restored to world dominance. The second angel's message occurs when the world accepts Babylon's false Sabbath (Sunday) as if it were God's true Sabbath (Saturday). This occurs when the universal Sunday law is enacted by the image to the beast, which is the United States, once it becomes a church-state union.

The third angel's message warns of God's wrath for those who obtain the mark of the beast on their foreheads or on their hands. These people are described as "worshipers of the beast and its image" (Revelation 14:11). This mark will occur at the enforcement of the buy-sell legislation described in Revelation 13:17. Once these civil penalties are applied to the Sunday law forcing compliance on everyone, this mark will occur. This mark can be obtained on the hand by outward compliance or on the forehead by inner commitment and belief in this false Sabbath. Revelation 14 ends with a description of the saints in the last days and the Second Coming of Jesus Christ. The saints are those who keep God's Ten Commandments (including the Sabbath commandment) and have faith in Jesus (rejecting the false Christ). Jesus Second Coming is described as a harvest of the grain (the righteous) and the grapes (the wicked).

Revelation 13 introduces a leopard-like beast with a mortal wound, which is described in Section II. This beast is the Papal kingdom restored to world domination after its wound is healed. This leopard-like beast will assist the lamb-like beast to form an image to the beast. The lamb-like beast with two horns speaks like a dragon. These two horns are religious and civil liberty. This lamb-like beast is the United States of America. When the United States loses its first horn (religious liberty) and becomes a church-state union it will become the image to the leopard-like beast, which is a church-state union. This will cause the censer to be thrown down (Revelation 8:5), which represents the loss of God's special blessings for the United States of America. This image will exist once the universal Sunday law is passed. This image will eventually pass additional laws to enforce compliance. Subsequent laws will not allow people to buy or sell unless they have the mark (keep the false Sabbath) (Revelation 13:16, 17). Once the buy-sell law is passed the United States (lamb-like beast) will have lost its second horn (civil liberty) and the mark of the beast will occur. The final law this image will enact will cause those who do not "worship the image of the beast to be slain" (Revelation 13:15).

Revelation 12 introduces a red dragon and a woman wearing a crown with 12 stars. This woman represents God's people through the ages and her crown represents God's victorious 144,000 at the time of the end. The 12 stars represent the 12 tribes of Revelation 7:4-8, which are the 144,000. The red "dragon" represents Satan (Revelation 12:9). The "male child" represents Jesus Christ who was caught up to God's throne (Revelation 12:5). The 1260 days of Revelation 12:6 represents the 1260 years of Papal supremacy (A.D. 538 to 1798) when God's people were persecuted by the Papal kingdom. Satan's angels are described as stars swept down from heaven.

The red dragon has seven heads and ten horns. The seven heads are crowned because they have already existed. The ten horns are uncrowned because they do not yet exist. This means that this vision represents the time of the eighth king's reign after the seven kings have completed their reigns but before the ten kings have come into existence. The ten kings will reign with the eighth king just prior to the end of time (Revelation 17:11, 12).

Revelation 12:10-12 next describes a celebration in heaven, which occurs at the close of probation, when God's kingdom and Christ's authority "have come" (Revelation 12:10). God's kingdom has come when His people are sealed. Satan is cast down because the investigative judgment is over. The world is warned of the woes, which are now to come. The three woes begin after the close of probation, when God's people are sealed (Revelation 9:4).

Satan is described as pursuing the woman (God's true church). The church is protected by "the two wings of the great eagle" (Revelation 12:14). These two wings represent God's Law and faith in Jesus (Revelation 12:17). These will protect God's people from the false Sabbath and Satan as the false Christ. The eagle represents God's protection. The time period of protection is "a time, and times, and half a time" (Revelation 12:14). This represents the three and one-half years of Satan's reign as the false Christ, the eighth king, and the abomination that makes desolate. This is the one-half of the week described in Daniel 9:27. This is the three and one-half years described in Daniel 12:7. This is the three and one-half years described in Revelation 11:9, 11 and the 42 months described in Revelation 11:2.

Satan is described as pouring "a river out of his mouth" (Revelation 12:15). This is a river of falsehoods to sweep away the world and God's people (the remnant). This can occur because Satan has killed God's word when he reigns as the false Christ. Satan is angry because he knows "his time is short" (Revelation 12:12).

Revelation 11 begins by describing the measurement of the temple. This measurement involves God's people "who worship there" (Revelation 11:1). This measurement does not involve the wicked. This measurement represents the ongoing investigative judgment, which involves only those who have attempted to serve God. This text suggests that the story of the two witnesses occurs after the investigative judgment has begun. This is proven in Revelation 11:14 because the story of the two witnesses ends the second woe.

Revelation 11:2 introduces "the holy city." This city is further described in Revelation 11:8 as the city "where their Lord was crucified." This city is Jerusalem, Israel in the Middle East. This city will be trampled over by Satan when he reigns as the false Christ (the eighth king or the abomination that makes desolate). This city will be ruled by Satan for 42 months (Revelation 11:2) or three and one-half years (Revelation 11:9, 11). Satan will minister in the rebuilt temple during this time period.

Revelation 11:3 introduces God's two witnesses, or two olive trees, or two lampstands (Revelation 11:4). These two witnesses represent God's Old Testament and New Testament. These two witnesses are described as in sackcloth or mourning for 1260 days or three and one-half years. They are later described as dead for three and one-half years in Revelation 11:8, 9. The 1260 day time period of Revelation 11:3 occurs prior to the beast (Satan) ascending his throne as the eighth king. The three and one-half year time period of Revelation 11:9 occurs after Satan is the eighth king. The 1260 days, during which the Old Testament and the New Testament are alive but in mourning, begins when the leopard-like beast and its image change God's Law. This occurs when the false Sabbath or Sunday law is enacted. This time period ends when Satan takes his throne as the eighth king. These two witnesses have power over fire, rain, and turning water to blood. These refer to the early trumpets, which will fall during this 1260-day period. The two witnesses also have power over every plague. The plagues will fall after the two witnesses are killed.

The two witnesses are killed by the beast that ascends from the bottomless pit. This beast is Satan. He will ascend when he takes the throne in Jerusalem as the false Christ. God's Word (the Old Testament and New Testament) will now be interpreted by Satan. God's Word will be dead to those who believe Satan's lies, but not buried because the world will think they now understand scripture better than before. God's two witnesses will be dead for three and one-half days representing three and one-half years. This is the time period of Satan's reign in Jerusalem. God's two witnesses will be raised at the end of this three and one-half years and ascend to heaven, since their job is completed. This resurrection will be marked by an earthquake in Jerusalem, Satan's capital city. This earthquake destroys one-tenth of the city, which is God's portion.

This earthquake signals the end of Satan's reign in Jerusalem and the destruction of the temple. This will occur during the time of the seven last plagues and Satan will be losing world dominance at this time. This loss of power will lead to the formation of the ten kingdoms by Satan in an attempt to maintain world domination. This loss of power will also lead to Satans attack on Babylon (the Papacy) (Revelation 17:16-18).

Revelation 15 describes God's wrath as the seven last plagues (Revelation 15:1). These plagues will occur after the investigative judgment has ended and no one can enter the temple (Revelation 15:8). The seven last plagues will be poured out on those "who bore the mark of the beast and worshiped its image" (Revelation 16:2).

The first angel "poured his bowl on the earth" and men developed "foul and evil sores" (Revelation 16:2). These sores will cause men to "long to die" (Revelation 9:6). This plague demonstrates Satan is not the creator he claims to be because he cannot cure mankind.

The second angel "poured his bowl into the sea" and it turns to blood (Revelation 16:3). This plague represents Satan's lack of power over the sea. Each plague will demonstrate that God is the true Creator and that Satan is not.

The third angel "poured his bowl into the rivers and the fountains of water" which became blood (Revelation 16:4). Satan is unable to cleanse this contaminated water. This water turned to blood represents the blood of the saints killed by the wicked, especially those killed during the second and third angel's messages.

The fourth angel "poured his bowl on the sun" and men were burned with fire (Revelation 16:8). Satan does not have power over the sun, which he claims to have created.

The fifth angel "poured his bowl on the throne of the beast" (Revelation 16:10) and his kingdom was in darkness. This throne represents Satan's throne in Jerusalem, which God now puts in darkness. Satan, the false god, is not able to restore the light. This will further weaken Satan's position as world leader. The world will now realize that Satan is vulnerable and can be attacked. This event will be associated with the earthquake described in Revelation 11:13, which will further destroy Satan's credibility as the god he claims to be. Satan will be forced to vacate Jerusalem (Daniel 11:44, 45).

The sixth angel "poured his bowl on the great river Euphrates, and its water was dried up" (Revelation 16:12). This drying up of the Euphrates will lead to the world's final world war called Armageddon. This battle will involve an attack on Jerusalem from the north and the east (Daniel 11:44) but will be global and kill "a third of mankind" (Revelation 9:15, 18). This world war will be interrupted by Jesus' Second Coming in order to save His elect (Matthew 24:22).

The seventh angel "poured his bowl into the air" which is followed by a voice from heaven saying, "It is done!" (Revelation 16:17). "The great city" is split into three parts (Revelation 16:19). This city is Jerusalem (Revelation 11:8) where Jesus was crucified. This plague is associated with the world's greatest earthquake, crushing hail, and Jesus' Second Coming. Each of the seven last plagues parallel creation week and are literal events, which prove God is the Creator and Satan is a liar. The seven last plagues parallel the purpose of the plagues of Egypt, which showed that Egypt's gods were false gods. The seven last plagues show that Satan is a false god. These events are outlined in the following graphs.

Section IV - The Time of the End Summary Outline

Revelation Chapter 14

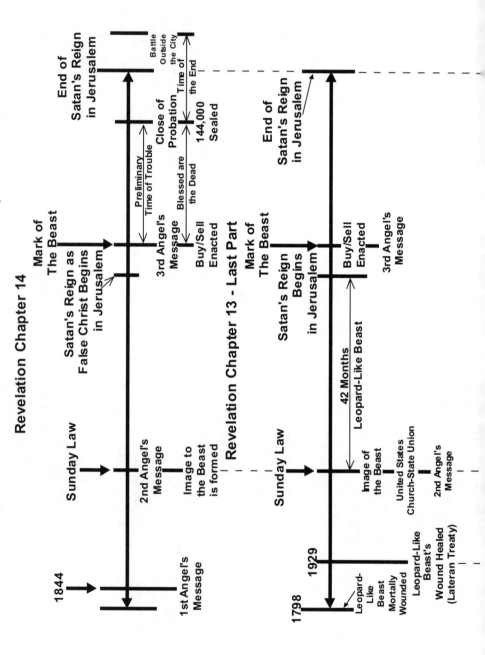

Revelation Chapter 13 - Last Part

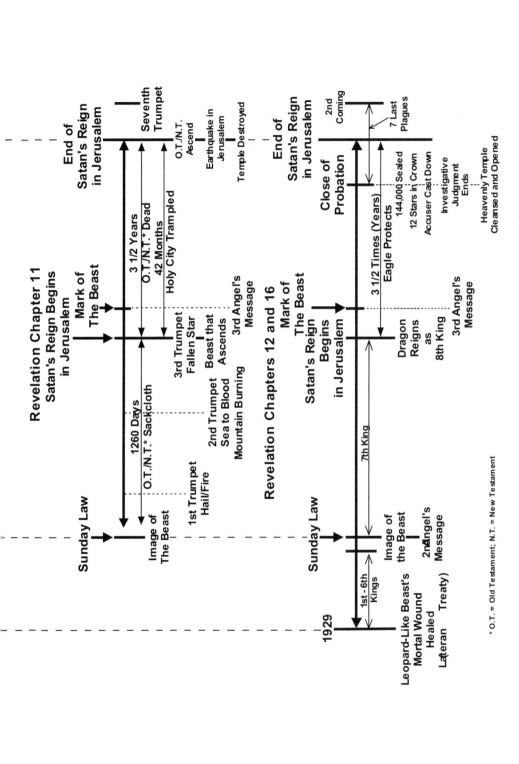

Revelation Chapter 11
Satan's Reign Begins
in Jerusalem

End of
Satan's Reign
in Jerusalem

Sunday Law

Seventh
Trumpet

Mark of
The Beast

O.T./N.T.
Ascend

Earthquake in
Jerusalem

Temple Destroyed

3 1/2 Years

O.T./N.T.* Dead

42 Months

Holy City Trampled

1260 Days

O.T./N.T.* Sackcloth

3rd Trumpet
Fallen Star

Beast that
Ascends

3rd Angel's
Message

2nd Trumpet
Sea to Blood
Mountain Burning

1st Trumpet
Hail/Fire

Image of
The Beast

Revelation Chapters 12 and 16

Satan's Reign
Begins
in Jerusalem

End of
Satan's Reign
in Jerusalem

Close of
Probation

2nd
Coming

7 Last
Plagues

144,000 Sealed

12 Stars in Crown

Accuser Cast Down

Investigative
Judgment
Ends

Heavenly Temple
Cleansed and Opened

Mark of
The Beast

3 1/2 Times (Years)

Eagle Protects

Dragon
Reigns
as
8th King

3rd Angel's
Message

Sunday Law

7th King

Image of
the Beast

2nd Angel's
Message

1st - 6th
Kings

1929

Leopard-Like Beast's
Mortal Wound
Healed
Lateran Treaty)

* O.T. = Old Testament; N.T. = New Testament

The False Christ
and
The Eighth King

SUMMARY
Section V

This book began with a simple question asked by Jesus' disciples in Matthew 24:3 "what will be the sign of your coming and of the close of the age?" Jesus' answer was to "Take heed that no one leads you astray" (Matthew 24:4). Jesus went on to warn the disciples of a coming false Christ which He further described as a "desolating sacrilege spoken of by the prophet Daniel, standing in the holy place" (Matthew 24:15). This desolating sacrilege or abomination that makes desolate would ultimately reign in Jerusalem and minister in the rebuilt temple. He would take "his seat in the temple of God, proclaiming himself to be God" (2 Thessalonians 2:4). This false Christ would reign as the eighth king (Revelation 17:11) and then become the king of the world (Revelation 9:11). His reign would be shared with ten kings just prior to Jesus' Second Coming (Revelation 17:12-14).

Jesus' answer to the disciple's question can be simplified to the following statement. The sign of My soon coming is a false Christ whom Daniel described as the abomination that makes desolate and John described as the eighth king. This false Christ will reign as the world's king at the time of the end and then I will return to save My people.

These events, as well as the other major events described in this book, are outlined on the summary graph: The False Christ—The Eighth King, which follows on the next four pages. This graph is a continuous time line beginning with Daniel's day and extending to eternity.

Section V - The False Christ

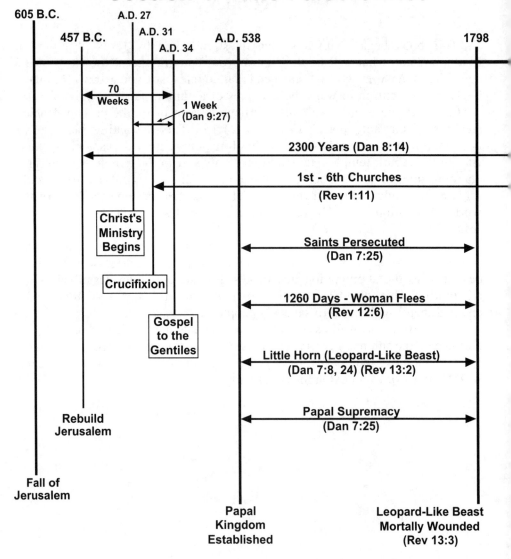

605 B.C.

457 B.C.

A.D. 27

A.D. 31

A.D. 34

A.D. 538

1798

70 Weeks

1 Week (Dan 9:27)

2300 Years (Dan 8:14)

1st - 6th Churches (Rev 1:11)

Christ's Ministry Begins

Saints Persecuted (Dan 7:25)

Crucifixion

1260 Days - Woman Flees (Rev 12:6)

Gospel to the Gentiles

Little Horn (Leopard-Like Beast) (Dan 7:8, 24) (Rev 13:2)

Rebuild Jerusalem

Papal Supremacy (Dan 7:25)

Fall of Jerusalem

Papal Kingdom Established

Leopard-Like Beast Mortally Wounded (Rev 13:3)

The Eighth King Summary Outline

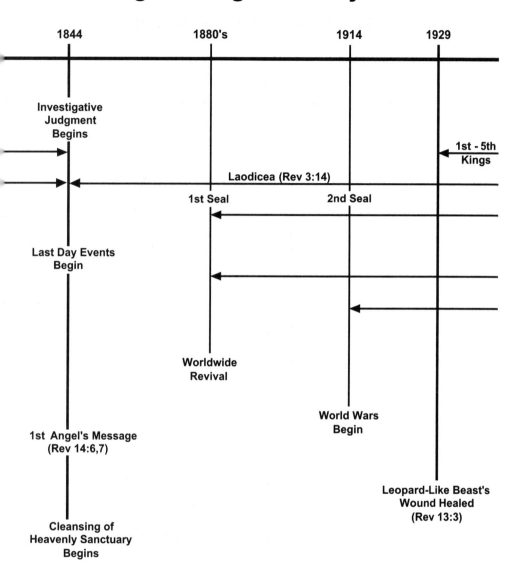

Section V - The False Christ

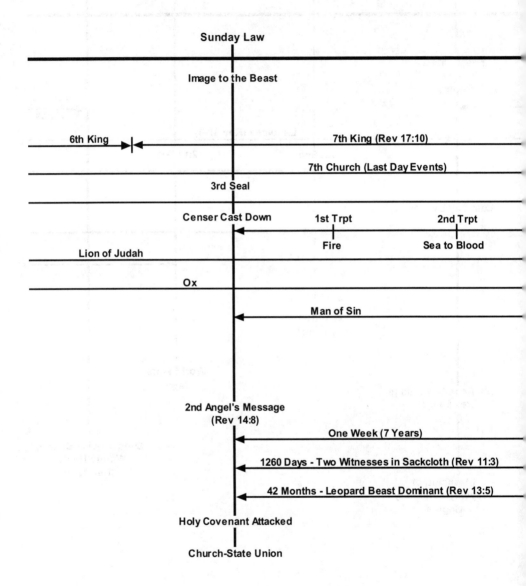

Sunday Law

Image to the Beast

6th King   **7th King (Rev 17:10)**

7th Church (Last Day Events)

3rd Seal

Censer Cast Down   **1st Trpt**   **2nd Trpt**

                       Fire   **Sea to Blood**

Lion of Judah

Ox

Man of Sin

2nd Angel's Message
(Rev 14:8)

One Week (7 Years)

1260 Days - Two Witnesses in Sackcloth (Rev 11:3)

42 Months - Leopard Beast Dominant (Rev 13:5)

Holy Covenant Attacked

Church-State Union

Legend: Trumpet = Trpt

The Eighth King Summary Outline

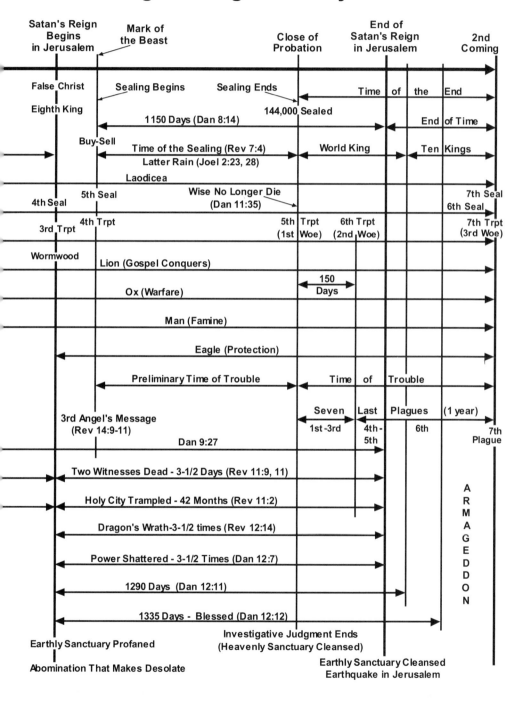

Appendix (5)
The Last Days

In order to understand the events described in this book the author has chosen to define the last-day events as the specific time period beginning in 1844 and extending through the Second Coming of Jesus Christ. The beginning of this time period occurs when "the hour of his judgment has come" (Revelation 14:6). This represents the beginning of the investigative judgment, which is the first phase of God's judgment process. This time period begins at the end of the 2300-year prophecy of Daniel 8:14, when the heavenly temple was to be restored or cleansed of sin. The 2300-year prophecy began in 457 B.C. with the edict to restore and to rebuild Jerusalem. This event was prophesied in Daniel 9:25 and began the 70 week or 490 year prophecy. This 490 year time period was set aside for literal Israel and was the beginning of the 2300-year prophecy that ended in 1844.

In this book the "last-day events" include all those events from 1844 through Jesus' Second Coming. This designation was made in order to differentiate these prior events from the events of the time of the end and the end of time. The "time of the end" events include only those events that Daniel included as "time of the end" events (Daniel 11:35, 40). The "time of the end" applies to those events after the sealing of the 144,000 and the close of probation. This designation was done to be consistent with Daniel's use of the term "time of the end" in Daniel 11.

The "end-of-time events" includes those events that will occur immediately adjacent to or at the Second Coming. Thus, "end-of-time events" would be included in the time of the end events and time of the end events would be included in the last-day events because each category extends to the Second Coming. This can be outlined as follows:

Last Day Events

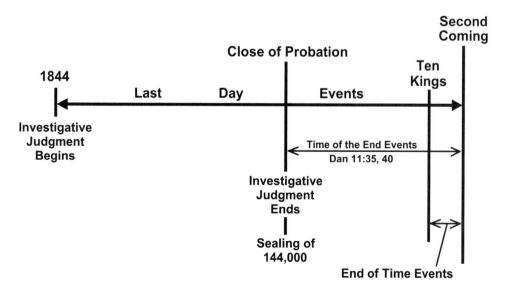

Therefore, the "last-day events" would include all of the seven seals, all of the seven trumpets, and all of the seven last plagues. The last-day events would occur during the time of the Laodicean church (the seventh church).

The "time of the end events" would only include the last year or so of the earth's history and the end of Satan's reign as the eighth king. The time of the end events would include the sixth and seventh seals and the fifth, sixth, and seventh trumpets as well as all of the seven last plagues.

The "end-of-time events" would include the sixth seal and the seventh seal. It would also include the sixth and seventh trumpets and the sixth and seventh plagues. These relationships, along with the other last-day events previously described in this book, are outlined in the graph labeled Section V—The False Christ—The Eighth King Summary Outline. The following appendix (Appendix (6)—The 1260-Day Prophecies and the Last Days) explains the relationship between the 1260-day prophecies and the last-day events. Appendix (7)—Revelation, the Book: Overview and Timeline is provided to demonstrate how the last-day applications of the book of Revelation make the book of Revelation an understandable and consecutive timeline. It is the author's hope and prayer that this outline will provide the reader with a clearer understanding of the last-day events and help the reader realize how close we are to our Lord's soon return.

Appendix (6)
The 1260-Day Prophecies
and the Last Days

There are seven texts found in Daniel and Revelation, which describe a 1260-day time period.[1] These texts are Daniel 7:25, Daniel 12:7, Revelation 11:2, Revelation 11:3, Revelation 12:6, Revelation 12:14 and Revelation 13:5. These seven time periods all refer to 1260 days but in different terms. In Revelation 11:3 and Revelation 12:6, these time periods are described as 1260 days. In Revelation 11:2 and Revelation 13:5, they are described as 42 months. Forty-two months is actually 42 times 30 days which equals 1260 days (there are 30 days in the Jewish calendar month). In Daniel 7:25, Daniel 12:7, and Revelation 12:14, these time periods are described as three and one-half "times." A Jewish time equals one year. Three and one-half times equals three and one-half years and three and one-half years equals 42 months or 1260 days. Many scholars have assumed since all of these time periods are equal to 1260 days that they are all describing the same time period in history. Therefore, some scholars have applied all of these time periods to A.D. 538 to 1798.[2] Using this approach none of these time periods would apply to last-day events. Another assumption made by some scholars is that all of these time periods represent prophetic time, which means that 1260 days is always interpreted as 1260 years. This assumes that none of these time periods are literal days. However, in relation to last-day events, 1260 years becomes meaningless since last-day events must be within a reasonable proximity to the Second Coming to be considered last-day events.

While the historical approach to these prophecies is certainly possible, it appears that many of these prophecies also have a dual application. In the context of last-day events, five of these seven texts have dual applications. The five texts which have dual applications are Daniel 12:7, Revelation 11:2, Revelation 11:3, Revelation 12:14, and Revelation 13:5.

Historically, the 1260-day time period described in these seven texts has been interpreted as 1260 years.[3] This is based on the day year principle, which states that one prophetic day equals one literal year. In Daniel 7:25, this 1260-day time period is linked to the little horn power, which would reign for "a time, two times and half a time." This little horn power would attempt to destroy God's saints during this time period. This little horn power would overthrow three kingdoms prior to its reign and would "speak words against the Most High" (Daniel 7:25). This little horn power represents the Papacy, which overthrew three European kingdoms prior to the beginning of its reign in A.D. 538. This Papal kingdom reigned for 1260 years until 1798 when it lost its world dominance with the capture of Pope Pius VI. Therefore, this 1260-day prophecy does refer to the 1260-year time period from A.D. 538 to 1798.

In Revelation 12:6, the 1260-day time period is described as "one thousand two hundred and sixty days." Revelation 12 is describing the woman who is being persecuted by the dragon (Satan). The woman is nourished by God in the wilderness for 1260 days representing the 1260 years of Papal persecution from A.D. 538 to 1798. Again, this 1260-day period is the same 1260 years of persecution of God's people described in Daniel 7:25 and does not apply to last-day events.

In Daniel 12:7, this same time period of 1260 days is described as "a time, two times, and half a time." However, the context of Daniel 12 is entirely different from that of Daniel 7 and from that of the first half of Revelation 12. Daniel 12 begins with the time of trouble, which is clearly a time of the end event. Daniel 12 also occurs after the abomination that makes desolate is set up, which occurs in Daniel 11:31. The abomination that makes desolate is a last-day event. Also, Daniel 12:1 refers back to the "time of the end" in Daniel 11:40, which further connects it to last-day events. Furthermore, the shattering of God's people's power is connected to this 1260-day period and this shattering is a last-day event. All of these facts suggest that the 1260 days of Daniel 12:7 is a literal 1260 days, which is part of the last-day events, and not a 1260 year time period.

In Revelation 11:2, we find a 42-month prophecy, which has been linked to the previously described period, A.D. 538 to 1798. However, the context of Revelation 11 is within the sixth trumpet, which is introduced in Revelation 9:13 and ends in Revelation 11:14. Also Revelation 11:2 refers to the trampling of "the holy city" which refers to Jerusalem. This does not fit with the A.D. 538 to 1798 time period but does fit within the last-day events. When Satan reigns in Jerusalem the city will be trampled. This will occur in the last days. Also, this 42-month period is linked to the two witnesses, which are involved in last-day events. Furthermore, Revelation 11:1 is connected to the investigative judgment and the measuring of God's people. This investigative judgment is ongoing when the holy city is described as being trampled on. This means that the trampling must occur after 1844 when the investigative judgment began. All of these facts suggest a last-day application of Revelation 11:2.

Revelation 11:3 describes another 1260-day time period which is linked to God's two witnesses. Historically, this time period has been applied to the time of Papal supremacy from A.D. 538 to 1798 when Roman traditions replaced God's Holy Word. God's two witnesses represent God's Holy Word (the Old Testament and the New Testament). God's Word is seen in sackcloth or mourning because it has been replaced by man's traditions. This application certainly does apply to A.D. 538 to 1798. However, in the last days God's Word will be attacked again. When the Sunday law is passed by the image to the beast (Revelation 13:15-17) God's Law will be changed and His Word will be in sackcloth again. This will occur in the last days and will signal the beginning of the seven trumpets. Also, the context of Revelation 11 supports this dual application. The two witnesses are linked to both the trumpets and the plagues in Revelation 11:5, 6, which are last-day events. Furthermore, the two witnesses are killed by the beast that is to ascend, which is Satan as the eighth king, which is also a last-day event (Revelation 17:8, 11). These two witnesses will be killed in Jerusalem, the city "where their Lord was crucified" (Revelation 11:8). This is also a last-day event. Further discussion of the last-day context for Revelation 11 can be found in the section of this book titled "Appendix 4—Revelation 11: A Last Day's Application ."

Revelation 12:14 describes a 1260-day period when the woman is "given the two wings of the great eagle" to fly into the wilderness for a "a time, and times, and half a time." This has also been applied to A.D. 538 to 1798 to describe the Dark Ages experience of God's people (the woman). While this application can apply, there is another last-day application that is also apparent. The last half of Revelation 12 is describing events after the close of probation and the end of the investigative judgment. This is shown by the 12 stars in the victory crown on the woman, which represent the 12 tribes of the 144,000 (Revelation 7:4-8), who will only exist after the close of probation. Also, Satan is no longer able to accuse anyone, which occurs at the end of the investigative judgment. Furthermore, the kingdom of our God has come (Revelation 12:10). This occurs when the investigative judgment has been completed and probation has closed. Also, Revelation 12 is linked to the woes in verse 12. The woes are time of the end events, which occur after the close of probation. This is shown in Revelation 9:4 because God's people are sealed when the first woe begins. Also, Satan is described as making war with "the rest of her offspring" which is the final remnant of God's people (Revelation 12:18). Furthermore, the dragon has seven crowned heads which means that the events described occur after the seven kings have reigned. Finally, Satan has only a short time (Revelation 12:12), which further connects this to last-day events. It should be noted that God protected the woman in the wilderness in Revelation 12:6 for 1260 days (years). However, in Revelation 12:14 God's people are protected by the eagle during their wilderness experience. The eagle is linked to last-day events (see Revelation 4:7, 6:7, and 8:13). Also, the two wings of this eagle are further described in Revelation 12:17 and relate to the remnant church in the last days.

Revelation 13:5 describes a time period of 42 months during which the leopard-like beast is given authority. This again has been applied to the reign of Papal supremacy from A.D. 538 to 1798. However, in the last days this 42-month period will occur again and will occur as a literal 42 months or three and one-half years. The context of Revelation 13 supports this interpretation. This leopard-like beast is introduced in Revelation 13:1-3 and is described with a mortal wound that has healed. This leopard-like beast refers to the Papacy and the mortal wound occurred in 1798 at the end of the time of Papal supremacy. This wound was healed in 1929 when the Lateran Treaty was signed by Mussolini. Revelation 13:4 continues the story with the world worshiping this beast whose wound has healed, and also worshiping the dragon, which is Satan. This event will only occur in the last days just prior to Satan taking the throne as the eighth king. At that time the leopard-like beast will be dominant in the world and Satan will be rising to dominance as the false Christ. These are clearly last-day events. Revelation 13:5 continues by describing the reign of the leopard-like beast as 42 months. It is clear that the leopard-like beast's wound has been healed because it is described as healed again in Revelation 13:12. Therefore, the leopard-like beast is being pictured in chapter 13 with its wound healed and shown as reigning for 42 months. This 42-month period will occur after 1929 and will actually occur as part of the very last-day events. The actions of this beast which are pictured in Revelation 13 are similar to the actions of this same beast pictured in Daniel 7:25. The characteristics of this beast are the same, because it is the same beast, and it will regain power in the last days for a short period of time. This leopard-like beast will regain power for three and one-half years just prior to the reign of the eighth king. This leopard-like beast will regain world supremacy through the help of its image beast (the United States). Thus, the context of Revelation 13 supports a last-day application of this time period.

There are two other texts in Revelation 11 that have also been interpreted as 1260 days or three and one-half years. These are found in Revelation 11:9 and Revelation 11:11 and describe the time period during which God's two witnesses are dead but not buried. These two verses apply to the three and one-half year time period of Satan's reign as the eighth king. Satan is "the beast that ascends from the bottomless pit" (Revelation 11:7), who kills God's two witnesses. Once Satan reigns as the eighth king he will interpret God's Word as if he wrote it. God's Word will be dead but not buried (Revelation 11:9) for three and one-half prophetic days or three and one-half literal years. This is the 42 months when the holy city will be trampled (Revelation 11:12). This is the same three and one-half years described in Revelation 12:14 when Satan pursues God's people. This is the time when the eagle will protect the remnant. The eagle is related to the very last portion of the last-day events. The eagle is linked to the three woes (Revelation 8:13) and the seven last plagues, which occur during those woes. The two witnesses (Old Testament and New Testament) are raised and return to heaven, which can only occur at the time of the end when their work is completed and probation is closed. This did not occur at the time of the French Revolution, as some suggest, because clearly their work was not completed then.

There is one other text in Daniel 9, which also relates to the 1260 days involved in the last-day events. Daniel 9:27 describes one-half of a week during which the sacrifices and offerings will cease. This half of a week or three and one-half days represents the three and one-half years during which the desolator will reign as the eighth king. This is the "desolating sacrilege" Jesus described "standing in the holy place" (Matthew 24:15). This is what Jesus was referring to in Daniel that he wanted the readers to understand. This is the time period during which the abomination that makes desolate (Daniel 11:31) will reign in Jerusalem. This is the same time period described in Revelation 12:14, Revelation 11:2, Daniel 12:7, and Revelation 11:9, 11. The following graph outlines each of these 1260-day prophecies in Daniel and Revelation and shows how they relate to last-day events.

1260 Day Prophecies

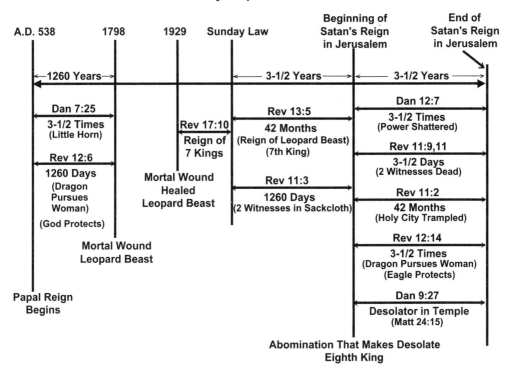

[1] Nichol, Francis D. (Ed.), *The Seventh-day Adventist Bible Commentary* (Review and Herald Publishing Association, Washington, D.C.) 1957, Vol. 7, p. 809.

[2] Ibid.

[3] Ibid.

Appendix (7)
Revelation, The Book:
Overview and Timeline

Many Bible students have struggled to understand the book of Revelation. The book of Revelation has many symbols and time prophecies which can appear quite formidable. One of the reasons that the book of Revelation is difficult to understand is the apparent absence of a recognizable time line. Historically, the first three chapters, which cover the seven churches, have been applied to the time from the 12 apostles (the first church or Ephesus) to the Second Coming (the seventh church or Laodicea). The seven seals and the seven trumpets have been applied by some to this same time period beginning with the apostles and extending to the Second Coming. Revelation 11 has been applied to the French Revolution and Revelation 12 and 13 to A.D. 538 to 1798. Revelation 10 has been applied to 1844 and Revelation 9 to the fourteenth through the nineteenth centuries.

This historical approach has assumed the book of Revelation was not written with a consecutive timeline and that the events described in one chapter do not necessarily connect to the preceding or following chapters. This assumption was necessary in order to interpret certain chapters and be consistent with a historical approach. However, if one assumes that the book of Revelation was written especially for the last days, then the assumption that there is no consecutive timeline must be re-examined. As has been shown in this book, the last-day events are linear and indeed are described in chronological order with only slight overlap. The overlap is necessary in order to describe different events which occur at the same time. In the light of last-day events the book of Revelation is much clearer than it has been made to appear. This simple progression is a very strong argument that these events are all interconnected.

Revelation 1-3

Revelation 1 through 3 introduce the timeline. This timeline begins in the Apostolic Era with the first church (Ephesus) and extends to the seventh church (Laodicea). The Laodicean church time period began in the 1840s with the first angel's message that the hour of judgment had come. This Laodicean church will continue to exist until the Second Coming.

Revelation 4-5

Revelation 4 and 5 describe the judgment that began in 1844. This is called the investigative judgment. This is also the cleansing or restoring of the sanctuary in heaven predicted in Daniel 8:14. This judgment process involves a book or scroll that only the Lamb Slain can open.

Revelation 6-7

Revelation 6 and 7 describe the seals and the victorious "who can stand" (Revelation 6:17). The seals are on the scroll described in Revelation 5. The scroll is part of the investigative judgment. The seals must be opened in order for the judgment to proceed. The seals began after 1844, which marks the beginning of the judgment process. The first seal occurred in the late 1800s and early 1900s. The second seal represented the world wars which began in 1919. The seals will continue until the Second Coming, which is the seventh seal.

Revelation 8-9

Revelation 8 begins with the casting down of the censer, which symbolizes judgment on God's favored nation (The United States of America) because it has rejected freedom of religion and passed a mandatory Sunday law. This passage of the Sunday law precedes the seven trumpets. This passage of the Sunday law is also the third seal. Thus, Revelation 8 parallels the seals beginning with the third seal or Sunday law. The first four trumpets are described in Revelation 8 and are warnings. The third trumpet represents Satan as the eighth king called Wormwood. Revelation 8 ends with the introduction of the three woes, which are the last three trumpets. Revelation 9 discusses the first two of those woes. The first woe represents Satan as the world king, which occurs at the end of his reign as the eighth king. The second woe describes the world once God has released His four angels. The third woe or seventh trumpet describes the Second Coming (Revelation 11:15-19). Therefore, Revelation 8 and 9 are linked to Revelation 6 because the trumpets begin after the third seal (the passage of the Sunday law) and continue on to the Second Coming (the seventh trumpet) paralleling the last three seals of Revelation 6 and Revelation 8:1 (the seventh seal).

Revelation 10

Revelation 10 describes a bittersweet experience for God's people. This experience will occur when the Sunday law is passed and God's people expect an immediate Second Coming only to be disappointed. The sweet expectation will turn bitter in the reality of the delay and tribulation.

Revelation 11

Revelation 11 describes two witnesses. These two witnesses are God's Old and New Testaments which will first be in sackcloth for three and one-half years and then be dead for three and one-half years. This seven year period begins with the passage of the National Sunday law. The reign of the eighth king marks the midpoint of this seven-year period and his reign is the fourth seal and the third trumpet. Satan will reign as world king near the end of the second three and one-half year time period. The two witnesses will be resurrected just prior to the Second Coming. The Second Coming is described in Revelation 11:15-19 as the seventh trumpet. The events of Revelation 11 parallel the events of Revelation 6 and 7 as well as Revelation 8 and 9.

Revelation 12

Revelation 12 begins with the story of the great controversy between God and Satan in order to identify who the dragon is and where he came from. It then describes Satan's reign as the eighth king, which includes the close of probation. The close of probation is described as the accuser being cast down (Revelation 12:10). Satan is also pictured as making war on God's remnant for three and one-half years. This three and one-half years correlates with the reign of the eighth king and the latter seals and the latter trumpets. This also parallels the three and one-half years when God's two witnesses are dead in Revelation 11.

Revelation 13

Revelation 13 covers the time period when Satan attacks God's people using the leopard-like beast for three and one-half years described in Revelation 13:5-10. Then Satan will make war on God's people described in Revelation 13:15-18 using the power of the image of the beast, which will parallel the three and one-half years of the reign of the eighth king. Revelation 13 first covers the time period of three and one-half years when the leopard-like beast is dominant. This is described as 42 months in Revelation 13:5, which correlates with the time when the two witnesses are in sackcloth. This also correlates with the reign of the seventh king. The latter half of Revelation 13 describes the world situation once the image of the beast enforces the buy-sell law and ultimately passes and enforces a death penalty. These events will occur during the reign of the eighth king. Revelation 12 and 13 are actually paralleling the description of events in Revelation 11, which parallel Revelation 6, 7, 8 and 9.

Revelation 14

Revelation 14 describes the 144,000 who will not receive the mark described at the end of Revelation 13. Revelation 14 then describes the three angel's messages with emphasis on the third angel's message, which involves the mark of the beast. This mark was introduced in chapter 13. Revelation 14 closes with the description of the Second Coming as a harvest of the righteous (grain) and the wicked (grapes).

Revelation 15-16

Revelation 15 and 16 describe the seven last plagues, which occur just prior to the Second Coming. These plagues fall on the wicked that have the mark of the beast. The mark of the beast connects chapters 15 and 16 to chapters 13 and 14. The seven last plagues end with the Second Coming, which is the seventh plague.

Revelation 17-18

Revelation 17 describes the judgment of Babylon the "mother of harlots" (Revelation 17:5). The beast (Satan) is described as the eighth king who will take over from the seventh king. The seventh king reigns during the first portion of Revelation 13. The time of the eighth king's reign is described in the second portion of Revelation 13 when the image to the beast enforces the buy-sell law. The eighth king is also described in Revelation 12. Revelation 17 describes ten kings (Revelation 17:17) who will reign with the beast (Satan) at the end of time and destroy Babylon (Revelation 17:16, 17).

Revelation 18 describes the destruction of Babylon (apostate Christianity) by God with His plagues (Revelation 18:8) and also describes the destruction that the ten kings will bring upon Babylon (Papal Rome), which will occur in "one hour" (Revelation 17:12 compared with Revelation 18:10, 17, 19).

Revelation 19

Revelation 19 describes the Second Coming as a bride made ready for her Bridegroom and then describes the battle between Satan and Christ which allows the bride to be taken home. The earth is pictured as a battleground with all the wicked slain. This is a clear description of the Second Coming.

Revelation 20

Revelation 20 pictures Satan bound in an empty world for 1000 years in a pit of circumstances with no one to tempt. Satan is loosed for a little while (Revelation 20:3) at the end of the 1000 years and then can "deceive the nations" again (Revelation 20:8). This occurs because God raises all the wicked just prior to the final return of Christ (Third Coming). Jesus' Third Coming occurs when He brings the saints and "the beloved city" to the earth (Revelation 20:9).

Revelation 21-22

Revelation 21 describes the Holy City "coming down out of heaven from God" (Revelation 21:2). The New Jerusalem is described further in Revelation 22. Thus, it can be seen that the entire book of Revelation is a continuous story and simply progresses from one event to the next. The story ends with God's people re-established on earth in the Holy City—The New Jerusalem.

The following timeline (Appendix (7)—Revelation Overview) outlines these events for the entire book of Revelation. It should be noted that almost all of the timelines of each chapter extend to the Second Coming prior to Revelation 19, which is the Second Coming. Therefore, what we see is a progressive shortening of the timeline from a long timeline beginning with the apostles and extending to the Second Coming to very short timelines when we are dealing with the seven last plagues and the ten kings who are involved in the destruction of Babylon. Finally, the timeline extends beyond the Second Coming for the one thousand year millennium and then to eternity.

Appendix (7) - Revelation Overview

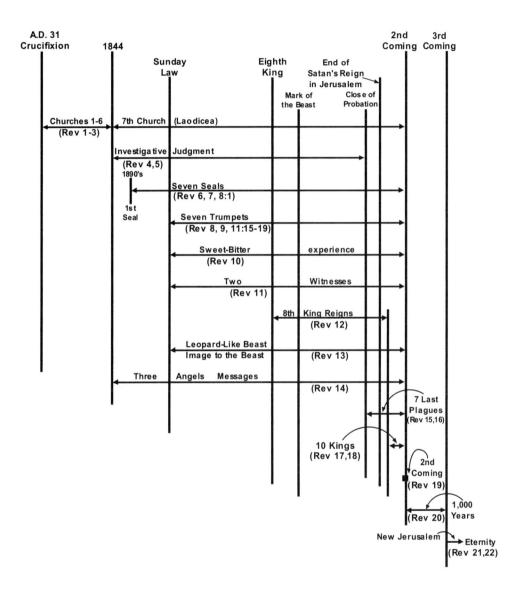

EPILOGUE: THE FUTURE OUTLINED

On a sunny and extremely hot day in the not too distant future, the eighth king is seen ascending to his throne in his new capital city. He had been waiting impatiently for this day for many millennia. He had claimed this world as his own for centuries but had not been allowed to take the throne. He had been held back by God's rules of engagement. Those rules had kept him from his rightful throne and he was angry over the delay. He would have destroyed the followers of Christ long ago if it hadn't been for those very same rules of engagement. He often remarked on how foolish Christ's followers were for not availing themselves of God's full protection under those rules. However, their lack of protection just made it easier for him to overcome them.

Now, some of those restrictions had been removed and he has gained his long awaited throne. He was able to accomplish this by deceiving the world into believing he was the Son of God, Christ the Messiah, who had returned to save the world from destruction. He achieved this by working miracles and doing wondrous things which humans could not explain. He could have done these things years ago but God had held him back. Through his miracles he had been able to convince most of the religious leaders and so-called Christians that he was Christ and that he could save the world. Ironically, he knows that the world's current problems originated with him. He had also been able to convince the Catholic Church to accept him as their leader and the previous Vicar (the seventh king) had given him his throne. This occurred because the Pope, as Vicar for Christ, was no longer needed now that Christ was here.

Almost all of the Protestant denominations had also accepted him as Christ and their leader. He would now rule approximately one-third of the world's population and Jerusalem was where he must rule in order to fulfill the Old Testament prophecies. In order to take his throne and rebuild his temple he had to eliminate Israel's control of Jerusalem. This required destruction of most of the Jewish nation. Even the Moslems had accepted him as their Messiah, because he had helped destroy the Jewish nation.

The world has no idea how he has manipulated events, in order to reach this throne. Recently he was able to change the Law of God by enacting a new worship day (Sunday). He will soon be able to enforce the sanctity of this day with a worldwide requirement for all Christians. This will show his power over God's Word. Now as the eighth king he will be the sole interpreter of God's Word. How ironic that Lucifer, God's enemy would now be asked to interpret God's Word. As the false Christ reigning in Jerusalem, he has now met one of his greatest ambitions. However, he craves more.

Being leader of approximately one third of the world is not sufficient for one who claims ownership of the entire world. His ultimate plan is to be world king and not just spiritual leader of the Christian world. Unfortunately, God is still holding him back. However, he knows God will soon release him and then he will be able to do anything he wishes. His plan is to make the world accept him as king of the world. When this occurs, he will have been further released from God's rules of engagement. Shortly thereafter, he knows that God will release him completely from all the rules of engagement and withdraw his angels, which are holding him back. Then he will finally have total control of the world.

This day of his inauguration as the eighth king, the spiritual king of the world, marks the beginning of increased persecution for God's true followers. This persecution will be unparalleled in history because he is now in control. God's Word, the Old Testament and New Testament, will be effectively dead once he assumes his throne. As spiritual king of the world he will now be the interpreter of God's Word. Satan also knows that once he becomes temporal king of the world, he will be able to put into motion his final plan, a death penalty for God's people. Unfortunately, he must wait until God releases his four angels that are holding him back.

Author's Footnote

As this book is going to the printing press Pope John Paul II, the sixth king, has died. The seventh king has been chosen and is Pope Benedict XVI. By the time you read this book the seventh king of Revelation chapter 17 will be reigning. The seventh king will reign for "only a little while" (Revelation 17:10) and then the eighth king will begin his reign as the false Christ. We are rapidly approaching Jesus' real return. Are you ready to meet Him?

ACKNOWLEDGMENTS

In each person's life there are certain events that stand out. One of those signal events in my own experience was the reading of Dr. Robert Smith's book, *The Sixth King*. I am indebted to Dr. Smith for his book, and several of his ideas were used in this book. I want to extend my heartfelt appreciation to Dr. Smith. His concept of the abomination that makes desolate is incorporated into this book and expanded upon.

I would like to thank my previous Pastor, Terry Johnson, for his support and encouragement. Terry and I had many discussions over Daniel and Revelation and these discussions both encouraged and prompted me to continue my studies.

I would also like to thank Pastor Richard Harbour, who provided welcomed guidance and criticism when needed.

There are many others who encouraged me to write when I was uncertain whether to proceed. I particularly want to thank my Sabbath school class who allowed me to test my theories on them. They were especially kind and helpful as we worked through many of these issues. Special thanks go to Debbie King for her many hours of help in reviewing the manuscript and improving its content. I would also like to thank Carla House, Lacy Brown, and Sherry Bice for their help in preparing the manuscript. Also I wish to thank Tonya Desmaris for all her help throughout this entire process.

I especially want to thank Paul and Gail Pelley, who not only encouraged me to persevere, but also provided excellent critical reviews of the manuscript.

A special thanks also goes to Toya Koch and Meredith Siems for their technical assistance in the final preparation of the book.

Most importantly, I want to thank John Hagensicker for all of his work on this project. John not only gave freely of his time but also gave important advice as we attempted to clarify many of these issues. John helped me with my research whenever I asked and his help was critical in creating all of the tables and graphs included in this book. John, I am forever in your debt.

Finally, I want to thank my wife Rosalyn for her patience and support. Being a physician's wife is hard enough but then to have to endure many hours while I was writing and editing is certainly going the extra mile. Thank you dear, I love you very much.